EMOTIC INTELLIGENCE 2.0 & MANIPULATION
The Most Powerful Collection

---

6 Books in 1

Dark Psychology, How to Analyze People, Master Your Emotions, Enneagram, Social Anxiety Solution, Mental Toughness

---

Dr Henry Campbell & Dr Daniel Watson

Legal & Disclaimer

The information contained in this book and its contents is not designed to replace or take the place of any form of medical or professional advice; and is not meant to replace the need for independent medical, financial, legal or other professional advice or services, as may be required. The content and information in this book has been provided for educational and entertainment purposes only.

The content and information contained in this book has been compiled from sources deemed reliable, and it is accurate to the best of the Author's knowledge, information and belief. However, the Author cannot guarantee its accuracy and validity and cannot be held liable for any errors and/or omissions. Further, changes are periodically made to this book as and when needed. Where appropriate and/or necessary, you must consult a professional (including but not limited to your doctor, attorney, financial advisor or such other professional advisor) before using any of the suggested remedies, techniques, or information in this book.

Upon using the contents and information contained in this book, you agree to hold harmless the Author from and against any damages, costs, and expenses, including any legal fees potentially resulting from the application of any of the information provided by this book. This disclaimer applies to any loss, damages or injury caused by the use and application, whether directly or indirectly, of any advice or information presented, whether for breach of contract, tort, negligence, personal injury, criminal intent, or under any other cause of action.

You agree to accept all risks of using the information presented inside this book.

You agree that by continuing to read this book, where appropriate and/or necessary, you shall consult a professional (including but not limited to your doctor, attorney, or financial advisor or such other advisor as needed) before using any of the suggested remedies, techniques, or information in this book.

CONTENTS

DARK PSYCHOLOGY

REVISED AND UPDATED

Guide to the Secrets of Dark Emotional Manipulation, Mind Control, Hypnosis and Brainwashing. Proven Psychological Techniques to Identify Dangerous People and to Achieve your Goals.

Dr Henry Campbell & Dr Daniel Watson

PREFACE TO MENTAL POWERS

The following chapters will discuss dark psychology. This form of psychology and understanding of the human mind can be found all around us. No matter how much we may hope that those around us are good and would never try to harm us, there are still people who are going to use our psyche and our emotions against us. This guidebook is going to go into depth about various dark psychology techniques and can arm you with the understanding to keep dark manipulators from taking advantage of you.

There are many different ways that a dark manipulator can try to take control over your mind and get you to react in a certain manner. They can often get in close with you, befriend you, and get you to act in certain ways. And many times, a rational and even an intelligent person will get caught in the trap, without realizing what is going on until it is too late to do anything about it. This is what makes dark psychology so dangerous and why it is so important to learn the signs and understand the different methods early on.

This guidebook will give you the information and the understanding that you need to recognize and defend against dark psychology. We will discuss some of the different methods that are used with dark psychology, why a dark manipulator will use these techniques, and more to help you understand what signs to look out for.

One of the best things that you can do to protect yourself from dark psychology is to know as much about it as possible. Take a look through this book and learn the main types of psychology that are out there that fit into this realm of darkness and manipulation.

INTRODUCTION

Psychology, as a whole, focuses on the brain, the mind, and behaviors of individuals within several different fields of study. Everything from how our brains develop through the seasons of life, to the way social cognizance and process molds the very fabric of our society, are separated and examined. Modern science has had influence over psychological processes and studies for around 150 years. However, the study of the human mind and how we interact, socialize, and even manipulate, dates back to the times of ancient Greece.

The Grecian Empire hails the intellectual and thought-provoking minds of philosophers such as Socrates. Socrates' thoughts and ideals have rolled through history-making way for other philosophers like Plato and Aristotle to sculpt profound theories that many of our current day sociological views and understandings are founded upon. While this wasn't an in-depth look at the human brain, the philosophical ideas of these greats, and many others, began the human curiosity into such things as memory, behavioral shifts in youth and adults, and even the ideas of attraction and free will. But even more so, the Greeks found a strong interest in what is now known as Dark Psychology.

The ability to bend and mold another's actions and thoughts to create a positive outcome for the manipulator has been something that most likely outdated even the Grecian greats. Human nature binds itself to one simple idea, at the root of all life, and that is survival. Survival has evolved through the ages as we are no longer hunters and gatherers, warriors, or even primitive human life forms existing on whatever we could find, hiding from predators, and taking what was needed.

Humans have existed on this planet for 2.5 billion years, and our idea of the modern Homo Sapiens have been here for roughly 0.3-0.8 billion years. However, our brains, the same brains that have created rockets, sent a man to the moon, and cured diseases have not changed from the first human to ever exist. Within that psyche, we still push to be the best, have the best, and be the strongest among us. Since times have changed, so have the avenues to succeed. And in addition, so has the propensity for violence, mischief, and psychological warfare. This is where we find Dark Psychology.

CHAPTER 1: DARK PSYCHOLOGY

Dark Psychology is the study of criminal behavior in order to decipher the potential of evil that could be found within all of us. This is going to be about studying of the conditions of humans relating to the people preying on others motivated by criminal intentions that lack drive and general expectations of primitive purposes and theoretical social sciences.

The idea with this one is that everyone, even if they realize it or not, will have the potential, if it is going to benefit themselves and even their families enough, to victimize other humans and creatures. Some people are just more willing to do it than others. For example, you may not think about doing this to just get a promotion at work or to get someone to notice you, but you may be willing to hurt other people if you knew it would save your life or save the life of someone in your family.

While many of us are going to restrain or hide this kind of tendency, there are those who are going to see these impulses and decide to act on them. The idea of dark psychology is to seek to understand these perceptions, feelings, thoughts, and even the particular system processing that lead to the destructive behavior which is unethical and is seen as normal or good by modern society.

Dark psychology is going to assume that any abusive, deviant, or criminal behaviors that are showing up are done for a purpose. They may be seen as bad or evil, but the other person is doing them for some purpose, and not just because they feel like it. They are going to have a rational goal most of the time. Someone may use abuse to keep their partner in their place to ensure that they are able to get the love and attention that they need. Is this something that the majority of society would do or see as normal? No, but it is a rational excuse in the mind of the person doing it.

Dark psychology is something that we can all learn from and benefit from. We just need to take some time to understand it a bit more. It is found inside all of us in some form or another, but most of us are willing to follow the laws and the moral codes in our world and will follow these to not use this latent personality trait. Then there are others who are going to fall onto the continuum and who will find that it is easier for them to use dark psychology in order to get the results and benefits that they are looking for.

CHAPTER 2: UNDERSTANDING DARK PERSUASION

Persuasion is an interesting topic. There are lots of persuasions that are considered just fine in society. They are acceptable, and even some people hold jobs where they will spend a lot of time trying to persuade others. Any attempt by one person to influence someone else to do some action can be persuasion. A salesperson at a car dealership is using persuasion because they try to persuade someone to purchase a new vehicle. This isn't seen as something sinister or bad. The difference here is that this persuasion and other similar examples of persuasion benefit both parties. The car dealer makes a sale and some money, and the "victim" is going to get a new vehicle.

There are a lot of legitimate types of persuasion that aren't considered part of dark psychology. The car dealer above is an example. If a negotiator uses their skills to persuade a terrorist to let their hostage go, this is a good form of persuasion. If you convince someone to come along to an event that they will enjoy, then this is a good form of persuasion. This type of persuasion is seen as positive persuasion. But then, what would count as dark persuasion?

Understanding Dark Persuasion

The first difference you will notice between positive and dark persuasion is the motive behind it. Positive persuasion is used in order to encourage someone to complete an action that isn't going to cause them any harm. In some cases, such as with the negotiator saving a hostage, this persuasion can be used to help save lives.
But with dark persuasion, there isn't really any form of moral motive. The motive is usually amoral, and often immoral. If positive persuasion is understood as a way to help people help themselves, then dark persuasion is more of the process of making

7

people act against their own self-interest. Sometimes, people are going to do these actions begrudgingly, knowing that they are probably not making the right choice, but they do it because they are eager to stop the incessant persuasion efforts. In other cases, the best dark persuader is going to make their victim think that they acted wisely, but the victim is actually doing the opposite in that case.

So, what are the motivations for someone who is a dark persuader? This is going to depend on the situation and the individual who is doing the persuading. Some people like to persuade their victims in order to serve their own self-interests. Others are going to act through with the intention just to cause some harm to the other person. In some cases, the persuader is not going to really benefit from darkly persuading their victim, but they do so because they want to inflict pain on the other person. And still, others enjoy the control that this kind of persuasion gives to them.

You will also find that the outcome you get from dark persuasion is going to differ from what happens with positive persuasion. With positive persuasion, you are going to get one of three scenarios including the following:

• The benefit goes to the person who is being persuaded.
• There is a win/win benefit for the persuaded and the persuader.
• There is a mutual benefit for the person who is persuaded and a third party.

All of these outcomes are good because they will involve a positive result for the person who is being persuaded. Sometimes, there will be others who benefit from these actions. But out of all three situations, the persuaded party is always going to benefit.

With dark persuasion, the outcome is going to be very different. The persuader is the one who will always benefit when they exercise their need for influence or control. The one who is being persuaded often goes against what is in their self-interest when they listen, and they are not going to benefit from all this dark persuasion.

In addition, the most skilled dark persuaders are not only able to cause some harm to their victims while also benefiting themselves, but they could also end up harming others in the process.

The Psychology of Persuasion

When you hear the word persuasion, what do you think about first? Some may think about messages used in advertising that they see all the time, the ones that focus on trying to get the viewer to choose a certain product or go after a political candidate. A powerful force called persuasion is what we are going to see in daily lives, and it does have a level of effect on society as a whole, as well as on the individual. Mass media, legal decisions, news, politics, advertising, and more are all going to be affected by the persuasion power, and that same persuasion is going to influence us as well.

Many people believe that they are persuasion resistant. They think that they have the ability to just see through any sales pitch that comes their way, and actually have a good comprehension about what the truth is in any given situation. This can be true some of the time, but there are so many different types of persuasion, and they aren't all going to be a aggressive salesman who wants to sell you something or even a commercial on the television.

You will find that persuasion becomes really subtle. And it can come from people we are close to, ones we wouldn't expect at all. The way that we are going to respond to these influences is going to depend on our background, along with many other factors.

When most people think about persuasion, they are going to focus on some of the negative examples of it. This is the way that a manipulator would try to use persuasion. But there are times when persuasion can be used in more of a positive way. for example, if you have ever seen a public service campaign that urged people to stop smoking, or to recycle, then you have seen an example of positive persuasion.

Persuasion is a figurative process in which people who are communicating try to persuade other people to change their actions or thoughts regarding an issue at hand through communicating a message in a situation where one is has the freedom to choose.
Always remember that no matter how strong the persuasion is, the victim does get a choice in how they act. The manipulator may work to take away this choice or make it seem like there aren't any choices, but there is still that freedom of the choice present.
There are a few key elements that come into play when we are talking about persuasion. These are going to include:

- Persuasion is something that is symbolic. It is going to use a variety of features, including sounds, images, words, and more.
- Persuasion is going to involve an attempt that is deliberate by one person to influence another person or a group of people.
- Persuading yourself is the key. The person is going always to have the freedom to make a choice, and they will never be coerced.
- Approaches of conveying persuasive messages can happen in many various ways. For example, verbal and nonverbal options and through radio, television, internet, face to face and other communication channels

What is Subliminal Persuasion?

Subliminal persuasion is going to be the technique of convincing your target, or your group of targets, to do something, without them knowing. There isn't going to be any outward suggesting of the idea, and often the victim isn't going to realize that you were trying to influence them at all. It is one of the types of persuasion that manipulators and others can use, and it is going to use words, along with some gestures, in order to get ahold of different people. So, you may find things like smiling, use of the head, eye expression, and more being used, both in a positive and a negative manner. It is a powerful technique, but often a difficult technique, that not only uses words, but uses the meaning behind the words, and body language, to ensure that the victim does what the manipulator wants.

In our modern world, the techniques that are used for subliminal persuasion are going to be powerful weapons that can really help you get ahead. They can help you to manipulate others, or even gain an advantage in a market where there is a lot of competition, and you need to stay ahead of the game. According to some experts in the field of marketing and persuasion, many people are resulting in subliminal advertising because it is more effective. As they say, "Persuasion that looks like persuasion isn't persuasive anymore."

Even a manipulator is able to use this information to help then take control of the victim. If the persuasion that they use is too obvious, then the victim is just going to walk away. We see so many examples of persuasion in our daily lives that it is easy to recognize the more obvious signs and stay away from them if we don't want to purchase something or do something.

If a manipulator comes at their victim with a big sales pitch, lots of bright flashing lights, and other obvious techniques of persuasion, then they will get nowhere. The victim is smart enough to recognize these signs, and they will get away from the manipulator, and this is where subliminal persuasion can come in.

Every time that the manipulator communicates with their victim, they are going to be very careful about the nonverbal signs that they are sending out as well. While they still have to say words (your victim is going to notice if you just stand around sending out nonverbal cues and never talking), the manipulator is going to try and send out extra messages and extra persuasion through the body language and the nonverbal cues that they are sending out as well.

Since subliminal persuasion is going to deal with the feelings that the victim has, there is going to be some kind of subconscious element in this kind of persuasion. As a manipulation or another kind of person who needs to use persuasion, you will provide the victim's mind with some feelings of enthusiasm and comfort about doing a given task. Those thoughts and emotions are going to be sent out to the subconscious mind, but then we have to take to the logical mind to. You can then talk to this part of the mind by discussing the things that are rational about the choice.

Subliminal Persuasion Advertising

One topic that we need to take a look at this topic is known as subliminal advertising. This type of advertising aims to use our subconscious minds against us in order to profit another company. The business is going to sneak different emotions, feelings, and thoughts into the things that we consume, in the hopes that we are going to want to purchase more of that same products. In some countries, the idea of subliminal advertising has been banned because it has been recognized how dangerous this kind of manipulation tactic can be against the consumer.

However, it is pretty common that an advertiser is able to get into the head of the consumer, and most of these advertisers are really good at doing it. They sometimes even pay to have potential consumers what the advertisement in order to monitor how the brain functions while watching that commercial. This helps the advertisers to get a better idea of how the brain is going to work while watching the advertisement, and then they can make adjustments to really make it stronger.

During these times, the advertisers are going to monitor several things. For example, they may decide to track eye movement in order to see what part of the commercial is drawing the attention of the crowd more. The advertising company can then use this information in order to really sell a product and to be as effective with the subliminal persuasion as possible. This shows just how powerful advertising can be, and how it has broken into our brains, understanding how to sell us something better than our understanding of capitalism, and what it means to be a consumer.

Compared to the other forms of mind control, persuasion can be performed on just one victim to change their mind; it's also possible to apply persuasion on a larger scale to persuade an entire group or society to change the way they are thinking. Hypnosis and brainwashing will require the victim to be in isolation to change their identity and minds.

Persuasion is more effective and perhaps dangerous because it can change the minds of many people all at once rather than the mind of just a single target.
Most people fall under the false impression that they are immune to the effects of persuasion. The act of persuasion is going to be very subtle, and it can be very hard for the victim to form their own opinions about what they are being told.

Elements of Persuasion

These elements assist in defining what persuasion is so that it is more recognized. One thing that makes persuasion different from the other forms of mind control is that the victim is often allowed to make their own free decisions in the matter even if the techniques of persuasion are going to work to shift the subject's mind in a specific direction.
These elements include:
• It involves the agent deliberately trying to manipulate the victim or group
• It is symbolic, and it utilizes words, sounds, and images to get the

point across

- Self-persuasion is a vital aspect of this process. The victim is often not coerced, and instead, they are given the freedom to choose their own decision.

For you to persuade a person to think or act in a particular way, you need to be able to show them why they should alter their thoughts. For you to achieve this, you will include the use of images, words, and sounds to get your new point across. You can use words to trigger an argument to show your new point. Pictures can be a great way to show the evidence that is needed to persuade a person to go one way or the other.

You will consciously apply persuasion to manipulate the ways other people think or act. The persuader will apply different tactics to get the victim to think the same way that they do.

The Difference Between Persuasion and Dark Persuasion?

The difference between persuasion and dark persuasion is in the intention. A persuader might try to convince a person to do something without thinking through particular motivation or techniques or without any real understanding of the target they are attempting to persuade.

A dark persuader often understands the bigger picture. The persuader understands who he or she is trying to persuade, what motivates them, and how far they need to take the technique for them to be successful. A dark persuader is typically unconcerned with the morality of his/her manipulation. He/she see doing the right thing as a perk, but it does not have to be his/her biggest motivation. In the Venn diagram of self-gratification and morality, dark persuader actions will not often fall into the overlapping section. A dark persuader will see the person or thing he or she wants and devise a way to get it by all means.

Techniques Used in Dark Persuasion

Masking the True Intentions

The idea of masking your true intentions. Sometimes when we are using dark psychology and the different methods that come with it, it makes more sense when we are able to hide our true intentions. Maybe they are bad intentions that the other person will want nothing to do with. Maybe hiding our intentions makes it easier to get what we want. Sometimes, even if the end goal is not that bad, people are not going to be happy to find out they are being used by someone else, and masking the true intentions ensures you are more likely to get what you want in the process.

There are a few different tactics that you are able to use in order to help you mask some of your true intentions. Some of the options include the following:

Use a decoyed object to help throw the target off from what you are doing.

Your goal with this one is to support a cause or some kind of idea that is going to be different from your opinions but are going to help you achieve your goal. Use this method in a safe and cautious manner. You want to make sure that you are able to keep away your intentions by not closing up, but be careful not to be too secretive because this is going to make other people feel suspicious about you. You can do this by talking a lot about your goals and your desires, just not the real ones.

This is going to benefit you in a lot of different manners. First, it is going to make you appear open, trusting, and friendly to the other person. It will help you to conceal some of your true intentions, and you will send your competitors on a wild goose chase that is just going to take up a lot of your time.

False security

People are going to mistake the idea of sincerity with honesty. Remember, the first instinct of most people is to believe the appearances and given that they really value honesty, they are going to try and believe that there is a lot of honesty in the surrounding people. This means that even if you are only able to show the idea of honesty to them, they are going to want to believe that you are always going, to be honest to them.

Stick with facial expressions that are going to be bland

Behind a plain and unreadable kind of exterior, you are able to get through all kinds of chaos. And since no one is able to read the facial expressions and more than you are giving, you can plan out a lot of trouble for the other person, without them having an idea of what you are doing. This is defense that is going to do you well, so practice going with some of the blandest body language cues and facial expressions that you are able to find.

Using noble gestures

The next thing that you are able to do is to work with what is noble gestures. Remember that people want to be able to trust what you are saying, and they believe that there is some good in all people. They have to believe that any kind of gesture that appears noble is something they can trust in because this is a pleasant belief to have. They are rarely going to take a look at some of the deception that could be happening behind the scenes with this.

Find a way to have a group to belong to.

The act of people making appearances for reality, that feeling that when someone belongs to your group, they must be real in their belonging and it's a habit which is going to make it easier especially for a dark persuader to come in and have the opportunity they need for their ideas at hand

The trick that comes with this one is going to be simple. You just need to blend in with those who are around you. The more that you are able to blend in and appear to be a part of the group, the less suspicious you are going to be in the process. Remember that it is going to take some patience and maybe a little bit of humility in order to do this. But it is going to ensure that you are able to get in with the group that you need and that others are not going to harm you in the process.

Leading Questions

The next option that we can look at when it comes to dark persuasion is the idea of leading questions. A leading question is going to be a question that will contain or imply the answer that the persuader wants you to answer with. It is going to make the other person feel like they need to answer in a certain way if they want to be right.

Usually, when we ask a question, we are going to ask a neutral one. This is going to be a type of question that is not going to suggest its own answer, allowing the target to answer in any way that they choose. But leading questions are going to pretty much tell the target how they are going to need to respond, and that is why they are turned into a form of persuasion that you need to be careful about. They are going to be rhetorical in a sense because they will imply answers that can attempt to shape or determine a response.

Now, this one is not always going to be a hostile kind of question or one that is meant to put the other person on the spot. At least not all of the time, instead it is going to just say what answer you want the target to use, and sometimes these can be hostile but often if you don't want to put the other target on their guard, and then you will not ask the question in a hostile manner.

Let's look at an example of how this is going to work. Let's say that a salesperson wants to be able to sell a piece of furniture to someone. It wouldn't really help them to say something like "So buy it already. It's just a sofa!" This is going to make the other people mad and they are going to walk out without making the purchase. Instead, they may say something like "How soon would you need your furniture delivered?" No matter what answer the customer gives they are implying that they are going to go ahead with the purchase, whether they need it right now or are perhaps waiting until the end of the month when they move to get the purchase.

Leading questions need to be used in a good manner. They need to be in a more friendly tone so that the person who is hearing it doesn't feel like they are being attacked or that they are going to give out the wrong answer. But they also need to be done in a manner that is not going to hide the intentions as much. They will push the other person, the target, into making a decision, and hopefully, if it is done in the proper manner, it is going to work well and to their advantage.

CHAPTER 3: HOW TO USE DARK PSYCHOLOGY

Love flooding

This would include any buttering up, praising, or complimenting people to get them to comply with the request that you want. If you want someone to help you move some items into your home, you may use love flooding in order to make them feel good, which could make it more likely that they will help you. A dark manipulator could also use it to make the other person feel attached to them and then get them to do things that they may not normally do.

Lying

This would include telling the victim an untrue version of the situation. It can also include a partial truth or exaggerations with the goal of getting what you wanted to be done.

Love denial

This one can be hard on the victim because it can make them feel lost and abandoned by the manipulator. This one basically includes withholding affection and love until you are able to get what you want out of the victim.

Withdrawal

This would be when the victim is given the silent treatment or is avoided until they meet the needs of the other person.

Restricting choices

The manipulator may give their victim access to some choices, but they do this in order to distract them from the choices that they don't want the victim to make.

Semantic manipulation

This is a technique where the manipulator is going to use some commonly known words, ones that have accepted meanings by both parties, in a conversation. But then they will tell the victim, later on, that they had meant something completely different when they used that word. The new meaning is often going to change up the entire definition and could make it so that the conversation goes the way the manipulator wanted, even though the victim was tricked.

Reverse psychology

This is when you tell someone to do something in one manner, knowing that they will do the opposite. But the opposite action is what the manipulator wanted to happen in the first place.

CHAPTER4: IDENTIFYING A DARK PERSUADER

At this point, you may be curious about who is using these dark methods of persuasion. Are there actually people out there who are interested in using this kind of persuasion and using it against others to cause harm?

The main characteristics of a dark persuader are either an indifference toward or an inability to care about how persuasion is going to impact others. Such people who use this kind of persuasion are going to be often narcissistic and will see their own needs as more important than the needs of others. They may even be sociopathic and unable to grasp the idea of someone else's emotions.

Many times, this kind of dark persuasion is going to show up in a relationship. Often one but sometimes both partners are going to be inclined towards trying to use dark persuasion on each other. If these attempts are persistent and endure, then this type of relationship is going to be classified as psychologically abusive, and that is not healthy for the victim in that relationship. Often, they will not realize that there is something going on or that they are darkly persuaded until it is too late, and they are stuck there.

There are many examples of using this kind of dark persuasion in a relationship. If one partner stops the other partner from taking a new job opportunity or doesn't allow them to go out with friends, then this could be an example of dark persuasion. The dark persuader will work to convince the victim that they are acting in a way that is best for the relationship. In reality, the victim is going through a process that harms them and the relationship.

CHAPTER 5: UNDETECTED MIND CONTROL

Your mind is your sanctuary. No matter what else can be lost to others, the mind is yours and yours alone. Or so we think. People like to believe that they are the ones in control of their own actions and thoughts. Many times our minds can be susceptible to the influence of others, and this allows others to control our minds if we're not careful.

Think about a time when you watched a horror movie. Your mind and your emotions are already being led and influenced in the movie. All the decisions of the director, from the camera shot, the lighting, and the music can determine how you are going to feel and react. Even though you are in full awareness that you are just watching a movie, the brain is going to respond to the prompts when they are given. If our brain can be so influenced by something that we are aware of, how strong would the influence of a dark manipulator be?

Undetected mind control is often the most deadly type of mind control there is. If someone is already aware that their mind is being influenced, then they have the option to object, either physically, verbally, or mentally. For example, they can choose to avoid any contact with the person who controls them. A lot of people are going to run at the first sign they see of a dangerous person trying to get inside the brain and take over. But if the mind controller is able to get into the brain of their victim without the victim detecting them, then the victim has no chance to put up their defenses before it's too late.

There are going to be two tactics that the manipulator can use to take over the mind of their victim without detection. This includes the use of media and interpersonal interactions. Traditionally, the media mind control was something that was only possible for the larger company. Most individual mind controllers were left to deal with just the interpersonal interactions. But with the changes in technology now, this is no longer the case.

Smartphones and laptops have allowed even individual manipulators to have media mind control. This can make it a very powerful tool that the manipulator can use. While the undetected mind controller is going to be able to use all these methods, they are often going to be more deliberate and only take their actions after some careful consideration. They are sometimes seen as a big more coward compared to some other controllers, such as psychological manipulators, but they will take deliberate actions in order to find the right victim to do the attack on.

Undetected Mind Control Tactics

Now that we know a little bit more about undetected mind control, it is time to learn about some of the methods that are used by manipulators in order to control the mind of a victim in a way that is undetected. We are going to explore both the media and the interpersonal techniques that are in the toolkit of the manipulator. Let's take a look at some of the different undetected mind control tactics.

Finding Those Who Are in Need

The first principle that comes with undetected mind control is to find a victim who has a goal. It has been proven that a person who has a pressing desire or need is someone who will be more susceptible to this type of mind control compared to someone that feels satisfied and at ease. This could range from a small physical goal, such as someone who is thirsty and looking for a drink. Or it can be a more psychological goal, such as someone who is craving affection and love.

A good example of this is the experiment that was conducted to look at subliminal influence or undetected mind control. In this study, there were two sets of people who were shown a film, but this film had a hidden image of iced tea. One set of people in the study were thirsty, and the second group wasn't.

After the movie, when the participants were given the chance to purchase a specific drink from a selection, the ones who were thirsty would purchase the iced tea in greater numbers compared to those who weren't thirsty. This shows that, when the brain is desperate for something, they are gladly taking suggestions on what they should choose.

So, how would you be able to use this principle with an individual on more of an interpersonal level? If the mind controller is able to find a victim who is already craving something in their life, then the manipulator will find that it is easier to control that victim. One example is a victim who just got out of a long-term relationship. They may crave the company again and the mind controller would be able to influence their target into thinking that they are the savior for the victim. In reality, they are going to cause harm and even ruin for the victim, but the victim will crave attention so much that they will fall for the mind control that is put on them.

There are a lot of needs that a manipulator is going to seek in order to exploit their victim including their need for company, their need to belong, and even monetary stability. These vulnerabilities are going to be exploited by someone who is more experienced for a number of purposes. They may want to financially or sexually exploit the victim. They may want to gain the victim's allegiance to form a cult or other extreme movement. Some manipulators just go through this process in order to toy with their chosen prey over their pleasure.

Limiting Choice

Controlling choice is form of undetected mind control. It can be a form of this because it is going to provide the manipulator with a range of built-in "get out clauses" if the victim ever starts to get suspicious. The key to this type of mind control is to take away any real choices that the victim has in a specific circumstance, while still providing the illusion that the victim is the one who has the control. Let's say that there is a woman who is being asked to go out on a date. A regular guy is going to spend some time to ask the question and then stammer out a question that is open-ended. They may say something like "Would you like to go out with me?" This question allows the woman to say yes or no based on their personal preferences. This is the way that people who aren't using manipulation will behave.

But someone who is trying to use mind control will approach all of this in a different way. They will confidently and smoothly work to charm the victim. They will get that person to laugh a bit and lower their guard. Then, with a lot of confidence and assurance, the manipulator will ask something like "So, am I taking you out on Thursday or Saturday?" This limits the choices that the victim can go with. The answer of no really isn't an option here, so the victim will pick one of the dates they are given. The victim can't really say that they weren't in control, but the manipulator had complete control the whole time.

Now, if the manipulator is caught, or the victim realizes that they are limited on the choices they are allowed to make, the manipulator can backtrack and still look innocent. They could say something to their victim like "I can't believe you're analyzing my words so much. That really hurts me and makes me not want to open up to you." This can make the victim feel like they were being mean, and they will likely give in.

Media Control with Images

Just like our five senses can be guides in our lives, they can also be our enemies. Our sense of sight is very powerful. This is why we

order to exploit their victim including their need for company, their need to belong, and even monetary stability. These vulnerabilities are going to be exploited by someone who is more experienced for a number of purposes. They may want to financially or sexually exploit the victim. They may want to gain the victim's allegiance to form a cult or other extreme movement. Some manipulators just go through this process in order to toy with their chosen prey over their pleasure.

Limiting Choice

Controlling choice is form of undetected mind control. It can be a form of this because it is going to provide the manipulator with a range of built-in "get out clauses" if the victim ever starts to get suspicious. The key to this type of mind control is to take away any real choices that the victim has in a specific circumstance, while still providing the illusion that the victim is the one who has the control. Let's say that there is a woman who is being asked to go out on a date. A regular guy is going to spend some time to ask the question and then stammer out a question that is open-ended. They may say something like "Would you like to go out with me?" This question allows the woman to say yes or no based on their personal preferences. This is the way that people who aren't using manipulation will behave.

But someone who is trying to use mind control will approach all of this in a different way. They will confidently and smoothly work to charm the victim. They will get that person to laugh a bit and lower their guard. Then, with a lot of confidence and assurance, the manipulator will ask something like "So, am I taking you out on Thursday or Saturday?" This limits the choices that the victim can go with. The answer of no really isn't an option here, so the victim will pick one of the dates they are given. The victim can't really say that they weren't in control, but the manipulator had complete control the whole time.

Now, if the manipulator is caught, or the victim realizes that they are limited on the choices they are allowed to make, the manipulator can backtrack and still look innocent. They could say something to their victim like "I can't believe you're analyzing my words so much. That really hurts me and makes me not want to open up to you." This can make the victim feel like they were being mean, and they will likely give in.

Media Control with Images

Just like our five senses can be guides in our lives, they can also be our enemies. Our sense of sight is very powerful. This is why we can even dream visually, even when all the other senses are missing, and we can use our sight in order to see images of past memories. This can make imagery as well as visual manipulation a really powerful technique to use with media mind control.

Because of the changes in technology, impactful imagery techniques are in the hands of manipulators all over the place, and they can even take these techniques and tailor them to their specific victim. So, if their victim seems to have a fear or an aversion to something, the manipulator is able to use the feared images to help access and then warp the emotions of a person without the victim even realizing what's going on.

Let's look at how this type of mind control can work. We are in an age where there are lots of smartphones, videos, and more. Everything is shot in high definition clips and can be sent at fast speeds to someone else. This means that a high-tech manipulator is able to allude to the feared image. For example, if a boyfriend who is manipulative knows that his girlfriend has a big fear of insects, they could "accidentally" put a book with a picture of an insect on its cover in the background somewhere during that video chat. While the girlfriend may not consciously register that the book is there, on an emotional and subtle level, she is going to feel the impact.

Media Mind Control with Sound

Sound is another method that the manipulator can use in order to do mind control. But personal experience and experiments can confirm this. Have you ever had a song that seems to get stuck in your head? How easy did you find it to get that song out of your head? The sound may have had a big influence over yourself, even though you knew it was there.

The power of an audio manipulation is even greater when it is undetected. Experiments have shown that if customers are exposed to music that comes from a specific region, then they are more likely to order wine from that country. When they were questioned about it later, they had no idea that the sound around them was what influenced them for their decision making.

While there are examples with the media mind control with sound in the media and with the government, even individual manipulators are able to use this kind of mind control as well. One of the creepiest forms of this mind control is to subliminally influence the victim when they are asleep. A skilled mind controller can get their victim when that victim is at the most vulnerable, such as when they are sleeping, and then can implant the dark and devious commands in the ear of their victim. This allows the commands to sink into the lowest layers of the brain of that victim. Another form of this auditory mind control is to mask the words with other words or noises that sound similar. Sounds that are outside the range of human perceptions can be this type of mind control. These sounds will reach a particular frequency, and they can be known to impart a feeling of unease, dread, or terror in those who are unknowingly exposed to them. Once the victim feels scared or trapped, the manipulator can then take control and do what they want from this point.

As you can see, there are a lot of different types of mind control that the manipulator is able to use on their victim. The one they choose will depend on the victim and what the end goal of the manipulator is at the time. The important part is that the manipulator needs to know their victim enough in order to do this type of mind control without worrying that the victim is going to find out what is going on. All of this can come together in order to ensure that the manipulator can get what they want, and the victim often won't realize what is going on until it's too late.

CHAPTER 6: DARK PSYCHOLOGY AND MIND GAMES

Mind games may be something that you think you understand and are able to recognize in your daily life. And it is probably true that someone has tried to play these games on you, and you were able to catch on to them. However, a true manipulator is able to use these mind games in a way that can build up sympathy for themselves, without the victim ever realizing what is going on.

It is common to attribute a lot of normal behaviors to mind games. If someone is hinting that they have a surprise for you or they are teasing you, you may say that the person is using mind games. In the world of dark psychology, this isn't really true. The intentions of the person who uses genuinely dark mind games are never friendly, positive, or good. Therefore, these innocent games, like surprises and teasing, are going to not fit this category right from the beginning.

If the innocent games that we usually associate with mind games don't fit in this category, then what actually constitutes a mind game? Mind games are going to be any type of psychological scheme on behalf of a manipulator towards their victim. These schemes are intended to play games with the willpower or the sanity of the victim.

This is seen as different from the other forms of manipulation we have discussed because the manipulator is toying with their victim. They probably aren't as invested in how this form of manipulation plays out compared to the other methods, and they don't really care about the severity of the situation.

A dark mind game is often one that the manipulator is just going to play for their delight or their amusement. The manipulator isn't going to have any regard for the wellbeing of the victim. Depending on the type of mind game, the intention will often be to test the victim and explore the psyche all at once. The best mind games here are going to be played without revealing the true nature of the manipulator ever being shown. This can really make it hard to detect the mind game, and it is very destructive once the manipulator decides to employ it.

What is the motivation behind these dark mind games?

The motivation behind the mind game can make the difference in whether it is seen as something positive or if it is part of dark psychology. The range of motivations that come with these manipulative mind games is going to be determined based on what the manipulator wants to do and who their victim is at the time.

One reason that a manipulator may choose to play mind games is to manipulate their chosen victim into performing a specific behavior or getting that victim to feel or think a certain way. The manipulator, with this case, may feel that the other forms of manipulation are not all that effective, and they may try to use something that is less obvious to their target, such as a mind game. The manipulator also has the choice to influence the victim in this way just because it amuses them and not because they are really trying to gain something out of the manipulation.

The specific types of influences that can be gained from playing these types of mind games will be explored here in a bit. But basically, these mind games are useful to a manipulator because they are going to reduce the amount of certainty that the victim has, and the psychological strength that the manipulator gains are very subtle and hard to see. Many times, these mind games are going to be used in a way to achieve influence while maintaining the illusion of autonomy with that victim.

Influencing a victim is not the only motivation behind someone using mind games. Many manipulators will choose to play these mind games just to entertain themselves. They like and get pleasure from plotting out ways to impact the psychology of the victim, and they enjoy watching the victim succumb to their intentions. This is similar to what a sociopath may do. The manipulator is not going to see the other person, their victim, as someone who has feelings and thoughts. Instead, they will see them as a system that is there for the manipulator to learn about and use for fun.

Sometimes the dark mind games are played because they are learned behavior, rather than as a conscious intent by the manipulator. This is when the manipulative individual has been exposed to these mind games throughout the course of their life, and they don't know how to act in any other way. This may seem innocent, but it can be just as dangerous because they learned how to act this way and have developed even more methods to really trick their victims into behaving a certain way.

Some Methods Used in Mind Games

Now that you know a bit more about the differences between regular mind games and dark mind games, it is time to explore the different types of mind games that a manipulator can use. The specific games can sometimes have innocent variants in them, but sometimes these variants are dark. Let's take a look at the different types of mind games that a manipulator may try to employ to get what they want from their victim.

Ultimatums

An ultimatum is when one person is able to present the other with a severe choice. It is often going to take the form of a demand such as "Do this... or this will happen." Some examples of how this may play out include:

"Lose weight...or I will see other people."

"Quit smoking...or I will leave you."

Ultimatums are like a request, but it has turned itself more into a demand. They pretty much leave the victim without any choice in the manner. With the example above, the other person will have to lose weight, or they won't be with the person they love any longer. They either need to quit smoking, or the other person is going to leave them. If the victim states that these ultimatums leave them with no choices, the manipulator can always come back and state that the victim had a choice, even though the manipulator knows this isn't true.

There are three factors that are going to determine if the ultimatum is considered dark psychology. First is the type of person who gives the ultimatum, the intention of the other person when giving the ultimatum, and the nature of the request or the ultimatum itself.

First, let's look at the person who is giving the ultimatum. If the ultimatum is a legitimate one, then the person who gives it may have a valid and genuine care about the person they want to help. They may say something like "Lose weight...or you are going to end up with a lot of health problems in the future." There is still an ultimatum because something is going to happen to the victim, but they aren't saying it to be mean or to take away love and care for the other person.

The motivation that comes with that ultimatum is going to be another important element of how you can understand it. Those who issue ultimatums with some good intentions will do it because they want to help make something better in the other person's life. These ultimatums are going to be issues with the intention and the purpose of helping the other person make a good choice and make positive life changes.

Judging the intention of these ultimatums can be difficult, which is sometimes why it is so hard to figure out if the ultimatum is dark or not. But with dark ultimatums, the request is often going to go against what is in the best self-interest of the victim.

The Eternal Breakup

One of the fundamental requirements for a good romantic relationship is that both parties need to have a feeling of contentment and security. People in happy romances or happy marriages are going to feel at ease and will not deal with a constant threat that the relationship is going to end at any time. Masters of manipulation understand these principles and will do everything in their power to invert them. By cultivating a sense of negativity, chaos, and instability in the relationship, the manipulator is able to keep their victim powerless for a long time.

So, what is the eternal breakup is a prolonged and persistent use of threatening to leave someone. This could be a promised, an implied, or an actual breakup that is never followed through on.

With an implied breakup, they will not actually involve the overt mention of the breaking up. Instead, the manipulator is going to hint at the breakup to put some doubt in the mind of their victim. The manipulator calmly mentions upcoming plans, ones that don't involve the victim at all. Any type of sentence or action that could make the victim doubt if the relationship will last can be counted as an implied breakup.

There is also a promised breakup. This is a step between the two types of breakups. This is going to happen when the manipulator issues a threat to their victim and then overtly states that they intend to break up with their victim in the future. The manipulator may resort to saying something like "I am going to leave you soon, and then I won't have to deal with this anymore." Any instance where the manipulator brings up the idea of a divorce, separation, or breakup, but they don't actually carry out this step is going to be a good example of the promised breakup.

Then there is the actual breakup that never occurs. This is the most severe option with the eternal breakup mind game. This is where the manipulator is actually going to break up with their victim without following through with it. They may decide to pack their bags and leave, recognize that the victim is sad or uncomfortable, and then not follow through with it. They may even break up with the victim, without any intention of following through. They will then "accept" the victim back after the victim shows enough sadness or beginning.

The reason that this tactic works is that the victim has often been used and manipulated by the other partner for some time. They are often vulnerable and susceptible to the influence and the power of the manipulator. This makes them more eager to preserve the relationship, even though it has only a dark psychological playground that is fun for the manipulator but hard on the victim each day. If this type of mind game goes on for a long time, it can result in the victim developing trust issues and other options that are not so good for the health of the victim.

Hard to Get

This is another one that can be part of normal and healthy behavior, but then it can also be a part of dark psychology. An example of a hard to get mind game would be the following: a person wants to seem like they are a bit of a challenge to someone they are interested in. They will decide not to be available all the time. This may involve them not accepting every suggested date, taking their time to reply to calls and messages, and other behaviors. The intention here is to make sure that the other person stays interested, and it can help to give them a happy and healthy relationship together.

But the dark psychological use of hard to get can be a lot more dangerous. Those who use this as a form of manipulation are going to play hard to get games at times other than at the beginning of the relationship. Their intention is not going to lead to a positive situation, and they don't really care at all about the wellbeing of the other person. When this continues onto the later parts of the relationship, it can result in a manipulator in the relationship who is unreliable and very evasive.

There are a lot of different ways that the manipulator can choose to be hard to get outside of the relationship. They may decide to become unavailable or unreliable after the two partners made an agreement to be in a committed relationship. This is an inversion to what is seen in most normal relationships. When you meet someone and decide to be in a relationship with them, this usually means that you are both moving in the right direction and that you become more reliable and available compared to the beginning. This does not happen when a dark manipulator is using the hard to get mind game against one of their victims in a relationship.

With a normal relationship, you will find that things are elusive at the start, but then they become firmer over time. A manipulator is able to artificially make the relationship firm in the beginning. This helps to force a sense of connection with their victim. Then, over time, they are going to become less and less available. This will happen once the victim is hooked and already attached to the manipulator.

When a person decides to play the hard to get mind game later on in the relationship, it is going to put the victim on the defensive, and they will need to put in some extra work. The victim is going to work hard to reconnect with the manipulator, who seems to be pulling away from them.

The point of this is that all this work on the part of the victim is going to gratify the manipulator's ego and can place the power back in their hands. The professional manipulators are able to balance out the actions that make them hard to get with those that convey some reliability and closeness. And when they do this successfully, it is going to lead to a lot of deep psychological confusion and even some instability in the mind of the victim. This allows the manipulator to get in there and exploit the situation in any manner they would like, without the victim realizing.

As you can see, there are many different mind games that a manipulator is able to play against their victim. Depending on the type of relationship that they have with their victim and the end results they are trying to gain, the manipulator can use a combination of these techniques to force the victim to act in the way that they want. This can be really hard on the victim. They often don't realize that they are being used and toyed with until it is too late, and by then they are often so stuck in the situation that they can't really do much about it.

CHAPTER 7: UNDERSTANDING DECEPTION AND DECEPTIVE TACTICS

Deception is a hot topic in today's society. At the root, deception is making claims that are false in nature which lead people to believe an idea or concept that isn't true. Deception comes in many forms, from propaganda to simple conversation from the aggressor to the victim convincing them of something that is false. In today's society, we are faced with deception at all angles. Some of the ways we are regularly deceived include:

The Media- Often times in the media we are given half-truths instead of the full picture. These half-truths lead us to complete the idea on our own. This is often used when it concerns public offices, racial inequality, world events, and even your local weather.

Food- With labels reading everything from, no hormones added to healthy and fat-free, we are unable to fully discern what we are eating and what the real regulations are.

Religion- For some, religion is a huge contention of deception. Whether it's the belief as a whole or the misinterpretation of religious text.

Personal Relationships- When we are deceived by the ones we love, it is hard to believe anything anyone says anymore.

The Interpersonal Deception Theory was developed by David B. Buller, and Judee K. Burgoon, both communication professors. At the time of its inception, deceit was not considered an actual form of communication. The IDT is an attempt to relate how people handle deception at both a conscious and an unconscious level. In order to fully understand deception, you have to know some of the forms in which it is presented.

- Misinterpretations of the Truth
- Downplaying of the Truth
- Stretching the Truth
- Holding Back All of the Information
- Contradiction
- Ambiguous Statements
- Lies

People and larger entities use deception for many reasons. The three main motives for deception include avoiding punishment or protecting someone or something, to keep relationships intact, and to preserve the aggressor's self-image. On top of those motives, things like propaganda and media acts of deception can oftentimes be linked to larger goals. For example, a country might put out propaganda in order to trick the people into believing that everything is okay, or that another country is the enemy when there is no truth behind it. A media outlet may put out misleading or half-truths in order to broaden their base of supporters for a specific cause or political candidate.

In today's political market deception can be found across party lines, both in the media and directly from the sources. It is a game of back and forth, telling mostly half-truths in order for you to draw your own conclusion based on your predetermined political ideals. These half-truths can lead to separation of the people and battles back and forth within the community based on political thoughts and notions.

On a smaller level, deception from person to person can lead to broken relationships, financial loss, loss of property, and even death. There are also forms of visual deception. They come in both nature and through man-made efforts. Disguises are another form of visual deception. As you can see, many of these types of deception are for survival purposes. It is when they move into personal gains or selfish reasonings that they become dangerous across the board.

Detecting deception can be difficult, especially when the deceit has no real grounding in physical proof. You could have a he said/ she said battle and the only proof are the words being spoken. How then is one supposed to know which side is deceitful and which is telling the truth? Oftentimes these decisions come down to your personal viewpoint and how well you know the people that are telling you the possibly deceiving stories. Other times, as it is with media and propaganda, research can be done to find out what the entire truth is.

Beyond the boundaries of nature, psychologists have studied deception for many years. They have cataloged, listed, and researched the different types of deception and what the psyche behind it holds. Those with a high likelihood of using their dark psyche often turn to deception for personal gain and to hold onto the lifestyle they have created.

The Psychology of Deception

Deception, boiled down, is essentially lying. Whether the truth is only half the truth, or the information is twisted to fit an agenda, it is a lie. But how often do we find ourselves lying? While no one likes to admit that they have lied or lie on a regular basis, is has been found to be a regular part of life.

Bella DePaulo, Ph.D., a psychologist at the University of Virginia, conducted a study in 1996. The study used 147 people ranging between 18 and 71 years of age. Each person was asked to keep a journal of all of the lies that they told during the course of one week. The study had the following findings:

1. Most people lie once to twice a day.
2. Men and Women, equally, lie in a fifth of their social interactions that last more than ten minutes.
3. In the course of one week, both sexes deceive thirty percent of the people they interact with face-to-face.
4. Some relationships attract deception more than others.

While we grow up being taught that lying is bad, and telling the truth is always the best way to go, as adults we don't follow that rule at all. Even some of the most influential professions such as lawyers, accountants, and politicians lie and deceive on a regular, or even daily, basis. Oftentimes, lying keeps you from receiving punishments. For example, if you are late to school, telling them that you overslept will give you detention, but telling there was an accident will usually let you off the hook. For such small insignificant occurrences, we are pressured into lying to not pay unneeded penalties when nothing is changed by our lateness.

DePaulo's study also included breaking down the types of lies, and the types of relationships most affected by them. She found that couples that are dating lie to each other about a third of the time. Most couples lie from the beginning about things like prior relationships and sexual history. Within marriage, the lies go down to about ten percent, and usually about small everyday things. DePaulo stated, "You save your really big lies for the person that you're closest to."

There are other types of lies as well. The small lies we tell others to avoid hurting their feelings. When we tell someone we like their new haircut or the color of their new magenta shoes. We tell people that they are good people, that their mistakes don't define them, when we know they often do in our society. People with extroverted personalities tend to lie more, especially when under pressure. We also, when facing mental health issues such as depression, have a tendency to lie to ourselves. Those lies can go either way. We can deceive ourselves into thinking everything is fine, or we can further dwell in our own pits of self-loathing, creating lies about ourselves that drag us down further.

The cold hard truth is that we, as a society, have set boundaries and expectations that are rigid enough that every single person lies. Most people, put under enough pressure and fear, will lie about anything. There are those that deceive in order to hurt others. Child custody court is a very good example. The father gets up and makes up complete untruths about the mother in an effort to discredit her. The only thing the judge listens to are the words from both parents and has to decide which one is being deceptive and which one is not. This can often highly affect a child's life.

With all the ways around things these days, what is the real reason that we lie? If there is an easier way to avoid discontent and deception everyone should use it, but we don't. We use lies to quickly put out the fires in our lives, only to find out those lies often start new ones. It is an endless cycle that everyone has gone through in their life.

Top Ways to Effectively Deceive

If you really want to know how to be an effective liar, the answers are all over the place. First, sit and think about a time you have been lied to, but the liar was terrible. Think about the things that were dead giveaways to you. It might have been body language, it might have been their inability to repeat the lie, it could have been filled with absolutely ridiculous information that anyone would have known was a lie. Whatever it is, take note of that. Those are things you do not want to make the mistake of doing. Beyond knowing what not to do, there are several things you want to make sure you always have in line before lying.

Reasoning is Everything

By reasoning, we don't mean your motive. Reasoning means, is it worth it? Pathological liars have a mental condition that triggers something in their brains that is almost a reward for telling a lie. Most pathological liars no longer have any idea what they are saying, and whether it is truth or lies. They will lie about anything at any time for no reason. To be good at deception you basically have to be selective. Keep your lies to a minimum. This will not only save you from having to remember all of your lies, it will create a persona of trustworthiness so when you do lie, no one will really question it. Pick the best times to lie, the times you will get the most out of it.

Have Your Story All Laid Out

There is nothing worse than telling a lie and then having someone ask questions, especially when you don't have the entire story and all the details laid out ahead of time. Making spur of the moment decisions on your stories can often lead you down a bad path. Things don't line up, timelines are off, and lies don't seem to fit together. On top of that, all of the lies you told spur of the moment now have to become cemented into your mind. You have to remember what story you told. In order to have a fluid deception, you have to lay out your story from the beginning to the end. Look at it from an outside perspective and think about all the questions that could be asked. Integrate that information into your mind and then test it for inaccuracies. Compare it to any proof that might be brought forward.

Create a Lie That Is Not Completely a Lie

There are always some truths to lies. One way to get around getting caught in a lie is to tell the truth but leave it short storied. Allow the other person to draw conclusions based on how your lie is told. Give a false impression when you tell your truth, one that pushes the other person in the direction that you want to see them go. Creating a lie from a truth will also help to avoid questions which can significantly increase your ability to successfully carry out your venture.

Really Know the Person You Are Lying To

As is with manipulation, deception works so much better if you are able to tell your lie to a person that you know well. You can incorporate a personal touch that uses emotions, experiences, and thoughts that you are aware that person has. This will automatically help the other person take your statement as truth without overthinking it. When it is something foreign to the person, they will oftentimes begin to question things, search for answers, and ask a lot of questions. All of these things can lead to your lie being found out.

Focus, Focus, Focus

Don't let distractions mix you up. If you already know your story from beginning to end, stay focused on telling it. Don't allow the other person to knock you off track. Look for those signals that show the other person is beginning to question what you are saying and steer them back in the direction you want them in. If you're not focused you could easily say something that throws your whole story out of whack. If you are faced with a question that you didn't think of when putting your story together, either concrete a new lie, if it's simple, or simply tell them you don't remember or you'll have to think about it. If you've already thought about your story from beginning to end, those specific instances will be such small details that it won't seem at all strange that you wouldn't have remembered them.

Don't Let Your Body Betray Your Lie

It is normal for a person to have a physical reaction when they are lying. People tend to have certain eye movements, avoid eye contact, fidget, scratch their faces, touch their noses, and even stutters. If you are going to lie you need to practice it and remember that the real moment may bring pressure with it. As you are telling your story, remember to stay conscious of your body. Keep your eyes glued on the other person and don't break away. Keep your hands comfortable in your lap or start with twirling a pencil, or tapping so that the action doesn't begin when you are telling your lie. Be calm in the face of adversity.

Even the best liars sometimes find themselves caught in a lie. If you find yourself caught don't panic. Don't get angry or violent. Begin to break away from the responsibility of that lie. Think of all the situations or people you can place the different parts of your lie on. Act as if you yourself are just finding out that it's a lie. Be ashamed and wild-eyed because of it. Don't allow the lie to take you over. Back away as quickly as you can and let the person believe you were simply telling it how it was told. That you yourself were deceived.

CHAPTER 8: BRAINWASHING AND DARK PSYCHOLOGY

This technique of mind control was first used in the 1950s during the Korean War. Brainwashing was applied to explain how the totalitarian regimes were able to complete the indoctrinate American troops via a process of propaganda and torture.

Brainwashing is the concept of a person's core affiliations, values, ideas, and beliefs are replaced, so much that the victims have no autonomy control over themselves and can't think independently or critically.

Who is vulnerable to Brainwashing?

From the book of 'The Manchurian Candidate,' a very prominent politician is held hostage by the Korean army during the war, and the senator is brainwashed into becoming a special sleeper agent for the Korean military, to assassinate the presidential contender. From the book, you can learn that even the most intelligent and powerful many can be easily brainwashed, but in the truth, the opposite is very likely.

This includes people that have:
• Been forced to live on the streets
• Lost their loved ones via death or divorce
• Been made redundant or sacked from their workplace
• Suffered or are suffering from an illness that they can't accept
•

How can one be Brainwashed?

A person who is attempting to brainwash you will want to know every detail about your life for them to manipulate your beliefs. The person will want to find out what is your weakness, who you trust, and what your strengths are, who is vital to you and who you listen to for advice.

After doing so, the person will begin the process of brainwashing, which will involve five steps:

Isolation
This is the first tactic towards brainwashing because when you have family and friends around you is harmful to the manipulators. The last thing that they desire is someone with a different idea to their idea, asking questions about what you are being asked to believe. This technique begins in the form of not allowing you to access to friends or family or constant checking where someone is and who they are with.

Attack on Self-esteem

When a person wants to brainwash someone, the manipulators can only do so if their target is in a vulnerable condition and has a low level of self-confidence. A person who is broken is much easy to rebuild with the manipulator's beliefs.
The manipulator requires to break down the target's self-esteem. This could be done through intimidation or embarrassment, physical abuse or verbal abuse, sleep deprivation. A manipulator will begin to regulate everything about the target's life, from the time they sleep to even using the washroom and from food.

Us versus Them

For you to break down a person and reshape them in a different image, an alternative way of their livelihood must be introduced that is more attractive than the present livelihood.

Blind Obedience

This is the ultimate goal of a manipulator, where the target follows orders without question.
Chanting a similar statement over and over again is a good way of controlling a person. Not only is repeating the same statement a tip of calming the mind, but studies have shown that the analytical and the repetitive parts of the mind are not interchangeable. Meaning that you can only do one or the other, so how perfect for halting those doubting thoughts by chanting.

Monopolization of Perception

The abuser utter things that causes you to be introspective, you look deeper, to solve issues of your soul.

The abuser keeps your attention on them

The manipulator makes it not possible for you to do off-limits things

The abusers try to remove anything from your world that they can't control.

Induced Exhaustion

Brainwashers tries to weaken your capability to resist their control by:

Finding tactics to make you feel guilty for not agreeing to their demands.

Keeping you often busy meeting their very high standards of holiness, parenting, and cleanliness

Claim your character is sub-par and they insist that you correct it

Demand that your friends with their boss's spouse, attend social events that improve their professional career

Add tasks to your life that are beyond and above what is often expected in a normal relationship.

Threats

The brainwasher threatens to leave you. The threats are credible to you. The abusers deliver the threats via body language too.

Degradation

The brainwasher harms you more when you resist their demands or question their ideas and stand up for your right. Any moment that your anger rises, the manipulator must deal with your fury, the punishment is more severe than if you just did the damn thing, to begin with.

The brainwasher will tend to degrade you with mere words, via physical or sexual abuse and humiliate you in the presence of their coworkers or friends at any time. The humiliation tears down your sense of self-worth to a lower level.

Demonstrate Omnipotence

Most Brainwashers will stalk you during relationships, use their friends, or they will exploit lucky coincidence to prove that they know everything you do even when they are not present.

Testing

Brainwashers can never think of their work as accomplished, as there are often situations where the target could begin to regain control of their autonomy and begin thinking critically for themselves again. Testing their targets not only shows that they are still brainwashed, but it allows the brainwasher to see just how much control he or she still have over his/her targets. The test could involve doing a criminal act, for example, burglarizing a home or robbing a store.

Healing From Brainwashing

Can one heal and overcome brainwashing? Yes. So long as you know that you have experienced brainwashing, you will be able to heal from it and improve from domestic violence and regain total control of your mind.
First, you should learn ways the manipulator used brainwashing techniques to put you under their control.

Steps that you can follow:

End Isolation. The fast method to get over any fear that you are feeling is opening up about the issue. It could be very wise for you to begin speaking about that manipulation to a therapist. I know that not all are always ready for this, but you can start by conversing about the weather state or the last night's match, this will help you to gain some confidence first. Isolating yourself does not completely end brainwashing on its own. Be around people that know about your abuse and who can be a voice of reason in your surreal, brainwashed world.

A. Learn more about various kind of abuse. Power is in knowledge, and you can make use of it to deny your manipulator's attempts to humiliate and degrade you. There is a lower probability of feeling worse about your manipulator's actions and words when you are aware that the reason your abuser harms you is to control you.

Understand and learn as much as possible about domestic abuse and violence. Soon you will learn how to recognize the kinds of verbal abuse on you by your partner. By learning to identify the types of verbal abuse will give you the ability to detach from harmful behaviors and words as you will tell specifically when your manipulator attempts to harm you. Get to learn what kind of abuse is out there, and how they sound like and look like, and note how the abuse makes you feel.

A familiar question that you might have ever asked yourself is, "Why does he or she abuse me!" Do not spend much of your time to research the answer to it.

B. Accept painful anxieties and thoughts. You will go through unpleasant feelings as you recover from brainwashing. What you should do to your mind is to deprogram it and leave your manipulator's world.

As you accept that the manipulator intends to harm you and mask themselves with a nice face, fear will be experienced. One of the most irrational and rational emotion is fear.
A good domestic attorney for violence or a therapist can assist you in dealing with or overcoming fears in a more healthy, productive manner.

Relieving Stress From Anxiety And Fear

One of the appropriate stress relievers for manipulation victims is them leaving the manipulator. That way, peace will be experienced in a way never imagined.
Most people are not prepared to quit, maybe they choose to stay there forever. Other ways that you can deal with anxiety and stress include:
• Listening to good music
• Proper nutrition.
• Hypnosis for abuse victims
• Techniques for deep breathing
• Meditation techniques
• Better medical care
• Have some spare time for some walk

Manipulation involves force. Physical force does not apply, but at least there is social and psychological force incorporated in every manipulation case.
It is also important to also note that mind manipulation is different

from brainwashing. In cases of brainwashing, the victim knows that the aggressor is an enemy. Brainwashing was used in wars to make prisoners change their belief systems. Besides, brainwashing normally involves physical force, and the victim is literally persuaded to do things he/she would not normally do. However, when he/she escapes the enemy, the effects of brainwashing disappear.

Mind manipulation, on the other hand, is sophisticated and more subtle because the manipulator is considered a friend and does not want to blow the cover. Because the victim is unaware of the selfish intentions, he/she will not apply any defensive techniques. In fact, most of them are willing participants who actually give the manipulator assistance, unknowingly. So long as the victim thinks he/she is in control of the decisions, and that the victimizer has the best interest at heart, then no resistance will be faced.

This aspect makes mind manipulation more dangerous and effective than physical coercion, torture, abuse, and brainwashing. Note again that mind-manipulation does not involve physical coercion, but it is in most cases more effective than other brainwashing and other techniques. This is because coercion (brainwashing) can change behavior, but mind manipulation, which is also referred to as coercive persuasion, will change the entire personality- attitudes, beliefs, behaviors, and thinking processes. Additionally, the victim will actively and happily participate in the process of change, believing it is best for him/her.

It is very hard to admit that a person you trusted, liked and helped was actually manipulating you. That is one reason why it is hard to help a person in a manipulative relationship. They just cannot believe the victimizer is manipulating them. Even when the victim is free of manipulation, he/she will not easily let go of the changes that had already occurred because of the belief that they made the decision to change. Technically, the decisions we make for ourselves have a longer-lasting effect than those we were pushed to make. And it is hard to admit that a close person made us make certain decisions.

Though you will learn how to use manipulation to get what you want, ensure that you do not ignore the desires of others, or cause harm to them. Manipulation will involve charm, coaxing, persuasion, and maybe some bits of misdirection and trickery. The idea of using manipulation should not be to fool everyone into giving you what you want regardless of the consequences. It should be about getting what you want and also leaving the other person in a better place than you found him/her. Do not be fooled into thinking you are smarter just because you can influence other people using mind manipulation tools, more so if you are doing it for selfish gains.

Once you realize that the manipulation techniques are working very effectively for you and are a sure ticket to getting what you want, the temptation to use them more may occur. Consequently, you might find yourself falling into negative manipulation. You might catch yourself failing to give attention to the needs of other people, not listening to the ideas and opinions of others, ignoring the consequences of your actions, and pretending that the other person is not suffering because of you. You might even hear the people around you commenting that you have become selfish and entitled. Some will even begin to avoid you. Know that you have crossed the lines.

To use manipulation effectively without hurting others, do not assume that your desires are the only important issues. Trust that the people around you have needs that might align to yours so that you can find a win-win situation. It is easier for people to trust you if they do not feel manipulated, and when they feel that their needs count too.

CHAPTER 9: HYPNOTISM

Hypnotism is a state of consciousness that involves the focused attention together with the reduced peripheral awareness that is characterized by the participant's increased ability to respond to suggestions that are given.

Major Myths of Hypnotism

Myths are untruths or exaggerations regarding the definition, process, and purpose of something. I will list some myths along with their refutations about hypnotism.

Is Hypnotism Sleeping?

No. The hypnotic trance is a modified state of consciousness called the Alpha state. In this state, other than physiological sleep, there is strong electrical activity in the brain due to the very high level of concentration that the subject is performing. Simplifying hypnosis to the maximum, we can define it as monoideism, that is, absolute focus on the imagination.

Hypnotism Is Conditional

A trusting partnership between the hypnotist and subject is required, so if the subject does not want to be hypnotized, they will not be. In the old days, it was said that the hypnotist became the operator of the mind of the hypnotized subject, but I would say that the hypnotist is another facilitator of the trance. He bridges the conscious mind and the unconscious, thus allowing the subject to access a state of consciousness which allows the subject to experience the full potential of their own mind.

Hypnotism Works

If this is true, 100% of the people who can pay attention are mentally weak. After all, if you "dream awake", have fun reading a good book, "travel" listening to an interesting story, or go to the movies and get emotional about them, you go into a trance.

Have you ever encountered a person who has a lost, seemingly distracted look and when you catch her attention, she takes a little fright? This person is not distracted, in fact, she is hyper-concentrated, that is, in trance.

The truth is that once in a while, our brain "hibernates" for a few minutes to save energy. Have you ever wondered if you needed to be aware of everything you do all the time? Consider someone who drives a car, when he was learning, he found it all complicated — steering, gears, brakes, throttle, clutch and all at the same time!

But now, he operates so unconsciously (or automatically) that he even commits himself to reckless talking on a cell phone while driving. Basically, if a human being is able to concentrate and obey the instructions, he can be hypnotized.

The Hypnotized Subject Will Do Whatever the Hypnotist Says

The human mind is not "mother's house". There are particular moral principles of each person and these principles are obeyed and protected by the subject's unconscious mind. Thus, it is true to say that a hypnotized person will do nothing against their moral principles (religion, family, values, physical integrity), that is, if you would not perform an action while "awake", you will not do so while hypnotized.

The Hypnotized Subject Will Tell All His Secrets to the Hypnotist

Hypnotism is a Physiological Phenomenon

It is a legitimate neuro-physiological phenomenon, where brain functioning has very special characteristics, such as muscle relaxation, anesthesia, dilation of the pupils, and memory enhancement.

During the trance, there are actually changes in the brain and this has already been confirmed in a study by examination of volunteers using an encephalogram. Perhaps in mysticism, there is a little hypnosis, but in hypnosis, there is nothing mystical.

Can a Person Not Return From the Trance?

Back from where? You're not going anywhere. The advantage of being hypnotized is that you can travel the whole world without leaving your body, just with your mind.

Finally, hypnosis is a safe method for both entertainment (street, stage) and clinical applications (hypnotherapy and the like). If you believe in God, see the ability to be hypnotized as a divine gift for your self-improvement, but if you do not believe in a deity, see hypnosis as a very powerful tool that nature has given to the human being to accelerate positive changes in life.

Hypnotism Techniques

There are 3 main techniques of hypnotism used in clinical treatment. Clinical hypnotism, that is, hypnotism performed in the office by a trained professional, can follow different methodologies or concepts, depending on the line of work of the hypnologist. Today, we will present the three most known lines and their main characteristics:

Conditional Hypnotism

Created and patented by Luiz Carlos Crozera, conditional hypnosis is a technique used to rid the patient's mind of blockages that directly interfere with his physical and emotional health.

In this technique, deep body relaxation is done so that the patient has a decrease in his brain frequency and, with the purest mind, can be led by the hypnotist to the traumatic records that accompany him. At this point, the professional removes the registered emotional charge, disassociating the trauma from the given situation.

Upon returning from the trance, the patient already has an important behavioral change when faced with what caused him anguish. Thus, the hypnotist uses the post-hypnotic suggestion, a technique that executes the commands inserted during the trance, in order to achieve the best possible results. In conditional hypnosis, the patient does not interact with the hypnotist.

Eriksonian Hypnotism

In this technique of clinical hypnosis, described by the American psychiatrist Milton Erickson, the patient is suggested to seek within himself new learning that leads to a reformulation of thoughts and truths. Thus, the patient is led to the trance and suggested to relive, in a metaphorical way, the situation that causes him pain and suffering but with a completely different outcome, aiming for the trauma to be forgotten.

The idea is not to change what has been experienced, but to give other responses to the trauma since it is believed that the patient has all the resources necessary to solve his own problems.

Classic Hypnotism

This method is mostly in disuse because it presents less efficient results than the other methodologies. Classic Hypnosis consists of searching in the memory of the patient for the facts that bring him suffering and making him understand that it is part of the past and should no longer reach the present.

How to Hypnotize Someone Without Them Knowing

Have you ever heard of a method that many claims to be able to achieve through repetitive motions, with the help of pendulums or finger movements, which allows them to stay in a state of trance? Is it possible? Well, some people believe so. Texts produced in Egypt in 1550 BC show evidence that older people already used these practices.

Well, the name of this method is hypnosis and, in fact, this is a psychological state, which brings together several phenomena that occur in our mind, and which can produce different impacts. It can be conducted by a voice and has been used as an instrument in the treatment of different diagnoses.

While there are those who believe in past lives and those who do not, it is true that hypnosis can cause the patient to return to a certain age. For example, hypnosis may return someone up to an "x" age, when he may have contracted some kind of trauma.

Let's look at a situation to illustrate: A patient is in a hypnotized state. The doctor puts his hands on the patient's arm and warns that he is applying an ointment, when in fact, he is not applying anything, he just touches the patient's hands. Despite this, the patient has the feeling that the doctor is actually applying an ointment, even being able to smell the ointment as it passes through a positive olfactory hallucination. The patient, who is hypnotized, really believes the doctor's words.

Another example is the case of a patient who smells a scent. When they smell the gunpowder, if this smell happens to be strongly associated with when they were 10 years of age, then the patient can regress until the age of 10 to try to solve some kind of childhood problem. Not everyone is able to perform this practice because a badly done hypnosis session can cause great harm. This is because hypnosis is not restricted only to the return to time but also the treatment of certain psychological problems, which can be aggravated if not treated by a specialized professional. For this reason, only those who have technical knowledge of the use of hypnosis should practice it.

How to Hypnotize a Person

However, if you would like to learn this technique in order to know the principles of hypnosis and then go deeper into the subject, follow this step-by-step guide:
1. The first thing to do is to make the person quite relaxed. Sitting comfortably and getting ready for the session in peace is a good start. It is not good to lie down because it can lead to sleep and prevent hypnosis from reaching the person's mind.
2. The second step is to start speaking very slowly so that the person pays attention to your voice and begins to relax at the same time. Then you can use a pendulum (swing the pendulum at the height of the person's eyes) or your own finger, making repetitive movements also at eye level. You could also use the moving image of a spiral. Continue the movement until you see the person become half asleep.

   Ideally, the person should not close his or her eyes. One way that helps create concentration is to blink and focus the mind on what is being said. Talk about certain things, slowly, that cause you to relax and ask the person to imagine a feeling of warmth and comfort all over their body.

3. You need to always be in touch with the person who will be hypnotized. Ask him to take a deep breath and breathe out slowly through his nose. Ensure that the participant always stays relaxed during the hypnosis.
4. Ask him to imagine himself levitating and also to pay attention to all parts of his body, trying to perceive any discomfort or pain starting with his head and working downwards. Tell him to let the pain go away. Ask him to repeat this kind of thinking for each part of his body.
5. As soon as you realize that the patient has reached a state of relaxation, have him imagine a spiral staircase. He should fully visualize this thought and go down the stairs. With every step he

takes on that ladder, he must feel he is moving ever deeper into his thoughts. A few steps later, as many as you think necessary, let the patient know that there is a door at the end of the staircase and that it is time for him to cross that door.

6. The person must open the door and enter the next environment. Direct the person to imagine that this environment is a room, which can be decorated in any way that he would like to imagine. Then direct the thoughts of the person saying that he should look in this room for a place to sit.

7. Say you will count from 1 to 10 and that, in the end, the participant will be in a deep state of hypnosis. This is the time to ask the questions that will bring the patient to the result that you want to extract from that experience. This is also the time to cause sensations by the suggestion of taste and smell, among others. For example, you can ask him to find some chicken in this room and eat it. The hypnotized person will actually believe and feel the taste of eating the chicken.

8. After the experience, let him know that he will wake up in a few moments. Ask him to rise from the place where, mentally, he is sitting and walk back down the same path. When he reaches the last step, he will be awake and relaxed. Then count to three and say wake up!

Remember that this experience needs a lot of care and attention to be put into practice. After all, there are proven cases of poorly done hypnosis practices that have caused mental problems in patients. Therefore, seek the guidance of a professional !

CHAPTER 9 PART 2: ENERGIZING THE MIND

Humans spend countless hours seeking new ways to work just about anything. Through endless hours of research, they pour over books and journals looking for the message that will tell them the secret to harnessing mind power. Many never realize that the most powerful mind power tool is already on board and just aching to be used. It is the human brain, the mind itself.

Every time a person practices a new habit or thinks a new thought, they make a new pathway in the brain. Every time the habit is used, or the idea is thought, the nerve pathway becomes even stronger. The human brain is wired at birth to be an efficient machine and it is ready, from birth, to make an ever increasing amount of nerve pathways and to strengthen the pathways that are used the most.

Sometimes thoughts and habits need to be changed for the improvement of the person. When people decide that they would like to make a change in their lives, there will be a period of adjustment. This is true whether the change is mental, emotional, or physical. During this period of adjustment, there will be some level of discomfort. When a habit or a thought is already formed, it has made its own path in the brain. When a stimulus is seen or heard, the message travels along the preset nerve pathway to the spot in the brain that controls that thought or habit. In order to change a thought or a habit, it is necessary for the nerve path to be changed. Until the nerve path is changed, the old nerve path will remain in the brain. The discomfort comes from the brain trying to automatically access the old pathway and the new pathway at the same time. This is painful for the brain to do.

It is easy to become frustrated when the brain goes back to its old patterns of thought and habit. Never fall into the habit of placing blame on a lack of willpower. Willpower has nothing to do with it. It is a very difficult thing to override preset pathways in the brain. The brain is a very powerful tool. When will power fails and mistakes happen, remember to use kindness and compassion in dealing with the failure. The brain is very efficient at doing what it does. The only way to change the pathways in the brain is to keep working on new pathways that will eventually obliterate the old, undesirable ones.

The brain needs a clear understanding that changes are about to take place and new pathways are about to be laid down. Remind the brain that new habits and new thoughts will be replacing the old ones. Blaming failure on a lack of willpower is a self-defeating statement. The process of making new nerve paths in the brain takes hard work and time. It will help to keep reminding oneself of the impending change. By doing this over and over, it makes the process no longer about possible character flaws. The focus is now put on the habit of thought that is being built.

Is it possible to build new nerve pathways in the brain? Yes, it is possible, and it can be done. If more proof is needed, just compare the adult brain to the baby's brain. Every current habit and thought a person has is the direct result of having spent time practicing them over and over until they created a pathway in the brain. New pathways can be created. Think of it this way: they already have. The baby's brain has no idea of anything. It has no thoughts or habits. Every nerve path currently in the brain was practiced until it became a part of the brain. Think of the baby. The baby lies around day after day and does baby things. Then one day the baby notices the shiny rattle that mommy is waving in front of its little face. The baby wants the rattle. As the baby is waving its tiny arms around, the mommy puts the rattle close enough so the baby can touch it with its wavering hand. After a few of these sessions, the baby gets the idea that if the arm is in the air it can touch the rattle. A nerve pathway is beginning to grow. So the baby decides to lift its arm to actively reach for the rattle. The baby will be unsuccessful at first because the arms will wave wildly and will not connect with the rattle. One day, the baby will actually grab the rattle, and the nerve pathway is then complete.

While this may seem like a very simple example, it is exactly how nerve pathways are created in the brain. Every action, thought, or habit has its own nerve pathway. All pathways must be created. No one was born knowing to sit in front of the television and mindlessly eat dip with chips. No one was born lamenting the excess pounds they carry in strange places. No one was born hating their body. All behaviors are learned, good and bad. And the bad ones can be replaced with good ones.

So if the ability to program negative thoughts into the brain exists, then the ability to disrupt those negative thoughts with positive thoughts also exists. The brain can be reprogrammed. It is a powerful tool, and its main function is to turn thoughts into reality. The brain is always working, so why not use the power of the brain to benefit rather than harm? Just because a particular habit or thought has been around all forever does not mean it needs to stay. Use the power of the brain to choose new habits and thoughts to focus on and replace the old, negative thought pathways in the brain.

CULTIVATING CONCENTRATION

The first step to be more compelling is to be more authentic. Authenticity is the act of being the individual you are. Write a short sentence or paragraph to describe your ideas, your beliefs. Try to catch the essence of who you are as opposed to describing yourself with your economic wellbeing (I'm a king) or employment (I'm the president). Those are worldly in nature and shaky foundations for your character because they can change. Instead, concentrate on your tendencies, your inherent nature; for example, are you mindful, engaged, keen, supportive, shrewd, thrifty, or empowering? Likewise, consider causes, traditions, or hobbies that characterize your life in your statement.

Being who you are is one of the most important things to being more compelling. This effort can lead individuals to trust in you and enhance your capacity to persuade those you look to impact. Building a sound and steady individual character is fundamental for individuals to bolster you, your thoughts, or your cause.

It is anything but difficult to connect compelling individuals to charismatic personalities. Ailes worked with U.S. presidents and motion picture stars throughout his long profession. He understands charisma, and likewise understands everybody can use some level of charisma if they are to have any impact on others. However, he indicates that it isn't something reserved for a few. He expands our view of the charismatic individual by stating that charisma doesn't require a man to be noisy or ostentatious. The best test is whether individuals respond to you rather than you responding to them.

Inspiring others to listen and respectfully respond is a genuine sign that you have a compelling impact. So how would you do this? Consider these attributes charismatic individuals normally display.

- They comprehend and acknowledge who they are and present a strong personality. This helps them identify with others and listen to others respectfully.
- They accept life as it is and live authentically.
- They have a mission and objectives for life that are greater than themselves. Compelling individuals don't live by the

expression "it's all about me."

- They anticipate good faith without entitlement. They take a long-term approach that may require a great deal of effort, yet it doesn't require a blind leap of faith for more difficult cases.

- They respect the contributions of others to their authority or work. The very meaning of charisma is comfort. A positive reaction does not boost their inner self, but rather prompts them to share credit.

- They understand the value they bring to a situation and don't question their capacities. They are skilled individuals who convey confidence and show others how it's done.

- They focus on their central goal or mission, and the associated objectives. This is only possible when these goals and objectives are consistent with their characteristic inspirations.

Certain lifetime accomplishments, one of a kind encounters, or individual qualities can boost your charisma. Consider the visually impaired man who climbs Mount Everest, a lady surviving a horrifying plane crash, or being raised in an environment that produces personality traits such as boldness, authority, and confidence as illustrations. These are things that you don't really have control over in your life. You can be more compelling by taking dynamic strides other charismatic individuals have taken to enhance your own personality.

HYPNOTIC TECHNIQUES WORLD'S TOP HYPNOTISTS USE

You have heard of hypnosis. You have surely seen it used on television where the hypnotist tells the person they are getting sleepy. They usually swing some type of pendulum in front of them and then the person falls asleep, completely under the control of the hypnotist. While it happens a bit differently in real life, the end result is the same. Once you are able to successfully hypnotize people, you are able to control what they do and think.

Once a person is under hypnosis, you can make suggestions. For example, you want a person to buy you something. You hypnotize them and suggest they buy it for you. Once they come out of the hypnosis, chances are they are going to get you what you suggested in the very near future.

Now, when you are using hypnosis in this way, you want to do it without the person knowing you are. You will not swing in a pendulum in front of their face to induce the trance state.

Stages of Hypnosis
There are four stages all people go through when you are working to get to their unconscious mind:
Stage One: You have to make sure that you have their undivided attention.

Stage Two: You have to get them to a state of compliance.

Stage Three: You have to activate their unconscious response.

Step Four: They are now under your control and you simply need to lead them to the outcome you desire.

Be Powerful
You can create a hypnotic state for people by simply exerting power over others. Look at how people are likely to blindly follow a person who appears to be powerful. When you do this, you can get a following and the people following you will do what you say because they want to please you and stay in your presence.
You can use this technique among your friends, family and coworkers. Basically any person that you have a pre-existing relationship with. You want to exert your power over time so that it does not feel too aggressive. Once you notice you have followers, start small with what you are asking. They will do it without even thinking twice about it. Over time, you can ask for larger things and you will have no trouble getting them.
Mirroring
Now, the powerful approach works for people you know, but what about strangers? This is where mirroring comes into play. This allows you to quickly develop a rapport with someone once they see you both have someone in common. This can almost put them into a trance because they will naturally like you and want to please you since they will perceive the both of you as very similar.
To successfully use this technique, pay attention to the stranger's common phrases and body language. Look at their behaviors. Exhibit these things back at them. As you continue your interaction with them, it will not take long for them to notice the similarities. You do not even have to lie about things you have in common. Simply mirroring their language and behaviors is enough to get them under your spell, per se.
Use Stories

The right stories can put people into a trance-like state. Think back to when you were a kid and your parents would read you stories before bed. This would induce a deep state of relaxation. The same is true when you are an adult.

As you are talking to people each day, add in some anecdotes. This shows you on a more personal level and can even give you a sense of power and authority. You want people to be able to visualize what you are saying, so use imagery when you are telling your story.

For example, you want a person to move something breakable for you because you just do not want to take the risk. Do not just ask them to move it carefully. State that you do not want the vase to be dropped since it can shatter. They will visualize the vase shattering, forcing them to not only be careful when moving it, but they will volunteer to do it. They will almost see completing the task successfully as a type of personal challenge.

Lengthy Speeches

When you want to induce hypnosis on a large group, lengthy speeches are the way to do it. Think about the television evangelists you have seen. They essentially use this form of hypnosis to get people to hand over thousands of dollars every time they hold a service.

When they are delivering their speech, they take few pauses. They use varied voice tones to annunciate points and keep people completely engrossed in what they are saying. They know what their message is, and they repeat it frequently. They often do it using different phrasing, however, so no one in the audience ever feels like something is being forced on them.

It is not uncommon for them to tell you exactly what to do without directly telling you to do it. When you are in this type of situation, you are so enamored with the speaker, that you will do just about anything they ask. They always present their lengthy speech and then they just pass the collection basket. They do not ask you to donate because they know you will because you feel dedicated to them.

This is a technique that you can use too. You do not need an auditorium for it either. If you need something from a person, or a group of people, plan out a speech. Make sure that those you are talking to feel empowered throughout the speech. By the time you get to the end, you have already subconsciously implanted in their minds what you want. You will not need to ask for it. You will just get it.

For example, you want people to invest in your new business idea. Give them a speech about the business, about how much starting it would mean to you and then insert a bit of a sob story about how this is your dream, but financially, you cannot swing it. After listening to your dramatic speech, they will feel compelled to invest.

Stacking

This is a hypnotic technique that works because you essentially overwhelm the people you are talking to. With this technique, you essentially bombard people with information. They are learning so many new things that they do not have time to sort through it. They do not feel they need to check facts because you are speaking with such authority that they automatically believe what you are saying. By the time you end your thoughts, you have essentially put them into a trance.

They are completely overwhelmed and defenseless at this point. So you can tell them anything now and they are going to believe it. This is when you step in and use their trance-like state to your advantage. You do not directly ask for something. At this point, you just need to make a mere suggestion and you will get what you want.

Eye Cues

You learned in a previous chapter how important body language is when you are looking to persuade someone to do something. The same is true when you are seeking to induce a state of hypnosis. You can look into a person's eyes and be able to tell if someone is essentially under your spell. You can also use your eyes to do it.

When you are seeking to hypnotize, look at where their eyes are. If they are directly focused on you, you know that you have their undivided attention and you can start implanting ideas and suggestions into the subconscious.

Cold Reading

This is something that psychics use to convince people that they can actually read their mind and predict their future. You will start by making a vague statement. For example, if you know a person to be shy, you will state this. You know it is true and they will elaborate, giving you further information. You will use this further information to essentially make other predictions. Once a person feels that you have this almost clairvoyant ability, they are more prone to believe anything that you tell them.

BETTY ERICKSON'S 3-2-1 SCRIPT

This is a type of hypnosis that involves the use of stories and metaphors in controlling the mind of the subject. The stories are often didactic and are told in a way that drives home a particular point by creating a clear picture in the head of the subject in order to enable the subject to change a behavioral pattern or attitude. For example, when a parent decides to tell a lying child a story that typically deploys lying as a grievous offense with drastic consequences, the child becomes emotionally drawn to the story and automatically becomes influenced positively by the story.

This is a form of hypnosis which an individual undergoes without the physical supervision of a hypnotist. The process mostly involves the use of instructions whether that is in the form of a video or audio format. Self-hypnosis is a very effective type of hypnosis because the subjects are often very determined to be subjective to the entire procedure. A person may self-hypnotize when a professional hypnotherapist isn't available. It involves the use of auto suggestions (because it might be difficult to achieve the altered state). This form of hypnosis helps people get over smoking addiction and various other forms of addiction. It can also be used to get over stage fright and anxiety. People who have undergone severe stress may decide to self-hypnotize in order to relax their minds.

Stage hypnosis: This is the most common form of hypnosis. This is the idea of hypnosis the majority of people have in mind when the topic 0f hypnosis comes up. It involves a scenario whereby a hypnotist stands before a large crowd to entertain them by giving some members of the audience a ridiculous set of instructions for the sole purpose of entertaining the audience. This could be done in a club or a theatre. No one knows why this type of hypnosis is often very effective. It has been recorded that most people who carry out these ridiculous instructions do so because, they are excited about performing in front of a large audience, while some do it because of the pressure that comes with it. Others do it because they jump at the opportunity to get over their stage fright under the guise of hypnosis. This form of hypnosis often combines several methods such as tricks, psychological wits, and other mediums. This form of hypnosis is sometimes not very popular with people as some subjects may become really annoyed when they realize how they have made a fool of themselves.

Medical hypnosis: Over the years, hypnosis has been used for medical purposes. The process of using hypnosis for the betterment of certain health conditions is known as "hypnotherapy." Hypnotherapy is a form of psychotherapy. Hypnotherapy has been used to help several patients overcome certain health conditions and addiction. Some of the use of hypnotherapy are:

The use of hypnotherapy in curing skin diseases.

The use of hypnotherapy during surgery. Some patients are naturally anxious before the commencement of a surgical operation. Hypnotherapy has been used over the years to allay the fears of patients during surgery or before surgery. Hypnotherapy has proved effective in the area of reducing anxiety and calming the human mind. Patients undergoing chemotherapy could also find hypnotherapy effective in the reduction of pain and getting over pain in general.

The use of hypnotherapy in overcoming addiction. Hypnotherapists have successfully helped people overcome their smoking habits and other several addictions. However, you must note that hypnotherapy isn't for everyone. Hypnotherapy works best when a person is willing to overcome an addiction themselves. No matter how much you try to hypnotize someone who isn't willing to get over an addiction, they will only keep going back to their addiction as soon as their hypnotherapy session ends.

The use of hypnotherapy for wellbeing purposes. Hypnotherapy has also helped people become more confident and more at peace with themselves and their surroundings. Helping the mind relax and calm can improve the general wellbeing of individuals.

A COMPLETE SCRIPT TO TAKE SOMEONE FROM BEGINNING TO END IN A HYPNOTIC SESSION

Hypnosis is something that many people consider to be fake or a myth. Many skeptics don't take it seriously, but others think that hypnosis is another form of mind control. Hypnosis is a type of legitimate therapy used for many patients. Some patients will use it to stop overeating, while others will use it to stop smoking. Many people do misunderstand it and its uses because it is not used everywhere and on everyone. There is medical research that has shown that it can work and it can be used in therapy.

Some people view hypnosis as the man waving the clock back and forth and saying, "you are getting very sleepy." This is an old image of how hypnosis used to be done, and there are new ways that it is done today by therapists. Hypnosis is used to make suggestions to the patient who is looking for help. This is why many think of it as a type of mind control. The power of suggestion can help people think just about anything they want, and we saw that in the Jim Jones case.

As a treatment option, hypnosis helps people to treat their problems and cope with issues that they have. The therapists will make slight suggestions on how they can do this while they are under hypnosis. Patients are put in a trance-like state, and this is when the therapist will start to give them suggestions on making their lives better. When you are under hypnosis, your brain goes through some changes. There are two major areas that are affected during hypnosis. These two places in the brain help you to process and control the things happening inside of your body. When your therapist tells those parts of the brain to stop eating whenever you're bored, the brain takes this information and moves it around your entire body. This is how hypnosis can work and be a great way to treat grief or other ailments. Many people will use hypnosis when nothing else has worked for them.

Many people believe that hypnosis is a type of mind control. This mind control comes in the form of suggestions. These suggestions can be verbal or non-verbal, and we will dive into each of these to show you what is done in hypnosis. We will start with verbal hypnosis and the suggestions made during a session. Verbal hypnosis is also known as conversational hypnosis. This type of hypnosis is a way to communicate with someone's unconscious mind. This is also done through a conversation with a patient. Verbal cues in this type of hypnosis include using some keywords that will unfasten the mind. Depending on what secrets the patient is holding, this could end up pretty dangerous, especially if the patient doesn't want these secrets coming out. This is why many people do not trust going to a verbal hypnotist.

Verbal hypnosis also uses vague words and phrases to try and get more out of the patient. This type of hypnosis has occurred in history with leaders and rulers all over the world. When these patients were given cues, they exposed more than they ever thought that they would! This type of hypnosis may have you a bit worried, but if you are going to a therapist to be hypnotized, you are perfectly safe. Never let someone hypnotize you unless they are a trained professional.

There is a non-verbal way to practice hypnosis as well. You probably guessed that this type of hypnosis is done without conversation. The eyes are what is used the most in this type of hypnosis. This is the type that many people will associate with mind control. The eyes are said to link the patient with the hypnotist, and this can help the patient get through their problems. A lot of people are not sure if they should trust this type of hypnosis because it is not used very often.

Hypnosis Tactics

When trying to hypnotize someone, there are many tactics that the hypnotists will use. We will explain these to you and show you just how they could be in the realm of mind control. One of these is called NLP, or neuro-linguistic programming. This is a type of hypnosis that is unlike anything traditional. In NLP, our behaviors are said to be associated with all of the sensory experiences that we have had. NLP focuses on olfactory, gustatory, auditory, visual, kinesthetic, and digital.

There are a few basics in NLP. First, there is a focus on ambiguity and the power it holds for us. For example, those who practice NLP will say things that help the patient with the best and most useful content for them at this very moment. The therapists will say, "do what is right for you" instead of telling them exactly what to do. There is a rhythm and tonality to NLP, along with a good and even flow. NLP therapists will use a lot of sounds to help their patients. They also use different language patterns with their patients, and that helps to change the commands that they are giving when their patient is in their trance-like state.

The tones that are used all have different meanings. The voice is giving commands, instead of asking questions. The command is given more emphasis, and the voice is changed when it is more important. The voice gives the patient a full reflection and meaning of the words that the therapist is using. There is non-verbal communication used in NLP, but the therapists will generally use their voice to give commands.

Anchoring is another popular tactic that is used in hypnosis. When an anchor is used, this means that the therapist is using a living memory to make an association with the patient. These anchors can be made of any senses, and when an anchor is used, therapists notice that the life memory becomes stronger as the senses are added in. An example would be mentioning a word like "daisy."

Some people will see the flower, while there are others who may see a pet or a woman. They may have fond memories of the flower, and this helps them to make the association and get the life memories more vivid in the therapy session.

There are some things to understand about using an anchor, though. Sometimes an anchor can trigger bad memories for a person. This is when you need to explain to them that their life memory is meant to be a safe place and not something that brings them pain. You must be able to understand just how intense the anchor you are using is. Your timing needs to be right as well. If you use an anchor for someone during a bad time for him or her, the hypnosis may go the opposite direction that you want it to. You will also need to figure out if any of the senses they used are a direct correlation to a trigger or stimulus for them. This is key when you are working with an anchor.

To make their patients feel as if they have a safe place, they let them get into their favorite position to relax in. If they are not comfortable in the office, the therapist can suggest other options for them. Many patients with severe triggers like to spend their therapy sessions outside and feeling the fresh air. The therapist will also ask a string of questions that will help them to determine what the patient's triggers are. This will help them to determine what senses they will try and stimulate and what anchor to use.

There are a few principles that therapists use when they put anchors into their sessions. The first is trust and interpersonal absorption. This is making sure that the trust of the patient is secured. This needs to happen before there is any anchor applied to the sessions. This may take one visit or many. If the patient stays with the therapist, then they can determine that trust is locked in. Uniqueness is also a part of the therapy. This means that anchors will be linked to the therapists, and they will have to be anchors that are not ones that bring up triggers or life memories for them. They are only to bring up life memories for the patients. This can be tricky for a therapist, so it is best for them to bring up the unique anchors they can produce. This does take a lot of work on the therapist's part as well.

Reframing is another tool that therapists use when they are with patients who are being hypnotized. This is a way to get them to look at a situation differently. It seems like many therapists do this anyway, so what makes it so different in hypnosis? Many therapists call this positive reframing because they are trying to get their patients to have a more optimistic view of their life and what has happened recently in their life. Many will try to do this after their patients have had a death in their family or a traumatic event has occurred. When reframing is used, it doesn't change the situation for the patient. It just helps them to reduce the damage that has been done already. It will put the situation in a different perspective, and it is usually a healthier way for them to look at it. Many therapists will try to use this technique to break the ice with their patients and try to add humor into their sessions. Those with open minds will love this type of therapy, but some do not want to add humor into their sessions until they feel better from their grief or sadness.

Lastly, we have the future pacing technique. This is a way that therapists will use the anchor in the sessions and connect other changes and resources to it. When you hear the words mental imagery, this is a type of it. Future pacing generally will happen at the end of an NLP session and helps to guarantee that the changes made in the patient's mind are feasible in the outside world. Future pacing is used only when patients possess certain traits. When a patient is calm, their breathing has slowed, and their blood pressure is then therapists can use this technique. Much like anchoring, if future pacing is used at the wrong time, there could be triggering effects that could do damage to the patient.

When future pacing is used, the therapist will think about a few things. First, they will think about all of the different situations for the future for their patient. They will use the senses to explain to the patient how to change their current situation. They will also talk to their patient about the positive changes that this will have on their lives. They will also walk them through the many ways that they can respond to any sudden changes in their lives.

All of these techniques can be used in hypnosis. If you feel that you want to try it, we suggest finding a professional who can walk you through it step by step. It is important to check their credentials and read the reviews. If you know someone close to you who has used a hypnotist, ask for their opinion and if it did work for them.

CHAPTER 10: PROTECTING YOURSELF AGAINST HYPNOSIS

Beware of Matchers

The first thing you're going to want to do is take in and apply everything you've just learned. Remember all that stuff about matching and mirroring? Well, now you need to be on the lookout for it. When you are speaking to someone who you think is trying to control you, make a point to note how they are reacting to your body language. Are they sitting in the same pattern you are? Are they copying your movements as well?

If you're unsure, try testing it out by changing your posture and then wait to see if they mimic it. The mimicking may be a bit more subtle and a bit more delayed, but the unskilled ones are a total giveaway. They'll copy the posture right away, and automatically, you know what you're up against.

Now that you know, you can either call them out on their behavior or, if you want to have a little fun, Not only will you catch them off guard, but if you can pull it off, you can get them to tell you what their whole ploy was all about and who put them up to it. Total win!

Consciously Infuse Randomness in Your Eye Movement

When it comes to confusing your opponent and playing them at their own game, there is little that is going to give you the same amount of satisfaction as random play. Random eye movements are like going to the gym with your iPod on shuffle. Nobody knows what's coming on next. It's basically like trolling your manipulators in real-time, and it can be quite fun.

Any user worth their salt is going to go in hard with the whole eye movement thing. This is because your eye movements tell them how you assess and store information, which is precisely why some people can tell if you are lying or cheating just by looking at your eyes. When they say your eyes speak volumes, this is what they mean! Simple, use random eye movements. As you are speaking, make a point to look left or right or up or down. You can even make a game of it. Left for every complex sentence, down for every question, and simple sentences can go right or up, depending on whether they start with a vowel.

Be Attentive

Another thing you need to be very careful about is how much attention you are paying to your surroundings and to what's going on in them. This may sound a little extreme because obviously who stays alert all the time, you're hardly a cop on the stakeout, and even if you were, how are you supposed to be attentive all the time! Okay, so look, we get you can't always be super alert, but you need to know that when you aren't alert; you are vulnerable. So, an important tactic that employers use when negotiating salary packages is waiting until the employee in question seems a little off and then jumping in and saying that they haven't negotiated a pay difference for Tom, Dick, and Harry, and don't foresee a lot of change in the other employees as well. Not much change at all, they repeat.

Automatically, now that you are asked how much change in salary you expect, you say not much change – Congratulations! You've just been programmed!

Watch Your Mouth

Another important tip? Watch what you say. Master manipulators tend to create a false sense of urgency where they will make you feel that you have to do this particular thing by this specific time or else something drastic will happen. You don't have a choice. You have to do this now! What do you do? Well, nothing.

Yes, seriously nothing. Never make any important decisions at the drop of a hat. Chances are you're not the president of the United States, meaning no nuclear codes lie with you, which of course means that you don't need to make any immediate decisions without consulting people. Really, you don't have to make any immediate decisions at all. Sit tight.

Getting you to commit is a classic dark psychology move to create a sense of obligation that can later be exploited. Don't fall for it!

Trust your Gut

And your final rule, which also happens to be your most important, is to trust your gut. Your instincts know a lot more than you do, mostly because your subconscious mind is processing signs and symbols at a rate your conscious brain can't even begin to fathom. So if it is out there telling you that something is up and that something needs to be done about it, then you need to make sure that you are on your guard ready to get things done because like a used car salesman, you are more likely than not in the hands of a master practitioner.

CHAPTER 11: THE DARK TRIAD

The dark triad is a collective term for three types of power characters that all bear signs of lack of empathy and with potential for recklessness, omnipotence, and extraordinary selfishness.

Research on "the dark triad" is practiced in applied psychology, especially in the fields of law enforcement, clinical psychology, and business management. People who, in tests, get high values for these traits are more likely to commit crimes because social distress and managers can pose serious problems for an organization, especially if they have significant leadership function.
• Narcissistic (personality disorder)
• Psychopathic (Psychopathy)
• Machiavelli (cynical/manipulative)
• Clinical description
All characters have the potential for highly demanding power, control needs over others, and emotional cooling for other people's misfortune or sadness. The picture also includes myth mania, i.e., the inability to adhere to the truth. There is also coexistence where certain traits of character are expressed depending on the situation. A Machiavellian person should also suffer from narcissism and psychopathy.
Narcissism

Narcissism is a mental disorder that can cause severe injuries (physical and mental) to the victim, especially in high-sensitivity and highly-sensitive, highly susceptible, more susceptible to their physical and emotional environment than others.
Most highly sensitive people have at some point in their lives come into contact with a so-called wounded narcissist (henceforth narcissist), and there are certainly many highly sensitive children who grow up with a narcissistic caregiver. In this type of relationship, the highly sensitive ones can find it difficult to understand why they are beginning to feel exploited, which makes them increasingly puzzled. They feel helpless and find it hard to put a name on what happens. They don't understand that they have suffered from a narcissist because they may not know or even suspect that something like that can exist! Some situations may be worse than others; sometimes, there is no other solution than to withdraw completely, simply to break the relationship.

Narcissists are supposed to make up 2-3% of the global population, but it has been found to be 6%. People with this disorder are difficult to detect (except for specialists), especially as they don't behave in the same way as outside the home. It is rare for narcissists to seek psychotherapy themselves. A narcissist can be anyone, the least you can imagine: a parent (or both), a sibling, a partner, an employer, a work colleague. It is not excluded that a narcissist in himself is a highly sensitive or much sensitive person, who in his youth became so affected by something negative or traumatic that the person in question developed this personality disorder.

Characterizes Narcissists:

Narcissists:

- Has a grand picture of its meaning; are concerned with thoughts of unlimited success, power, grandeur, beauty, or ideal love.
- Believe that they are unique and that they can only be accepted or understood by people who are unique or at a high level.
- Has an excessive need to be admired.
- Believe that they are entitled to everything, except that they have the right to receive any special favorable treatment and that their wishes will automatically be fulfilled.
- Exploit others in mutual relationships; make use of others to achieve their own goals.
- Lacking empathy is not inclined to recognize or share someone else's feelings or needs.
- Are often jealous of others and believe that others are jealous of them.
- Uses arrogance and high-minded attitudes and behaviors.

Machiavellianism

The term "Machiavellian" actually came into use during the 16th century when people used the word to describe the practice of using manipulation to get what you want. It stems from an individual name Niccolò Machiavelli who wrote the infamous novel The Prince. In this book, Machiavelli described the philosophy that a ruler should implement force, brutality, and whatever means necessary to ensure control, glory, power, etc. It is the ultimate dark interpretation of the phrase, "The ends justify the means." In modern psychology, there still exists a test used to measure the degree to which a personality involves the Machiavellian trait, and this facet of the Dark Triad is mostly consumed by the tendency to use manipulation for personal gain.

Any of us, to be honest, has selfish goals: make more money, make a career, win the competition. Everyone has their list. But still, most of us don't forget about decency, and from time to time we behave like altruists. For example, if someone helps us, we will try to respond with the same, donating, if necessary, with our time and money.

But there are people for whom these rules don't exist, those who consider others only as a tool for achieving their goals. And here all means are good - be it treachery, treason, stab in the back. Their principle is every man for himself; no one can be trusted.

Machiavellianism enters (along with narcissism and psychopathy) in the so-called "dark triad," which unites negative, malicious personality traits. There is also a special text on the level of Machiavellianism, developed in the 1970s by Columbia University psychologists Richard Christie and Florence L. Geis. It is a set of statements that the respondent may agree or disagree with. People with a high level of "Machiavellianism" more often than others admit statements like "Flatter important people — wisely" and "The best way to build relationships with people — tell them what they want to hear.

Recently, a group of Hungarian researchers from Pec University experimented with the participation of people who have passed this test 1. The subjects were supposed to play a game of trust, and during the game, they scanned the brain. It turned out that the "Machiavellian" brain began to work with a vengeance when they met a partner who demonstrated a willingness to play fair and cooperate. Why? They immediately began to figure out how to benefit from this situation for themselves.

The game had four stages; students participated in it, part of which had high, and part - low scores on the scale of "Machiavellianism". At first, participants were given a sum of money equal to about $5, and they needed to decide how much to "invest" in their partner. And he got three times more than they invested. Then the partner had to decide how much money to return.

The trick was that the partner in the game was not some other student (as participants thought). This role was played by a computer that was programmed to choose one of two options - "honest" (return about the same amount plus or minus 10%) or obviously "dishonest" (return a third less). For example, if a participant invested $1.6 in a partner, the "honest partner" returned about $1.71, and "dishonest" - about $1.25.

Then partners changed roles. Now the computer has invested a certain amount, which has increased three times, and the participant-person has decided how much to return. Accordingly, he had a chance to punish a partner for dishonest behavior or to reciprocate his honest cooperation.

It is not difficult to guess that the "Machiavellians" at the end of the game had more money than the other students. This is how it happened. On the one hand, both groups of participants "punished" the partner for unfair play. But the "Machiavellian," unlike the others, did not reciprocate the fair game at all.

Psychopathy

Psychopathy (from psyche "soul," "life," and pathos "suffering") is a general term for a disturbed personality in terms of emotional life and willingness to follow social norms. It's sometimes counted as a personality disorder, but it doesn't exist as a diagnosis in any standardized diagnostic manual. Psychopathy is often associated with crime, but the personality must not be unable to live lawfully. Many are committing acts that are perceived by the majority as evil because of the disturbance; the psychopath is unable to feel regret but, on the contrary, can boast of having been sentenced to death. The proportion of psychopaths is estimated at a small percent of the population.

When people with psychotic diseases often have bizarre behaviors, the psychopath is instead well aware of getting right, being pleasant, and giving a good impression it is part of the disorder. However, the behavior can be theatrical or articulated; the person can express perceptions of his excellence, simulate feelings that are considered appropriate, all to manipulate and achieve certain personal goals. A person with a psychopathic disorder usually has difficulty understanding the nuances of shade in emotions, for example, the difference between sexual attraction and true love. In combination with this, psychopaths often suffer from impulse control disorders and lack patience; they seek adventure and behave irresponsibly.

The rise of psychopathy

The rise of psychopathy can be studied biologically and partly socially. Adult psychopathy often correlates with behavioral disorder and ADHD during childhood. However, it can be questioned whether this should be seen as comorbidity without an essential link, or whether the disorders during childhood precede psychopathy. However, it's usually seen as a connection without relevance to the understanding of psychopathy.

People who are inclined to emphasize social factors for the onset of abnormalities have usually explained psychopathy with poor social and emotional upbringing environment. In that interpretative tradition, psychopathy was replaced for a while by the term sociopath, for emphasizing the influence of society on personality development. Thus, the evil associated with psychopathy could be placed on society, and not on the character of any individual.

Another explanation model is based on the personality genetics with its regulation of hormones and neurotransmitters that affect personality with life, emotions, and mood. One argument for this model is that psychopaths are found in all social environments and that different social environments only affect the expressions of psychopathy.

The different approaches to the emergence of psychopathy lead to different views on whether the psychopath himself is a victim or not. By explaining psychopathy with social structures, the criminal or the evil self becomes a victim, while emphasizing the biological place causes the behavior of the psychopath himself.

The concept of psychopathy

Psychopathy as a disease

Psychopathy is a condition that differs from normal personality development in man. The psychopathic character traits are not perceived as the cause of the suffering of the psychopath. The psychopath can admit that there is suffering in his life, which psychopathy has caused.

On the other hand, the psychopath lacks insight into the causal relationship of suffering that the debt is in its character. It is common for them to develop abuses of various kinds because they often think they can handle and tolerate alcoholic beverages and drugs. It's also common for the psychopath to present himself as a victim when it is favorable.

Psychopathy, which almost exclusively affects men, probably largely has a biological etiology, including through testosterone regulation. Of all of these biological conditions, those who grow up in socially vulnerable environments risk becoming to a greater extent violent criminals, that is, the expressions for psychopathy become tangible and direct, those who are educated in environments where violence is unacceptable tend to manipulate others more often and commit other forms of crime as a result of psychopathy.

Neurobiological and Other Physiological Characteristics

There are several medical studies on what characterizes psychopaths. An often stated hypothesis is that they don't have the same recognition for threats as others and thus they, therefore, don't feel fear. Some evidence of this is that they lack the startle reflex that spontaneous muscle tension in fear fails, that they don't read fear in the behavior of others, and that their way of flashing differs from those who are not psychopaths.

In depression, by comparison, individuals have overactivity in the amygdala, hippocampus, ventromedial cortex, and anterior girdle swelling, which due to the signaling system of the limbic system causes endocrine disorders. But in psychopathy, an under activity is seen in the same areas, which likewise produces altered hormone levels. However, psychopathy, unlike many other conditions, is resistant to treatment.

Neuroendocrine studies have shown some abnormal hormone levels. There appears to be a correlation with high levels of triiodothyronine in combination with normal or low levels of thyroxine. Psychopaths also appear to have high testosterone values in combination with low cortisol values.

Psychopathy is associated with hyperactivity in the reward system of the accumulator core, that is, the dopamine secretion. This explains drug abuse, impulsivity, and antisocial behavior in the disorder. The exacerbating aggression in psychopathy correlates with sub-function of the serotonergic, and hyperfunctioning of the dopaminergic system, as well as high levels of other catecholamines.

People with psychopathy generally have a lower resting heart rate than the rest of the population. They also have a higher heart rate variability than the general population. However, when meeting a stimulus that arouses aversion, psychopaths tend to get a faster pulse. In this, psychopaths remind of the physiological responses of impulsive persons.

Psychopathy and Relationships

Psychopathy is not a uniform concept, because, to some extent, it appears that people exhibit some but not other traits of psychopathy. There is, therefore, a differentiation between primary and secondary psychopaths. Primary psychopathy is psychopathy characterized by empathy, lack of guilt and compassion, and the level of anxiety is lower than the average population. Secondary psychopathy is the character trait that is mainly about the ability to complete plans, impulsivity, irresponsibility, a pattern of life that in the long run, is self-destructive. Psychopathic traits can, to a varying degree, be found in many people who don't meet all the criteria of psychopathy because the boundary between normality and pathology is fluid.

There are several personality traits in psychopathy that affect the interaction with others. Such characteristic features make it difficult to maintain relationships, but there is, nevertheless, psychopaths who are socially adapted, even though such an adaptation is superficial and only included in the psychopath's deceptive attitude. The psychopath doesn't necessarily lack the ability to follow learned rules and imprinted norms (in his grandiose self-image, the psychopath can't identify with anything negative), the psychopath lacks the ability to feel deep, genuine feelings and to have selfless motives for relationships, whether his actions are superficially considered seems sympathetic or not. Regarding love relationships, a manipulative charm is often a successful tool for acquiring a partner, especially when the partner is young. In other words, what is expressed in that primary psychopathy doesn't adversely affect either stable relationships or friendships (but research doesn't correlate positively with being popular). Secondary psychopathy, on the other hand, affects the ability to maintain all kinds of relationships very strongly negatively.

Psychopathy in Women

Limited number of (detected or diagnosed) persons with psychopathy are women. Women's psychopathy is similar to men's, but there are gender differences. Women's psychopathy is usually characterized by impulsive antisocial and histrionic or narcissistic personality types. There may also be associated with borderline personality disorder, trauma, and post-traumatic stress disorder. However, there is no complete consensus on the question whether this so-called female psychopathy is a variant of the male or whether it is completely different from this segregated syndrome, and whether the prevailing notion of men's dominance within the personality type would actually be a rash of a gender bias (clarify) when it comes to observing women's disorders. Personality traits such as impulsivity, violence, manipulation, and so on can be expressed differently by the sexes.

Like male psychopaths (according to Hare's definition), female psychopaths deviate from the startle reflex, which, in particular, applies to cases of negative emotional images of victims, which reflects the women's compassionate insensitivity and lack of compassion, several studies have suggested that female psychopaths suffer from worse alexithymia than male psychopaths.

CHAPTER 12: THE DARK TRIAD TEST

What all of these personality traits and disorders tend to have in common are the methods which these individuals use to get what they want out of life. The desires and pursuits of people with these Dark Triad personalities often necessitate the cooperation, willfully or not, of other people in their lives. In order to secure this operation, they've learned what it is about people that makes them tick—then, they exploit this to the best of their abilities.

As we continue to explore dark psychology, we will be diving deeper and deeper into these strategies and tools. So, for now, let's take a look at a vital factor involved in the success of these individuals' manipulation techniques—the victim.

While there are lots of things that tie humanity together in terms of human nature and tendency, there also exist vast differences in the demeanors and temperaments, characteristics, strengths, and weaknesses among people. For this reason, an individual with the intent to manipulate and use another person to his own ends must be secure in his decision on a target or targets. You'll remember that the critical component in all dark psychology strategies is observation and the gathering of information. The practitioner must observe the intended target and become familiar with the aspects of his/her personality, behaviors, routines, values, and relationships—the list is endless. The more information he has before taking action means that success is more likely to follow. Let's take a look at an example using the narcissist.

Max is a full-blown narcissist who intends to climb the corporate ladder at his business. His boss has an attractive daughter, and he decides that he is going to form a relationship with this woman in order to get close to the boss, thereby securing a high likelihood of promotion in the future. What makes those on the Dark Triad spectrum so dangerous is that the smart ones will quickly learn that they have to be able to feign universal human emotions like empathy, love, and humility in order to get on people's good sides and to earn their trust, even though they don't really feel this way. Max knows that in order to form a relationship for this woman, let's call her Susan, for whom he has no real feelings for, he will have to go through an elaborate performance of courtship. He may take a few days, weeks, or months to prepare himself for this undertaking with a single-minded and quite impressive amount of focus and determination. When he takes action, he will be well-prepared and will have constructed an alternate personality which is designed to be as attractive as possible from the point of view of this woman.

There are lots of different ways a narcissist might go about instigating this relationship. He may approach her directly, fabricating a scenario in which the two meet "by accident" and start a conversation. He may begin by approaching and ingratiating himself to her father, casually mentioning how he has tried dating and has insofar been unsuccessful and prompting the father to mention his daughter, whom he might enjoy meeting. Let's say Max decides to approach Susan at a casual business function to which employees are invited to bring their significant others. Max might create an impression in Susan's mind that paints Max as an attractive bachelor who is perhaps slightly self-conscious about being alone at the party, thereby prompting Susan to approach and offer him some company. Or, probably Max has discovered through close observation or conversation with her father that she prefers strong-willed and powerful men. Max might instead begin commanding the attention of the room by following a preconceived set of steps which result in his having the undivided attention of a large group of people who have been charmed by his outgoing and entertaining personality. Seeing that this man is the center of attention, Susan will be attracted to his influence and apparent charm and power, and she may take the lead herself.

The narcissist is more likely than others to invest a great deal in his schemes in anticipation of a sizable payoff at the end for his troubles. Max may go through the motions of this relationship for months or years, and finally having secured a position for himself, might choose to, all of a sudden, drop the relationship without warning, or perhaps undermine the aging CEO in order to take his job and leave his whole family in the dust. The narcissist would not think twice if he saw the opportunity to gain what he desired at the cost of others' wellbeing. Though the narcissist is not above feelings of guilt, shame, and even remorse to some extent, they simply prioritize their own wellbeing and status above anything else, and so, like the Machiavellian, he will simply believe that the ends justify the means.

Let's say we're dealing with a sociopath who simply wants to find an attractive girlfriend for the sake of status within his social circle. The ideal target for him will be someone who is highly sensitive and also suggestible, perhaps someone quite young and naïve. Again, the sociopath here will need to spend some time observing and gathering information about potential targets before selecting his victim. Perhaps he is at a dance club where there are lots of attractive women. Will he choose the girl who is surrounded by lots of friends and swooning men? Or will he go after the young tag-along who seems slightly uncomfortable and inexperienced? The sociopath might see this second lady as a potential victim because he can see himself charming her to the point that he gains her trust. From there, all he has to do is practice what he's learned about forming an emotional dependency. At that point, it will be quite possible to get what he wants from her without too much trouble.

CHAPTER 13: DARK SEDUCERS

When it comes to dark psychology and mental manipulation, the single most common use of both of these tactics is the exploitation of sexual favors or sexualized conquests. Where dark psychology has been used to control subjects superficially to guide them into various actions, or for both monetary and power-based gains, the whole issue of dark seduction goes beyond anything we have experienced until this point.

Dark seduction deals with the intense influence that mental manipulation can have on the intimate specifications of one's sex life and, by extension, their love life. It is what gets young women to fall for older, more experienced men and, conversely, which allows younger men to follow experienced women around like obedient little puppies.

The darker the personality is, the more intense the appetite of the seducer becomes. Henry VIII is commonly seen as a Casanova or a seducer of women. The British king, played by Jonathan Rhys Meyers in modern adaptations, is seen to not only seduce women and control his wives but also to manipulate his court into allowing him to marry multiple times just so that he can follow through on his dark seductions. With most of his wives ending up headless, it is easy to see what the king's real intent was.

But that is still not the darkest form of seduction.

Remember Ted Bundy? Yup, the insanely smart, insanely good-looking serial killer that was played by Zac Efron in the Netflix series. If there was one person who effectively crafted himself into the icon of dark seduction, it would be this man. Unlike uncouth or uncultured seducers who ineffectively pursue women and land themselves with a restraining order, Ted Bundy was all about the finesse, and as such he used dark psychology to not only pursue but also to seduce his prey, all while maintaining his carefully crafted facade of a normal human being. His little hill of dead bodies was something only he knew about, and he kept it that way, only finally being caught because of a parking ticket on his way back from another kill.

The chapter goes on and deals with dark seduction in a clear open manner so that individuals can see how basic the entire ordeal is. Dark seduction is neither uncommon nor is it necessarily a bad thing. It is a throwback to natural forms of seduction and is important because it allows readers like you to realize how good seduction techniques are almost exactly like calculative ones, as are embodied by on-screen Casanova's like Ryan Gosling in the hit film Crazy, Stupid, Love.

Like most other manipulation techniques, there is no basic good or bad for seduction, not even dark seduction. The nature of the pursuit or seduction changes based on the intention of the seducer. So like a knife that can be a tool for a cook and a weapon to a thief, dark seduction is also at the mercy of its implementers and nothing more.

Covert Emotional Manipulation in Seduction

Covert emotional manipulation, or CEM as it is more commonly known, is a critical part of dark psychology, particularly in terms of emotional manipulation. And although most dark psychology tactics already use some form or variant of covert emotional manipulation, the basic core of CEM is something that you are going to need to be better acquainted with if you truly want to understand and equip yourself with these techniques.

So, what exactly is covert emotional manipulation?
Covert emotional manipulation is a form of mind control where the primary controller moves to influence and control the thoughts and feelings of the subject in a discreet manner that goes undetected by the subject themselves.

The word covert here is a reference to the manipulator's attempt to hide or, more importantly, to mask the true intentions of the manipulator. The subject is not only unaware that manipulation is taking place but also, and perhaps more importantly, unaware of the manipulator's identity, which is kept a secret so that even if the manipulation is discovered, the subject has no way of understanding the source. It's like having a rat in the mob family. The manipulator slowly and carefully leaks information that gets the subject to act by their will, but the subject doesn't know where the leak is coming from. When done by a skilled manipulator, the subject will consider themselves to be the source of the manipulative thought, and as such, will not even seek to blame anyone.

Then what does the emotional issue represent? Emotional manipulation is all about the side of the manipulation the manipulator has chosen to pursue. There are numerous ways in which a person can manipulate a subject: religious beliefs, willpower, physical empowerment, and even greed. Emotion is just another side that can be opted to control. Emotional circuits are more often chosen because CEM-using manipulators are generally close to the subject, so much so that they are well acquainted with the subject and know what makes the subject "tick," so to say. As such, it is easier for the manipulator to tap into these emotional aspects and take control. What's more, emotional control is one of the complete forms of control. Whereas other control ventures may or may not work, an emotional control station is like taking over the helm of a plane. You are officially in control without autopilot.

This, of course, brings us to our last core term: manipulation. Now, manipulation, which is distinctly different from influence or encouragement, deals with the secret, underhanded process of influencing a person without their knowledge in a manner that benefits the influencer rather than the influence-ee.
Whereas an influencer would encourage a subject to open their mind and see the situation for what it is and then guide them to the morally right path, the manipulator would seek to cover and hide the whole picture and would instead befuddle the subject with fragmented bits and pieces designed to control their response.

The Morality of Dark Seduction

That, of course, brings us back to the morality issue of dark seduction. So, given that dark seduction can be so convoluted it must be a bad thing and, ergo, should be banned.

Unfortunately, the whole thing is hardly that simple.

Like most other seduction techniques, there isn't much morality attached to the process or methodology of dark seduction. It is merely what it is.

The methods of dark seduction that are chosen, as well as the extent to which they are used, and of course the intent with which they are used, ultimately are what determine the moral value of dark seduction. While on one hand, dark seduction can be used to help and benefit the people the seduction is practiced on, it can also conversely be used to cause harm to the same people. Dark seduction isn't just about benefiting or harming the subject, though, sometimes dark seduction can be used to create a benefit for the applicator of the technique. That is to say, sometimes dark seduction is more about the manipulator, where the intent and benefit of the manipulator is central to the application.

So let's take a deeper look at these three branches, starting, of course, with the "help the seduced" mindset. Now, as hard as it may be to believe, given that seduction has built up a bad rap over the years, one of the core tenants of seducers is to leave the subjects in a better position (be it mentally, emotionally or physically) than they were before being seduced. This is a general but positive form of seduction where the seducer doesn't feel the need to wield the power they have negatively. Their objective is to get something out of it, but they also don't believe that just because they are getting something out of it, the opposite party can't get something out of it. Win-win solutions are common here and are often displayed to mark the benefits of emotionally triggered seduction.

This doesn't mean, however, that it's always roses and unicorns. In fact, for most people, most acts of seduction are not about mutual benefit. Instead, they focus on the method of undermining or destroying a person through seductive techniques. This is generally done by jealous or over-possessive lovers who believe that they have a form of ownership over the subject and are entitled to treat them however they want. This kind of behavior can also stem from rage or revenge motives, which is why dark seduction is often closely linked with negatively tinted issues such as manipulative seduction.

The final form of seduction, however, is currently the most common. Here the individual not only deals with the possibility of hurting or benefiting the subject, but they also have the issue of self-development. For these people, seduction is more about them using a tool to derive whatever it is they want and then getting what they want. The whole seduction angle is more of an afterthought—it's more like getting to point A to B for them.

CHAPTER 14: THE TECHNIQUES TO MAKE DARK SEDUCTION WORK

This, of course, brings up to the major dark seduction techniques that are in existence now. While there are tons of other seduction techniques out there that both help and ensure seduction, the reason people are opting for seduction over attraction is simple. It is no longer enough to have attraction because attraction has become a dime a dozen.

What you need is emotional addiction—so much of it, in fact, that you are no longer afraid of your subject leaving or doing anything but what you've asked. How can you ensure that emotional state you seduce your prey? You take over complete control and force your subject into mental slavery, where you control their every move.

Love Bombing

Meet love bombing, the most common dark psychology seduction technique on the planet and, as a result, probably the most difficult to control. Love bombing is a form of seductive terrorism that stems from a person, usually the dark personality in question, using a combination of affection, material gifts, and promises to establish a strong sense of appeasement. People who are faced with love bombing find it hard to overcome or get past the apparent seductiveness of their manipulator, so this technique has a lasting impact. Long term exposure to love bombing has even shown a lack of self-validation later on once the relationship has ended.

Spot a Love Bomber

How do you spot a Love Bomber? Well for one, look at how long the relationship has been going on. With love bombing, the effect is quick and dangerous. The materialistic over-the-top manipulator doesn't have a whole lot of time before he is caught. Initially, though, love bombing can be difficult to identify, since the initial honeymoon period is almost identical to regular relationships.

Do, however, make a note and check out if the relationship feels a little suffocating. Why? Well, because love bombing may seem like any other relationship, but it quickly leads to difficulties, particularly when the manipulator suddenly starts lashing out at the subject when the subject gives time to any other individual. Love bombers may seem kind and giving, but they are extremely cruel and restrictive, meaning they hate when the subject is attentive to anyone but them.

Difficulty in Spotting a Love Bomber

Why is it so hard to deal with a love bomber, and why can't we simply up and leave? Well, because they won't let you. You see, love bombers have a way of setting up deep destabilizing roots in a very short period. The subject easily becomes drawn to them due to their apparent self-confidence and ambition and because of how self-sufficient they are. But because they are so used to these three factors and the whirlwind nature of the courtship, victims of love bombings just can't seem to imagine life without their abusers.

Breaking Free

With love bombing, though, it is important for victims to want to break free. If the subject of the love-bombing is adamant about sticking it out with their abuser, it is almost impossible to save them. This is because the valuation system of how the subjects view themselves and the manipulator is often intricately related. To admit that they were conned would mean that they would have to admit that they were mistaken. This, to the subject, leads to a sense of devaluation that negatively impacts their idea of self-worth.

The most important thing to keep in mind as a potential subject is because love bombing is so hard to escape, you need to be wary from the start. If something seems too good to be true or like a Hollywood fantasy, it is probably both of these things, meaning in no way is this realistic. If you find yourself in the middle of a situation where you are the target of a love bomber, instead of trying to escape, first focus on protecting yourself. Remember, love bombers are emotional terrorists, so the better you protect yourself mentally, the more likely you are to come out of this experience unscathed.

Reinforcement (CEM Stacked)

Love bombing is commonly followed by this procedure called intermittent positive reinforcement. Here the subject is forced to face what seems like a period of happy and positive reinforcement, which is then followed by intermittent positive reinforcement to prevent the body and mind from going into positivity starvation. It is essentially the same technique used by intermittent fasters to lose weight. They trick the body into thinking that they are going to be receiving constant food and then, just as it is about to go into a protective starvation mode, they give it so much food it does the same thing all over again.

Reinforcement is the same. So, this starts with love bombing, which is, of course, the over pouring of an insane amount of positive manipulation. Love bombers begin by tapping into everything the subject could imagine themselves receiving in a relationship, and then they do all that and more.

The only goal that the love bomber has is to soften up the subject's defenses so that they are more likely to be open to the manipulator and, as such, are more open to suggestion. This is, of course, where the whole positive reinforcement trick comes in to play. After weeks or months of being a strong positive influencer who has provided relentless unconditional positivity for the subject without a break, the manipulator suddenly switches off so to say and stops giving out positive reactions of any sort until the subject complies with a desired form of behavior.

The victim or the subject is at this point addicted to the positive reinforcement and is desperate be validated, so much so that once they start to pick up that certain activities can lead to positive reactions, they go back and continuously keep performing those same actions. It's like a dog realizing that if they pick up a bone, you'll give them a dog treat. Not only will they pick up the bone when it's thrown, but they'll also actually encourage the manipulator to throw that bone so that they can fetch it and then be rewarded.

So in terms of a relationship, the manipulator will only be kind and positive when the subject is doing something positive for the manipulator, such as the subject calling them every night instead of going out with friends. The idea is to take away the feeling of happiness or joy when the subject does something that the manipulator doesn't want them to do. This reinforces a negative emotion with that task even though no negative action has been taken. This is predicted positive reinforcement, which the manipulator slowly begins to change as well.

Now the subject doesn't receive positive reinforcement, even when they have done the task the way the manipulator wanted them to. This is because now the manipulator is applying CBT to force the subject to respond to reward-based behavior sometimes so that to gain validation or positive reinforcement, the subject begins to put himself in a constant state of pleasing the manipulator. This works because, in order to get some positive validation at some point, the subject is continually doing what the manipulator wants. Eventually, the subject replaces their wants with their need for positive reinforcement.

Reality Denial

This is then followed up by reality denial. Now, if you thought love bombing and intermittent positive reinforcement were terrible, you are about to be shocked. Reality denial is the most underhanded trick in the book, and it is a critical component of how stress-related issues can be used to trick the subject into thinking that they are dealing with a situation that they aren't.

Reality denial has almost always been seen to be an inner self-protection tool that is used to allow a person to feel that their sanity is still intact, not knowing that the procedure they are using to test their sanity is what will cause them to lose it. A close cousin of the gaslighting technique, generally reality denial was always used to protect a person's mind above all else. The idea was that reality denial only ever took place when acknowledging a reality was so physically or emotionally damaging that the subject simply couldn't bear to deal with the reality as it was presented. Often the subject feels responsible for the reality they are faced with, and as such, they develop an even stronger unwillingness to admit to their contribution to this now unbearable conundrum.

This is where reality denial as we know it comes into play. The subject starts by pretending they had nothing to do with the wrongdoing in question. This attempt to feign ignorance and innocence is a classic way to have subjects try to go into a public relations mode and control the image they present to other people. The idea is to come off as innocent to other people so that they are not held accountable and, subsequently, so that they can, in the future, convince themselves that they are not at fault. The denial, however, must be perfect.

No gaps, no ifs, but, or maybes are allowed. And if there is even a chance that the denial isn't reinforced strongly, the entire mental castle will cascade and fall apart. If the denial being enforced by the manipulator is strong enough, it can actually confuse the subject into thinking that they are the ones who made a mistake.

A good dark manipulator will not only not admit to the act, but they will also refuse to concede to any wrongdoing and, at the same time, refuse to admit any failure in their standards of behavior that may have contributed to the issue at hand. Instead, they will exaggerate and lie to themselves about the toxic demonstrations being put on by other people as they point to those as excuses for the problem that is being faced. If executed properly, the whole denial of reality tactic can be used to effectively and convincingly persuade masses as well as the subject that the manipulator is unaware of the charge, much less guilty of it.

Long story short, be wary of people who won't admit to their own mistakes. These people need to find someone to blame for their own mistakes, and a classic way to do it is to deploy the classic reality denial trope.

Gaslighting

Gaslighting is a tactic used to induce a strong power-play between individuals. When properly applied, the method leads to a person or entity questioning their reality and everything they know to be true. Shocking as it may sound, gaslighting works far better than you might think. It's a common technique of abusers, dictators, narcissists, and leaders of cults. It's done slowly, so the victim doesn't realize how brainwashed they are. In fact, multiple psychological syndromes have gaslighting as a root cause.

Gaslighting occurs in individual relationships, specialized relationships and even in public relations. Political leaders, for instance, are well known for using gaslighting techniques such as those used by Donald Trump in the 2016 presidential elections.

There are a bunch of common gaslighting techniques used and refined by pro-gas lighters, but we're just going to walk you

Dependence Growth

A significant trait that dark manipulation focuses on is that of the whole process of emotional motivation and, in particular, psychological dependence. From a human perspective, the dependence that a person develops on another human being stems mostly from their need for some positive reinforcement from that person. Psychological dependence is like any other random narcotic dependence. Just as the dependence on drugs and the desperate need for them can drive a person to do anything and everything to obtain the drugs in question, the desperate need for approval or positive reinforcement of any type can also trigger the same reaction in a person's mind.

Generally, these needs manifest as cravings or anxiety issues that present when detached from their source or positive reinforcement. They can also, however, result in depressive behavior, irritability, and restlessness, all of which show as withdrawal symptoms from the positive reinforcement in question.

Skilled manipulators know that true dependence can evolve into a psychological need and can, if deeply embedded enough, lead to a psychical need as well. The individuals knowingly use these tactics to develop the bond further and enhance the dependency so that they can use the addition in their favor much like a dealer would use a drug to get a client to do what they want.

Unfortunately, once a dependence reaches the level at which it is addictive, it is hard to move forward and detach from it. This is exactly what skilled manipulators bank on. As a subject, you need to be aware when anyone is fostering dependence on you; not only can you stop it much more easily at this stage, but you also have a better chance at recovery. If, however, it is too late and you've realized that you're already in too deep, the first thing you need to do is make sure that your manipulator doesn't catch on to the fact that you know. Now, carefully start finding a different route to deal with your issues. If your manipulator has made you financially dependent, you can use this time to slowly build up a personal nest egg or a secret income source. Find a job or start squirreling away money so that you don't feel as reliant. The objective is to carefully siphon off the need and uncover your true worth.

Playing on Narcissism

Narcissistic manipulation is one of the most common and easily one of the most prominent forms of mental abuse and manipulation. Narcissists are language masters who not only use the words they use to mislead and coerce but also to seduce their subjects. They are like snakes; they'll say two things at the same time and still maintain two faces. What is worse is that narcissists are also almost exclusively lacking in empathy. They feel nothing. They want nothing but themselves, and as such, it is hard to tame them as well.

A narcissist's bread and butter is their ability to have a million faces. Trust us, Arya Stark has nothing on these people. Verbal trickery and gaslighting is child's play to them, and their trademark move is to devalue and desensitize their victims so that they can continue their abusive habits without facing any obstacles. Once targeted, a subject will leave a narcissist's den feeling subjugated and worthless. The narcissists' relentless mind games are unbelievably harmful to the people on the receiving end. Not only do the victims of narcissistic abuse deal with anxiety and depression, but they are also prone to a host of other psychological effects, including paranoia and insomnia.

This is why educating yourself about the sadistic language of narcissists is so important; only once you learn it can you recognize it when you're faced with it.

Always remember, knowledge is power, and knowing how narcissists think and work will help you shape your shield against their attacks and prepare you for a quick escape if you are ever lured in by one, which, to be honest, you most likely already have been.

Don't' believe me? Why don't we run you through a list of common characteristics and you tell me if you don't find them shockingly similar to some of the people you know.

Numero uno is the constant verbal attacks that are such a common part of your day. Every single meeting you have with them, every single encounter, you leave with a bitter taste in your mouth. Admittedly, you can't always figure out why and what has caused the bitterness, but if you have the time, try to trace back your thoughts. You'll find to no one's surprise that the entire thing stems almost entirely from that one person, who is a certified narcissist.

Another common hook that narcissists use is the whole special relationship concept. A narcissist will make you believe quite convincingly all day and all night that the bond and the relationship you have with them is so unique and so uncommon that it cannot possibly be replicated by any other person in any other situation, ever! They use a system similar to love bombing to groom the subjects before absolutely destroying them with a quick "Oh, it was only a joke" or "But we were just kidding; why are you getting so worked up about it?" Remember, narcissist are masters of manipulation, so as you deal with them and the people around them make sure you are being consciously aware of their manipulative language and how they are using their power. It'll help you see a lot of things you hadn't noticed yet.

Mood Swings

The mood swings of an emotional manipulator are, without a doubt, one of their most basic weapons. Whereas most abusers can outright be caught because of their physical or controlling behavior, the emotional mood swings of a dark psychopath make the whole thing much harder to deal with.

But first off, let's try to figure out precisely what a mood swing is.

Mood swings are rapid changes in mood generally attributed to some medical or hormonal imbalance. The chemistry of the brain gets a little messed up, and soon enough, the hormones not only cause pain and hot flashes, but they also take over the brains nervous center and one second your happy and the next you're a hot mess. Generally, this balance is maintained by a hormone called serotonin; serotonin imbalances are common in women when they are on their period, but that is not what we're looking at right now.

Now, imagine the following: You are dating a person who is constantly changing their mind and their moods. It's like being on an emotional rollercoaster. Not only do they always want to know what you're doing and who you are with, but these people can also be very invasive. You'll come home to your partner checking your phone or asking you why you went to see a particular friend and all of a sudden you find yourself apologizing multiple times over something that you didn't even do. What's worse is you will also find yourself apologizing for things that you should not have to apologize for. Nonetheless, you apologize just to get them off your back and to bring peace back to the relationship and your partner. Your partner knows this and chooses to exploit this knowledge. What may seem like a simple end to an argument is actually a deliberate power play where the dark psychopath has effectively created a position of power from which they are controlling you.

But that's not all. Manipulative psychopaths also have a desperate need to cut down a person's self-esteem. They do this consciously so that they can control the subject more easily. Another common tactic used by dark psychopaths is the faux forgiveness tactic. Even though it is normal for all couples to fight and you and your partner seem to have made up, a dark psychopath may accept your apology, but they will then continue to hold the situation over your head and use it to emotionally blackmail you on a regular basis so that you constantly feel like you have to apologize. This is done so that the subject is constantly behind, and the dark psychopath continues to wield the upper hand. Ultimately, you will feel like you have to change parts of your entire personality to fit in with their mood and how they want you to be. As a subject, you will be made to feel like you always have to adapt, and that adaption is not only unfair to the subject in general in the long run, it also causes the subject to lose sight of their true self.

The Guilt Trap

The final weapon in the arsenal of a dark manipulator is guilt. As American novelist Erma Bombeck puts it, guilt is the gift that keeps giving, and a dark psychopath, particularly a skilled one, knows this. To simply put it, guilt is the natural and social way to control an individual who has behaved in a manner that is outside of the constraints of society. Guilt is the form of mental punishment, which is naturally occurring.

The problem is not with guilt, but with the people who are wielding it against normal individuals such as you, dear reader. Now think about it. Don't you already feel bad like you've done something that you shouldn't have done? Is it really necessary for someone to constantly badger you and remind you of your feelings and shortcomings?

Unfortunately, a dark psychopath does not care about what they should or should not be doing. The mere fact that they find giving another individual a guilt trip to be a mentally satisfying exercise is another reason for them to continue to use that as a weapon. After all, in the dark psychopath's world, the only thing that matters is self-satisfaction.

Fortunately, however, there is a way to escape dark psychopathy, particularly when it comes to guilt-tripping.

The first thing that you need to do is decide that you are going to put your own needs first. Making room for yourself and putting yourself first is extremely important because, as a subject, we generally tend to avoid putting our individual needs first as doing so makes us feel selfish or entitled. Once you have found room for yourself, explain to your mind that putting your needs first does not make you a bad person regardless of what society may say. Instead, point out to yourself that it is hard for a person to be a good-hearted person if they are suffering on the inside. As such, in the interests of being a better person, it is essential for you to take better care of yourself and then to take better care of those around you. After you have done so, then start to talk to others around you about your choice. Explain to them how you choose to put yourself ahead of others in the interest of your sanity and watch as they also agree with your choice. This instant validation will be a real eye-opener for you, mostly because the dark psychopath has already spent so much time explaining to you how you were a bad, selfish person. The manipulator has gotten you to the point where you expect other people to think the same.

Dark seduction is a very complex area in terms of manipulation, not just for the manipulator but also for the subject. It is complex because, while on one hand, the entire act is filled with malice and selfish intent, the act is also more often than not welcomed, since it makes the subject feel good about themselves and their surroundings, even if it is just for a little while.

CHAPTER 15: DARK SEDUCTION CASE STUDIES ON

Adolf Hitler

Adolph Hitler was responsible for one of the largest wars in history. He murdered millions of innocent Jewish people because he believed that he and all other Germans were superior. He never showed an ounce of remorse or empathy for the lives that were lost and regularly instructed the German Army to spread constant propaganda, enriching his own self-worth. The entire Nazi regime was required to have pictures of him in every government building and salute those pictures every time they left the room. Even to his dying breath, he argued his case, ultimately killing himself and his girlfriend to avoid a pointed claim to his death by the opposing forces.

Rasputin

You can't go through case studies on dark psychology without taking into account Rasputin and everything that this monk represents. Rasputin is an interesting figure because the type of power that he wielded in this field has echoed way into the future and it even inspired the aspects of many charismatic influencers that came around later on.

Rasputin was a spiritual figure who was able to use his powers to gain some influence over the Russian rulers of that time. He was able to project an intoxicating mix of sensuality and piousness that appealed to almost any side of a person that Rasputin wanted to work with. Those who may have been more inclined to follow religion were very impressed by the powers of healing the monk seemed to have. But those who enjoyed the sensual pleasures of the world were also able to find things to admire in the character of Rasputin. The most influential part of Rasputin's character was the fact that he was able to be an angel and a devil at the same time.

Many parts of the influence of Rasputin can be found in modern-day users of hypnosis. Rasputin was one of the most infamous, and perhaps earliest, figures to induce something similar to a trancelike state of suggestibility on the minds of any victim he chose.

What were these healing and hypnotic powers that were rumored to belong to Rasputin? It is believed that he was able to induce in his victims some deep feelings of relaxation, ease, and calm. He is well known for his abilities to ease the aches and pains anyone in the Russian family dealt with at that time. This helped to add some more to his mystique and really increased the amount of influence that he had on everyone near him.

Rasputin also did many things that are now common in covert emotional manipulation. One of the reasons that Rasputin had such a big impact on those around him is that it never seemed like he was trying to control the victims. Instead, he was able to come across as someone who had an unexplainable power that people would just succumb to. These are all hallmarks of cover emotional manipulation as it is used in modern times.

The case study of Rasputin is relevant when it comes to those who are learning more about charismatic influence. Like Rasputin, many modern-day dark psychological manipulators are able to attract followers, often because there is a perception out there that these manipulators possess a secret or some special knowledge.

This principle was way more effective back in Rasputin's time. The world was not used to this form of deception like it is today, and rational and science were less developed. This help to give some more credence to the idea that Rasputin was divine as well as a powerful person. Students of this dark psychology are going to be able to draw a lot of parallels between the power of a supernatural portrayal and similar charismatic leaders of the modern world who would feign spirituality in order to gain the control and influence that they wanted.

The link that is present between sexual expression and psychological power is very clear in the story of Rasputin. Similar to what many others did throughout history, Rasputin was able to leverage his dark influence into a life of decadent indulgence and even promiscuity. It is not a coincidence that many cult leaders, no matter where they are found or practicing throughout the world, are often found enjoying their choice of followers in any manner that they choose. While Rasputin may be an infamous example of this, he is not the first person to ever use these techniques.

Napoleon Bonaparte
Napoleon Bonaparte was well known for his short temper stemming from his short stature. He was incredibly full of himself and did whatever he could to receive the attention of others. The Napoleon Complex is no joke; he had serious issues with being that short and felt he had to overindulge in personality and wargames in order to earn that recognition. Today, Napoleon is used as the butt of many jokes and always portrayed as a tiny, very angry man.

Amy Bishop
Amy Bishop was a is a former professor at the University of Alabama. She had killed her brother using a shotgun in 1986. That incident was ruled as an accident.

In February 2010, while on a departmental meeting at the university, she pulled out a handgun and started shooting at the people present at the meeting starting with the one closest to her.

It was established that Bishop was denied a tenure while she was at the university on her last semester. This might be the reason she went on a shooting spree.

Bishop is also a suspect in a case where a letter bomb was sent to her the supervisors at Harvard.

Charles Manson
Manson was a cult leader and also a criminal. He was born on November 12, 1934. He formed the Manson Family cult.

The Manson Family cult gained followers and was responsible for a murderous campaign where nine murders were committed in 1969 at different places.
Several Hollywood residents were murdered by his followers including actress Sharon Tate.

Mansion was sentenced to life imprisonment where he died in 2017 while still in prison.

Albert DeSalvo

Albert DeSalvo was born in Massachusetts on September 3, 1931. He is best knowing for admitting that he was the "Boston Strangler". The Boston Strangler had killed 13 women between 1962-1964 in Boston area. Most of these women were elderly.

He was sentenced in 1967 to life imprisonment. He was stabbed and died in prison in 1973.

Jeffrey Dahmer
Everyone knows the name and everyone has heard the stories. Jeffrey Dahmer is one of the most notorious serial killers of all time. He was also known as the Milwaukee Cannibal after murdering, raping, dismembering, and oftentimes eating, over seventeen young men over a fourteen-year span. At one point, he admitted to the court that he attempted to turn his victims into sex slaves by drilling a hole in their heads. Dahmer was beaten to death in prison before he could be put to death.

CHAPTER 16: MAKE DARK PSYCHOLOGY KNOWN TO CHILDREN

Young people are naturally more inclined to be influenced, leading them to be a target group of malignant influencers for centuries.

Take Hitler, for instance. Back in Nazi Germany, Hitler set up a youth organization that was meant to make the youth feel more empowered. For the rest of their lives, these children grew up following the dictates of Hitler simply because that was all they knew. At just thirteen or fourteen years old, these children were given uniforms and posts and made to feel as if they were part of the Nazi Party, which at that time was the most powerful party in all of Germany. The children's discipline and loyalty came from the false sense of importance that the Nazi's were nurturing.

It is the same thing that every other dark psychopath does. They prey on the young because it's easier to persuade children, to shape their minds, or to convince them to do something than it is to do so to a grown adult who will ask questions. There is even a legal term for abusing power over individuals. It's called abusing fiduciary power and is a criminal offense such as fraud in many cases. Imagine how often it has to happen to be a part of a law written hundreds of years ago. Isn't it daunting to realize how inherent dark psychology is?

Some parents manipulate their children in the name of discipline. What they do not realize is, they are setting these children up for depression, guilt, eating issues, anxiety, and other mental complications. Some studies have revealed that children who are manipulated by their [parents at a young age are more likely to use the same techniques in their adulthood to get what they want from others. These children grow up thinking it is okay to twist people's arms to get what they want. Some of the signs indicating that a child is manipulated by the parent include; Lack of accountability, the victim tends to feel guilty, the child's achievements are not recognized by the parent, and the parent making all decisions for the child.

CHAPTER 17: MICRO EXPRESSIONS AND BODY LANGUAGE

Arms
Nonverbal cue: Arms crossed over the chest.
Often indicates: Unless it's cold out, this is typically a defensive posture. You won't see it so often with figures of authority who tend to display arms comfortably at their sides, or perhaps with a hand in one pocket to indicate ease.
Nonverbal cue: Complete stillness of the arms in conversation.
Often indicates: This is one to watch for, as the stillness of the arms can indicate purposeful masking of body language or tenseness at the very least. Proceed with caution.
Nonverbal cue: The gripping of one's own arm.
Often indicates: Gripping one's own arms is a gesture of self-comfort with typically negative connotations. You'll see this one a lot when people are waiting in a government office to renew a license and the wait is long, on airplanes from those with a fear of flying, or quite commonly, in doctors' offices.
Nonverbal cue: Their arms and hands are held low in front of them, with hands clasped.
Often indicates: This is a position of defense and can indicate that the subject is feeling vulnerable or otherwise insecure about their position in the conversation. Keep in mind that dark psychology practitioners are also aware of this and may adopt this stance to appear more vulnerable. You see this pose adopted often when people are asking for help.

Hands
Nonverbal cue: They have their hand resting on their cheek.
Often indicates: This can indicate that someone is thinking or perhaps evaluating the situation.
Nonverbal cue: Touching the nose or scratching the nose.
Often indicates: This can indicate disbelief or, in some cases, may indicate that the person is deceiving you. Watch for how they do it. Usually, a genuine scratch is going to be quick and efficient. If it is

occurring a lot and it's not the cold season, then this may be a nonverbal cue to watch for.

Nonverbal cue: Someone is rubbing one eye while you are speaking.

Often indicates: This is another indicator that someone may not believe what you are saying. Take the weather in consideration and, if the rubbing of the eye seems a bit fishy, then note it to yourself.

Nonverbal cue: Someone approaches with their hands clasped behind their back.

Often indicates: This can indicate frustration, irritation, and anger in many cases. It is sometimes adopted as a domination posture in the workplace, as well as a way of showing aggression.

Nonverbal cue: Someone has their head resting in one hand and their eyes looking down.

Often indicates: This one typically just indicates that the subject is bored.

Nonverbal cue: Someone is sitting with their hands clasped behind their head and with their legs crossed.

Often indicates: Confidence, superiority.

Nonverbal cue: Someone presents open palms when they see you.

Often indicates: This is a gesture meant to show sincerity and to inspire openness in a conversation. It is also a way of communicating symbolically 'I have no weapons in my hands, you can trust me.'

Nonverbal cue: Someone pinches the bridge of their nose, closing their eyes momentarily.

Often indicates: This generally indicates that someone is responding negatively to the subject at hand.

Nonverbal cue: Someone is playing with their hair.

Often indicates: If this behavior is not in an atmosphere conducive to flirting, then it can indicate that the person is feeling insecure.

Nonverbal cue: Someone is moving around excessively.

Often indicates: If someone you are speaking with is playing with their pencil, tapping their feet, or playing in their chair, basically any excessive movement as if distracted, is a common indicator of impatience.

Nonverbal cue: Someone is stroking their chin.

Often indicates: This is commonly associated as an evaluation gesture and indicates that someone is coming to a decision.

Fingers

Nonverbal cue: Someone is steepling their fingers while speaking to you.

Often indicates: This is typically a gesture of authority where the person that you are speaking with feels they are the dominant presence.

Nonverbal cue: Someone is drumming their fingers on the table or tapping.

Often indicates: This is something we've all seen and merely indicative of impatience.

Head

Nonverbal cue: Someone quickly tilts their head slightly during a conversation.

Often indicates: This is an indicator that what you have just said or something they have noticed in the environment has suddenly gotten their attention. It is always a good thing to notice when leading a conversation or ascertaining motives.

Nonverbal cue: Lowering of the head in conversation.

Often indicates: There are a number of meanings to this depending on a few factors. For instance, a quick lowering of the head is a mini-nod, indicative of an agreement or feigned agreement. If eye contact is maintained, it can be a sign of flirtation or an indication of distrust, depending on the context. If lowering the head so that the chin is covering the neck, then it is a defensive gesture. It can also indicate frustration or exhaustion, although, in such cases, it is often followed with a sigh.

Nonverbal cue: Their head is perfectly still while speaking to you.

Often indicates: This can indicate that the person is serious or feels they are speaking from a position dominant/in authority of you. This can also be indicative of anger or potential violence.

CHAPTER 18: HOW TO COME OUT AS WINNERS AND TO ACHIEVE ALL YOUR GOALS

Doing what it takes

How important are your goals to you? How much do you want that dream house or that dream job or the kind of life that you desire?

Always remember to take the high road and treat yourself and others with the utmost care and respect. Never break the law or do anything immoral to get what you want. That is like cooking rice in dirty water. It is never a good idea to not respect yourself or others in life. Your rewards will be far sweeter if you reach your goals with hard work and planning and help from God.

Another warning is to not get so wrapped up in what you want to be or think you should be that you devalue yourself or the life that you have today. If you live in a run-down apartment, and you can't change that overnight, remind yourself of all of the other good people that are in the same situation. And remember, you don't have to stay poor if you have friends that are poor. You don't have to stay a certain weight if you have friends that are that weight. You don't have to go out to dinner every night because your friends invite you. You have a goal, and you are responsible for reaching that goal.

Break your goals into actionable stages

Break the goals into small ones because this helps you to track your progress. Recognize the most difficult stages of achieving your goals because this allows you to revise and practice them until they are achieved.

Plan your victory

Create a victory schedule for yourself and get organized by having daily, weekly, monthly and yearly goals and always check to see if you are achieving them and if you aren't able to achieve them in one week, try again during the next week.

Surround yourself with winners

Make friends with the people you admire because success is contagious. If you want to achieve certain goals, join a team of people who have achieved such things. Welcome the company of people whose success you appreciate and are envious of. It is usually tempting to be in the company of people who will make you look good, but you lose focus of your goals if those people aren't in the category of the success or goals you want to achieve. And more so, you will enjoy friendship more with the people you admire and look up to.

Turn the negative feelings into inspiration.

If you realize you are feeling unsuccessful or envious, that a good sign that you are ready to set a new goal for your life. Begin by realizing the cause of that negative feeling and set a goal that will propel you beyond that feeling. You get more satisfaction from achieving that goal that you have set than from showing up for another person.

CONCLUSION

The notion that dark psychology is prevalent and that it is part of our world can be a scary thought. People have centered their whole lives around using these tactics, whether at work or at home to get people to do what they want and to harm them.

Those who suffer from narcissism, Machiavellianism, and psychopathy suffer from mental diseases that can be harmful to their loved ones, and as well as their friends. Not all of these people harm others intentionally. However, some do, with or without the excuse of feigning a mental illness diagnosis.

We defined Dark psychology at the beginning of the book and indicated that it falls into the same category as general psychology. However, it does deeper into the human mind and helps pinpoint tactics that people use to motivate, persuade, manipulate, and coerce to get what they want from others.

The Dark Triad is a term in dark psychology that can be helpful when trying to pinpoint the beginning of criminal behavior.

Narcissism exhibits these traits: egotism, grandiosity, and lack of empathy

Machiavellianism uses a form of manipulation to betray and exploit people. Those who practice this do not practice morality or ethics.

Psychopathy is a trick to those who put their trust in these types of people. They are often charming and friendly. Yet they are ruled by impulsivity, selfishness, lack of empathy, and remorselessness.

None of us want to fall prey to manipulation, persuasion, deception, reverse psychology, brainwashing, or even hypnosis, especially from those who we love. The result is that we often are. Dark psychology tactics can be used on a regular basis to harm us for the pure joy of experiencing a type of joy of fulfillment for others.

The fact that people can be used as pawns on a chessboard makes all of us want to understand dark psychology more and to figure out what it is, and how we can save ourselves from it. This book was written as a guide that provides a list of tactics within each chapter so that the reader would know how to educate themselves on the devious actions of others and how they could go about protecting themselves.

Knowledge is a key element in protection because the more you know, the more you can read behind the devious acts of others within your life or who you find yourself trying to coerce you into purchasing something that you really didn't need.

Out of all of the methods we discussed in this book, the art of hypnosis has been used by medical science for something good. There are many ailments that hypnosis can make better or even cure. And we are not just talking about mental ailments, but physical as well. Hypnosis can be used to help cure some of the side effects that are caused by chemo and radiation in cancer patients.

We all know that there has been a lot of skepticism for this alternative medicine due to the quacks that use it as a laughingstock. However, when used correctly, this type of medicine can do a lot better than harm because it wakes peoples subconscious up to letting go of things that they are holding on to that might be causing a plethora of problems in their lives.

With this being said, all of these methods can be used for good; it is just based on their intentions and the overall outcome. Those who use manipulation tactics do not use them for the intention of helping anyone. Manipulating is changing someone's thoughts, actions, and behaviors to fit someone else's (the manipulator's agenda). There is no way to sugarcoat some of these techniques. And that is why they fall under the dark psychology umbrella because they have been used by criminals to get what they want as well.

We hope that you have used this book as a sort of guideline to help you understand these methods more, and be able to spot them, as well as have a list of tactics that can be used in order help you protect yourself in the future.

Because we all know that someone is going to try to make us a victim of one of these methods again, sometime in our lives, and I for one would want to be as ready as I could possibly be.

Thanks for reading this book. I really hope it has left you some valuable notions to exploit in everyday life;

I wish you all the best!

HOW TO ANALYZE PEOPLE

REVISED AND UPDATED

The Complete Guide to Instantly Read Like an Open Book, Body Language Through Innovative Behavioral Psychological Techniques and Analyzing Personality Types and Patterns

Dr Henry Campbell & Dr Daniel Watson

PREFACE TO MENTALISM

Wouldn't it be nice to be able to read people like books? You could know their hidden intentions and true feelings. You could avoid all miscommunication and deception. The guesswork would be taken out of social interaction. This sounds like a dream come true, right?

While it is not possible to read minds, you can get pretty close to clairvoyance with the tips in this book. This book is your guide to the fundamentals of reading people like books. You will learn everything you need to know about body language, facial expressions, nuances of speech, and other signs that reveal what a person is trying to conceal.

It may seem very difficult to figure out what a person is trying to hide. People may seem like obscure, impenetrable mysteries. But that is just because you don't know the cues and signs to watch for. Once you learn them, reading people is actually very easy.

Some people make a living out of reading others. FBI profilers, cops, job interviewers, and even dating profile matchmakers are excellent reads of character who are adroit at finding out who people really are without being told. These people are not in possession of some secret superhuman talent. Rather, they have mastered tips and tricks that you can master yourself. This book will help you become as good as an FBI profiler at reading other people.

You first have to learn some of the main tells that people exhibit. These tells not only betray when someone is lying, but they also indicate what a person is not saying. Tells give away what a person is hiding inside, whether or not the person is being dishonest. One of the best tells is any inconsistency between someone's talk and body language. Eye contact is another great tell. Fidgeting can indicate nervousness.

You can glean a lot of information about people by what they do directly say, however. People are surprisingly open. You just have to pay attention. Learning to read people involves learning to really listen and absorb what someone says to you.

Furthermore, you must learn to make people want to open up to you. You can make yourself the type of person that people want to talk to. You want to project an aura of caring and compassion that make others trust you and feel comfortable around you.

There are so many different ways to read people. From being introspective to carefully observing others, this book will cover them all.

You may wonder why reading people is so important. There are countless benefits to being able to understand the people around you right off the bat. Your understanding of people can certainly make your life easier.

For one thing, you can become a more sensitive and empathetic lover and friend because you understand people better. You can read the signs of someone's emotions and respond appropriately. You will no longer be clueless about what those around you feel.

You also can avoid a lot of pain and problems by learning to identify the true intentions of people. Some people are just bad. Most bad people are good at hiding it, however. You can see through their ruses and protect yourself. On the flip side, you can spot good people who will treat you well. As a result, you can avoid bad friends and pick good ones. Your dating life will improve as well as you become more discerning about your partners.

Work can become easier. If you work in sales or customer service, you will be able to read your customers for clues about whether or not they are happy. If you work for clients, you can understand their wants better. You can become more empathetic and understanding of co-workers and superiors. This can help you satisfy people that you work with better.

In addition, you will get along better with your family. By being able to read your family members, you can tell what they are feeling and what they expect. Fights over "nothing" will stop because you will be able to spot the warning signs that a fight is coming. You will also be more empathetic, which your family members will appreciate.

Even on the street, you can become more discerning about the intentions of others. You can spot people who mean you harm and take steps to protect yourself. This is quite important for self-defense.

The life skill of people reading is very helpful and essential to your success in your social life. Therefore, you should start learning today. You have started in the right place with this book.

INTRODUCTION

Reading people is a technique most people wish they would master. To some, it is an inborn talent, while others learn it and it becomes an art. In many cases, as you struggle through different scenarios in life, reading people becomes a prerequisite for survival. In the modern workplace, for example, the ability to analyze people will help you get out of unhealthy situations or help in conflict resolution. These are skills that are useful to you in many spheres of life.

Psychiatrists learn to read people. Reading people is not just about listening to what they say; you must also read into their nonverbal cues. Many conversations today can be misconstrued to mean so many things when, in reality, the participants were talking about something different. From experience, you might have realized it the hard way already that people are not always who or what they say they are.

To tell the true story behind someone's actions, words, voice, and gestures, you need to be very keen. It is also imperative that you set aside your earlier preoccupations and ideas about them. Each time you interact with someone, start on a clean slate with them. Set aside your resentments, emotional attachment, and ego because these are some of the things that hold you back from truly seeing them for who they are.

To analyze someone correctly, you must approach them from a neutral perspective. This allows you to consume and interpret their information without distortion. Personal bias is one of the factors that prevent you from correctly analyzing people (DeDe, 2013). Once you can look beyond this, you are in the best position to analyze someone.

CHAPTER 1:WHY ANALYZE A PERSON AND IT'S ADVANTAGES

In the case of professionals like psychiatrists, they are trained to see beyond the ordinary. They attune their senses to greater heights, such that they can see things you take for granted yet mean so much. There are three techniques that professionals use to read people:

1. Monitor Body Language. Communication is a combination of tonal variation, body language, and spoken words. Of these three, body language is the most important element that determines how the message is passed across. To get the message, you need to embrace body language from a neutral perspective. Don't expect anything. In an attempt to analyze someone, you might go overboard and overthink the message.
It is advisable that you relax, observe, and allow you're subject to express they comfortably and freely. Allow your subject the same freedom of expression as you need to interact with them and understand them well.

There are a few things you need to pay attention to that can help you analyze their actions and body language and decipher the message in their communication better. Here are some of the things you should look at:

Body Posture
To analyze someone, you must be keen on their body posture. There are subtle messages you can identify from someone's body posture, like confidence, self-esteem, and ego. These have an effect on the message passed across or the inferences drawn from the message.

Appearance

Appearance matters when communicating with someone. It can influence your perception of the recipient or their message. Many people will assume someone is deeply spiritual if they show up in Buddhist attire, casual if they have a T-shirt and jeans on, and professional if they are in a power suit. By their clothing and appearance, you are already biased about their personality, hence the message you expect from them.

Motion

Physical movements can also influence the way you analyze someone. Some of the things you should focus on are feeble, but they can tell you so much. Someone who feels under pressure can pick their cuticles or bite their lips in a bid to ease the situation or to overcome an awkward moment.

This might not apply all the time, but in most cases, when someone is not forthcoming about something, they tend to pocket, put their hands behind their back, or place their hands on the laps.

Anger, defensiveness, or need for self-preservation is portrayed when someone folds their arms and legs (Hwang, Kim, and Lee, 2006). Look keenly, and you might also notice that people tend to lean toward those they feel more comfortable with or those they like and further away from their foes. It is amazing how such simple reactions can tell you so much about someone even without them uttering a word.

Facial Expressions

While it is easy to hold back from saying something, it is not easy to hide facial expressions. Facial expressions can also tell you a lot about someone's reaction. Someone who is overthinking a situation or worried might have deep frown lines. Contempt and anger are associated with pursed lips. The same can also be expected of a bitter person. In a tense moment, many people will grind their teeth or clench their jaws.

2. Emotional Attunement. Ever heard someone say you give off positive or negative vibes? This is true. Emotions express your energy about someone or something. When you are around them, you feel either good or bad. Some people drain your energy while others make you feel vibrant. The energy might be invisible, but it has a profound impact on your perception of someone, which also affects the way you analyze them.

To sense someone's energy, be keen when talking to them. Do you feel comfortable in their presence, or do you want to back off? Look at their eyes. You can tell whether someone is angry or content by looking at their eyes when they speak to you.

Another feature you should look at is the tonal variation. From someone's tone, you can tell whether they are annoyed or happy. You can also tell how their mood changes when they tell a story from their tone.

3. Intuitive Approach. Intuition is about gut feeling. This goes beyond the spoken word and body language. Intuition rises above everything you might have read or heard about someone. It is about what you feel about them the moment you meet them.

During your first meeting with someone, how easy are you around them? Gut feeling is a primal method your body uses to determine whether you can trust someone or not. After your gut feeling, think about the Goosebumps. Goosebumps represent striking a chord with someone or a sign that you resonate with someone who inspires you even if you have never met them in the first place.

CHAPTER 2: THE SECRETS OF THE HUMAN MIND

Psychology is defined as the study of the functions of the human mind, most specifically pertaining to behavior. It studies how we think, our mental processes, what makes us "tick," as it were. The human psyche consists of our mind and soul. It is what makes us individuals; we think differently and act differently, making the ability to accurately analyze basic human behavior a very valuable skill.

Key Psychological Concepts

Here are some specific areas of study used to answer the questions surrounding behavioral influences.

Study of the brain and behavior

Psychology helps to simplify the complexities of human behavior and mental processes through the study of perceptions, learning, cognitive development, emotion, and memory. Behavioral psychology focuses on physical and mental processes that can lead to various behaviors.

Study of individual differences

Personalities, motives, and intelligence level differ from person to person. One of the essential roles of psychology is to investigate how these different aspects interrelate to help define how individual identities are developed.

Personality

Personality, of course, refers to an individual's unique cognitive functions and behaviors. Psychologists have developed many different theories to explain how personality traits work. The theories of Carl Jung on personality are particularly popular; the

Myers-Briggs Type Indicator tool has arisen from further study on his research.

Motivations

Motives deal primarily in regard to rewards and value. The theories on motivations lean towards the assumption that learned responses result from one type of motive or another.

Intelligence

The subject of intelligence is commonly discussed in the study of psychology. Not all psychologists agree, however, as to what it actually consists of and there are many different views on the topic. Some would say that intelligence encompasses a variety of skills, talents, and abilities while others hold that intelligence lies in one single, overall ability.

Study of Group Behavior

Humans are naturally social, and our behavior will change depending upon the setting. We act differently when we are alone compared to when we are in a social setting. The study of human behavior will most likely cover both anti-social as well as pro-social behaviors. These different behaviors usually result from some type of outside influence from other people. Social psychology helps to discover how individuals may conform to social norms or submit to others in authority. It can also show gender roles and how culture can mold a person's behavior.

Five Main Goals of Psychology

We all use psychology in our everyday lives, sometimes without even realizing it. Studying psychology doesn't mean we have to become psychologists. Rather, understanding some of the innate behaviors we use will give us a better understanding of people as a whole. Here are some of the main goals of psychology.

To describe

The study of psychology strives to first observe and then describe different behaviors as objectively as it can. The data is logged in great detail in order to provide as much information as possible on the findings.

To explain

Data gathered by observations would probably do us no good without knowing what we are looking at. Once a psychologist observes and gathers the information, they must then explain their findings. It is not enough to know that a certain behavior was observed; we want to know why it happened.

To predict

Past behavior often predicts future behavior. Knowing the "what" and the "why" in psychology may be able to help predict future outcomes based on the behavioral trends that have been observed.

To gain control over situations

Being able to understand behaviors and speculate on the most likely outcomes will then give us a better chance of controlling said outcomes. Knowing that we may be repeatedly making the same bad choices based on past behavior means we are that much more able to change our negative behavior.

To improve

The control factor of psychology is meant to be a positive thing. Controlling negative behaviors will improve our lives; at least, that is the goal. It may not always serve us as it should, but when the knowledge of psychology is used correctly, we will most likely see great improvement in our lives.

Psychological Theories

Years of combined research have provided a plethora of theories that study the human mind from different angles. The evidence gathered works to back up an educated hypothesis on the motives behind certain behaviors. A functional theory follows two main guidelines: they must define a specific behavior, and they must be able to predict how behaviors will change in the future. Such theories include (but are not limited to): cognitive theories, behavioral theories, developmental theories, and personality theories.

Cognitive Theories

Cognitive theories are exactly what their name suggests. They concentrate on internal cognitive states such as our motivations, how we solve problems, thinking and concentration, and decision-making processes.

Behavioral Theories (Behaviorism)

Behaviorism suggests that human behaviors are developed through conditioning. These techniques were very popular during the first part of the 20th century and are still commonly used at present to aid individuals in learning different behaviors and skills.

Developmental Theories

These theories explore the human development, growth, and learning processes. Understanding theories behind human thought can offer valuable insight, especially in the workplace.

Personality Theories

These theories study what makes us individuals and unique from one person to another. Feelings, emotions, and thought patterns are as different and personal as fingerprints, and a firm understanding of individual personality is extremely beneficial.

How Psychology Improves Our Lives

Psychology is a theoretical and applied subject making it an easy and appropriate topic for anyone to learn, not just for professionals in the field. It can open the doors to so many more opportunities if given the time to apply what is learnt about psychology. Here are some of many various benefits we can gain from a better understanding of human behavior.

Better motivation

Why is it so hard to get things done sometimes? Barring any

physiological symptoms or disabilities, many of us just simply lack the motivation. Types of self-improvements such as losing weight, getting back into shape, quitting cigarettes or other addictive behaviors can be overwhelmingly difficult.

Some tips to boost motivation based on some cognitive theories are:

- Keep searching for new interests to hold your attention better.
- Do things randomly to keep your brain from getting bored.
- Learn new things! Expand your knowledge. Do not get stagnant.
- Make sure the goals you set for yourself are clear and relate to the task.
- Find ways to reward success.

Improved leadership skills

Being a good leader is a valuable trait to have. As we will learn in the next chapter, there are some personality types that are more suited to leadership skills than others. But don't let personality stand in your way; we can always be better. Here are some tips to help improve leadership skills no matter what your job entails:

- Remember to let the group have a voice while maintaining clear guidance.
- Brainstorm with the group and come up with solutions to problems.
- Keep the ideas inspirational and reward creativity.

Improved communication skills

Good communication is a must in any situation when dealing with people, both written and verbal. Non-verbal gestures are also important when attempting to communicate clearly. You can use these tips to learn how to better express yourself non-verbally and to learn to notice others' non-verbal cues:

- Maintain good eye contact.
- Take note of what non-verbal gestures are normally for different people.
- Use the tone of your voice when you speak to help emphasize what you are trying to say.

Better understanding of other people

A big part of what this book entails is learning how to use psychology to read people's emotions. Understanding other people's emotions, as well as your own, has a vital role in personal and professional relationships. This is known as **emotional intelligence** or **emotional I.Q.** Here are a couple of useful tips to boost emotional intelligence.

• Take note of your own emotional reactions to changes within an environment.
• Make an effort to view situations from another person's perspective.

Better decision-making skills

Another aspect of cognitive psychology is our decision-making process. Research has given us a multitude of tools that can help us make better choices.

• Use an approach called Six Thinking Hats to view a situation from all angles: intuition, rationality, creativity, emotion, negativity, and positivity.
• Weigh the pros and cons of big decisions.
• Try using a grid analysis technique to determine which decision will best meet the needs of a situation.

Improved memory

Don't forget to remember! Memory is an extremely important factor in our lives, especially when we begin to lose it. Thankfully, psychology has given us some ways to improve it.

• Teach yourself to focus on the information you are exposed to.
• Practice the things you have learned.
• Try to eliminate as many distractions as possible.

Better financial choices

There is a type of research called behavioral economics. It examines how different people manage risk and uncertainty in their decision-making. Here are some key tips to make better choices with regards to money management:

• Do not wait too long to wisely invest your money.
• Make an effort to regularly put a portion of what you earn into savings and retirement.
• Be aware of biases you might have that can cause you to make bad financial decisions.

Improved grades

Many people hate taking tests and quizzes in schools. However, research shows that testing, which is a form of repeated learning, does help in retention and learning. Take every opportunity to test yourself when learning something new.

Improved production

Our livelihood depends on our jobs and our success in the professional world, and on the level of our productivity. Some may believe improving productivity includes multitasking but researchers have found out that multitasking is actually counterproductive. Trying to do several things simultaneously can have a negative impact on our accuracy and speed in completing a task. Here are some ways we can use psychology to improve productivity:
• Avoid multitasking.
• Focus on one thing at a time, especially when doing complex or risky jobs.
• Get rid of as many distractions as you can.

Improved health

Keeping your body healthy will, in turn, keep your mind healthy. A healthy mind leads to improved understanding and cognition, and psychology is a great tool for achieving health goals. Here are some ways to apply these strategies:

• Stay in the light! Research has shown that both natural and artificial light can actually reduce occurrences of Seasonal Affective Disorder (SAD).
• Exercise releases endorphins which contribute to your psychological well-being.
• Helping others understand the risks of unhealthy behaviors can help them make healthier choices.

This brief look into the basics of psychology and its benefits by no means covers the whole of the study of the human psyche. However, it does provide a good introduction into what will be discussed in the following chapters.

CHAPTER 2 PART 2: MENTALIST TRICKS

You don't have to wait until you have a crucial meeting with someone before you can put your body-reading skills to use. Continuous practice will improve your people-reading skills. Every day try to devote some time to studying people's body language and compare what you see with the indications in this book. Also take the time to be aware of the verbal and nonverbal cues that you are emitting. Often times, the body language you get from a person will be a mirror of yours. Don't worry, we will talk about mirroring in the following chapters.

Attend parties and business meeting to help you study the flow of human communication. This will help you identify the powerful voice, the sly, and the cowed ones. Watching videos is another interesting way to hone your people-reading skills. Turn down the volume and try to analyze what the flow of conversation is by interpreting their body language.

Mind you, this is different from lip reading. Learning how to analyze people through their body language will liberate you from those who seek to manipulate and dominate.

It brings you the epiphany that others are also doing this same to you—reading your body language. It teaches you to be more sensitive to other people's feelings and to connect more with your peers and loved ones.

HIGHLY SENSITIVE PEOPLE

Have you always been told that you are too sensitive for your own good, that you need to "toughen up," or that you cry too easily? If you're a deep thinker who often feels as though you don't quite fit in, there's a good chance you might be an HSP.

This kind of sensitivity is more common than you might think. Dr. Elaine Aron, famous for her research with HSPs, states that approximately 20% of the population is highly sensitive.

Signs of the Highly Sensitive Person

How many of the following describe you?

1. A tendency to feel particularly overwhelmed in noisy environments.
2. A preference for smaller gatherings of people rather than large crowds.
3. A good track record of picking up on other people's moods and motives.
4. An ability to notice little changes in the environment.
5. A tendency to be easily moved by music, books, films, and other media.
6. Heightened sensitivity to hunger, pain, medication, and caffeine.
7. A need to recharge and relax alone on a regular basis.
8. An appreciation of good manners and politeness.
9. Difficulty in refusing others' requests for fear of hurting their feelings.
10. Difficulty in forgiving yourself for even the smallest mistakes.
11. Perfectionism and imposter syndrome.
12. Trouble handling conflict and criticism.

You don't have to answer "Yes!" to every item on this list to qualify as an HSP. Trust your intuition. If this list resonates with you, there's a good chance that you have a highly sensitive personality.

D.O.E.S. – A Useful Way to Think about High Sensitivity

The D.O.E.S. model is a helpful acronym that explains the HSP profile.

Depth of processing: HSPs have brains that work a little differently from the norm. They process incoming information—sights, sounds, smells, and so on—in a more thorough way. An HSPs mirror neurons—the cells in the brain that help us empathize with others—are more active than average. This explains why HSPs are especially sensitive to other people's moods and feelings and why they are readily overwhelmed in noisy places.

Overstimulation: Overstimulation is inevitable when you have a particularly sensitive brain! An HSP takes longer than the average person to process stimuli, so they soon become overwhelmed and drained in busy or crowded environments. This also accounts for their heightened sensitivity to pain and hunger.

Emotional reactivity: Emotional reactivity is probably what gets HSPs into trouble most often. As they are always "tuned in" to their environment, they cannot help but react strongly to both positive and negative situations. Unfortunately, their negative emotions can become all-consuming if not properly managed. Being so empathetic, they are also prone to picking up on other people's bad moods.

Sensing the subtle: HSPs do not have superhuman powers—they see and hear just about as well as anyone else. However, they do have a special ability to pick up on tiny details in the environment that other people usually miss. For example, if you are an HSP, you may find that you are the first to notice when a vase of flowers has been moved to a different place in a room.

This attention to detail also applies in social settings. An HSP can easily identify deception and ulterior motives in a friend or partner. Even when someone tries to conceal their true nature, an HSP will usually be able to see through the act!

High sensitivity isn't a disorder or an illness. It's just a natural variation that occurs in a minority of the human population. An HSP is born possessing this trait, which cannot be learned or unlearned. Men are just as likely to be highly sensitive as women, so don't assume that you can't be an HSP if you are a man.

HSP Myths

High sensitivity isn't well understood. Here are just a few of the most common myths debunked.

HSPs are empaths. All empaths are HSPs, but not all HSPs are empaths. You can think of an empath as an individual who meets all the criteria for high sensitivity yet has an additional set of abilities. An empath literally feels other people's emotions, whereas HSPs merely sense them. Empaths are also more vulnerable to negative energy and are more likely to report meaningful spiritual and intuitive experiences.

HSPs are all introverts. Whilst the majority of HSPs are introverts, almost one-third (30%) are actually extroverts! Don't dismiss the possibility that you are an HSP just because spending time with other people leaves you feeling energized rather than drained. In fact, HSPs can develop a wide circle of friends because they are so empathetic and intellectually stimulating.

HSPs are just shy. HSPs often like to take their time when processing social situations, especially if they are in a noisy environment. To an outsider, their measured approach might suggest that they are shy. This isn't the case. It's more likely that a quiet HSP is just taking a moment or two to reflect on what is happening around them. They might appear slower to speak than others, but this is because they believe in the power of words and therefore prefer to think about what they want to say before opening their mouths.

HSPs all have anxiety disorders and/or depression. This simply isn't true. High sensitivity describes a way of thinking and relating to the world, whereas anxiety disorders and depression are mental illnesses. However, it is true that HSPs can become anxious and depressed if they don't understand their own needs. They can also experience great suffering if those around them cannot, or will not, understand them. Later in this book, you'll learn how to keep yourself healthy and happy.

HSPs all have Autism Spectrum Disorders (ASD). People with ASD sometimes have problems processing sensory information, and they can become overloaded as a result. In some cases, those with ASD can experience "meltdowns" triggered by excessive sensory input. It's easy to see why people conflate "highly sensitive" and "autistic."

However, there is a fundamental difference between being an HSP and having an ASD. An ASD is a developmental disorder, not a trait or personality type. To be diagnosed with ASD, an individual must show "persistent deficits in social communication and social interaction across multiple contexts." HSPs do not have problems communicating with other people, and the majority are skilled at social interaction.

HSPs have Attention Deficit Hyperactivity Disorder (ADHD), or Attention Deficit Disorder (ADD), and that's why they are so reactive to stimuli. This is simply untrue. ADHD and ADD are psychiatric disorders that usually require treatment, whereas high sensitivity is a natural variation that occurs in one-fifth of the population.

This confusion arises because there are some points of similarity between HSPs and those with ADHD/ADD. Both groups tend to be perfectionists, they both have a well-developed sense of intuition, they both enjoy daydreaming, and they both like to help other people. They also share an appreciation for the arts, frequently feel the need to express themselves creatively, and believe in standing up for the oppressed. As an HSP, you may find that you naturally gravitate towards people with ADD or ADHD.

However, there are a few signs that separate an HSP from someone with ADHD. For the most part, HSPs have the ability to concentrate for prolonged periods of time, which is usually a difficult task for those with ADHD. HSPs are usually better at following the thread of a conversation. However, an overstimulated HSP soon feels overwhelmed, and they might find it hard to complete a task.

To complicate matters further, it's possible to be highly sensitive and be diagnosed with ADHD or ADD at the same time! However, as a general rule, you are likely to be one or the other. Reading this book will help you gain clarity on this point. If you are still unsure, consider consulting a medical professional to gain a definitive diagnosis.

HSPs are rare. Twenty percent of the population are HSPs. You could argue that this makes them relatively unusual, but it's hardly a "rare" trait. To put it into perspective, at least one child in every classroom is an HSP, and there might be a few dozen working in a large company! Assuming you know at least five people besides yourself, there's a good chance you know another HSP.

HSPs are more gifted, intelligent, or creative than the average person. This may or may not be true—we don't have enough information yet to know either way! Dr. Elaine Aron, highly-regarded sensitivity expert, takes the view that HSPs and non-HSPs are probably equally as intelligent and creative.

It's obvious when someone is highly sensitive. If you are an HSP, you have probably chosen to hide your trait from time to time. Most highly sensitive people have taught themselves to conceal their true nature for fear of being judged. For example, if your parents made you feel bad just because you happened to have a sensitive nature, it's almost inevitable that you would get into the habit of pretending to be "normal." As an HSP, you have been blessed with a strong sense of intuition, but don't beat yourself up if another HSP slips past you—over time, sensitive people can become highly accomplished at putting up a façade.

HSPs can be "normal" if they want to change. It's true that an HSP can act "normal," but this doesn't mean that they can turn their sensitivity on and off at will. They certainly don't choose to be more sensitive than the rest of the world.

All HSPs prefer a quiet, boring life with little stimulation. Most HSPs value the opportunity to retreat from the hustle and bustle of the world to relax and recharge, particularly if they've had to spend a lot of time in a busy environment. However, this definitely does not mean that they want to stay at home all the time! HSPs tend to be curious about the world around them, so they will happily go out and explore it. Not only that, but extroverted HSPs can thrive in social situations that entail talking to lots of people.

HSPs are weak. Sensitive doesn't mean "weak" or "frail." To survive as an HSP in a world that doesn't understand sensitivity requires strength and determination—in fact, you can't afford to be weak if you're an HSP!

HSPs don't have successful careers. It's true that HSPs have different requirements when it comes to the workplace. For example, as an HSP, you probably dislike jobs that require you to work in chaotic environments for hours at a time. However, as long as you understand and accommodate your own needs, there is no reason you can't enjoy a great career.

The key to having a successful career is noticing your strengths and making the most of them. For instance, as a diplomatic person who is reluctant to hurt anyone's feelings, you are in a great position to put forward constructive criticism and potentially controversial new ideas without causing undue offense. This will gain you respect at work.

There's a lot of information to take in when learning about high sensitivity. Fortunately, you don't have to remember all the finer details. Just bear in mind that, as an HSP, you can't help but process the world in a deeper, arguably more meaningful way than the majority of the population. Unfortunately, it's hard to manage your feelings if you don't have the tools to do so! Just because you feel emotions intensely doesn't mean you know how to deal with them. In the next chapter, we'll look at how you can develop your emotional intelligence and why these skills can make your life as an HSP much easier.

EMPATHY AND COMPASSION

One thing that we need to focus on a bit here before we move on is the importance of empathy. This is a skill that a lot of people are going to fail, especially when they start to analyze other people. They assume that everything is black and white and that if someone is showing a certain behavior, the result is the same each time. But people are unpredictable, and they have things that happen that can influence them often without even realizing how that projects out to another person.

For example, if you meet up with someone who has just gotten out of a fight with their partner, they may seem tense. You notice that their posture is tense, their hands are in fists, and ready to punch something, and their speech is tight and angry. If you are not empathetic, and you look at the body signals, you may assume that this person is mad at you when in reality, they are mad at something else.

In some cases, the nonverbal cues you pick up are going to be concerning you and how you affect the other person. But, there are also times when something external, something that has nothing to do with you or that conversation or situation is affecting the other person. Being empathetic will help you to look for and understand some of these things, and can make it easier for you to make that connection with them.

This brings up the question of why we should practice empathy. Some of the best reasons that you should always make sure you are practicing empathy with those around you will include:

You are more likely when practicing empathy to treat those you care about, and anyone else, in the way that you wish that they would treat you.

You will be better equipped to understand the needs of those who are around you.

You will then be able to more clearly understand the perception you create in others based on the actions you use and the words you rely on.

You will be able to understand how some of the nonverbal communication that you share with others is going to impact them.

In the workplace, you will be able to have a better understanding of the needs of your customers.

You will find that it is easier for you to predict, with a lot of accuracies, the actions and the reactions of those you are interacting with.

It is easier for you to motivate those around you if you can look at what motivates them the best.

You can show your point of view to others more effectively.

You will find that it is easier to see a higher resolution of the world around you because you can see the perspective of others and not just your own.

Even when some negativity comes from others towards you, it is easier to deal with it when you understand their fears and the things that motivate them to act this way.

Sometimes, we get so caught up in our little world that it is easy to forget about others and what they are experiencing at the time. Sometimes, we assume they are mad at us, and then we get mad and upset because we don't understand what we did wrong. In truth, if we took a moment to look at what the other person is feeling, and we understood that maybe an outside force that has nothing to do with us is causing the issue, it would be easier to handle that negativity!

Choose the Other Side

One thing that we often struggle with is feeling that when someone is mad at us or kind of mean, we see them as our enemy. Many times, we are told to see it from their point of view and become friends with them. But if you have been in this kind of enemy role with the other person for a long time, this is a hard thing to fight off very effectively.

To make this easier, rather than trying to side with the enemy, try to be an actual third person with this. We all have those loved ones and friends who will complain to us about how other people are treating them. It is part of human nature to complain, and sometimes, we see it as our duty to listen and be sympathetic, up to a point. The assumption is that the listener is going to be on the side of the one complaining, and someone supportive usually will.

With this exercise - any time you are struggling with being empathetic towards another person, practice internally while taking the opposing viewpoint. You should not jump into the default reaction right away. Start on the other side, and then work your way back. You may learn something new and find that you are feeling what the other person is going through a little bit more when you decide to go with this option.

It is hard to do an accurate analysis of another person, and learn as much about them as you can if you are not able to let some empathy in the door. You may not always agree with the people you are trying to analyze, and they may do or say something that doesn't make you all that happy. But when you learn to see things from their point of view, and you learn a bit of empathy, you will find that it is easier than ever to learn more about them and understand that person and what they may be going through in their life.

The next step is to sit down and evaluate your persuasion skills. Once you know where you are with your skills, it will be much easier to ensure that you are able to quickly get your skills to the desired level.

There's no doubt that there's a benefit to learning how to analyze people, although I'll advise you to keep your newfound "superpowers" under wraps since others might not feel comfortable if they think you are trying to constantly observe and analyze them.

It can make people clamp up around you, and this can deny you of the opportunity to practice these skills.

The essence of this book is to help you blend and survive better in a complex and largely unpredictable environment and not for you to become isolated. So carefully observe the gestures stated in this book.

Remember, the only way for you to fully grasp this information is for you to practice and refer back to the book as needed. By doing this, you will quickly get familiar with the common nonverbal and verbal cues from those around you.

It's important for you to know that there are some nonverbal cues that are not covered in this book. So practice reading people and observe the context in which they exhibit nonverbal and verbal cues. Remember, never stop learning. I wish you the best in your endeavors.

CHAPTER 3: MASTERING THE ART OF ANALYZING PEOPLE - BODY LANGUAGE 101

Body Language and the Importance of Nonverbal Communication

Body language is a kind of nonverbal communication where individuals use physical behaviors instead of words in conveying or expressing information. These kinds of behaviors consist of body posture, facial expression, eye movement, gestures, and use of space as well as touch.

Here, we will be focusing on how to interpret human body language. It is also called kinesics.

Body language is not the same as sign languages. Sign languages are complete languages similar to spoken ones that come with their complicated grammar systems. They are also able to show the basic properties you can find in every language.

On the other hand, body language does not possess a grammar system. You need to broadly interpret it as opposed to having an obvious meaning that corresponds to a specific movement. So, it isn't a language similar to sign language, and it is only called a language as a result of popular norms.

What is Nonverbal Communication?

Nonverbal communication is the act of passing across a feeling, idea, or thought using facial expressions, posture, and physical gestures. According to a study carried out at UCLA, it was proven that most of communication is not verbal. Although the precise statistics of the study, which showed that just seven percent of any message was transmitted via words, fifty-five percent via nonverbal components like gestures and postures and thirty-eight percent via vocal components like tone are doubtful.

How Does Nonverbal Communication Work?

Nonverbal communication has a crucial role to play in our lives. It can enhance the capacity of an individual to engage, relate, and create relevant relations in everyday life. When individuals have better knowledge of this kind of communication, it may aid them in developing more powerful relationships with others. Frequently called body language, nonverbal communication can take a range of forms and can be interpreted in numerous ways by various individuals, mostly across cultures. Even an absence of these nonverbal cues can have a meaning and is a kind of nonverbal communication.
Every movement and blend of body movements like changes in posture, eye direction, limb gestures, and facial expressions gives a signal to other individuals. These cues could either be obvious or subtle and might be conflicting. An individual may say something while the body languages transmit a completely different message, something that is usually the case when the person is being deceptive. Because nonverbal communication is frequently natural,

faking it is not easy, and it is a more accurate indication of how an individual feel.

Kinds of Nonverbal Communication

The kinds of nonverbal communication are numerous and varied. They can also offer broad perception into the feelings or thoughts of an individual. The kinds of nonverbal communication can be classified to better understand their place in daily interactions:

- Posture: the body's position on its own and the way it relates to others
- Gesture: the motion of the limbs or head
- Eye Contact and Movements: the focus and direction of an individual's eyes
- Body Movements: any movement of the body
- Facial Expression: any motion and changes of the facial structure
- Voice Tone: the variety of pitch in the voice that might communicate something aside from spoken words. For example, sarcasm may give the words of an individual an utterly distinct meaning.

Nonverbal communication is frequently used alongside verbal communication to support, repeat, contradict, and emphasize a verbal message. It is also utilized in replacing verbal messages.

Nonverbal Communication's Role in Relationships

The nonverbal cues of an individual may be less difficult to read by a family member, partner, or close friend. In close relationships, this profound understanding on a nonverbal level may encourage increased closeness or strengthen bonds. This understanding is the case when it corresponds with what is being said by one partner or friend in a relationship.

But when something feels wrong, it may not be as easy for individuals to keep things away from those they share a close relationship with, and efforts to do so may result in conflicts or miscommunications in the relationship. Since nonverbal communication is not often conscious, the way people interact nonverbally may reveal an underlying problem not readily obvious in the relationship.

Principles of Body Language Intelligence

The following are a few principles of body language intelligence:

Body Language Precedes Words

Individuals say and do things in response to what others say and do. These external happenings act as triggers or cues that inspire innate responses.

Cues could equally be internal. For example, where concerns and thoughts result in a change in the position of the body. You may also ask, "Considering their body language, what could they be feeling or thinking?"

Cues are a crucial aspect of conditioning where actions and emotions are paired with a cue such that when the cue shows up, it triggers a range of feelings and likely associated actions that the individual may try suppressing. This cue response could also be natural, like the way some creatures cause a fear response.

Context Is Everything

Context may impact how a person acts, feels, and thinks. What is happening in the immediate surroundings could have an obvious effect. For example, when men are around appealing young ladies, they will indulge more in posturing and preening.

The broader context of an individual's life may have an impact on their body language. It typically indicates excitement, anxieties, and anticipation. If you are not aware of such modifiers, it could have a severe effect on your efforts to read their body language.

Search for Clusters

While changes in body language can show up as single happenings, like the folding of arms, they often show up as a group of diverse movements that take place at the same time or one after the other. For example, an individual may cross their arms, change their posture, lean back slightly, frown, and purse their lips all as simultaneous evidence of disagreement.

Clusters of body movement send obvious signs when they all specify the same thing. This awareness may occur when each has a related meaning, or where the entire group of movement merges to create one definition.

At times, cluster movements oppose one another. For example, when an individual rubs his nose, which shows a possible deception, and smiles. The subsequently mixed signals will likely result in you feeling uncomfortable, and it would be smart to be vigilant for these kinds of gut feelings while searching for why you may be feeling this way.

Character

The general character of the other individual is a factor that can compound and explain a lot. An individual who is an extrovert, for example, may show regular and large body movements, while an individual who is more introverted may utilize more precise gestures.

Confusing these personality qualities for others like timidity is easy. In a bid to categorize others, we frequently misread limited body signs and then filter things we see using these inaccurate mental models.

Mood, temperament, and short-term emotions can also function as modifiers that have an impact on body language, making it much harder to interpret. If you can determine the present emotional state of a person, you will be able to apply this insight in your interpretation and attain a better understanding of the actual meanings of their motions.

Sudden Changes Are Relevant

A crucial thing to look out for is changes. For example, when an individual scratch their nose suddenly, it could be a sign of discomfort.

When you observe changes in body language, search for cues that may have caused the transition. For example, when an individual suspected of telling lies is asked a question and he looks away.

Individuals in sales are always on the lookout for body language changes like subtle cues, positive responses, and leaning forward as signs that a client is becoming persuaded. The salesperson then utilizes this knowledge as a sign to head to the next phase in closing the deal.

Rules for Accurately Reading People and Why Analyzing People Is Important

The capacity to read other individuals will have a great impact on your dealings with them. When you have an understanding of the feelings of another individual, you will be able to adapt your communication and message style to ensure it is attained in the best method possible.
But what are the things you should be watching out for that can aid you in reading someone accurately?

The First Strategy: Notice Body Language Cues

According to research, words account for just seven percent of how we converse, while our voice tone is thirty percent. The highest is the body language, which accounts for fifty-five percent.

Do not try too hard to read body language cues. Do not get too analytical or intense. Remain fluid and relaxed. Sit back, be comfortable, and observe.

Below are a few things to look out for:

• Take Note of Appearance
When you read others, observe the following: Are they putting on well-polished shoes and a power suit, dressed for triumph, signaling ambition?
T-shirt and jeans, signifying comfort and a casual look? A close-fitting top showing cleavage that indicates a seductive choice? A pendant like a Buddha or a cross indicating spiritual standards?

• Observe Posture
When reading the posture of others, ask yourself: Do they cower or walk indecisively, which is an indication of low self-esteem? Do they place their head high, a sign of confidence?

Does the individual swagger with their chest puffed out, which is an indication of a huge ego?

- Look Out for Physical Motions

Distance and leaning: Notice when individuals lean. Typically, individuals lean away from those they do not like and toward those they do.

Hiding hands: When individuals place their hands in their pockets, on their laps, or behind them, it indicates they are trying to hide something.

- Translate Facial Expression

Emotions can be written on our faces. Deep frown lines indicate overthinking or worry. Smiling with crow's feet close to the eyes is an indication of joy. Teeth grinding and clenched jaw indicate tension. Pursed lips signify bitterness, anger, or contempt.

The Second Strategy: Pay Attention to Your Intuition

You will be able to tune into an individual past their words and body language. Intuition is the feeling in your gut and not what your head tells you. It is the nonverbal data you observe through body language and images as opposed to logic.

If you desire to understand an individual, what matters the most is who the individual is and not their external trappings. Intuition gives you the capacity to see past the evident to disclose a richer story.

List of Intuitive Cues:

- Honor the Feelings in Your Gut

Pay attention to what your gut tells you, especially during initial meetings. It is a primal reaction that takes place before you have an opportunity to think. It lets you know if you are comfortable or not.

Gut feelings take place quickly; they are a natural reaction. They act as your truth meter and let you know if you should trust a person.

- Sense the Goosebumps

These are wonderful instinctive prickles that let us know we resonate with individuals who inspire or move us, or we are having a conversation that hits the spot.

Goosebumps also occur when you experience déjà vu, which is a feeling that you used to know a person even though you have not met before.

• Watch Out for Flickers of Insight
When conversing with individuals, a bulb may light up about an individual, which comes in an instant. You must remain alert, or you may miss it. We tend to head to the subsequent thoughts so quickly that we lose these vital insights.

• Look Out for Intuitive Compassion
At times you will be able to feel the physical emotions and symptoms of individuals in your body, which is a powerful kind of compassion. So, while reading individuals, notice things like whether your arm hurts when it did not previously or if you are upset or sad after a meeting. To find out if this is empathy, you need to get feedback.

The Third Strategy: Perceive Emotional Energy
Emotions are spectacular expressions of our energy or the vibe we let out. We record this using intuition. It feels great to be around some individuals; they enhance your vitality and mood.

On the other hand, others drain you; you impulsively want to leave their vicinity. You can feel this subtle energy feet or inches from the body, even though it is not visible. It is known as "Chi" in Chinese medicine, a crucial vitality to health.

Tactics for Reading Emotional Energy

• Sense the Presence of Individuals
Presence is the total energy we let out. It is not essentially consistent with behavior or words. It is the emotional air that surrounds us like the sun or a rain cloud.

When you read individuals, observe whether they have a friendly presence that draws you in. Or are you getting the jitters, which make you, back off?

• Pay Attention to the Eyes of Individuals
Our eyes convey commanding energies, similar to the way the

brain possesses an electronic signal that extends past the body. Even without research, we intuitively know that the eyes send energy.
Take a moment to observe the eyes of individuals. Are they angry? Caring? Mean? Is the individual at home in their eyes, showing an aptitude for intimacy? Or do they seem to be hiding or shielded?

• Notice How a Touch, Hug, and Handshake Feels
We send emotional energy via physical contact similar to an electrical current. Ask yourself whether a hug or handshake feels confident, comfortable, or warm.
Or does it make you feel so uneasy that you have the desire to withdraw? Are the hands of individual's clammy, indicating nervousness? Or limp, which suggests being timid or noncommittal?

• Pay Attention to the Laugh and Voice of People
The volume and tone of our voice can tell us a lot concerning our emotions. Vibrations are produced from sound frequencies. When you are reading a person, observe how the tone of their voice has an impact on you. Ask yourself whether the tone is whiny, snippy, or abrasive. Do they have a soothing tone?

Importance of Nonverbal Communication

Simply put, if you do not know how you are coming across to others, you are losing out on a huge part of human interaction.

If you are a young professional with ambition, discerning these cues could build or mar your career. And if you are in search of how to move up the ladder of your career, being able to take advantage of what you know about body language can give you an upper hand in the presence of your clients, in the office, or in other professional circumstances.

A fast, precise read could make a lot of difference when it comes to messing up in front of your coworkers or dazzling your boss.

CHAPTER4: HOW DOES BODY LANGUAGE REVEAL YOUR EMOTIONS AND THOUGHTS?

Reading and analyzing people is a skill. Like most skills, some people master them easily while others have to learn. Think about it like coding. Some children master coding skills at an early age, and by the time they hit their teenage years, they are very good at coding and can hack some of the most secure systems. On the other hand, some people learn to code later on in life. They get through life oblivious of their potential in computer science, but when they start learning, they become masters. This is what happens with reading people.

It does not matter when you learn to read people. What matters is how good you are at it and what you do to improve your skills. To be honest, this is an important skill that you will be well suited to learn. It can save you in many situations. You might not be able to read someone's mind, but you can read what you see in their actions and what you hear in their words. That counts for something because you have tangible evidence upon which you base your actions.

In as much as you will learn how to read people, you must also be aware of your weaknesses. Even some of the best analysts out there will, from time to time, struggle to set aside their experiences, unconscious bias, or normal influence and knowledge of human nature.

Before you claim awareness of what someone is thinking, you have to step back and question the basis of your knowledge. Do you have information or evidence to back your analysis? Are you sure you are not projecting your personal experience on the subject to conclude? Of all the information you have about the subject, do you believe you have thoroughly analyzed them all before making a decision? More importantly, is the information in your possession credible and thorough enough to rule out any other possibility behind the subject's behavior? If you can do that, you will have an honest and accurate analysis of the subject.

In many cases, when you believe you have a hunch about someone, it is no more than your personal bias clouding your judgment. From there, you can make an incorrect decision about them, yet deep down, you believe you are correct. Critical thinking must be an important part of such assessments. The ability to read people is a skill, an important one that we should all learn.

It is easier to read some people than others. In a powerful position, it is wise to make the participants feel comfortable. Relax the situation so that they feel comfortable enough to express themselves freely. This way, you have a better chance of analyzing their feelings and thoughts clearer.

How many times have you come across poker face in conversations? People throw it around randomly even when it's not necessary, but it alludes to someone who can conceal their emotions and feelings by keeping a straight face. Such a person can be sad but interact jovially with everyone, masking their deep pain. Many reports suggest that spoken words only account for 7% of communication. Further, they suggest that body language and tonal variation account for 55% and 38% respectively (Wiesenthal, Silbersweig, and Stern, 2016).

While the population samples for these studies might vary from each situation, the concept is true. Therapists and clinical psychologists read so much into their patients' lives by observing their facial expressions and body language while in session. Many patients are defensive and only come to therapy because they are made to. To get out of therapy, they spin tales of how they are doing well already and feeling better and can reintegrate into society. However, the therapist is trained to notice the disconnect between their actions and words.

The therapist will try to find an action pattern at different parts of the conversation, most of them unrelated, and use this to assess whether the patient is honest about their words or not. It is not just about telling whether the patient is healed or not; it is also about helping them heal. A lot of people also come to therapy as a last resort. Everything else has failed them, and they need to find solace in someone or something. By understanding body language, therapists can genuinely show empathy and encourage the patient to stay strong.

This is another technique of creating a healthy environment where the patient can knock down their boundaries and allow the therapist to understand their pain and distress and eventually help them overcome their tribulations.

Let's take another example—parenting. Many parents have a deep (if not intimate) understanding of their children. Despite the brave face that your child might show, you know something is not right. You can feel the depression. You know a certain behavior pattern in your child, and when that pattern changes abruptly, you are wise to know something is amiss.

Many children struggle in life, especially as they approach their teen years. They struggle because they feel no one understands them. This is how they end up finding help in the wrong places because someone was keener on their behavior than the people closest to them. Such people eventually exploit their innocence.

To be fair to parents, understanding and reading teenagers is not easy. They are at a point in their lives where hormonal changes and interaction with the rest of the world conflict with everything that they might have learned about life growing up. It is so confusing for them. Most of them embrace their true identity at this point, and it might be different from what you might have expected of them growing up. As the development advances, their ability to conceal their real feelings also grows, especially if they feel they are going in a different direction than what you expect of them.

CHAPTER 5: UNDERSTANDING AND ANALYZING PERSONALITY TYPES

A person's personality is the "fingerprint" of his or her soul, as some would say. It is what sets him or her apart from the rest of the world. Personality might make one person more assertive than another. It defines how we live our lives and the roles we assume.

There are multiple theories on the topic of personality, and we will be looking into two of them: the Four Temperament Theory and the more complex Myers-Briggs personality typing process.

Four-Temperament Theory

This proto-psychological theory proposes that there are four basic personality types: melancholic, phlegmatic, sanguine, and choleric. Research does not mean to imply that individual personalities only include one of these types; however it does suggest that at least one will be more dominant.

Melancholic: The melancholic person can be very analytical and detail oriented. They are often deep thinkers, and they tend to be somewhat introverted. Their reserved personalities and attention to detail make them fairly self-sufficient. They are also reserved and thoughtful; the type to think before they speak or act.

Phlegmatic: The phlegmatic is a bit more relaxed and easy-going. They are caring individuals but prefer to hide their emotions. They also tend to generalize issues and can be prone to making compromises.

Sanguine: The sanguine individuals tend to be very extroverted and social. They are more comfortable in crowds and can be very charismatic. Sanguine personalities thrive in staying active and can lean towards some risk-taking behavior.

Choleric: Choleric personalities are also more outgoing. They are often very independent, goal-oriented, and tend to have very good leadership skills.

As stated before, individual personalities typically include a mix of these personality types, making it more difficult at times to accurately analyze without developing personal relationships.

Myers-Briggs Personality Type Indicator

The Myers-Briggs personality typing is considerably more complex than some of the other personality theories. This typing system is taken from the psychological types first described in Carl Jung's personality theories in the 1920's. Jung's theory was founded on the idea that there are specific attitudes and functions of our consciousness. Jung felt that whichever trait dominated the consciousness would also have a repressed offsetting attitude. He believed that these repressed tendencies could be recognized in dreams or under extreme duress. For example, if a person were dominantly introverted, the subconscious mind would then try to offset the introversion by communicating extroversion. The opposite would also then be true. According to Jung's theory, he categorized four functions of consciousness: intuition, thinking, feeling, and sensation.

Intuition

Intuition is a deep insight of possible inner meanings. It generalizes information and tends to overlook details. Intuition does not directly mirror reality; it reads into possible situations that are not immediately evident.

Thinking

Thinking focuses primarily on the true or false nature of a situation. It is intellectual and rational and sees reality through logic and analysis.

Feeling

Feeling is, as it suggests, very sentimental. It forms opinions based on likes or dislikes and categorizes experiences into pleasant or unpleasant, good or bad, acceptable or unacceptable.

Sensation
This function alludes to a person's objective experience to the world, without any kind of extraneous evaluation. It sees objects

160

for what they realistically are. Sensation does not take into account meanings or implications but represents the fact readily available to the senses.

Jung then took these four functions and assigned them to two offsetting functions. So sensation and intuition have two perceiving (non-rational) functions and two judging (rational) functions for feeling and thinking. Using this formula, Jung identified eight main personality or "function" types. The Myers-Briggs tool includes eight more.

These types are based on a theory that suggests what is seen as random variations in a person's behavior actually has an orderly and consistent explanation. The behaviors in question are simply differences in a person's preference in how they use judgment and perception.

Each of the sixteen personalities is made up of four of the different preferences.

1. ISTJ (Introversion, Sensing, Thinking, Judging)

ISTJ's tend to be serious and thorough. They are very dependable, practical, and realistic. They are also very responsible and can get a job done in spite of distractions. They thrive on keeping things orderly in every aspect of their lives. They are also extremely loyal and traditional.

2. ISFJ (Introversion, Sensing, Feeling, Judging)

ISFJ's are personable but quiet. They are also responsible and careful, they are dependable, and they fulfill their obligations. They are painstakingly thorough and accurate. They make an effort to remember specific details about the people who are important to them and they are very concerned about the feelings of others. They crave neat and non-confrontational environments both at work and at home.

3. INFJ (Introversion, Intuition, Feeling, Judging)
INFJ's look for meanings and connections in ideas, relationships, and possessions. They strive to understand motivations behind people's decisions and can be very insightful. They tend to have

firm values and stick to them rigidly. They will search for a concise vision on how to serve the common good, and they are structured and decisive in making their visions a reality.

4. INTJ (Introversion, Intuition, Thinking, Judging)

INTJ's are original minds, and they have an intense drive for getting their ideas implemented and achieving goals. They notice patterns easily, and once they have committed to a task, they see it through in an organized manner. They can tend to be skeptical, and they hold high-performance standards, for themselves as well as others.

5.ISTP (Introversion, Sensing, Thinking, Perceiving)

ISTP's are typically laid back observers unless there is a problem to be taken care of. Then they will work quickly to find a solution. They are flexible and tolerant and have great analytical skills. They can handle going through large amounts of data to get to the core problems. Cause and effect is interesting to them, and they categorize facts with logical principles, and they strive to be efficient.

6. ISFP (Introversion, Sensing, Feeling, Perceiving)

ISFP's are personable, quiet, kind, and sensitive. They are able to enjoy things at the moment, and they prefer to work in their own space and have their own deadlines. They are also very loyal and committed to the people close to them as well as their values. Conflicts are very distasteful to them, and they resist forcing their values or opinions on others.

7. INFP (Introversion, Intuition, Feeling, Perceiving)

INFP'S are loyal and idealistic, and they desire their external lives to be compatible with their values. They are naturally curious and can easily spot possibilities. They are often catalysts behind establishing new ideas; they strive to understand people and are happy to help them achieve their potential. They are flexible, able to adapt easily, and are very accepting only if their values are not in jeopardy.

8. INTP (Introversion, Intuition, Thinking, Perceiving)

INTP'S like to cultivate logical explanations for anything that is interesting to them both theoretical and abstract. Their interest leans more towards ideas than actual social interaction. They are quiet, demure, and adaptable. They have an uncanny ability to focus deeply on problem-solving if they are interested in the topic. They never stop analyzing, and can sometimes be critical and skeptical.

9. ESTP (Extrovert, Sensing, Thinking, Perceiving)

ESTP's are tolerant, flexible, and logical when it comes to their approach in getting immediate results. They quickly lose interest in conceptual explanations; they prefer to take action and enthusiastically participate in problem-solving. They enjoy being active and spontaneous, and they know how to live in the moment. Material comforts are important to them, and they tend to be more hands-on learners.

10. ESFP (Extrovert, Sensing, Feeling, Perceiving)
ESFP's are friendly and accepting towards new things. They love life, material things, and the people around them. They are able to and even enjoy working with others to get a job done. They approach work realistically and with common sense and often find ways to make the job more fun. They adapt easily to new environments and people, they are flexible, spontaneous and they learn best by experimenting with new things alongside other people.

11. ENFP (Extrovert, Intuition, Feeling, Perceiving)

ENFP's are very imaginative and passionate. They can see possibilities in life that perhaps others cannot, and they connect information and corresponding events very easily just based on the patterns they have detected. They need to feel affirmation from others, and they readily return the favor by appreciating and supporting others. They can rely on their verbal eloquence and ability to improvise, and they are flexible and spontaneous.

12. ENTP (Extrovert, Intuition, Thinking, Perceiving)

ENTP's are creative, quick, and vocal. They are very resourceful and can successfully tackle challenging and unfamiliar issues. They can conceptualize different possibilities and analyze them accordingly. They are adept at reading other people's behavior, and they can get bored with routines very quickly. They constantly change the way they do things and can tend to jump from one new interest to another.

13. ESTJ (Extrovert, Sensing, Thinking, Judging)

ESTJ's see things as they are. They are logical, practical, and realistic. They can make decisions quickly, they are able to organize people well to get a job done, and they can find the most efficient way to complete a task. They have a strong group of logical standards and semantically stick to them and desire to see others follow them as well. They can at times be somewhat forceful in fulfilling their plans.

14. ESFJ (Extrovert, Sensing, Feeling, Judging)

ESFJ's are warm and careful, and they tend to cooperate well. They desire a harmonious environment, and they work very hard to form it. They enjoy working with other people to complete jobs and they are usually precise and on time. They are loyal; they obtain a good follow through no matter how large or small the matter is. They can see what is needed by others in their daily lives and they strive to fulfill those needs. They desire appreciation for their contributions, both as who they are as a person and what they contribute to the world.

15. ENFJ (Extrovert, Intuition, Feeling, Judging)

ENFJ's are warm, approachable, empathetic to others, and responsible. They can easily ascertain the feelings and emotions of others around them and can find the potential in everyone. They desire to help people succeed and grow and can be the instigator in growth both in individuals and groups. They are very loyal, and they respond strongly to both criticism and commendation. They are sociable and able to organize others into groups; they know how to listen and make for inspiring leaders.

16. ENTJ (Extrovert, Intuition, Thinking, Judging)

ENTJ's are blunt, and to the point, they can easily take over leadership, and they are decisive. They quickly notice inadequate methods and procedures and work to develop more cohesive ways to resolve organizational issues. They set long-term plans and goals. They keep themselves well-informed; they are often well-read and enjoy learning and teaching new things. They can at times be forceful in getting their ideas heard.

The test used to discover one's personality type is reliable and accurate and can actually be very useful, especially when job searching. Many have used this tool to determine what career paths would best suit them. Here is an interesting list of careers that researchers have found to match well with the different personality types:

- ISTJ: Systems administrator, accountant, office manager
- ESTJ: Sous chef, general manager, loan officer
- ISFJ: teacher (especially younger children, possibly kindergarten age), social worker, executive assistant
- ESTP: Military, contractor, detective/investigator, financial advisor
- ESFJ: Nurse, teacher, nutritionist, childcare director
- ESFP: Bartender, receptionist, dental hygienist, recreation director
- ISTP: Police/law Enforcement, mechanic, computer engineer, analyst
- ISFP: Jeweler, veterinary technician, surveyor, equipment repair
- INFJ: Veterinarian, school counselor, interior decorator, writer
- INTJ: Microbiologist, technical writer, judge, software developer, surgeon
- ENTJ: Doctor/physician, engineer, lawyer, architect, executive
- ENFJ: Pastor/minister, health educator, PR specialist, charity director
- INTP: Professor, psychiatrist, software engineer, mathematician
- ENTP: Media reporter, producer or director, planner, real estate agent, entrepreneur
- INFP: Artist
- ENFP: Landscape Architect

Many corporate HR departments have taken advantage of this

typing tool in an effort to help their employees succeed in the workplace, including many Fortune 500 and 100 companies. Not all psychologists agree on the accuracy, but it has been proven beneficial for some employers.

It is hard not to have the mindset that one personality is superior to another. It is important to note that they are all equal and this is simply a tool to get to know oneself and other people better. These differences in personalities are what help make successful relationships, both personal and professional. The knowledge gained from understanding a person's personality and how they operate can help employers and managers decide how to assign people to jobs or positions that are the best for each of them. They can determine which individuals can successfully work on their own and which ones can work together in group settings.

Employees can gain from this knowledge as well. Learning how to survive in the workplace is a vital skill, and it takes more than just following orders. Knowing how an employer or supervisor thinks and operates can make it easier to predict what they are looking for to get a job done. Proactive employees are valuable assets and may have more of a chance of moving up the ladder in their career.

CHAPTER 6: INTROVERSION AND EXTROVERSION TYPES

It's safe to assume that the majority of workplaces and careers will involve working with a variety of other people. Some will work with more than others and understanding personalities, including your own; can give you a significant advantage.

Many supervisors will ask what a prospective employee can "bring to the table." The answer to that question requires having a firm grasp of your own strengths and weaknesses. The Myers-Briggs personality typing process provides valuable insight into understanding personalities. Take the test to discover your dominant personality traits. Some tests even include suggestions of the types of careers a given personality would do well in.

Extrovert

If you're an extrovert, you will probably do well in front of people either in a leadership position or perhaps even giving a presentation. You will be comfortable heading up a team and will be able to effectively resolve conflicts. Most extroverts naturally like to meet new people, which mean they most likely have an extensive network, giving them an advantage as they try to advance. Take advantage of the traits of the extrovert but be careful to remember to balance workload with inter-office socialization.

Introvert

Introverts have a much harder time in group settings. If you're an introvert, you most likely thrive in working alone and probably prefer written rather than face-to-face communication. Because introverts prefer to stay in the background, they can be overlooked, which is not a good thing when trying to advance in a career. Find solo jobs to work on that are detail oriented and will show well-rounded work that shows how much effort and thought went into it. But don't stay silent; learn to be more assertive, speak out in meetings, and make a conscious effort to connect with colleagues as best you can.

Sensing

A sensing person relies on the truths of a matter in their decision-making processes. If this is your more dominant trait, you will tend to be very logical, wanting clear, hard facts before deciding on results. Sensing qualities can be very beneficial in getting ahead in your career. This is due to your ability to pay close attention to details, which helps in picking up cues from the people you work around. Learn how your colleagues act and operate; use this knowledge to build a bond and maintain clear avenues of communication. Be careful not to focus so much on the small details that you fail to see the whole vision being laid out.

Intuition

Intuitive individuals assemble information through deep introspection. They strive to understand the concepts behind decisions or situations. If your personality leans towards intuition, you will be invaluable for your ability to think outside the box and provide unique ideas. However, unlike the sensing individual, you will often focus on the bigger picture rather and forget about the finer details. Those details could be vital components to succeeding and advancing in your career so be careful not to leave them out. Learn to pay attention to every aspect of the job or project being worked on.

Thinking

Obviously, all decisions require thought, but the thinkers in the group will be more interested in the facts rather than the feelings of a given situation. If you're a thinker, you will tend to approach problems in a rational way, taking the emotion out of issue in order to solve the problem. Thinkers are often very fair when it comes to dealing with conflicts and, like the extroverts, can make very good leaders, which gives them significant advantages. However, take care to not take too much emotion out of situations. Rationality can only go so far when dealing with people and thinkers can often be seen as cold and insensitive.

Feeling

Feeling personalities bring in the emotional approach behind decisions. If you tend to consider the feelings of other during a decision-making process, feeling is most likely your dominant trait. You have a distinct advantage in your ability to get along with almost any personality types, which is definitely another great quality for a leader. You will most likely be very aware of others' emotions and will be able to act accordingly. Be aware that you will not always be able to make everyone happy. Put any certain number of people together in one place, with their different personalities and even cultures, and there will be conflict. Accept that fact and learn conflict resolution to avoid further issues down the line. Be careful not to show favoritism and teach yourself how to make hard decisions, even the ones that will leave some people displeased.

Judging

Judging personalities make their decisions based upon a certain set of rules. Those rules could simply be defined by social norms, or they could be rules established by the company. If you're a judging personality, you most likely crave order and strive to follow the rules. Supervisors will definitely be quick to notice and appreciate those traits, which are also beneficial in aspiring for a leadership position. It can be difficult for judging personalities to bend so you must learn to be flexible. Don't be too rigid and understand that sometimes the rules must change in order to succeed. Deadlines should be met, but in a group setting it's important to be able to be flexible with the others in the group rather than insisting on structure.

Perceiving

Unlike judgers, perceiving individuals are prone to being much more naturally flexible. Flexibility is good, but it is important to also be able to come to a conclusion without taking too much time. You may not be as good with deadlines as some of the other personality types which will require extra effort in that area in order to maintain an advantage in the workplace.

CHAPTER 7:WHY WOMEN ARE MORE INTUITIVE THAN MEN

When next you are out, pay attention to the things you see. Do you observe any body language that suggests attraction? When people are speaking, do they lean away from each other? Do they lean into each other? Is the lady curling her hair around her finger?

These are a few subtle cues to look out for when spotting romantic interest. These clues are almost unnoticeable, and you really need to concentrate on seeing them. They may not seem important, but once you identify what they are, they will change the game forever.

Below are a few subtle cues that imply attraction:

• Dilated pupils
• The nostrils of men slightly flare
• Men have the tendency to touch their lips or chin
• Women have the tendency to touch their hair or face

Subtle cues that portray disinterest are:

• Men keep their distance when standing
• Men keep their arms closed around themselves
• Women are distracted or fidgety
• Women hold their purses in front of them

Now, let us take a further look at some romantic body language cues and what they mean.

Posture

There are moments when body language, mostly posture, does not properly communicate the signals we understand. We may interpret slouching as a sign of disinterest. We may believe shoulders down relays sadness.

What is crucial about posture when it has to do with attraction, however, is whether your love interest leans away from you or into you. Are their feet facing you or pointed away? Do they look closed or uptight?

Posture is even crucial for your online dating profile pictures. The way we walk, stand, and even head into a room may say a lot of things about us. We may be able to attract interests and attraction with this simple act.

Preening

Preening typically occurs when women fix themselves, usually when they are close to a man with whom they have an interest. Part of it has to do with her wanting to look better for him. It also has to do with her nerve. Another part of it is that there is something amazing about a woman fixing herself up, so watch out for this subtle sign.

Touch

Many men overlook touch when it comes to spotting romantic interest or attraction. Most women do not touch men with whom they have no interest. For a lot of complicated reasons that have to do with evolution, men have the tendency to initiate while women have the tendency to hold back.

While men initiate an obvious touch, women will touch by "accident." If a man brushes against the arm of a woman or gives her a quick pat on the hand or shoulder during a chat, he may be indicating interest.

It is best not to relate every accidental touch as a sign of romantic interest or attraction. What one should be searching for is not a solitary example. One should be looking for a recurrent pattern. If she keeps hitting her elbow against his in a room that is totally empty, she may have a level of attraction for him. If her arm brushes against his in a crowded room, she may be attracted to him, but she may also be lacking space.

Position of Feet

The feet position portrays the path of interest. For example, if a man has an interest in a lady but is too anxious to walk up to her, his feet may remain pointed in her direction. The same is applicable for women. However, women tend to stand with both feet facing inward or pigeon-toed to assume a posture that is more approachable.

Palms Up

When an individual makes gestures with palms facing upward, it is an indication of openness. Revealing the wrists divulges a readiness to be vulnerable, but hands facing downward divulge an attitude that is slightly defensive.

Eye Contact

A brief stare, which lasts for around five seconds, is typically an attraction sign, especially if it takes place recurrently. It might be an offer to approach and begin a conversation. An upward look from a tilted forehead is a gesture that is quite flirtatious.
A long stare or downward look can pass a threatening message.

Natural Smile

A natural smile, creating wrinkles around the eyes, may indicate real interest. When a person smiles just to be polite, the smile only moves muscles close to the lips.

Leaning

Leaning toward a person when seated is an indication of interest. On the other hand, leaning away indicates irritation or disinterest. This move implies that the individual would prefer to be anywhere else.

Mirroring

Copying the posture or gesture of another individual suggests interest. Mirroring does not have to do with copying each movement exactly. For example, if a lady leans forward and smiles, a man who is attracted may lean in as well.

Learning subtle cues changes the game. But you need to practice continuously. The best method of practicing is to continue observing. Observe individuals and the way they interact. Listen to what their body language says, and if you are able to get close enough, hear what they have to say. Do their words match what their body language says?

You can learn a lot from body language. You can use body language in business, dating, and communication among others. Body language is one of the solutions of connecting with individuals and developing relationships.

CHAPTER 8: THINKING AND FEELING

As philosophy developed in the West, we became obsessed with separating the mind and body. The indecent philosophers of greatness like Aristotle and Plato have provided the foundation for thousands of years of philosophy that sought to state that we had been prisoners of the body and that the mind was the holy part of the human.

This attitude basically makes it seem like the mind is the godly part of the human and the body is the animal type part of the human. This is a classically Christian view, as the Christian view states that man was made in God's image. If we are made in God's image but as humans, we must have some part of both, and to the ancient thinkers, the mind seemed more god-like. Of course, the body has to deal with waste and food and sights and smells that seem quite unsavory. The mind, in contrast, deals with matters of cognitive ability and feelings and reason and science. This was the classical attitude toward the mind-body split, and it was a good thing because the mind is godly and the body isn't.

What these ancient philosophers forgot, though, is that our most human part is not the brain or the mind or the hands, but actually the big toe. Not just any of our toes, but particularly the big toe. The big toe is what separates us from the other animals physically. It is what lets us stand up, and not be all wobbly, and lets us develop incredible athletic feats like running and sports.

Mindfulness is interwoven into almost every subject discussed in this book, and it is definitely interwoven into the mind-body connection. Most of us these days grow up with a relationship far too focused on the mind. We must remain positive and working for capital gains constantly to be able to have our lives go on. We are subjected to modern media, which is all-pervasive, and this affects our cognitive structure as well. We are mostly told to ignore our bodies in order to work eight-hour shifts standing or sitting. When you do this kind of work, you have to do extra to keep up with the demands of the body, because the body is not designed to be happy when it is inactive for most of the time. The body craves engagement and interaction in the world. The body needs to be a part of the world and to do that, it must interact with the world in a physical manner. This can be accomplished in many ways but the easiest is directed exercise, whether just running or walking or some other form.

For most of us, the transition that needs to happen is to be more toward the body from the mind. This is because we are slanted too far in one direction. Therefore, we need to make up for this disconnection and find a way to be more oriented toward the experience of the body in different moments to take information in.

The mind/body connection is important because you can't be integrated without it. An integrated person is not only one who has experiences and knowledge but also has the ability to synthesize different ideas and concepts to build beliefs and success through behaviors. This is the difference between knowledge and wisdom. Knowledge is a knowing of some information and data. Wisdom is the ability to really know what the information means, for them and for others and the ability to employ information in different ways.

The mind-body connection is an illustration of the ultimate integration that a human could hope to achieve. By achieving high levels of awareness and mindfulness, a person can develop their personality beyond their current state of development towards self-realization.

Self-realization is the concept that a person can be so integrated and truly act in their authentic self, rather than keeping it rewrapped in layers of repression and denial. It is when a person is no longer concerned with what the world thinks about them, and they act totally honestly. It is a state where you do not doubt yourself because you are confident and ready to engage with whatever comes along. It is a state of being you. Most people are far from this, and they have things that stand in the way. One thing that stands in a lot of people's way is youth. When we are young, we don't have experiences in the world to look back on and draw information from. This makes us so confused about where to go and dealing with our problems.

Self-realization, then, is something that probably comes later in life than adolescence and young adulthood. It is usually someone somewhat advanced in their years, who has do a lot of soul-searching, tried a lot of things out, and done a lot with their lives. These are people who are usually good candidates for this type of transformative experience.

Part of getting there, besides experience, however, is awareness of the body. Awareness of the body has been so demonized in our culture that we are only rewarded for what is visible in our cognitive accomplishments and we are torn desperately away from things that will keep us healthy being connected to our self and earth.

The mind-body connection is extremely important because, in order to read body language, a person must have a balance between their cognitive mind and their emotional mind. The emotional mind is more focused on the unconscious, which is giving us information as to our animal selves. This is really where the rich analytical body language stuff comes into play, but it has to be tempered by the cognitive state of mind, the thinking mind. The thinking mind is able to take the information from the emotional mind and really interpret it into something that actually means something for us. We can't be working in either of these minds exclusively, and that's why you need to foster a balance in the mind-body connection. A person who is too much in the mind will over-process things, and a person who is too much in the emotional mind and the body will not be processing enough. They will be taken over by the impulses of the animalistic side of our minds, and they will not be able to process body language information, but rather be overtaken by the information and too involved to have a sense of self around it.

You see the first one all the time: people too much up in their heads. These are people who worry a lot and can't be in the present moment. You may know someone like this. They might come off as whiny or complaining or too self-oriented. This is because they are a slave to their mental habits, and their mental habits just happen to be thinking negative thoughts about themselves and others. This is fine, and they are not bad people for it, but it isn't the healthiest way to live and if you search deeper and connect with the body, you can change his fate and be a balanced individual. There are some who are too in the body and they never process in a cognitive manner that they are experiencing. This may include addicts or people who have trouble with eating or sex addiction. The addict is not concerned with the future when they are taking a drug; they are only thinking about the present. This is obviously not good for them, but it doesn't line up with the idea of being present. Why? Because we are not doing things in the present moment with enough intentionality. Intentionality is the difference between an addict's mind and a well person's mind. The well person is able to act with intentionality because they know that if they partake in a certain experience; they will know that it will affect their day. They have that knowledge and they use it. An addict does not have the knowledge, and when they do, they are not able to use the knowledge.

An addict is not only exclusively in the body and emotional mind, however, and sometimes, they are skewed too far towards the head; they are always up in their thoughts. This is the type of addict who is good at rationalizing and hiding things. This is the addict who is functional and smart and capable but never changes. If this type of addict chooses to get more in touch with the body and address the mind-body connection, they will start to come out of their heads and they will start to realize that we all have a common experience in our bodies. Once the addict realizes that we all have a common experience and we are all trapped in our bodies, they start to realize that they no longer have to suffer from their condition like they used to. They can learn new ways to deal with their condition.

CHAPTER 9: COLD READINGS

Cold reading is when a person tries to convince you that they know more than they do. Mentalists, mediums, fortune tellers, and psychics will often use this technique to convince you that they are more aware of you and the information pertaining to your life than they actually do. Those that know how to cold read can quickly pick up on your body language and verbal cues to gain a quick understanding of who you are and how you work. These cold readers will use a set of guesses to figure out information, analyzing body language and other responses to figure out whether they are right are not.

For instance, a psychic might start by telling a group of people that they are speaking to someone that has passed with a name that starts with "J." Most people in the audience likely know someone that has died with a "J" name, so they will start to assume the psychic is talking about the person they know. An audience member might speak up by saying, "my uncle Joe just died,' and then the psychic will play off their body language, making small general guesses that the audience member can relate to their life.

The psychic will use verbal cues to tell if they are making the right guesses. If a participant sounds sad, they know they have hit on their emotions and can use this to their advantage. If they seem confused or distant, the psychic knows that they still need to use caution when proceeding with their readings. Anyone who states that they can talk to the dead, see the future, or make predictions and assumptions about yourself is likely highly trained in reading verbal and facial cues in order to produce a convincing cold reading.

Once your world is defined, it can be easy to pinpoint all the things that make your world unique. Some people will start to exploit this individuality, trying to connect with you on a personal level. For example, someone might notice that you like henna tattoos, so maybe they get one in an attempt to get closer to you. They end up only doing this because they want something from you. The manipulator is breaking into the person's individual world, disguising themselves as someone they can relate to, when really, they're just trying to distract them to get close.

People will make you rethink your choices based upon your own world. They might make you question, does this fit in with your beliefs? Are you sure you're not going against anything you believe in? These master manipulators will make you question your own morals, and when your beliefs become vulnerable; they'll swoop in and try to take advantage of that.

If someone knows that you're a religious person, they might use religion against you. They'll play on your weaknesses, knowing that as a religious person, breaking your moral code can cause great pain. They can use guilt and other manipulation tactics pertaining to the things that matter to you in order to get what they want.

Those using NLP tactics will often begin to mimic the body language of another person in order to feel connected to them. If a person is standing with their hand on their hip, the NLP user will do the same thing. If someone is overly confident, puffing their chest with their arms tightly crossed, the NLP user will do this same thing. They'll try to match their body with the other person to make a connection; letting them know they're someone they can trust and depend on.

They might even start talking like them, and they'll certainly give into other ideas as well. If someone is overly enthusiastic, an NLP user might feed on that enthusiasm, exerting a good mood and overall happiness as well. The opposite is true too in terms of personality. If someone seems overly pessimistic, complaining often and sharing negative views, the NLP user will try to match this, giving off the same attitude.

They might even touch the other person in order to gain some sense of connection. This can be very violating, but some people feel so thrown off by this touch that they don't even notice they're being manipulated. This can happen a lot in the workplace and even in school. Maybe a teacher or boss comes up behind a worker and places a hand on their shoulder, their way of exerting their power over the other person. In order to not create an uncomfortable situation, most people just allow the other person to touch them, giving the power to the person that did the touching in the first place.

In order to avoid this, try to do strange things you wouldn't normally do, and see if they begin to do the same thing. Find a funny trick to do with your hand, like maybe tapping the top of your head lightly. Move your eyes around rapidly and tilt your head to the side back and forth. If the person you're talking to begins to do this as well, there's a good chance they might be using NLP tactics. The same goes for anyone that touches you. If you don't want to be touched, call that person out. Ask them to not touch you nicely, and you'll be surprised to find that they'll let up. The teacher or boss that always seems to put their hand on your shoulder likely won't after the first time you ask them not to because they know it's strange behavior.

Some people actually just adopt the behaviors around them because that's part of their personality. This is a result of codependency, and not always necessarily a manipulation tactic. In order to decipher someone's true intentions, you have to look at what they might gain from the situation. If they don't seem to be taking anything from the other person, it's usually harmless behavior.

CHAPTER 10: STRATEGIES TO READING BODY LANGUAGE

Can you read someone? Many people believe they can. Whether this is true or not is a matter of perspective. If you have been in a situation where you saw through someone's lies, you can feel enlightened. This makes you feel confident about your ability to analyze someone and know what they are about. Perhaps it was luck, or maybe the person you read was the easiest read ever. If this happens frequently and for different people, you can start to believe you are good at it. Are you?

It is important to understand that there is a difference between reading and analyzing someone in your presence and telepathy. Many people confuse the two. Science fiction fans are more than conversant with the concept of telepathy. You are thousands of miles away, yet somehow, just when you are thinking about someone, they call you. This is a different story altogether.

Analyzing someone is about being in their presence. You must be aware of their role at the moment and yours to accurately analyze them. How many people can do this? Not so many. If you consider the level of training that the FBI and other specialized security departments go through to enable their operatives to learn how to read their targets and suspects, it is safe to say that not so many people can read and analyze someone instantly.

However, another thing we learn from the FBI example is that while it might be an innate talent to some, you can also learn. Reading people is primarily about awareness. You must be observant and note the tiny details that others might ignore. When things are tough, it is the subtle details that give away lies from the truth.

While reading a situation and telepathy are different, one thing that they might both share is empathy. It is through empathy that you can feel the emotions in someone's story. You can tell when you watch them or read their body language to know they are uncomfortable about the situation. Empathy allows you to see things from their perspective, instead of forcing them to operate within yours.

Indeed, some people are born with the ability to read situations better than their peers. Each time you interact with someone, it is not just about meeting them in person; it is about observing how they behave, how they react, and what they say. If you can strike a connection between their words and their actions, especially how they respond to specific stimuli or words, you can accurately analyze them.

In most cases, such individuals are capable of embracing an internal representation of the sensations, emotions, and actions of the people they interact with in such a manner that might suggest they are the ones feeling, sensing, seeing, or moving the way the subject does. Scientists believe that such people not only share the sensations, emotions, and actions of their subjects but also mirror the neuron circuits that enable the subject to behave the way they do.

CHAPTER 11: DETECTING SPECIFIC PERSONALITY TRAITS THROUGH BODY LANGUAGE

Self-awareness is truly the key to analyzing people. Before you go to understand someone else, you must have a pretty deep understanding of yourself. First, you can ask yourself a few questions to see if your level of self-awareness is up to par. Ask yourself, what have I been through in my life? Your story will tell what you think about your life and this may illustrate your level of self-awareness. If your answer is something like, "I don't know, I had a pretty normal childhood, I got kind of lucky getting this job that I have now, I'm not really certain about my future," then this will tell you what you need to know. You are a person who has not really integrated their life story and identity. You may find yourself lacking purpose or direction, or understanding why you do the things that you do.

A more self-aware answer might go something like this: "I am a 32-year-old man who was born in the Northwest and moved to California for college. A bright and talented programmer, I was offered a variety of jobs, and I decided on the one I have now because it seemed like the best option. I hope to meet someone that I can settle down with soon." This is a more mature and honest answer. The person who is answering these sounds like they know who they are and they know where they want to be.

Unfortunately, self-awareness is not something you can attain intentionally. It is something like wisdom that comes with age and experience. The best way to become self-aware is sometimes to get outside of yourself and experience things that go against what you are typically used to. For example, if you have never been to see a certain type of music, you should go check it out sometime and see why you like it or don't like it. This will give you some context and information links to what kind of music you like and the reasons that you have for liking it or not liking it.

We sometimes get too comfortable where we are in many different ways and we start wanting not to change. This is an understandable human condition, but it cannot be the one that we go forward within our lives. We must get outside of our comfort zones. I'm sure you've heard this many times before. Most people don't realize how accessible the outside of the comfort zone is. Maybe, you take a drive downtown with some friends, because downtown is a little far and you usually don't feel like driving the distance. That's okay! You can do it. Try something different from the usual routine. This will aid in self-awareness because you will experience things that might broaden your scope.

There are tons of things that you can do to open yourself up to new experiences. You can take up a new hobby, for example. Maybe, you've always wanted to learn to play. You can take up this hobby fairly easily if you purchase an inexpensive instrument and use online resources. This will provide you with a new outlet for expression as well as the cognitive tasks to help your mind stay limber and focused.

Another one of the essential tools and traits for analyzing people is an understanding of behaviorism and particularly the structure of the reward system with regard to the reinforcement and punishment of certain behaviors. In behaviorism, this is done to examine the phenomenon of how we learn. Behaviorism has pretty much established that we learn from rewards and punishment in regard to honor our behavior. When we are rewarded for a behavior, in any way, whether it is an emotional release or a physical enjoyment such as a piece of candy, we do that action again and again. When we have punishment for an action we will tend to do that action less. This is the main force of our learning as human and animal creatures, and sometimes, is much more complicated than it might seem. For example, the activity of running has a specific brain reward that comes with it. It is when we are exerting ourselves running or doing other strenuous activities that we get chemicals in our brain that make us feel good. This might make you think that we would have a natural tendency toward running and physical activity, right? Yes, but we also have a natural tendency to be influenced by other things. For instance, the reward of sugar is an intense feeling of pleasure, and we sometimes become addicted to that. There is also the pain and difficulty associated with running when you are not in the best of shape, so this is acting as a concurrent punishment for the activity. If a person can cognitively understand that when they are running they will experience some pain but feel much better afterward, they will understand how to participate in the activity for the ultimate reward.

There are some states, like long-term addiction, that can change how the brain works. The brain starts to get hold of the same substance over and over, whether it is sugar or fat or happiness or whatever else, and it starts to get used to that as a reward. However, after a while, these reward centers get burnt out and they start to fail to recognize the substances as rewarding any more. After this, the brain perceives the object of addiction not as a reward at all. Yet, the person still engages in the activity over and over and over. The person is caught in a cycle where they are motivated to engage in the activity but they are no longer receiving the reward. This is a common state that many people get into many different substances and activities.

Another important skill in the work of analyzing people is being able to understand the aspects of their childhood development and family of origin that came with their lives. This is important because the family of origin is where we first develop all of our ways of interacting with the world and being in the world. These people are the people that we grow up emulating. They are examples of masculinity and femininity in our lives. They are, in fact, the examples for all the behaviors that we understand at first. It is through this lens that we can actually understand people's motivations because people don't grow up in a vacuum. They grow up with fallible people who make mistakes and are unpredictable.

Visual observation is an important trait in the practice of analyzing people. Visual observation will give you what you need to look in a body language and understand people's true intentions. It also helps to analyze facial expression, hygiene, clothing choices, and other visual cues.

Another key trait and skill for analyzing people are writing skills. You should start to record your observations of people whom you come across in life. If you start to do this, you will develop a voice that affects your view of the world. At first, the voice might be scared or overly assuming. This can be adjusted though, and first, you might not know what to do about it, but in the future, you will get used to your voice and you will learn to work with it. As your voice progresses, keep wiring, and eventually, this voice will become something that you have even when you are not writing. What is the voice of intuition? We all have it, we just have to get used to following it.

Many people have problems following their intuition. They might second guess themselves for a variety of reasons, one being the feeling that they are not good enough to do anything. Another reason might be that they think of themselves as failures. Whatever the reason, you have to get over it and start trusting your intuition. Your intuitionis an abstract concept, but it basically means to trust your gut. The word trust gets thrown around a lot in this topic because you have to be able to trust yourself not to have the "wrong" intuition if there is such a thing. Over the years, as you learn to follow your intuition, you will find more trust in it, and you will find yourself going along the path towards self-realization.

Self-realization happens when there is no separation from the real you and the one you present to the world. Self-realization happens when you are completely honest with yourself and the world. This will be when you're able to analyze others completely because you have gone through every possibility in yourself. You have enough experience to know how people usually act when they are experiencing something.

CHAPTER 12: HOW TO ANALYZE PEOPLE VIA NONVERBAL BEHAVIORS

The Arms

The arm is made of a ball up top, a hinge joint in the middle, and a very complex toolset at the end. The arm makes for an interesting appendage in the study of body language signs as it provides a lot of information about the person. The subtle signs given out with the arms are below.

Still arms

Still arms are usually the first telltale sign of a deceiver. A person wanting to deceive tries to keep his intentions in check through the act of maintaining still arms. He usually holds one arm with the other while going through the motions of his deceitful plan.

Arms Expansion

A smart way to appear friendly or as a threat is by the mere usage of the arms as expanding devices. They can help one appear bigger or smaller than one actually is, which is dependent on the situation one is being faced with at the point in time. Arms can offer or show support and comfort when expanded in a curved shape.

When faced with a threatening position, the arms can engage in quick, direct motions toward the threatening source.

The arms also portray the level of a person's confidence or aggressive pose when they are expanded in a lateral manner.

Arms Shaping

Arms shaping is a means of literally telling people the state of one's feelings by the act of waving the arms. The shaping of the arms indicates many things in the study of body language.

In an excited or confident mood, waving the arms in windmill fashion is a telltale sign. In a less confident or depressed mood, the arms aren't waved about wildly but are waved much closer to the body.

A person can be viewed as clumsy when he waves his arms and bangs objects during the act.

Raising Arms

The body language cues shown by raising the arms varies from exaggeration to frustration to confusion. These gestures are shown when the person throws up his hands.

Frustration is shown when a person throws both arms in the air, a sign that indicates that whatever is troubling the person at that point in time is being thrown up into the air.

Confusion is a state of mind shown by the arms when a person shrugs his shoulders in tandem with the arm-throwing gesture.

Reaching Forward Arm Gesture

An aggressive pose is shown when the arms reach forward in a sudden, direct thrust, especially if the hand is shaped like a fist. Reaching forward with the arms can also be seen as a supportive or affectionate gesture as portrayed by spouses or lovers when they seek to engage in intimacy with their partner.

Pulling Back of the Arms

The first thing that intuitively comes to anyone's mind when faced with a threatening situation is to pull back the arms because the arms are usually the first body part used to gain an advantage in such a situation when grabbed.

Hidden Arms

Hidden arms, which literally expose the torso, indicate a state of vulnerability in some cases. They may mean one is submissive and can't do anything about the situation with which he is faced. Hidden arms may also mean the person is comfortable with the other party as he believes his open torso isn't vulnerable to attack. Additionally, they may indicate a position of power as the person believes what is before him is not a threat in any way.

Hidden arms may also be indicative of a person's threatening intentions as the arms could possibly be hiding a weapon.

Arms Crossing

When the arms are crossed in front of a person's torso, they act as a barrier or pathway to one's body. Crossing of the arms is used to form a defensive shield when a person feels his personal space is being invaded. Not all crossed arms are signs of

defense, however.

- The crossing of the arms could indicate the state of anxiety of a person's mind. It could be that the person doesn't trust the person with whom he is in contact, it could be a feeling of discomfort or pain and, in some cases, and it could portray a sense of déjà vu or vulnerability from an experience of personal trauma.
- The extent to which the arms are crossed is an indication of how closed off a person really is. The gesture can vary from a light arm cross to folded arms to crossed arms wrapped around a person's torso. In extreme cases, the person would have their arms wrapped tightly around their torso with their hands or palms formed into fists, which is an indication of hostility. When the legs are also crossed, it further hints at an extra measure of hostility.
- The crossing of the arms while wrapping them around one's torso could be a sign that the person is trying to rein in his temper or is merely trying to keep his body still.
- Hands in an arm-cross gesture mean the person is in a relaxed, comfortable mood as he is engaged in a self-hug.
- Crossing of the arms is also seen as a compliment in some climes. A person who engages in such arm crossing while listening to the other party is seen to be giving his full attention to the party.
- When the arms aren't crossed, it is indicative that the person is very comfortable with the person or people in his immediate surrounding space. It could also mean that the person feels in a

position of power as he feels absolutely no threat from the person he is in contact with at the time.

- When a salesperson comes in contact with people who engage in the arms-crossed gesture during their marketing gig, they usually employ the technique of having such people make use of their arms. For example, they could give them a pen to write with to loosen them up and make them more comfortable while they sell whatever product they intend putting in the mind of the person.

Arms as Weapons

Arms as weapons are usually used as a means of defense or attack depending on the situation faced.

The legs

Finally, the legs and feet are the last important aspect of the body to make note of. The large muscles in these parts are often used to manifest excessive psychological distress that might be particularly pronounced. Significant nervousness often presents itself as a shaking leg.
The ways the legs and feet are positioned also give away some information about a person's disposition. Feet that are spread slightly apart creates an open impression, which means that an individual is prepared and willing to take on conversation.

It's often normal for the feet to move and sway gently during a conversation, especially if you're seated. But take note of sudden changes in movement as they could indicate a point of interest during your conversation. For instance, a foot that suddenly points downwards as you shift topics might indicate excitement or disdain. You can confirm this by assessing how the person approaches the conversation after the switch.

The hands and palm

How someone uses their hands and arms is another way that body language can be interpreted to get a better understanding of the people you're interacting with. Our hands represent so much about ourselves. They're a way of expressing out stories, putting different emphasis on various parts. If someone's telling a story, they're going to use hand gestures to keep people interested. Think of someone engaged in a conversation as someone that's directing an orchestra. They'll lift their hands to keep up a rhythm and pace for those listening around.

Someone's hands and arms can also express how open or closed off they are. They can be like the doorway into someone's body. If they're crossed tightly in front of someone's chest, that person might be a little more closed off, not wanting to engage too much in conversation. Having their arms crossed doesn't always mean that someone is necessarily closed off. They might also just want to rest their arms, so if they're loosely hanging in front of their chest, they're likely just casually listening to you.

Someone that has their arms outstretched, maybe over their head, will likely be very open and possibly even trying to exert power over a situation. Someone with their hands on their hips might also be trying to assert their power.

CHAPTER 13: ANALYZE PEOPLE THROUGH THEIR HANDSHAKES

Similar to the way a person writes, the way they shake hands offers a clue to their inner nature. So if you are aware of what every handshake says about the people with whom you are interacting, you can make good use of this information.

Below are a few kinds of handshakes and what they mean:

- **Dominance** is displayed with one hand placed above the other, extended holding, and holding the individual using the other hand.
- **Affection** is displayed with the duration and speed of the shake, touching using the other hand, and smiling enthusiastically. Affectionate and dominant handshakes are similar and may result in a confusing situation where a dominant individual act friendly.
- **Submission** is displayed with a floppy hand, palm up (which may be clammy at times), and a fast withdrawal.

Kinds of Handshakes

- **Dead fish**: This form of handshake has no energy, no squeeze, no shake, and no pinch. It makes you feel as if you are holding a dead fish as opposed to a hand. This handshake is associated with low self-esteem.
- **Sweaty palms**: When a person is anxious, their nervous system often gets overactive, which in turn leads to sweaty palms.
- **The two-handed handshake**: This handshake is typically common with politicians. It is a form of handshake that brings to mind words like "friendly," "trustworthy," "warmth," and "honest." If the hand remains on your hand, the handshake is sincere. But if the hand moves to your arms, wrists, or elbows,

195

they want something from you.

- **Brush off**: This kind of handshake is a fast grasp then a release that seems as if your hand is being pushed aside. The handshake implies that your agenda is not essential.
- **Controller**: If you feel the other person pulling your hand toward him or directing it to another direction or a chair, this kind of person is a controller. It implies that they need to be in control of both animate and inanimate items in the room, including you.
- **Bone Crusher**: This kind of handshake, which has to do with squeezing your hands until you begin cringing, aims to intimidate you. For these individuals, you don't need to pretend to be weak. They might even respond positively if you display your strength.
- **Finger Vice**: When a person grips your fingers as opposed to your whole hand, the aim is to keep you far from them. These individuals are usually secure. If they crush your fingers, they are including a display of personal power aimed to hold you at a distance.
- **The Top-Handed Shake**: As opposed to holding his hand vertically, this shaker does so horizontally so his hand is above yours. This gesture implies he feels he is superior to you.
- **Lobster Claw**: Similar to a lobster claw, the other individual's fingers and thumb touch your palm. This individual is scared of deep connections and may have issues in developing relationships. Give them time and let them open up when they want.
- **The Pusher**: While this individual gives you a handshake, she stretches her arms so you are unable to get close. This kind of individual requires space and is not allowing you in. You must provide them the emotional and physical space they want if you plan on building a friendship with them.

CHAPTER 14: HOW TO ANALYZE PEOPLE VIA THE NONVERBAL

The Face

The face consists of about forty muscles. It utilizes many of these in sending numerous nonverbal signals. Alongside muscles, the dampness and color of the skin can also be crucial in communication.

Below are some of the body language meanings and cues given by facial expressions?

Facial Colors

You will be able to tell what a person is feeling by the color of their face. The face generally can switch between colors, all with diverse implications.

Red

- A red face may signify that the individual is hot as the blood heads to the surface of the skin to cool down. The red may also be from either emotional arousal or exercise. It can either be when a person is energized or excited.
- A red face is also typical of individuals who are angry. It is a clear sign of danger, and it is a way of warning the other person that they may be injured if they refuse to back off.
- Other times, individuals blush when they are embarrassed. The necks of some individuals go red, while for others it is the cheeks. Other times, the entire face goes red.

White

- White skin may be an indication of coldness as the blood heads deeper into the body to prevent further cooling.
- White skin may signify fear, usually extreme fear. It also occurs as

the blood leaves a surface that has been injured, heading to muscles where its power is required more.

Blue

The skin also can go blue as an indication of extreme fear or cold.

Facial Moisture

- Sweating is the natural cooling mechanism of the body when it gets hot. It can occur as a result of emotional arousal and excitement.
- Sweat is also linked with fear. It is probably to help the skin become slippery to stop an opponent from getting a firm hold.

Facial Expressions

- Trustworthiness

According to Helman et al. (2015), it was proven that a face that is trustworthy is one that has a slight smile, with the mouth corners turning upward and the eyebrows a bit raised. This expression implies being friendly and confident without being nervous as to whether others will like us, making us more appealing as friends.

- Intelligence

According to Kleisner et al. (2014), it was proven that individuals who have a narrower face with a lengthy nose and thinner chin are a typical stereotype of how a person who is very intelligent looks. On the other hand, a person with a broader, oval face, with a smaller nose and larger chin is seen as having lower intelligence.

They also pointed out that higher intelligence is discerned when a person is showing joy or smiling. On the other hand, lower intelligence is easily linked with untrustworthiness and anger.

The Eye

Every time we like what we see, our pupils tend to dilate, and they constrict when we find something, not to our liking. In truth, we can't control our pupils as they are responsive to external stimuli such as changes in light and internal stimuli as well. A good example of this is our thoughts. A response occurs in fractions of a second.

When we are surprised, aroused, or suddenly confronted by someone, our eyes tend to open up and widen with dilated pupils in order to let in maximum light needed to send maximum information to the brain. Once the information is processed and we perceive it to be negative, our pupils will constrict in a fraction of a second.

Any decrease in the size of the eyes is a subconscious blocking behavior which indicates a concern, disagreement, dislike or perceived a potential threat.

You can tell if a person is telling a lie through their eyes. This part of the body bears a tremendous amount of data relating to their emotion, particularly about telling the truth. Often we can detect how others feel towards us through the look in their eyes.

When Attracted

When a person likes you tremendously at first glance, their eyes turn big and round trying to take in your presence through his vision. Those are greatly attracted to you will have visible eye cues like looking to the left then sweeps your face with his gaze, turn his look to the right and repeat the same procedure. They will never look at you directly. As they delve with their attraction, they will barely raise their eyebrows. As they continue to scan and absorb your facial expressions, eyes and brows tend to mimic yours.

When Lying

A lying person finds it hard to look someone straight in the eyes. Even when that person smiles, grins, or show some teeth, their smile can give away their lies. Lying eyes never squint or crinkle along with the smile. This indicates that the outward display of happiness never reaches the person's eyes. This is because the eyes of a deceiving person are stressed. Here are some of the eye responses when the eye is attempting to display false body language.

- Shutting up when a critical question is being asked.
- The long duration of eye contact in an attempt to cover up the sense of guilt
- Rapid eye blinking while listening to critical issues
- Sudden and uncontrollable muscle twitching due to the automatic muscle response triggered by the autonomic nervous system.

A person who is lying tends to fix their stare on the ground or floor because of their guilt and embarrassment being caught lying. They look down and avert their gaze to avoid your judging them, which can be seen in your look of anger, disgust, or disappointment.

When in Doubt or Unbelieving

When someone is doubtful of your words, you can observe the following body cues and signals:

- Narrowing set of eyes
- Wrinkles on the forehead
- Slightly squinted eye
- Lip sides are pulled back tightly as a sign of discomfort or thinking of manufacturing a story
- Eyes suddenly open wide when presented with crucial information

Suddenly opening wide when crucial information is presented

Quickly shifting their look to the left or right, up or down, or could be simply looking around. This is because they believe that untruthful presentation of facts isn't worth their time to listen.

Here are a few of the facial signals and eye movements you may see for various emotions. Note that these are just possible indicators. Not all signals are required and not all indicated signals here necessarily show the emotion linked to them.

- Anxiety: Damp eyes, eyebrows pushed together, head tilted down slightly, lower lip trembling, and chin wrinkled.
- Fear: Eyes opened wide, pointing down, or closed. Eyebrows raised, white face, head down, open mouth or corners turned down.

- Anger: Wide eyes and staring pulled down eyebrows, forehead wrinkled, red face, clenched or flattened teeth and flared nostrils.
- Desire: Dilated pupils with eyes wide open. Eyebrows raised slightly, head tilted forward, slightly puckered or parted or smiling lips.
- Sadness: Cast-down eyes that is tearful or damp. Pinched lips, head facing downward or to the side.
- Happiness: Sparkling eyes with crow's-feet wrinkles by the sides, mouth smiling, eyebrows slightly elevated, head level, and possible laughter.
- Envy: Eyes staring, jutting chin, nose crooked in sneer, and corners of the mouth turned down.
- Surprise: Eyes open widely, eyes elevated high, head tilted to the side or held back, and mouth dropped open.
- Interest: Fixed eye gaze at an element of interest, could be squinting. Eyebrows a bit raised, lips pressed together slightly, head pushed forward or erect.
- Boredom: Eyes looking in another direction face generally not moving, head upheld with hand, lips drawn to the side.
- Disgust: Eyes and head turned to another direction, closed mouth, sneering nose, jutting chin, and protruding tongue.
- Relief: Tilted head mouth either smiling or tilted down.
- Pity: Eyes probably damp and in extended gaze, head tilted sideways, eyebrows pulled together slightly downward at edges or in the middle.
- Shame: Head and eyes facing downward, blushing red skin, and eyebrows held low.
- Calm: Facial muscles relaxed. Eyes in a steady gaze, mouth possibly turned up a little at the sides in a calm smile.

The Lips

When you just pay close attention to people's lips, it can tell you how the person feels about you. It can tell you much about the person - that is if he is truthful and honest. If you just take the time to practice regularly, you can become a lip reader and learn to read lips based on how people move their lips, tongue, and teeth.

While sweating on the forehead is a visible sign that the person is tense and also indicates possible deception, so is the perspiration seen above the lip. As the autonomic nervous system is triggered in response to a sudden body change, the top of the upper lip and the forehead were perspiration suddenly appears. When the temperature of the body rises, it starts to release perspiration.

A smile can be a sign of being polite. Other people are forced to give out a smile even when they don't feel like smiling, but if you can read what the lips are telling you, you can easily tell if the smile is genuine or not.

Celebrities are often exhibiting tight-lipped smile during a photo shoot. Most of the time, they aren't really happy with the invasion of their privacy, but they need to be polite so they can please their fans.

Watch out for a genuine smile at an inappropriate moment. An example is when someone smiles to see someone who is injured. It could be that the person is happy to see the injured person suffers.

Sometimes, a smile is an indication that the person is withholding some information. They would pursue their lips into a tight smile to show that they know something but is not willing to tell you. Ever seen some showbiz personalities who are asked about their love life? When they have an ongoing romance, they don't want to reveal, they simply give out a smile as an answer. It means that they are enjoying their romance but is not willing to share it to the public.

Lip biting is another subconscious way of holding yourself from giving out any information. This is a natural reaction of the facial muscle when the person has told a lie. Notice how the lower lip recoils while the upper lip clamped it down.

On the other hand, lip blowing is a facial expression that occurs before or after an attempt of deception and when the person is tensed. As the autonomic nervous systems work hard in blood pumping - there occurs a respiratory change in the body in order to maintain a homeostatic balance. This is what makes the individual take in a huge breath of air through mouth and nose before audibly release it through their lips in a big blow.

Lips That Lies

It is common to see people covering their lips with their hands when they tell a lie. This is to prevent them from telling the truth. This is a subconscious attempt to shut up.

When you observe people in the habit of licking their lips due to the dryness of the oral mucosa, be on the lookout when the muscles in the throat of a person tightens, and there is that evident up and down movement of the neck or Adam's apple as the person is literally trying to swallow his lie.

When a person manufactures a story in an attempt to cover up something, it is common to see the lip swing - lip pulled to one side of the face - as they are trying to concoct the story. Such an expression is also seen in people who are confused about what to do next.

Blushing And Blanching

A person's forehead can tell us a lot of information about them that reading the facial language of the forehead can be more difficult with eh introduction of facial fillers that hides wrinkles. The advent of Botox technology further hampers the effective reading of a person's forehead as the chemical used in Botox paralyzed muscles in the face while attempting to make people look younger.

Whenever possible, reading wrinkles can tell you more about a person.

A wrinkle that ran horizontally across the forehead and raised upward means the person is surprised. These are likewise evident when a person likes you at first sight and greets you. Often accompanies by raised eyebrows and wide-opened eyes, the presence of these lines is telling that the person is pleasantly surprised to see you.

A raised forehead signified surprise when the person is caught lying or doing something, not right.
A wrinkled forehead can also be an indication that the person is not pleased to see you. The same signs or expressions are also evident in people who are worried, in pain or showing deep concern about something. The same wrinkles are those vertical lines found in the middle of the forehead just above the nasal

bridge.

When you see moisture or perspiration in the forehead before any other parts in the body, it is a sign that the person is lying or distressed. As the autonomic nervous system kicks in stress are manifested in the physical sense, a sudden shine of sweat will appear in the forehead of the person.
When a person shows signs of embarrassment as in blushing, red pigments appear first on the forehead, which may also indicate that the person is emotionally or sexually aroused, agitated, or excited.

Once a person also experienced sudden tension, they tend to rub their forehead either to remove the moisture or relieve themselves of the tension. This is evident in people who feel uncomfortable in certain situations. Rubbing the temples also helps relieve oneself from arising stress.

Another sign of stress or tension is the bulging up of veins in a person's forehead. However, a pulsating vein can also be an indication of anxiety, stress, or deception.

When people realize a mistake, this is shown by slapping their middle forehead with an open palm.

CHAPTER 15:HOW TO DIFFERENTIATE BETWEEN REAL AND FAKE SMILES

Smiling is one way of showing your availability and interest to another person. A genuine smile shows your teeth, lifts your cheek and reaches your eyes. If you see a person genuinely smiling at you and can't stop doing so, it simply means that they're attracted to you. On the other hand, some smiles look forced and awkward. This kind doesn't convey attraction but might mean that the person doesn't know how to feel about you or that they're just shy.
Compare the smiles of the two subjects below:

Which one do you think has a genuine smile? How do you describe the smile of the man on the right?

Let's analyze the photo of the couple below:

Even though the couple is close to each other, you can notice that the woman appears to be more interested in her man than he is to her. Her smile is genuine, which is characterized by smiling eyes, raised cheeks, and visible teeth. She leans her head into his, signifying her display of affection. On the other hand, he has an uncertain smile with lips pulled tight. Despite the visibility of his teeth, you can't see his eyes smiling. It might be a signal that he feels hesitant about their relationship.

A smile is a body attraction technique that can be used as a powerful gesture. Making a simple smile is a vital nonverbal cue that you have to pay attention to. There are two types of smiles— the fake smile and the sincere smile. A sincere smile suggests that the person you are interacting with is happy, and he/she is enjoying your company. On the contrary, a fake smile is used to suggest pleasure or approval, but it shows that the person making the fake smile is really feeling something totally different.
A half-smile is also a familiar facial expression that only involves one side of the mouth and it suggests uncertainty or sarcasm.

CHAPTER 16: HOW TO DETERMINE IF SOMEONE IS LYING

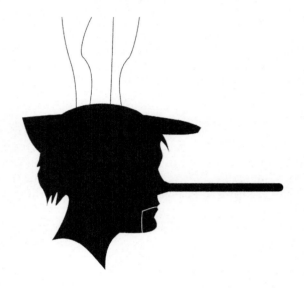

Why do people lie? Everyone who is caught in a lie offers an immediate apology or remorse for what they have done. Lies are as complicated as human nature. Some lies are necessary to protect the greater good. Take the example of a security operative captured in a foreign country. Should they tell the truth about their true identity and objective of their mission? Should they maintain their story that they are just tourists who happened to wander in the wrong place and took one too many photos?

When you are caught in a lie, and you apologize, do you apologize for the lie or for the fact that you were caught in the act? If you were not caught in the act, would you have kept doing the same thing, knowing that it is wrong? What is the difference between someone who lies and someone who doesn't? Is it one's principle or the absence of opportunity? (Meibauer, 2018).

There is so much that we can discuss lies, their nature, and their impact. One thing that is true about lies, however, is that they distort your ability to analyze someone correctly. To be fair, the person being laid to forms an opinion of the deceiver based on information that they believe is correct.

Lies are also about communication, so there must be a recipient, sender, and the context of the message. When the deceiver represents themselves falsely, the person reading them becomes a part of the lie. It could be as a result of overconfidence, ignorance, learned apathy, or personal bias.

Most people who tell lies try to appeal to your weakness so that they can get away with something. The gullibility of humans explains why lies are easily perpetuated. Many people believe that everyone they come across is telling the truth. They don't see why it would suit someone to lie to them. It serves no purpose because they never tell lies themselves, or at least they believe they don't.

Lies can be perpetuated as one of the following:
• pertinent omission
• exaggeration
• half-truth
• deception

Whichever of these you are a victim of; the deceiver will lie because they believe they have more to lose in telling the truth than telling a lie. It is also possible that people lie because of a mental defect, making it impossible for them to permanently or temporarily discern a lie from the truth. The individual might be suffering from compulsive lying disorder.

Why Do People Lie?

It is not easy to understand or tell in confidence why people lie because there is always a reason why they feel the lie is better than the truth. Some people lie because they want you to see them in a different light than who they are. Others are impulsive liars. Some lie so that they don't have to hurt your feelings with the truth, while others lie so that they don't have to deal with the consequences of their actions.

The statements above do not give a complete explanation as to why people tell lies, but you have probably come across them, or you might even have lied to someone along those lines. The fact is that in this life, everyone tells a lie at some point. How frequent you lie or the magnitude of the lie might differ from one person to the next, but everyone tells a lie. Here are some reasons why people find it easier to lie than tell the truth:

The Desire for Control. Telling a lie is about control. You need to change people's perspective on something. You need them to see things your way. Nothing else matters. By influencing your perception with a lie, the liar can then get specific reactions that they needed, and hopefully, they can use this to sway important decisions their way.

This is a psychopathic way of addressing issues. The liar has no proof that telling the truth might have them at a disadvantage, but they are not willing to take the risk either. Because of this reason, it is easier to lie so that they gain control over the discussion and box everyone else into a corner. Without knowing it, participants become pawns in their game.

Sustaining a Lie. Lies, like most stories, need and have a life of their own. You need a new story to sell a lie better each time. The moment you tell a lie, you must remember it the way you told it, and make sure the details never change. When someone reminds you of the lie, which they believe is the truth, you are at pains to explain it accurately, and as a result, you might add some details that were not part of the original lie.

To keep it convincing, you create something else to support the new information and keep the original lie convincing. This is how lies grow. What started as one small lie eventually turns into so many lies. The problem is that over time, people will keep poking holes into the lies. As soon as any single lie has been debunked, the rest of the lies associated with it will fall apart.

To Serve Their Own Needs. People tell lies because they feel it is important to them that you get their version of the truth at all costs. They feel the issue at hand is more important to them than you know, and it might probably be insignificant to you. Many people lie because they feel the issue they lie about is very important, especially if told from their perspective, while in most cases, this is never the case.

Need for Affection. Someone who is not comfortable with themselves will find it easier to lie so that they can impress you. They crave your attention or approval, and the only way they can get it is to lie. People do this all the time, hoping you like them and hang out with them more.

There is also the issue of self-esteem and lack of confidence. When someone does not believe in themselves, they don't think they can do much. They feel they are not worthy of your attention, yet they need it. To solve this problem, they spin lies so that you can see them in a different light, embrace them, and accept them. What they don't realize is that it is not them you are embracing; it is the lie they spin.

Easiest Way Out. When facing some challenges, some people lie because they feel it is the easiest way out of a situation. Unfortunately, lies eventually get caught. It is wise to face the consequences of your actions instead of looking for the easiest way out. This creates a problem because as time goes by, you get used to lying as a means to an end. There is no easy way in life. Some things are best tackled as difficult as they are.

Covering Up for Mistakes. Reproach and reprimand might be too much for some people to handle. Because of this, they choose to cover up for their mistakes by lying. In so doing, they hope that the truth never comes to light, and they keep living a lie. We have seen this happen in many cases, especially in the corporate sector. Someone makes a mistake, and they cover it up with a convenient lie. Everyone believes in the lie until a whistleblower unveils the truth, and their house of cards crumbles.

To Progress in Something. It is possible that some people tell lies to help them progress in life. In the TV Land comedy series Younger, a 40-year-old woman pretends to be a 26-year-old millennial so that she can get a job in publishing. This comes after several unsuccessful attempts at finding a job in the cut-throat industry. Her truth is that she left the job market to raise a family, hence the huge career gap in her résumé. However, she hides it and takes on a new persona as a 26-year-old, gets the job, and builds a successful career out of it, in the process causing havoc and pain in the lives of those around her.

While this might be a fictional character in a sitcom, it is something many people are too familiar with. People tell lies out of necessity so that they can progress in life and their careers.

Egotistic Gratification. Some lies are told to make the liar feel better about them. This is about satisfying their ego and making everyone else see them as accomplished people when, in reality, they haven't achieved much in their lives. This character is common with narcissists. By inflating your ego and image, you want people to see you like something, someone else, bigger than you are.

Create Their Version of the Truth. A lot of people tell lies to create their unique version of the truth. When the truth doesn't sound juicy enough, it is easier for someone to create their truth. This might start with something subtle, but over time, it grows and becomes bigger than they thought it would be. Some people believe that once they tell a lie, it is easier to repeat it until it becomes the truth. This never works out in the long run.

Excuses. People tell lies to act as excuses so that they are not held accountable for their actions. When they make a mistake or intentionally do something wrong, they realize what the consequences are, but instead of facing them boldly, they lie so that they can get away with it.

Out of Malice. One of the worst reasons why some people lie is to hurt others around them. This act of malice will see them intentionally tell lies, hoping that someone will pick it up as the truth and result in their downfall. Others also tell lies about people so that others can see them in the wrong light while they gain from it.

We have heard of many people in the past who fabricate stories about celebrities, hoping to blackmail them in the process. It is difficult for celebrities because of the kind of attention their names get online. One lie can spread faster than wildfire in a minute, especially when you consider how connected people are online today. By the time the truth comes out, some of the damage the lie does might be irreparable.

White Lies. Have you ever told a white lie? Parents get away with this all the time. A white lie is one of those lies people tell with a good reason. In many cases, these lies are perpetuated to avoid hurting someone's feelings. These lies are, in most cases, harmless, and no one stands to benefit from them in any way.

While people normally find white lies to be harmless, it is important to understand that these lies are just like any other lie. They might seem harmless right now, but they form the perfect foundation for you to build on to bigger lies. After all, once you get away with one lie, another small lie might not hurt, right?

Identifying a Liar

Lying might come naturally to some people, but it is a psychological construct. Some signs can alert you to lie whenever you are speaking to someone. You can tell it in their tone, in the way they speak, and how they insist on selling you the truth. The difference between the truth and a lie is that lies take effort, while the truth is effortless.

When you tell a lie, you know it is not true. You worry that perhaps the other party might know it is a lie or that they might have heard something similar before. Because of the uncertainty around your lie, you are not comfortable with it and will do all you can to sell it as the truth. At the first sign of displeasure, you will probably go on the defensive to dissuade your audience from poking holes into your narrative.

At some point, you might defend the lie so much that you end up not sure what you believe in either. The difference with the truth is that the truth is real. You don't have to think about it. It is something that happened. Your imagination is vivid, and even if someone woke you up in the middle of the night, the narrative would not change. This is why the truth is always effortless.

Telling whether someone is lying to you or not is not easy. There are, however, some cues that you can focus on that might give them away. Here are some ideas you should keep in mind when talking to someone:

Stutter. Stuttering, unless the individual has a speech defect, is one of the common examples of being caught in a lie. When you are trying to sell someone a lie, your brain might be caught up in the lie too. It is thinking about the truth while at the same time trying not to process the truth, but instead, send out the lie.

In this confusion, the disconnect between the truth and the lie in your brain might cause you to stutter. Stuttering might be accompanied by filler words, especially when the liar is aware you are almost catching up on their lie. Stuttering is also associated with anxiety. Telling a lie is one good reason for someone to be anxious because they are not sure what you know or whether you might have spoken about the issue at hand with someone else. It gets worse if they know you have intimate knowledge of someone who is a part of their lie.

Change the Subject. People change the subject to cause a distraction, especially when they realize they said something they were not supposed to. Say you are catching up with your partner, and they start giving you details about the previous night when they were hanging out with some friends. It's all fun and games as they go into details about the movies, the bars, and the music. However, they suddenly shift and start talking about something the house manager said, or they remember they haven't compiled a report they need ready before they go to work tomorrow.

If you are keen, you might also realize that there is a lot of distortion in everything they say from the moment they changed the subject. These are signs that they need you to forget everything that they just said and focus on something else. This is the problem with lying. Most of the time, the lie feels easy and right in your head until you start telling it to someone and you realize you can't sustain it.

Lying is not easy because you have to come up with a story and make it convincing at the same time. It gets difficult if you are trying to lie to someone who knows or has known you for a long time. This is someone who knows how you communicate and what you do when telling a lie.

Tonal Variation. Whenever someone is trying to sell you a lie, you will notice it in their tone. Most liars are aware you might be informed, but they take the risk anyway. As they speak to you, their tone might change each time they try to prove something.

The change in their tone might also be associated with the fact that they are nervous and anxious. You have them in a situation that they are uncomfortable with, and it causes them more distress than you are aware of. They need to get out of the situation as fast as possible.

Liars might also change their tone around certain words or phrases. These are the points in the conversation when they are trying to convince you (Soderberg, 2014). They believe these are their selling points, and they will try to capitalize on them.

It is also possible that some people change their tone so that they can distract you from thinking about something. If you start a conversation about something they are not comfortable with, they can use a tone that suggests displeasure or lack of interest, hoping that you can catch up on that vibe and drop the story altogether. In so doing, they managed to lie to you without actually telling a lie.

Rephrasing Questions. While it is okay to pause and get your mind straight in a conversation, liars do this for a different reason. The pause allows them to find new ideas to sell you their story. Other than pausing, they also like to rephrase questions.

If you ask them something, don't be surprised if they repeat your question. They did hear it right the first time you asked, but by repeating it, it gives them enough time to remember something that they can use to sway your opinion.

Here are some examples:
If you ask, "I already sent you the email in the morning. Did you read it?"

They'll respond with, "You did send me the email in the morning. I haven't gotten around to reading it yet."

If you say, "Did I see your car at the mall yesterday?"

They'll respond with, "My car was not at the mall yesterday."

In the examples above, they are not rephrasing your questions as a way of discipline or to try and understand it better. They are trying to make sure you don't probe further than you have already.

Using Filler Words. You need a lot of effort to sell a lie and make it convincing. Most of the time, everything you plan in your head before you lie to someone does not go according to plan. You have the entire conversation planned out, but when you meet someone, they say something different, and you are thrown off your game. The best solution is to think on your feet.

It is not easy to think on your feet and, at the same time, keep the story flowing and check all the points. To solve this problem, liars use filler words. These are words that don't add value to the conversation but somehow keeps it going.

Some of the common filler words that sell a lie include **um, like, er,** and **uh**. As the conversation drags on, the liar tries to fill in the gaps with new information so that it is credible. They might remember something that should add value that they forgot to mention, and take the conversation a few minutes back to prove that point, then move on to the current issue.

Defensive Approach. You have to defend your position whenever you are telling a lie. If someone seeks clarification about something, you feel you are being intimidated or attacked. Liars can easily go on the defense verbally and even accuse you of calling them liars when, in reality, they truly are.

It is not uncommon for a liar to say they are not lying. If you are weak in your resolve, they might also try to make you feel guilty. If you keep prodding, they might even get angry and walk out of the room in protest.

If there are other people in the room, liars can shift the attention from you to them. As they try to make you feel guilty, they will face the other people in the room, trying to appeal to them to see things from their perspective. At this juncture, they alienate you from the conversation because you are catching on to them, and they cannot let that happen. If someone else joins in, this works out for them because your thought process has already been distorted. In the heat of the moment, it might be more important to restore calm in the room than listen to the rest of the argument.

Pay attention to the difference between two people accused of lying. The person who is telling the truth will not be offended. Perhaps they feel your position is because you are not aware of the facts. They will take time to explain the facts and offer any explanation you need to validate the truth. They know the truth and will stand by it. On the other hand, a liar will not address the issue at hand by providing details or further explanation. It is easier for them to defend themselves than defend their claim.

Sudden Pause. A sudden pause in a conversation is not always about someone catching their breath. It might also be someone caught in a lie. Following the pause, they will pick up the conversation and respond slower than usual or in a low tone and then increase their tone shortly after. They hope that you are caught up and don't hear or pay attention to something they say after the pause.

Forget about Contractions. Contractions help to make conversations shorter and help people deliberate over something without spending too much time on it. The difference in application is that liars eliminate contractions. Instead of saying "wasn't," they will say "was not." The idea here is to slow down the speed at which you consume the information, which allows them enough time to think of the right lies to convince you.

Types of Liars

In the same way, there are different reasons why people tell lies. There are different types of liars too. Some people might lie because it is the easiest thing to do, while others might be sick. The following are three of the common types of liars you might encounter as you go about your day:
• pathological liars
• sociopaths
• compulsive liars

Pathological liars are individuals who lie as a response to anything. They have perfected lying down to an art, such that it comes so naturally to them. It might not be easy to detect their lies.

One of the defining characteristics of a sociopath is that they don't empathize. Their lies must persist whether people get hurt in the process or not.

Compulsive liars are very easy to identify because they lie for whatever reason that comes to mind. They are not the best liars and will, in most cases, lie to get out of a situation, often clumsily.

Let's take an in-depth look at each of these types so that we understand what makes them tick and how to identify them.

Pathological Liars

The scientific term for pathological lying is **myth mania**. You might already deduce from this that these are people whose lives revolve around myths. This is a chronic behavior to the point where it becomes a habit.

While most people can tell a white lie from time to time to prevent someone from getting hurt, pathological liars, on the other hand, don't need a reason to lie. Even when they don't have a reason to lie, they still do. Interacting with such people can be very difficult and frustrating because you are never sure whether to trust them or not.

Pathological liars tell tales that make them appear to be the hero of the situation or tales that evoke sympathy. There might not be anything for them to gain in telling a lie, but the attention matters to them anyway. The following are some of the characteristics that can help you identify a pathological liar:

Pointless Lies. Many people tell lies to get out of an uncomfortable situation or to avert a crisis or whichever reason. A pathological liar, on the other hand, is comfortable lying even when there is no clear benefit to the lie. It is very frustrating interacting with such people because even after you learn about the truth, you cannot reconcile their lie and any achievable gains.

As a result, most people who are victims of pathological liars are left wondering what their motivation might have been. Is there something they stand to gain from the lie in the near future? Are you still living part of the lie, or is it over? This level of uncertainty can be disconcerting and creates a painful experience for people who interact with pathological liars.

Complicated Lies. One of the defining characteristics of pathological liars is the lengths they go to sell a lie. They create stories that are too complicated, dramatic, and have a lot of detail. This is possible because they are also very good at telling stories. Their tales might be compelling because of how good they can spin stories in an instant.

Victim or Hero Stories. Another thing that defines a pathological liar is their desire for attention. They must be at the center of the story. In this case, they will either be the victim in the story or the hero, but never the villain. People should either applaud them or sympathize with them, hence their tales. They also tell these stories to gain approval and validation from their audience.

Strong Belief in Their Tales. The problem with pathological liars is that as the lie grows, so does the liar's belief in it. Pathological liars are known to be deluded with their version of the truth. It gets to a point where they strongly believe their lives are the truth.

The challenge comes in dealing with a pathological liar who is not aware of their lies. Some people lie too much to the point where medical experts who attend to them believe they might not be in a position to tell apart the reality from the lie they built their lives around.

Perhaps one of the key highlights of a pathological liar is the fact that they are naturals when it comes to pulling a performance. Their eloquence is amazing, and it is very easy for them to engage people and entertain the audience. They are blessed with astonishing creativity, and most of them are very quick thinkers, in which case they will barely exhibit some of the common signs of lying that we discussed earlier on.

They tend to get away with many lies because of how convincing and surprisingly lovable they are. Ask them one question, and they will go into a verbal tirade that might charm you instead of addressing the question you asked.

Different Versions of One Tale. A pathological liar is so creative that they need to make everyone believe in their stories by any means possible. As a result, they tap into their creativity to keep the audience entertained whenever they can. The problem with this is that they easily forget the previous details and, as a result, end up telling one story in different versions.

Quick Responses. We all love someone who can address our concerns as fast as possible. This is one of the traits of pathological liars. They will respond to any issues raised very fast. However, you might realize that their answers are vague, and instead of answering the question, they try to throw you off your line of thought.

Sociopathic Liars

The term sociopath sends chills down your spine. You might feel unsettled and afraid. There are very many descriptions that have been put forward for sociopaths, but they all agree on a few things; sociopaths lack moral capacity or standards, and they don't have a conscience, or if they do, it only exists to serve their needs (Lipman and Pizzurro, 2016).

To understand how sociopathic liars operate, it is important that we take a deep look at the definition of sociopaths. Sociopaths can be identified in four groups:

Affective. Sociopaths can't empathize. They don't feel or show emotions at all. It is pointless expecting a sociopath to see things from your perspective or to care about what you feel concerning their actions.

Interpersonal. They cannot form deep connections with people when it comes to social interactions. Most of their interactions are superficial. It is very easy for a sociopath to put on a show to impress someone, but it is no more than a smokescreen. They are the embodiment of antisocial beings. Their partnerships, friendships, and relationships are meaningless and can use deception when necessary to gain the advantage they seek.

Antisocial. The basic construct of a sociopath is that they are immune to normal social tendencies. They believe they are all alone in the world. This is how they live their lives, locking out any interpersonal connection or societal interactions. This also explains their penchant for breaking the law.

Behavioral. The behavior of a sociopath is unpredictable. They are unreliable, cannot be trusted to set goals, or take responsibility for their actions. They can't even understand the responsibility for their actions, let alone owning up to them. They are also very impulsive.

At this point, you can already understand how damaging sociopathic liars can be in your life. Sociopathic liars are extreme in everything they do. This is one of the main reasons why you should be wary of them. They feel no pain or remorse. If they are out to hurt you, they will keep at it until they think they have gained as much pleasure from your pain as possible.

Sadly, they are also very good impressionists. This is how they get people to fall for their charm. The first time you meet them, they are very likable. They can easily lure you into a trap, and by the time you realize what's going on, you are so deep into the web that getting out can choke you to death.

Other than the fact that they cannot feel emotions, they also have no desire to understand what their actions do to others. Your pain might be thrilling to a sociopathic liar. They are manipulative people and will never reveal emotions unless they do to trick you. There is always an explanation for that ill deed they subjected you to. Their explanations are in such a way that you might even feel guilty and remorseful, yet you are the victim in the situation. The following are some of the characteristics of sociopathic liars:

Strained and Difficult Relationships. Sociopathic liars struggle to establish healthy bonds with people in their lives. Because of this, most of the relationships they are in are full of chaos and are always unstable. One of the reasons for this is that instead of trying to establish a relationship, they try to exploit people around them through intimidation, coercion, or lying to them. All this is done for their benefit.

No Empathy. Are you hoping for empathy from a sociopathic liar? You are looking in the wrong place. Lack of empathy is one of the defining traits that identify people with antisocial personality disorder. Because they cannot empathize, sociopathic liars are a very dangerous lot. Someone who cannot feel remorse or pain for their actions is capable of doing anything and, to any limit, without care.

Dishonesty. Deceit and dishonesty come so easily to a sociopathic liar. If they are in trouble, it is easier to tell a lie than to admit the truth. They will also lie for any reason, as long as they can get what they want.

Gross Irresponsibility. Sociopathic liars tend to be highly irresponsible. From social obligations to financial prudence, they don't care about anything. They don't believe in recourse for their actions, and this is why most of them end up on the wrong side of the law.

Aggression. When interacting with a sociopathic liar, you should watch out for aggressive outbursts. This is someone who might not care what you feel, but they know what they want. If they can be aggressive and threaten you into submission, they will do it. It is common for a sociopathic liar to cut your conversation aggressively and interject with whatever they want you to hear.

Manipulation. Sociopathic liars are master manipulators. Everything they do is about them. They can charm and seduce their way into your life, but all this is aimed at a personal gain or for their pleasure. They take a lot of pleasure in hurting you for entertainment. While most of the manipulative sociopaths can be charming, this does not always apply to all of them.

Hostility. Hostility is an interesting principle when discussing sociopathic liars. While they might not necessarily be hostile by nature, it is easy for them to create a hostile environment and have you as an active participant without your knowledge. How does that happen? A sociopathic liar can respond to your reaction or behavior by interpreting it as a hostile response. As a result, they will seek revenge, in which case they become more hostile than the perception they created of you. Since they feel you hurt them, they will only be satisfied when they hurt you back.

Affinity for Risky Behavior. Sociopathic liars are very dangerous, given their desire for risky behavior. They don't care about theirs or anyone else's comfort or safety. It is easy for them to initiate or engage in risky behavior like crime, drug abuse, unsafe sexual acts, or gambling. Be wary of people in your life who are drawn to such activities because they might be trying to lure you in.

You might also realize that in a very dangerous or scary situation, they are uncharacteristically calm. Everyone might be freaking out after an accident, yet there is one person in your midst that doesn't seem to be threatened or afraid.

Impulsive Actions. Everyone makes an impulse decision from time to time. The difference between sociopaths and normal people is that even in your moment of impulse, you are still aware of the consequences of your actions. On their part, they have no disregard for consequences.

Laughter, Smirks, and Smiles. Sociopathic liars will speak to you with an evil smirk on their faces. They enjoy your pain and are thrilled by the fact that you are willing to go along. This is because they cannot empathize. They cannot help themselves from enjoying your pain.

You Are Special. Be careful with someone who makes you feel so special. They treat you differently from everyone else. When they are around you, they are emotionally astute and deep in their conversations and seem to pay attention to everything you want. However, at the same time, everyone else has a very bad observation about them. These are signs that you might be interacting with a sociopathic liar.

Sociopathic liars are very tricky because they have also perfected the art of telling lies. Whenever they talk to you, they can be compelling and come off as sincere, yet this is not their true intention. What they are really after is getting you to let your guard down and see them as genuine, yet they are not.

Justify Wrongdoing. It is difficult for a sociopath to admit that they are wrong. Instead, they will try to make you believe that you are wrong. This is someone who can do something so bad, but when you confront them about it, they try to make you believe it is okay to do what they did, and something is wrong with you if you feel otherwise.

Compulsive Liars

There is too much exaggeration in the world today. Social media has made it very easy for people to live fake lives. They try to portray themselves as something else; often opposite of who they truly are. Outright lies, distorted information, convenient truths, and half-truths—all these are common experiences you will come across today.

There is not much difference between compulsive liars and pathological liars. They both lie on impulse and will try to be as persuasive as possible. You might come across some literature that uses both terms interchangeably.

Compulsive lying is a situation where someone is used to lying that it becomes a habit. Even when they have no reason to lie, they still do. Compared to pathological liars, it is very easy to spot a compulsive liar. While pathological liars are creative and charming, compulsive liars try to get by. They spring a lie and hope it works. When they are lying, they will exhibit most of the common signs that someone is dishonest, like avoiding eye contact, breaking a sweat, or rambling over their words. They get anxious, especially at the slightest hint that you have them figured out.

Most of the time, compulsive liars don't have an ulterior motive behind their tales. As a result, they end up lying even about things that will hurt them. It might be difficult for them to admit the truth even if they have been figured out already. Persistent compulsive lying might be a sign that someone is suffering from any of the following:
• narcissistic personality
• borderline personality
• substance abuse
• attention deficit hyperactivity
• bipolar
• impulse control issues

Experts believe that compulsive lying is not necessarily a sign of psychosis. This is because most of the time, these individuals are not withdrawn from reality. Most of them can tell apart their lies from the truth. Many compulsive liars become what they are as a result of their immediate environment. For example, an individual who is brought up in a house or neighborhood where people gain advantage through deception will soon catch on, especially if those around them do not impose consequences on lying. As a result, to them, the benefits always trump the risks involved.

It is also possible that compulsive liars might spin tales to help them cope with previous trauma in their lives or lack of confidence and low esteem. Many of these are short-term approaches, which do not pan out well in the long-run. Keeping track of all the lies becomes a problem and stressful. There is also the risk of strained relationships if their lies unfold, and in some cases, they might have their day in court.

Given the closeness between pathological liars and compulsive liars, it is almost difficult to tell them apart. However, the following are some differences that can help you distinguish between the two:

Pathological liars:
• have a clear motive and intent
• show very few signs of lying
• appear to be in control of their lies
• might be defensive when their lies are challenged
• the lie is a function of their illusory reality
• extravagant and extremely detailed tales, which might be modified each time

Compulsive liars:
• are compelled to lie as a survival mechanism
• can admit to lying when confronted but might not stop lying
• are aware of the difference between their lies and reality
• tell stories that they believe the audience needs to hear
• spontaneous and don't put a lot of thought into their lies
• lie because they can, even when there's no benefit involved

To be safe, you have to learn to treat liars with caution. While most of the things they say might be lies, they might also tell the truth from time to time. The challenge lies in distinguishing the difference between their lies and truths. This is where your ability to read people comes in handy.

Study their body language carefully over time, and you will learn to know the signs of trouble. You can also learn some of the subjects that they love to lie about and dig deeper to understand why especially if these are people who are so close and dear to you. Understanding the context is important in helping you understand them and protect you from the impending risks. When dealing with liars, you must also try not to withdraw from reality. Irrespective of your affection toward them, you have to respect the fact that the lies will happen again. This is who they are, so try not to take things too personally. You can also recommend treatment for them, especially for liars whose plight is already diagnosed.

How to Deal with Liars

Most of the lies people tell are undetected. This happens because other than the fact that many people don't know how to deal with liars, they don't know how to read them in the first place. Some people don't care or don't think the lie is something worth causing a fuss about. Think about the number of lies you told your parents when you were growing up, for example. If you remember correctly, none of that will fly by you if your kids tried it on you today. How come your parents let you off easily?

The example above is about very simple lies, which, in most cases, cause no harm. However, some lies have far-reaching effects, and if you don't deal with them when you should, they form a recipe for disaster. When you keep getting away with lies, a pattern forms, and as time goes by, you embrace lies as the best option to deal with everything.

What do you do with lies? How do you deal with a liar in your life? Perhaps this is someone so close to you that you cannot get rid of them, but you can stand them somehow. The following are useful tips that will help you learn how to handle the situation better:

Prioritize Personal Safety. Your safety is more important than anything else. Even if you want to save the relationship, it means nothing if you cannot enjoy the results. Before you confront someone about their lies, always make sure you are safe. Scan the environment and ensure no harm can befall you.

You can never be too sure what the nature of the confrontation will be or what it might spiral into. Because of this, it is safe to bring someone else as a buffer, just in case things get out of hand. This is true because, many times, when people are confronted about their lies, they can be aggressive to scare you off and drop the issue altogether.

Differentiate Lies from the Truth. It might not be easy to read so much into someone's words, but you can tell so much from their body language. This is a good opportunity for you to tell the difference between the truth and the lies. Awareness of some of the symptoms you are being lied to can help you identify some pointers that someone is not honest with you. You need to be conscious of their behavioral patterns.

Exit the Situation. You cannot solve everything at the same time. In some confrontations, it is better if you know the right time to remove yourself from the equation. When you realize that things are getting heated, you have to take a step back and evaluate your position from afar.

If the relationship you share with the person you are confronting means anything to both or either of you, cooling off will allow you both to reflect on what has been said, and by the time you get back to discussing it again, you might have a better chance of handling the matter well.

Remember that even if you exit the situation and get back to it later, it might be a while before the liar stops lying completely. Some people never do. They just chose the people they lie to and those they stay true to. With this in mind, remember that if you decide to stay and keep them by your side, this is a journey that might take a very long time, and you might need to seek professional help. You should also notice whether they are willing to change or not. It is pointless trying to change someone who has no intention to do so.

Empathize. In as much as you are trying to understand and deal with a liar, remember that something is wrong with them, so you should empathize. There might be several reasons why they choose lies over the truth. Show them that you understand, especially if you know their lies are a self-defense mechanism.

Many compulsive liars need professional help. When it comes to empathy, in some cases, you don't even need to talk. Just be there for them and listen. As much as it is painful for you to see them go through this experience, it is also the right thing to do. Do not judge. Listen to them. Explain their reasons. If you realize they are lying about that too, call them out on it and implore them to take your concern seriously. At some point, they will have to come clean.

Identify the Type of Lies. People tell different kinds of lies. While some lays cause destruction and pain, some lies are just harmless. It would be ideal if you learned how to identify the difference between a harmless lie and a nefarious lie.

Of course, we contend that it is not okay to lie, but at times, it is inevitable. If you can tell the difference between these two situations, you are in a better position because you can determine how to handle the situation going forward.

For a white lie, while it might be harmless, don't forget to remind the liar that you know what they did. Warn them of consequences and remind them that they will not get away with it next time. It is unsafe to ignore such lies because if they get used to it, there can only be one outcome, and it's not a great one.

Ask for Help. You know them better than anyone else, so there is a good chance you might need help in handling the confrontation. Get help. Bring in professionals or other family members that you believe can help you handle the situation better.

Introducing someone else into the picture provides a third-party perspective, which provides common ground for all of you. Remember that if you are bringing in a third party, it should not be someone that intimidates the person you are confronting. Otherwise, they can choose to box their feelings and ignore the issue altogether.

Stay Calm. You need to stay calm whenever you are confronting a liar. Remember that you hold power in this conversation since you confronted them about it. Try not to lose your nerves because you might end up in an argument that will not solve anything.

Explain to them in the best way possible what their lies have done to your life, your relationship with them, and more importantly, trust between the two of you. Unless they are willing to put in the work and repair the damage, remind them that there will be consequences, and state them clearly.

As you confront them about the lies, remember that you need to keep the situation calm and welcoming so that they don't feel like you are ganging up on them or they are being ambushed. However much you feel they hurt you, yours is the voice of reason, so try to keep it calm.

Healthy Confrontation. Confronting a liar is not easy, especially for someone close to you. However, some part of their mind knows this, and they know how much you struggle to bring yourself to confront them. There is always a good way to confront someone about their lies.

First, make sure you do it in private. Never confront them in public because this only shames them. Before the confrontation, ensure you have sufficient evidence to back your claims. Pathological liars are performers, so you can expect that they will resist and try to play it out as something else. They might even insist you are out to harm them. However, you must be steadfast because you are doing this for the greater good, which is to help them.

Always Keep Evidence. At times the easiest way to help someone is to confront them in the most painful way—to expose them. You have to be careful about this because exposure can backfire if not done properly. A lot of people have suffered irreparable differences and never made up. The first thing you should do if you are to expose a liar is to ensure the environment is convenient. If you have to do it in front of people, do it in the presence of people who care for them, who are willing to support them if they are willing to change.

From the moment you discover their lies, gather as much evidence as possible. Document it if possible so that it is congruent with the story and will help prevent loopholes in their argument. Remember that the idea is not just about exposing them and shaming them in the process. It is about exposing them to make them realize their mistakes and encourage them to change their lives for the better. It is possible. You have to find a way to do it kindly without making them feel like they are outcasts. This is important because some habitual liars already struggle with mental conditions that make them feel they are different. Singling them out aimlessly might be counter-effective if not done properly.

Determine the Subject of Interest. Habitual liars might lie all the time, but if you are keen, you can identify a pattern in their lies. There is always something that triggers them to lie; especially something they feel closely and deeply about. More often, this happens because they are afraid of confronting the truth about their lives. In this case, lying becomes their go-to mechanism whenever they feel threatened or if their position on the matter is challenged.

Repetitive patterns indicate a systemic problem, which means whatever is bothering them about the subject is deeply rooted in their minds, and it would be advisable to seek professional help. If it is not a serious concern, perhaps it might be better to leave things as they are, and instead of giving them an opportunity to lie, you can beat them to their game and change the subject to something else.

In conclusion, one of the most important things you must understand is that lies are different and they depend on the kind of situation. Liars are triggered by different things in their environment. Just as much as every lie is different, so is the lie detection mechanism. There is no one-size-fits-all method in detecting or dealing with liars. More often, two things are almost always constant—your awareness of the situation and the context. If you can perfect these two, you can easily master other skills and learn how to identify liars by recognizing the verbal and nonverbal cues and other traits.

CHAPTER 17: ANALYZING PEOPLE IN DATING AND LOVE

Being able to detect if a person is truly into you can save a lot of time and heartache when dating. There are specific body movements that are unique to men and women that display attraction. Sure, words are powerful, but actions are groundbreaking. This form of body language is the most sensual in nature and inviting. Many of the common depictions on cartoons and illustrations are quite accurate when it comes to flirting. Women have a unique set of body language cues that are attractive to men. It complements their feminine role and can be used as a form of luring the man in. Men demonstrate a similar display of body cues that align with their masculinity. Oftentimes, the cues are so strong, they release certain hormones related to sexual attraction. The act of engaging in sexual pleasure is body language at its height. Since words are not commonly used as a sexual act, intercourse is the purest form of visually displaying that attraction. However, the journey from first date to the bedroom is filled with subtle clues that could alter the destination. Let's consider the primary difference between men and women when it comes to displaying attraction.

Common Female Dating Signals And Gestures

When a woman finds a male attractive, she may begin by locking eyes with him. She could give a subtle gaze and then look away. If this continues, the woman essentially wants the man to chase her. Simple touches to the body and even her curling her hair with fingers are used to flirt. This brings attention to the feminine qualities of a woman that may be attractive to the man. When a woman raises her eyebrows when talking with a man, they are signaling attraction. She may find the man to be physically handsome or admirable. Or she may be so caught up in what he is saying that it moves her to agree. The lips also indicate attraction especially in the biting, licking, or caressing them. When a woman looks intently at a man's lips and then makes direct eye contact, this is a subconscious invitation to kiss.

As mentioned previously, women tend to lean in toward their dates to show attraction. When her legs are crossed inward, facing her date, it's a suggestive pose that indicates sexual interest. This is heightened when the genitals are exposed and involve a light caress. Women may also arch their backs to further elongate their spines. The curvature of their spine is a feminine quality that is attractive to the man. Slight exposure of the breast is a sign of intense flirtation. She is drawing the man into her womanhood to express interest.

Women may also "bat" their eyes up and down rapidly as a sign of flirtation. This brings attention to the lashes which, when elongated, are physically pleasing to the man. She may pair this with a slight giggle to signal attraction.

Oftentimes, women tend to "mirror" the movements of men. This signifies submission as the woman is showing respect for the position of the man. Inadvertently, she is following the lead of her date. Many sensual dances rely on the man leading and the woman following. Women subconsciously perform these acts as a means to show respect for the men's masculinity.

Common Male Dating Signals And Gestures

When a man moves his head slightly, raises his brows, and allows his nostrils to flare, he is indicating attraction. When paired with a smile, the level of attraction is heightened. Initially, a man will avoid making direct eye contact as he may be nervous or unaware of the woman's attraction level. In addition, men speak with their chest. If the chest is pointing towards the woman, he is giving her his full attention. If his chest is pointing elsewhere, he secretly wants to escape the situation.

Men want to appear dominant, masculine, and strong to perspective dates. They may stand with their feet wide and their hands on their hips in order to appear sturdy. If his hands are gracing his waist line, he essentially wants the woman to look near his genitals. This is a silent invitation to a possible sexual encounter. Men tend to show their attraction through their hands.

Slight touches to the back, thigh, and arm indicates sexual attraction. However, a pat on the shoulder could be read as platonic.

There are universal signs of attraction carried out by both men and women. Smiling and a willingness to laugh without apprehension are valuable signs. Spatial awareness is a key indicator to revealing intent. When two people are attracted to each other, they tend to stand close. Their shoulders are raised and positioned inwardly which indicates interest. Even the positioning of the toes symbolizes attraction. As mentioned, the toes point to where they want to go. When the toes are facing each other, sometimes called "pigeon toed," they are subtle signs of flirting. The man or woman wants to appear cute and coy. This vulnerable position subconsciously boosts sexual attraction. The palms traditionally reveal truth. When a man or a woman is interested, their palms may rest in an exposed position. It promotes openness which indicates that the two would like to get to know each other.

The laws of attraction are traditional as they signify small psychological changes that are quite universal. When a person speaks their intent with body language cues to follow, you can guarantee their validity. By understanding these simple cues, you will be better equipped to make accurate perceptions about the intent of others.

CHAPTER 18:DETECTING LIES AND DANGER SIGNALS

Detecting deceit will give you the rare opportunity to choose your associates wisely without having to say a word. The body goes into an immense ball of anxiety when a person lies. The trained eye will be able to detect these small variances that occur. Although words may speak their version of the truth, the body never lies. Deceit is the act of covering up the way you truly feel through seeking control. Oftentimes, that control is executed in a sloppy manner, thus leading to dominant cues that signal deceit. Whether it's a large lie or a little white lie, the results of dishonesty come with a variety of consequences. Essentially, people lie as a subconscious form of protection. They are either hiding their negative behavior or protecting their reputations. Even when used to exaggerate a story, they may be attempting to protect the fact that their life is truly boring. They want others to find them enjoyable. Thus, various lies are told.

One organization divides deceit into four categories of explanation and uses:

Anxiety- seeking to hide the fact that they are nervous

Control- gestures or smiles that are forced or a grand attempt to stop the body from moving

Distraction- Frequent pausing or bodily actions in between answers is that person's attempt to distract you from their lie. By acting out these grand gestures, they believe they are making their stories believable.

Persuasion- Deceit may stem from wanting someone to carry out an action which will result in the liar's favor.

Joseph Tecce, a researcher at Boston College, exposed the six reasons why individuals lie in addition to their respective character traits:

1. Protective Lies: This protects the reputation of the liar or even the victim from undue harm. They seek to keep their social status by not revealing true behavior.

2. Heroic Liars: These individuals will lie in an attempt to uphold the greater good. For example, a popular episode of **Sex and the City** portrayed Carrie and her friend, Stanford, at a mixer. Stanford was interested in a handsome man across the room. He asked Carrie to go and find out if the man was gay or straight. She approached him and let him know of Stanford's interest. The man looked at Stanford from across the room in utter repulsion. As Carrie went back to her hopeful friend, she told him that the handsome man was straight. She wanted to protect her friend's self-esteem by not revealing the truth.

3. Playful Liars: Playful liars accentuate their stories in order to provide a means of entertainment for listeners.

4. Ego Liars: Ego liars will cover mistakes in order to protect their reputations or status.

5. Gainful Liars: These are people who lie for personal gain.

6. Malicious Liars: These are the individuals who are out to seek revenge and harm others due to psychological challenges.

Many individuals are so crafty at lying; they have mastered the art of concealing their body movements. Sociopaths and psychopaths alike are so deranged; they feel no emotional connection to the lies. It is quite difficult to detect their inaccuracies because they are so connected to the lies. They may even begin to believe the lies. When considering the deceit of mentally stable individuals, however, there may be concrete reasons behind their excessive lying. Let's consider a few signs of a deceitful person and consider their traits.

The head can offer a slight indication of a person beginning to lie. When being asked a question, a liar tends to quickly move their head prior to responding. Interestingly, the face holds many of the truest signs of deception. We express honest emotions through the theory of timing. Researchers have found that, naturally, we hold our expressions between one and four seconds. When a person is lying or faking an emotion, the expression is usually held for a longer period of time. In addition, their symmetrical alignment can play a huge role in detecting insincerity. To tell if a person is being honest, notice the purest emotions are evenly distributed throughout the face. However, a liar will typically express their emotions on one side dominantly. Our speech and body movements should complement each other. So if a person is telling you how beautiful you look while frowning and crossing their arms, it is safe to conclude that they aren't genuine.

Excessive body movements are often associated with nervousness. Naturally, though, the body engages in slight movements even without the presence of anxiety. However, Dr. Leanne Brinke, professor of the Haas School of Business, indicates that a person who remains as still as a statue should be further examined.

It is also key to notice where their hands go when being confronted. Do they cover their mouths? Throats? Chests? By providing this subtle distraction, they are protecting themselves from the truth. They have no intention of telling the truth, so they are, in effect, covering areas of the body that assist with communication. In addition, verbal cues also point towards deception. Excessive repeating, stuttering, and clearing of the throat are key signs of nervousness. They are desperately trying to buy time to respond.

Traditionally, the eyes have been closely associated with deceit. Previously, we spoke about the connection between dilation and interest. When we see something we love or are attracted to, our eyes dilate. When in a relationship, a key indicator of a loss of interest rests in the pupils. When you ask your mate if your outfit looks great, they may say it looks awesome, but the pupils tell the truth. Excessive darting of the eyes or an avoidance of eye contact signifies some level of deceit. The person may be attempting to put on the demeanor of aggression, but they refuse to look at another's eyes. Are they truly as tough as they say they are? Interestingly, the right side of the brain controls auditory processing, big picture ideas, and decision making. When a person darts their eyes downward and towards the right, they are attempting to envision something, perhaps visiting a place they have never been. They may look down and to the right when thinking about what it's like to live there. When someone is lying, notice how they may repeat this same motion. Interestingly, they are attempting to envision something that didn't occur rather than recall a memory.

The body is also a clear indicator of deceit. You may notice the person's breathing patterns significantly speed up. Their chest could move faster, and their breathing becomes louder. Their shoulders and elbows are stiffly raised. This movement represents being caught, as seen depicted in cartoons. The robber may inadvertently stop in their tracks with their shoulders raised. They are trying to protect themselves by growing defensive. Psychics and spiritual healers utilize exposed palms to reveal truth. Although controversial, many readers analyze the open palms to detect repressed emotions, predict future occurrences, and decode personality. When a person is lying, those palms of truth are suddenly closed and facing away from the subject. It's a subconscious way of not wanting to reveal their truth.

Although detecting liars is an essential tool to have, simply noticing a liar isn't productive. Effective communication in conjunction with understanding can help to reveal lies and reach solutions.

CHAPTER 19: LEARN TO LISTEN CAREFULLY

Most of us listen to others in order to gather information. We also tend to listen in order to respond. As others speak, we're much more focused on what we're going to say to them, than what they're saying to us. In this way, we miss much of what's being said, which is a pity.

Good listening skills mean actively hearing and processing what others are saying and how they're saying it. It means paying attention to nuances like subtext and facial expression. It means hearing what's not being said (which is probably more important than anything else).

We listen to:

• Gather information
• Get a sense of a situation or an issue
• For the sake of entertainment
• To formulate a response
But the truth is that most of us don't even manage to absorb 50% of what we hear, even when standing face-to-face with the person you're listening to. Some of us don't even manage to take in 25% of what we hear. This is a natural weakness with human beings, but it's something we can address. Imagine being able to capture all that's being said, instead of zoning out. Detaching ourselves from their agenda to focus on how we're going to respond, or finding something more interesting to think about means we may actually miss the point of what it is they want to say. When you come to think of it, we all do ourselves a great disservice by not listening attentively to what others are saying to us. We miss out on a lot – 50% in most cases!

We're missing out when we don't listen

Because many of us hear only ¼ to half of what is said to us, we're missing out on a lot. Our inattentiveness is costing us in terms of understanding those we interact with and the world around us, generally. While we're thinking about our witty comebacks, or doing a mental indicator of what's in our refrigerators, valuable information is being shared with us. The problem is that a lot of it is going in one ear and then, straight out the other!

Sharpening your listening skills means gaining access to important information you're otherwise missing and that includes information about the person talking to you. If you really want to learn how to read people, then you're going to have to listen.

Learning to listen attentively has numerous benefits:

• Being aware of what others are saying means you're open to change. That means you boost your chances of success in relationships and at work. "Sorry, I wasn't listening" is one of the most insulting things you can say to another person. It means you have more important things to think about than what they're saying. How do you like hearing those words after you've said something worth taking note of? Not much, I'll bet.

• Listening to people tells you a lot about them. This enhanced understanding can come in handy in terms of building relationships and developing your ability to influence the people you have those relationships with when it counts.

• Knowing where people are coming from, what matters to them and how people tick can make you a much more effective negotiator because you are seeing both sides.

• Listening provides you with all you need to know to help you prevent misunderstandings that lead to unnecessary conflict. Missed details can sometimes be the key to heading conflict off at the pass.

With so much to gain, you will readily appreciate the need to practice active listening. What's on your mind can be attended to when others aren't speaking. It's not just a matter of courtesy. It's a matter of benefit to you, also.

Being present

Listening actively allows you to get to the fullness of what's being said. It's not just about words. It's about gestures, facial expressions, posture, pitch and tone. Being attentive to all these factors can provide you with the unspoken truth that's really the foundation of what's being said. Being present to other people also prompts them to tell you much more in **actual words** than they might otherwise tell you. People like to be heard. Being known as a person who is attentive to what others are saying sets you apart and makes people not only want to tell you important things, but tell you them more often.

What gets in the way of listening?

There are numerous factors that can contribute to not hearing as much as we should when others are speaking. Our own thought processes and our attitudes to the messages we're taking in can get in the way of us hearing what's really being said. When your minds wander, it may be because you have already written off the contents of what you're hearing because you either don't like the person speaking, or have pre-judged the message. The following are some other factors that may impact your ability to hear all that's being said.

Environmental distractions

We're animals prone to seek out stimulation. That means if we're listening and something or someone moves, or a bright flash of color is seen from the corner of our eye, we can become distracted. Donuts on the credenza, an empty coffee cup, an itchy or runny nose, or the tie the guy across the boardroom table is wearing can all throw us off our game. Maybe we're out for dinner with our spouse and an attractive stranger walks by while we're listening. Our eyes unconsciously wander in pursuit of the pleasant apparition. I guess we all know how that one ends.

Maintaining focus to hear what's being said is a matter of practice and deliberate intention. If you decide that you're invested in hearing all that's being said, without succumbing to environmental distractions, you will. In a business setting, a good means of maintaining focus is note taking. The very act of writing things down prevents you from being distracted by other factors in the environment. The words you hear are being written by your pen. By taking the action, you are reinforcing the meaning of what's being said.

Formulating a response

Many of us listen in order to be able to respond. We do this for a variety of reasons. Sometimes, we're defending our point of view. Sometimes, we're trying to look clever. Sometimes, we want the person speaking to understand that we are engaged in what they're saying. Instead of listening, though, we're writing what we have to say in response before they've even stopped talking. That's not the same as engagement. It's a type of disrespect for what's being said. If you think what you have to say is so much more important than what's being said by someone else, then you may as well stay home and talk to yourself in the bathroom mirror.

Zoning out

Some people find it very difficult to concentrate. Others are impatient and find listening to others speak becomes a burden, or even a waste of time. Any time you allow this somewhat negative part of your personality to play out, you are likely to grasp just a small fraction of what is being said.

Now that you know what sabotages your active listening, you can avoid it. But we all know most things are easier said than done. Everything's a learning curve in this life and active listening is no different. It's something you need to actively and intentionally work on. It's not always your fault. Some people are difficult to listen to. They meander. They ramble. They speak in a monotone. The trick is to cut through all your own barriers to listening attentively, putting aside the quirks of the speaker. This is one of those times you need to get out of your own way – even if the speaker is a thundering bore.

CONCLUSION

Learning the skill to speed read and analyze people through their behavior is vital to your everyday life. As we are in contact with different types of people while engaging in our daily routine and tasks, we need to know how we deal with them.

While everyone is unique and distinct in their behavior, personality, and character, dealing with different people every day in our whole life won't be easy. Conflicts and pressures arise when we fail to understand them. Not only are we limited to connect with our families and friends and understand them, but we are likewise expected to involve in social interactions, thus expanding the range of connection and optimizing the need for understanding them individually.

As we are adding more people to our lives, the more types of behavior we see, and the more chances for conflicts to arise once we fail or neglect to understand each other.

Speed reading and analyzing people will give you a broad understanding of how people will behave under a certain circumstance while being aware of our own strength and weakness. The skills present to us the advantage of harnessing our potentials for success and a better life.

This book had provided you enough basic and advance knowledge in learning the skill, but the rest is up to you. Just like any other skills, although you can learn it quickly, mastering it can take time and religious practice.

Learning how to read and analyze people and their behavior can take so much time and concentration because of the diversity in all areas concerned. Although there are people who have inherent abilities or have stronger instinct working for them when it comes to reading body language cues and signals, yet the skill is learnable as long as you have the interest and determination to sacrifice what is needed – time and effort in earning.

ENNEAGRAM

REVISED AND UPDATED

The Complete and Scientific Guide to Increase
Empathic Skills, Discover Ourselves and Personality
Types, Gain Emotional Balance and Develop
Compassionate Relationships with Everyone

Dr Henry Campbell & Dr Daniel Watson

PREFACE

The goal of every person on earth today, is to become the truest, highest and best version of themselves. Even though career, social, and background paths may differ, this is the ultimate need of man. Some experts prefer to call this, "self-actualization."
The fact is that if you don't know who is, then how in the world are you going to become the best version of yourself? To actualize yourself, you must first discover yourself. When you discover yourself, the knowledge of your discovery will open doors for you to begin certain actions, steps and strategies that will commence the transformation process to become whom you aspire to be.

The Enneagram of Personality is an ancient tool that has set many people on the path of self-actualization. Due to the incredible impact, it has become very useful and popular in recent times. Many psychologists, life coaches, priests, spiritual leaders, therapists, and counselors have been using it to help their clients discover themselves and improve their life.
The Enneagram offers an exciting and thrilling way to start the process of self-discovery, and then take the necessary actions to develop ourselves. It is no wonder that the self-discovery tool has gained global popularity and has transformed the lives of millions of people across the globe.
By understanding the Enneagram and learning how to use it to improve your life, you will catapult yourself into the next level of progress in your life. Not only will you see changes in your life, but the progress that will be made will help you gain a deeper knowledge of yourself, maximize your potential and become the best of yourself.
The Enneagram classifies personality into nine types. Each human being has a core type and accompanying wing type. Each of personality has its own strengths and weaknesses. Through an Enneagram test, you can find your type and know your blind spots. The insight gleaned will also set you on track to develop yourself and maximize your potential.
Discovering your Enneagram type does not only help you but also the people around you. It changes the way you relate with others. When you discover your type and begin to work on yourself, you gain a deep sense of self-awareness which helps to connect better

with other people. This opens doors for you to empower yourself to form a strong relationship with others.

.

You learn to accept other people, as opposed to criticizing them. Instead of exhibiting the deadly sins of each your enneatype, you exhibit the healthy virtues. As Jim Rohn said, "Success is something you attract by the person you become." As you discover and work on your personality type, you develop an attractive personality that people like and trust.

In the following pages and chapters, you will discover how the Enneagram can change and transform your life and that of your partner forever. From discovering your Enneagram type, finding balance by developing a healthy personality and applying the wisdom of the Enneagram to all areas of your life, you will find exciting tips, advices, and strategies to take your life to the next level. Enjoy your reading!

INTRODUCTION

To begin with, the term Enneagram is a simple term which can be quite complicated in its understanding. However, with the help of this chapter, you will be able to create your definition on the concept. Being able to do so is essential in that it ensures that you understand the real meaning of Enneagram. The Enneagram can be defined as the study of human personalities, especially in their relationships or behaviors in a social setting. It is also a model for identification of who we actually are, and the nine personality types that are used in the analysis.

It is essential to know that because of how extensive the study is; it has different concepts aimed at different purposes but with a fundamental notion of "nine human personalities study." As a model, the Enneagram is understood to be a collection of interrelated personality types. Take for example, when you're around people, and you notice that some people are optimistic, happy and energetic, some are dull, or even in despair, some could be moving around aimlessly, while some remain quite still. Without knowing it, you have just conducted an enneagram study on those people.

As a typology of human personalities, Enneagram is referred to as the nine shades or sometimes called Enneatypes. This is indicated by a geometric figure known as enneagram points. It is the point where different personalities within a specified geometry meet with the reactions of different people at the same given scenario.

The growth of Enneagram has been tremendous and alarming at the spiritual and business levels as it had garnered momentum as regards these levels over the past few years. This is because they are the two significant social settings that deal with the co-existence of people for a relatively long time. The need to study Enneagram across the bounds of a specific geographical setting is pertinent. This is because even within two people, social relations can be established. Think about this, when you are in a conversation with someone, and suddenly their reaction dramatically changes - try to understand what caused this change.

In the long run, you will come to realize that everything boils down to your Enneagram. In other words, your personality and that of the other person's. It's little wonder why Enneagram is very important in our lives for a successful relationship with the people around us. These personalities are interwoven with yours, and they determine your relationships with people as well. In the line of business, Enneagram means the act of gaining more knowledge of how dynamic interpersonal thoughts affect diverse workers in their approaches to tasks at the workplaces. Interviewers use this Enneagram as a concept and a working mechanism in determining how the candidates will react to events surrounding them.

This will tell them the best candidates for their job. Instead of asking these workers about their job functions and responsibilities, Enneagram would focus more on the personalities of the workers as related to their line of duty. All of this is Enneagram at play. While in the spiritual setting, Enneagram is seen as what depicts a meaningful living and also an awareness of the state of living. This is how Enneagram operates spiritually in the real sense of the world. Be that as it may, we shouldn't forget that Enneagram is a broad concept with diverse settings and usage. Although they might seem to be an embodiment of these nine personality traits, they are also independent but interrelated. Furthermore, Enneagram is the best state or personalities believed to be true for all humans.

Additionally, the Enneagram is perceived as a personality system which combines nine different traits. Many accentuations have been made regarding the fact that humans have one of these personalities which consist of some subtypes as well. Well, you might wonder how these traits get to us; many people say we pick them up in childhood while other people say it is genetically related. Whatever your belief might be about these two assumptions, the fact that everyone behaves within specified traits in different ways remains true for every situation.

There are nine types of Enneagram generally. There are different attachments to these types, and they all have a placement within the symbol of the Enneagram. The nine personalities have different names, and they are as follows:

1. The Reformer,

2. The Helpers,

3. The Achievers,

4. The Individualist,
5. The Investigators,

6. The Loyalists,

7. The Enthusiasts,

8. The Challenger,

9. The Peacemakers.

In all the studies of Enneagram, one repeated and fascinating factor that has come up is that people within a given type of trait will be different from one another. The reason for this is yet to be ascertained, but it could be because humans are dynamic. In fact, everyone, including you, could be a challenger within a particular time and then change to an enthusiast some other times.

Many psychologists believe that every change in human traits premises on the state of mental health. Further opinions are still subject to researchers though. Healthiness or unhealthiness state is defined as what a particularly given quality finds pleasurable and natural to them against what they see and do as otherwise. The focus of this chapter is not to provide in-depth information about the personalities.

However, it is to open your mind and introduce you to the concept of Enneagram. That way, you will be able to understand the following chapters as you read them. There are different levels in the personalities' types which contribute to their healthiness as well. In order to explain Enneagram in total, there are separate wings created for them. These wings will be adequately discussed later in this book.

However, what they explain is the fact that many people have combinations of Enneagram personalities. Even though the nine personalities are true to humans, there are more combinations to these personalities than the existence of their singular presence. This makes postulation of rules that capture their behavior a mirage and vague.

It is pertinent to note that there are different names given to these personalities. This could be because they have different teachings, context, and usage of the information. Whatever angle enneagram studies might take in the future, one fact remains that it is a nine-personality study and a model to understanding the ways, actions, and reactions that occur in social relationships.

In conclusion, Enneagram encapsulates the system of the nine human personalities that determine the trait which signals why people react and act in the way they do. The people that developed it might have not even imagined it could be real Enneagram. This is because many people have altered the probability of having the Enneagram in its holistic nature. , but its reality is shown even in these non believers. This is the power of Enneagram.

Trust me -nothing is stopping you from becoming a better version of yourself - besides yourself. You are your own biggest rival and enemy towards achieving this fantastic trait. If only you can look past your weaknesses and emotions, understanding people's personalities would be at your fingertips. That way, you would be able to thrive in your workplace, relationships, and other social outings. The next chapter focuses on how Enneagram began as a concept, idea, and term. You don't want to miss it.

CHAPTER 1: ENNEAGRAM AND ITS HISTORY

As the old saying goes, everything that has a beginning has an end - and vise versa. Every process has a starting point, and every piece of history is felt in the future. This same situation extends to Enneagram. To fully understand what the term Enneagram means, we would have to go deep into its historical background and development. How did Enneagram begin? What led to its development? How was the idea of Enneagram conceived?

The word Enneagram is from two Greek words, ennea, which means "nine" and gramma meaning "written." The origin of Enneagram has been a notable controversy among scholars. The need arose because many people have found the personalities identified as being true to form even in their personal experiences. One of the earliest writings on the Enneagram, as opined by Palmer and Wiltse is found in the book of Evagrius Ponticus in the 4th century. In his book, Ponticus gave eight personalities, which he called logismoi meaning "deadly thoughts" with the critical thought as "love of self." This was created because Ponticus thought that whatever one does as a judgment of another person's trait is influenced by the personality of that person.

In other words, people with the 'challenger' personality will mostly take 'enthusiasm' as a negative trait simply because they don't exhibit it. To bolster this, Ponticus further says that;

"The first thought of all is that love of self (Philautia); after this [come] the eight."

These identifications given by Ponticus caused a lot of commotion as people wondered how true it was to equate love to personalities. How could love originate without being altered too? In response to that, Ponticus gave the "remedies" to the eight thoughts. These solutions will be used to answer whatever questions that has to do with or would erupt on the ideas. With these remedies, many people saw the need to adopt the thoughts of Ponticus with all carefulness. Whether the resources given to the eight thoughts are still relevant in today's world is debatable.

The eight thoughts didn't, however, get enough publicity. But with the works of G.I. Gurdjieff, the Enneagram was known everywhere. This could have been the origin of what Enneagram is, alongside its study today. It is pertinent to note that Gurdjieff still retained the eight thoughts from Ponticus. As a matter of fact, they served as the guiding tenets of his work.

In modern day, Oscar Ichazo, a Bolivian, could be said to be Enneagram originator. The nine personality studies in this contemporary age are from his lectures, most importantly, those that focus on ego-fixations, virtues, passions, and holy ideas, delivered by Oscar in the 1950s. Another report claims that Oscar's well-detailed self-development and orientation were actually how he started the teaching that begot Enneagram. The lessons on 'Proto-analysis' use the typical nine enneagram figures and ideas that are used today.

With the growth in awareness of Enneagram through Oscar's teaching, Africa institute based in Chile was established. However, it later moved to the United States of America when he relocated to South America. This is where the etymology of "Enneagram of Personality" can be traced to. Oscar later coined the term. As the enneagram personalities got enough establishments, Oscar needed to teach some of his students so that they would be able to take enneagram personalities around the globe and obviously to the next level.

In the 1970s, notable psychologists such as John Lilly and Claudio Naranjo went to Oscar to learn about the concept of Enneagram. Little wonder why these two were part of the earliest students of Oscar to understand Enneagram of personality. The Chilean and psychiatrist, Claudio Naranjo (from Arica in Chile) was in Africa Institute to take a course. Naranjo, having learned a great deal from Oscar, decided to start his teachings on Enneagram in the United States.

He took the teaching with a differing view from what his teacher, Oscar, taught him. He influenced some priest, the Jesuit, who adopted it to spiritual dealings. Enneagram took another approach against what Oscar wanted. His different approach, though friendly and straightforward, was perceived by Oscar as shrewd and misunderstanding. Because of this, Oscar disowned Naranjo and labeled his teachings as treacherous even though his lessons with other teachers spread like wildfire in the 1970s. Because Naranjo was teaching his understanding of Enneagram, his theory grew very fast and had students too.

As the saying goes, 'you shall reap what you sow,' Naranjo also witnessed the same thing he did to his teacher as his students also misconstrued and betrayed him in the end. Naranjo taught different things which were taken for spiritual dealings, and his students taught things that seemed to be more business inclined. Instead of preaching their teacher's teachings, they focus on a paradigm shift which saw them exploring the business side of Enneagram.

In the 1980s and 1990s, diverse authors such as Helen Palmer, Richard Rohr, Elizabeth Wagele and Don Richard Riso, started various publications on Enneagram. Meanwhile, the theories they taught and published are a mixture of how Enneagram erupted. In today's enneagram theories, attention to what the context of their application is, solely determined their usage and understanding. As part of the publishers, this book takes no particular view other than simplifying everything concerning Enneagram.

Maybe because enneagram founders understood and taught Enneagram at a different situation, many of Enneagram theories are basically on spirituality and business —as noted in the introduction. In fact, today, many authors would love to equate Enneagram to spirituality. This is very wrong, considering the history of the Enneagram. The account given here was confirmed from different authors and looking at it from different opinions. Enneagram is used in psychology and even neuroscience today. A lot of attention has been drawn to it because of how people have known about it lately.

Know that the historical background of Enneagram follows an intricate pattern. From one scholar to another, from one philosopher to another, and from one teacher to another, the Enneagram concept had followed a fantastic design which had led to its rapid development over the past century. Additionally, the idea is still being transformed and developed with new ideas coming from young minds. Now, our next chapter will focus on where the concept of Enneagram was developed.

Where Enneagram was developed

The exact nature of where Enneagram originated has been a mirage since its inception in the 4th century. As noted from the beginning of this book, contextual understanding of Enneagram has been developed through various conceptions and teachings from scholars with diverse ideas. Many people who published works to influence others on the nature of Enneagram never had the intention of the deduced meanings. Interestingly, one of the concepts of psychology that have suffered a lot of false conceptions is Enneagram.

Many people that start Enneagram do so with what could be considered diluted knowledge regarding where it was initially developed. Different conceptions of Enneagram have contributed immensely to what we know it as today. Here, the 'places' where Enneagram was developed are the most prominent ones throughout its history. They are where Enneagram can best be understood and found. They are the teachings of the notable more profound of the Enneagram personalities.

Since Enneagram has entertained different approaches and alarming concern from different professions —such as psychology, neurology, theology, and lots more —the need to understand where it was developed rose to some degree. It is pertinent to note that where Enneagram of personality developed from, as discussed here, is based on the diverse scholars of the Enneagram and not that there is a concrete building like a pyramid of Egypt or a monument center that begat it.

Additionally, Enneagrams development is based on the fact that there are different schools of thoughts with different terminologies. As well as approaches, conception, overlapping and merging, teachings, dealings, etc. The Enneagram we have today, though quite different from its original intention, is gotten from the places it evolved.

In past studies, psychologists have identified six basic 'places' where Enneagram originated. Keep in mind that this is different from the history of the Enneagram. The origins and places where it was developed to simplify the teachings of the developers. Below are the six 'places' where Enneagram was developed:

Don Richard Riso

Don Richard Riso is a neurotic approach to the study of the Enneagram. Its manner of dealing is to give a full description of the sequence in the nine personalities from the neurotic approach through to normal development and then to healthy emotion. The development of this kind of Enneagram was based on giving an analysis of how emotional health has evolved using the neurons in the body. Based on this approach and development, there have been many beliefs and teachings on this kind of Enneagram personality. It contributes to where the enneagram personality was developed.

Oscar Ichazo development of enneagram personalities

An approach that is based on Ichazo was developed in order to give the application of the nine personalities using varying schemata like ego and fixations in order to provide an analysis of self-development. Many books have used this approach where enneagram personalities had been developed both in the application and in actual teachings. The goal of the Enneagram in this approach is to provide the schema in self-development using the fixations theories.

Hameed A. Ali (A. S. Almaas) development of Enneagram personalities

Hameed A. Ali's development of Enneagram personalities is a psychological approach which evolved as another different kind of Enneagram. With this approach, Enneagram of personality is only a combination of studies from disciplines in the therapy of Gestalt through to that of Zen and the Reichian. It is purely psychological, thus studies the mind as well as how they affect human behavior. This particular type of Enneagram is probably the type that had received the most publications and teachings.

Claudio Naranjo development of enneagram personalities

Being a psychiatrist, Claudio proposed an approach that substitutes and replaces the usage of neurotic terms and strategies with psychiatric jargons and dealings. The total reliance on neurotic usage of transactions as a determinant of Enneagram personality was denounced and changed. Essentially, everything boiled down to the psychiatric approach. Well, because this approach is more or less synonymous to the disorder of humans and this is why many people reject it for a better approach – meanwhile only those within the field love to use it. Whenever you read a book relating to Enneagram that utilizes this kind of personality developed, adjust your attention to their terminologies only.

Helen Palmer

Helen Palmer is the sort of Enneagram that focuses on the overall narrative of prevalent teachings. Just like this book, this development is in learning the general idea as there is no particular niche given. On a closing note, this Enneagram developed here is based on the teachings and approaches it had from its inception. It is not to nullify that Enneagram is based on the nine human personalities in their social relations and reactions to things and people. Based on this general background, it is believed that the development of Enneagram is from the first developer.

Oscar Ichazo development of Enneagram personalities

The Oscar Ichazo development is an approach that was developed as a way to give the application of the nine personalities, through the use of varying schemata, ego, for example. Psychologists and other great developers of Enneagram have agreed, at least to some extent, that those enneagram personalities had been in man since childbirth. Noting that there were not many new insights found when they traced the origin of the Enneagram to inhuman sources. In fact, the only thing that was discovered was the naming, description, and teachings of the nine Enneagram personalities which have been believed to be an influence of different developers explained at the beginning of this chapter. The line of enneagram development is evolving, and the probability of having much more approaches in the future is very high.

Lastly, note that the development of Enneagram has followed several approaches; however, none has ruled out the context of birth in the perception of the concept by the developer. This is one of the reasons enneagram personalities have many misconceptions even from the onset. The approach given here is the underlying factor which proves that Enneagram is a model and also a system of nine human personalities, using the names mostly adopted and not the popularly known misconception because this book will give you a complete introduction to the Enneagram personalities.

This chapter should familiarize you with the knowledge of the different school of thoughts in regards to the Enneagram. Having a deep understanding of where the concept originated from would also go a long way in putting you through a straight path concerning this journey. This chapter will help broaden your horizon as regards this concept. Now, which Enneagram school do you fancy? Which do you find appealing? Once you lay this foundation, the rest will fall into place.

CHAPTER 2: BENEFITS OF USING ENNEAGRAM

The most important benefit that the Enneagram provides is that it will help you to understand yourself. It will help you to understand your inner self. It will also help you to understand others. When you understand others, you can be more compassionate towards them. The Enneagram will help you to not just access, but even expand your emotional, mental, and spiritual intelligence. You will be aware of your automatic responses and defensive reactions towards situations in life. When you are aware of the manner in which you react, you can change your reactions. The only thing that you can fully control in your life is your reactions. The difference between success and failure is your reaction. The way you react can decide the course of your life. Thus, the Enneagram will improve your efficiency when you interact with others. Not just that, it will help you to build meaningful relationships. It will help you to live in the present and not the past or the future. Well, it all boils down to self-awareness. Being aware of yourself will help you to change your life for the better.

Confidence

The eighth, and second to last personality that we will look at in this book is called the challenger. They are named this because they never turn down challenges. It is more like they feed on these challenges. Challengers are quick to make decisions and have high confidence in the choices that they make. This confidence has earned them the nicknames of Willful, Powerful and Self-confident. They always feel the need to control the environment because of their surety. Because of this, they have also known for being quite dominating.

Influential and inspirational but sometimes becomes intimidating; people of the eighth personality do not like to show weakness. They would rather challenge those around them in order to show their resourcefulness and skill. They never miss a chance at turning a challenge into a means to better them. They make advances at taking control before anyone else has an opportunity even to try let alone acquiring any form of rule over them. They fear to be vulnerable and possibly being hurt or dominated by others.

There is no way around it challengers are highly competitive people. They will do anything to win and ensure that the perceived opponent has no advantage over them. They feel a need to win at everything, and revel in their strengths, abilities, and work. They not only dislike human control, but they also hate being controlled by circumstances. Much like the seventh personality we looked at, challengers do not like feeling restricted. Sometimes these two personalities are mistaken for one another. This is especially true when an eighth's dominant wing is a seven, or a seven's dominant wing is an eight.

No matter how much contradiction challengers face, they only want to do what seems right to them and would go to any length to achieve their goals. Unlike the seventh personality that goes to extremes in order to get what they want because of a need for excitement, challengers go to extremes because they want to prove their worth and show their strength. They don't mind being forced out of their comfort zones because they like the idea that they have the opportunity to give more than they usually do and be even better than they already are.

Self-Awareness

Now that you have discovered your personality type, it is important that you consider actions and steps that will allow you the joys of personal growth to become more self-aware. As you would guess, different personalities have different actions and recommendations for the journey of self-awareness. Therefore, let us examine each of these individually in order to help you identify what works best for your type.

Benefits of self-awareness

Your coping skills will improve.

Life will always throw challenges at you. When you lack self-awareness, you may address obstacles from a place of reactivity, and it becomes much harder to cope. With awareness, you can handle these difficulties from a place of grace and acceptance, and it becomes easier to remain positive and relaxed, and to make empowering choices.

You will heal yourself.

When pain remains buried and unaddressed, hurt lingers on in your body, making you more likely to react to the present from the place of your past pain. Working through your challenges makes it easier to act consciously and frees you from the burdens you carry. People tend to feel much better each time an issue gets resolved.

Your internal sense of balance will increase.

Sometimes, you may feel as if you are on an emotional tightrope. Each emotion and reaction has the potential to hit you like a strong gust of wind, leaving you struggling to cling to the delicate balance you've created. Self-awareness gives you strength, and acceptance makes you even stronger. You can maintain your balance and weather internal storms.

Your relationships will get better.

You can make it easy for others to enjoy your company when you relate to them from a place of awareness. When you react to others from a place of unconsciousness, you have more conflicts, and greater hurt may arise in relationships. With self-awareness, you develop compassion for others' pain. It is easier to connect with others from a place of kindness.

You will develop presence and mindfulness.

Being present allows people to live in the here and now. When we are focused on only the current moment, we don't need to feel hurt by the wounds from the past or fear the unknown in the future. We find acceptance and joy in everything. We simply are. In presence, we see others and ourselves fully and compassionately.

Compassion

The enneagram allows for one to get on a journey towards self-enlightenment and acceptance for who you are. Everyone has a basic driving force and a preferred strategy set for unique talents and strengths that make us individuals. We look at the world and the present era with specific perspectives and we are drawn in particular directions as individuals. These preferences can harden into modes of behavior, which also strangle the ways in which we grow. At times when people first discover the particular type they are, they might say that they would like to change to another type. That is an indication they are judging one type to be more desirable as compared to another. The key to utilizing the enneagram would be exploration without the use of judgment. The question is if each pattern provided a large reservoir of talent, which is equally valuable. You are undoubtedly growing and maturing everyday so there should not be a limit to the potentials irrespective of your type. Every evidence points to the fact that no enneagram type is better than the other. In each archetype there are different levels of maturity and generativity. The level of maturity may vary though in different contexts.

Each type of enneagram represents a deep habit. It shows a theme that for a lot of people is constant throughout their life, though the possibilities for the mental, physical or spiritual developments have no bounds. The type is a fundamental form of human habit. With some technology and coaching, it is possible to utilize the information gained from this information to transform patterns for more effective behavior and perspectives.

As we study our types, it begins to dawn on us that there is a range of healthy to unhealthy behaviors we engage in unwittingly. When we are relaxed, we may feel safe and have natural gifts that are inherent to our type that are at our disposal. Similarly, when under stress, we have ways of reacting that may run contrary to the best intentions we have. When triggered we may also react in the best way to protect ourselves from pain, fear or shame and respond so quickly that we do not even acknowledge the effect that it has on other people. When growing to understand our type, we develop the right skills which are particular to that type and that may allow us to reduce the levels of stress we harbor through reactivity and our quick responses which negatively affect the ones that are around us. This also allows the illustration of the greatest gifts and as we continue to learn, there is an understanding that others also have unconscious patterns and reactions which are predictable during times of crises, happening beyond the level of present awareness.

With more study, one may start to develop valuable traits such as compassion and understanding for themselves and others concerning the patterns of the type and then grow to appreciate just how fast anyone can be triggered and how much it is not possible to note the patterns. Develop skills that would slow things down and bring us out of the trance that instilled patterns we engage. We can then become compassionate and sensitive to the emotional vulnerabilities of everyone and become skilled at holding space for them. Under stress, each category has a way they disconnect from their loved ones emotionally.

In depth exploration concerning the enneagram also assists one to navigate their relationships with more skill. Knowing the types of your family and colleagues can increase your understanding on their fears, defenses and motivations, allowing you to understand how they would interact with you and others. The other reason you should take this journey into self-exploration is the commitment to living a conscious and caring life though every day you may come across situations and people that could result in self-sabotaging reactions. Even if you had been on a spiritual path for some time, you may still be humbled by the manner that the unconscious reactions bring you to patterns that you had thought had been outgrown.

It could be that you tend to space when your spouse expresses painful emotions because it disrupts your carefree attitude, or you may turn to alcohol or other drugs when you feel like you are being shunned or things are not going your way. Irrespective of the pattern, everyone comes with habits that block self-expression and joy. All of these patterns which are negative because of their own suffering and they are linked to habits of the different enneagram types. Even in the event that you can recite deep spiritual truths when these patterns are triggered, you may still forget the bigger picture of who you are and the unique gifts that you can share with the world. The question then arises on how one can find clarity and free themselves from the fears, motivations and desires that fuel behavioral patterns and trigger other reactions from others.

Leadership

People who fit into the challenger category are both convincing and charismatic. Hence, they can be found in a variety of leadership positions. They tend to be the best in their different fields and can sometimes be seen as paragons of whatever it is they stand for. Because of their ability to exercise so much control and restraint, they significantly affect their society and believe they have a full understanding of how things should work. They expect that everyone follows them and will fight opposition at all costs. They also have powerful instincts that they'll follow at all costs rather than go along with someone else's or being convinced to ignore their instincts.

Much like people of the sixth personality, trust is not an easy thing to achieve for challengers, but when they do realize it, they make that person into a very close friend and give that person a level of importance in their lives. People of the eighth personality begin to use their protective instincts to defend these people who are close to them and would do anything to provide for those people.

Challengers do not appreciate any form of control over them. They fear allowing external factors to influence them and will fight no matter what to break that influence. They choose to always grow their power, resources, and skills, which puts them way ahead of any threats of being overthrown. They are the most independent of all the types of personalities of the Enneagram.

Challengers might listen to advice from others, but they ensure they have the final say. They like to make sure they and no one else is the decision maker in their lives. Because of this, they often have problems with hierarchy if they aren't at the top. They often come off as rebellious because they are so strong-willed and feel a need for their opinions to heard and acknowledged.

When it comes to fears and concerns, people of this personality fear physical harm. But their primary fear is the feeling of being vulnerable in any way. Sometimes, challengers find intimate relationships hard to participate in because it requires a level of vulnerability, and people of this personality do not like to open up. This, combined with a fear of betrayal, also makes it difficult for challengers to engage in intimate relationships with anyone. It's not like they are entirely unfeeling. They have sentimental sides but would rather keep those sites hidden so that no one can see them as vulnerable or see those sentiments as an opportunity to gain control over them.

People well known in their various fields or groups are most likely perfect examples of challengers. People such as Donald Trump, Queen Latifah, Serena Williams, Pablo Picasso, and Franklin Roosevelt, Ernest Hemingway, James Brown, Pink, Jack Black, and Humphrey Bogart all fit into this category.

CHAPTER 3: THE ENNEAGRAM ROADMAP

The path to spiritual growth, bluntly put, can be brutal and grueling. Not only is it difficult to know how to get started, but it also seems impossible for most to keep on that path toward their own benefit, their own success, their own greatness. It's difficult to stay determined, most definitely, as it is with everything and all kinds of commitment in life. However, with the help of some simple mechanisms, cheats, and the support of the people around you, taking that road and sticking to it is nowhere near impossible.

Of course, how people recover from trauma and move forward in life toward their most ideal versions of themselves depends heavily on the individual, their personality, their determination to change, and many other factors which vary massively from person to person. Keeping this in mind, it's sometimes actually fairly important to mind your personality type. Not just in the way you act and behave, but under the surface as well. Whether that be analyzing your test results on various reputable personality tests, or whatever method you individually see fit, understanding the deeper side of yourself—your motivations, your aspirations, the reasons behind your bad habits and your flaws—can and will help you take the first step forward into becoming a better person. This also helps you to learn love yourself and gives spiritually healing your mind, body, and soul.

To better heal, the first and most important step is often to understand ourselves better. To understand the mind of someone else, you must first have at least a general understanding of the inner workings of your own mind. This helps you to be able to project the observations about yourself onto someone else. Although there's much individuality when it comes to personality, it should be dually noted that in addition to all of these differences, there are also a number of similarities which join us together.

These similarities promote a sense of togetherness and camaraderie, and can sometimes help build empathy between people. After all, it isn't out diversity which helps us understand our common ground and forge relationships with others. It's those similarities which bind us together, as a group and as the human race. Because many of those similarities exist on the internal level, below the surface of most of the human psyche, we have to dig a little deeper to understand ourselves better, so that we can better understand others as well. After all, the motivations of others behind the scenes and behind their actions are often also our own motivations for the path in life we choose, and the roads of those paths which we walk as a result of those choices.

Although we have many similarities and as a result, many of the ways to spiritually heal yourself will work to a certain extent for everyone and any personality type—we have many subtle differences which make how we learn, how we process information, and how we cope with trauma and the daily stresses of life, intrinsically different from that of our peers; The way we heal in our minds and in our hearts is bound to at least be slightly different from the methods of those around us. The way our friends, our families, our spouses, is often going to be at least slightly different from what works best for us. Of course, using the methods of your loved ones or if anyone will guarantee you at least some success, depending on the situation and the exact method. However, they are tailored specifically to certain personality types and tendencies within those personality types.

Not all Type 1s are like, and nor are all Type 7s. Even within these groups and categories we make for ourselves, there are many ways that individuals that exist within those groups can manifest their individuality. Because we all choose to manifest that sense of individuality a bit differently from each other, the method that is tailored to your enneagram type may not necessarily be the one that works best for you. The Enneagram model included is no way to define yourself or your personality truly.

There are many different kinds of people who may have different motivations and different temperaments from one another who may actually be the same Enneagram type. In no way does this speak to the individuality of the people within the personality types, or lack thereof. It's an inescapable thing that a broad range of descriptions won't apply to every single person who falls under a certain name or type number.

With this in mind, let's move on into the lists of recommended methods to get started or stay determined on your path to spiritual healing, fulfillment, and bettering your life experience, depending on your personality type.

Introverts, don't push yourselves socially types like 4 and 9, the romantic and the dreamer with their head in the clouds, aren't the type who will constantly be engaging in a social activity. They usually aren't party animals or people who will actively search for a way to fulfill themselves socially or emotionally through interaction with their peers. That's absolutely ok! Not only are you the kind of person who doesn't need to be validated in this way, but trying to force yourself to be an extravert and push yourself to be someone who is constantly engaging in potentially dangerous activities simply for the sake of feeling like you're helping yourself, is the exact opposite. Not only is doing this going against your nature, but it's usually something that's exhausting for a lot of introverts, and it can even be physically unhealthy and dangerous for an introverted type like 4 or 9.

If you identify as one of these types or are otherwise a person who feels as though they're a very introverted person, don't neglect that fact! Nurture your introversions and engage in activities which aren't too demanding of your physically or emotionally. Of course, if you feel like you're holding yourself back from doing extraverted things and don't feel exhausted because doing extraverted things is uninteresting, but because your sense of social anxiety is holding you back, this is a different matter entirely. If you feel as though you may actually be someone who wants to do things like this and go to parties and that those extraverted activities may actually suit you more, it may just be a matter of anxiety or nervousness. Combatting this anxiety is something that must be taken slowly and carefully. This is another matter in which you can't overwork yourself or go too hard, too quickly. Anxiety is something that must be nurtured and gently disposed of.

Trying to violently or harshly dispel the nervous tendencies of an anxious person is more likely to simply cause them to revert back to a person afraid of their own shadow, crippled by the idea of being looked down upon or seen as too awkward by other people at a social function. If you're someone who struggles with courage or the self-esteem needed to pursue those interests and engage yourself in unfamiliar functions or social circles, you aren't alone. Be gentle with yourself and congratulate yourself on even what seems like the smallest and most insignificant victories on your path to becoming the person you most want to be.

Remember that the best things take time and that the fruit which is the ripest, is the hardest to be plucked.

For Type 4: The romantic who feels as though being different is the key to success. Here's a secret I've learned over the years; sometimes, trying to be unique can be the downfall of both a business and a person. Being different in a way that doesn't come naturally will only decrease your chances of success, and there's a big difference between being yourself and trying too hard to appeal to others. There's a strange kind of irony in your venture to be different so that you can escape the feeling that you're trying to get the attention and praise of others. In that venture, you're also trying to get the attention and the praise of other people who have pioneered their way through the world in their originality and their different perspective of the world. You want to be like them, and it's because of that desire to be recognized, to be seen, that you're tempted to try so hard to break the "status quo" and break apart from a majority you might look down upon.

Consider something else about that majority while you're at it; the majority that you might be looking down your nose at is probably more right than you are. Of course, it's never an especially accurate creed to always follow the crowd, but vowing to follow that crowd instead never at all, may actually be an even worse idea. After all, the effect that one person has to influence an entire crowd isn't infinite. There's a reason, and usually a good reason, that something becomes popular. Of course, there will always be cult classic movies and hidden gems of the media, but not everything that the majority of people enjoy is bad. This simply is because it's popular, and not everything you deem "underrated," because it's not well liked, is actually objectively good enough to be considered underrated by most other people, critics of that media included. While we're on the subject, a healthy amount of criticism of others is healthy, but taking it too far will result in conflict and poor relationships.

Speaking your mind is important, but not being willing to compromise with others, or to empathize with others, is even more important to work with others in society. Unfortunately for you, living off the grid in total seclusion likely isn't an option so I wouldn't recommend it. Learning to cooperate, collaborate, listen to the opinions or others, and take those opinions to mean equal value to you like yours, will help you become not only a happier person but a kinder and a wiser person as well.

To Type 1, the individual who can become obsessive, the things you are currently worrying about probably will not actually matter to you or to anyone else in a few years. To be concerned with something isn't in any way bad or something that will negatively affect you in the short term. However, your obsessive tendencies can and will come back to bite you in the long run. Take some time for yourself and dedicate that time to loving yourself and taking care of yourself. You are the only person you've got to live as, so you might as well enjoy the life you are trying to live. There is more to life, and more to your happiness, than your efficiency and how much work you've done for yourself.

Surely, your accomplishments in life so far are nothing to scoff at, and you're doing well for yourself in the literal sense, but what will those accomplishments mean when you feel yourself on the brink of departure from the earth? What will all the nights you could have spent resting, that you spent in the office or dedicating your being to work, mean at that moment when you look back? What it will mean, is that you've wasted a part of it. Of course, everyone will have different priorities in their lifetime, but the understanding that you are not meant to spend your entire life working until you keel over is universal, at least to most people. It's dangerous to your health, as well. There is, of course, nothing wrong objectively to educating yourself to your work or to your heart. However, there is something wrong when you become obsessive, constantly dedicating yourself to your work to please others, instead of for your own enjoyment.

You work as hard, as desperately, and as obsessively as you do, so that you can attain the praise and the affirmations of the people you respect and live up to. Of course, that's nothing to be ashamed of in and of itself. However, having that as the sole or main purpose for your hard work isn't normal or healthy. That fixation on the validation of your boss or higher-ups is going to be your downfall, the reason you may look back at the end of your life and finally realize your mistake. That mistake can cost you weeks, months, years, decades of your livelihood and of your career. And that career will likely be successful, but not fulfilling. If, after a deep and long period of searching your soul for what you want to do, you determine that you truly do value your efficiency and your career's achievements above your happiness and fulfillment, then the way you may be going right now is going to lead you to that exact destination. If, however, that's not the way you wish to go in life, be wary. Your obsessive tendencies can lead you down a dark and winding path that will surely lead you a place where you find it almost impossible to turn back from if you aren't careful and aware of yourself.

Take some time for yourself, whenever possible in between work and assignments you may have. Learn to do work for yourself, not for others. Ultimately, it's you who will reap the emotional reward of the way you live your life, not your boss and not your teachers, your mothers or anyone else. It's you alone who will have to deal with the melancholy and the regret, or with the acceptance and peace of what you did and why you did it. There are times when you will have to prioritize your work, but try not to make it a habit.

Habitually making yourself and your health take the back seat to your work and productivity will ultimately lead to you suffering majorly because of those choices, both mentally and physically. Take care of yourself, as your future self is depending on you to do so. You are the most precious cargo you have.

To Type 3, the performer who might not know when to quit. You are the spotlight of your life. You are the main actor, the star of your stage. You are not, however, the same star to others as you are to yourself. You are bound to give bad performances, have botched lines, have to improve every now and then; it happens, it has happened, and it will most certainly happen again. You're going to have to get used to it now before you let the fear that comes with the prospect of making a mistake on stage swallow you up a whole. You're a performer, an achiever who knows what it's like to struggle in the face of adversity. Remember that your performances, the you that you are on stage, is not the "real you."

Take care of yourself off stage, as all performances must come to an end. Come to terms with the fact that the person you become on your mental stage is little more than a façade. Although it's a coping mechanism, one that isn't necessarily unhealthy, the danger arises when you begin to lose the recognition of what is a performance and what are truly you, what is truly happening around you and what is happening in the play of your life. Remember to come back down off the stage every now and again, because the stage will be there for you when you get back.

When we develop a coping mechanism that works for us, we allow it to act as our crutch and are then hesitant to get off of it. We sometimes are tempted to let that mechanism that crutch consume us and take us over. We don't know what's too much, how much we can rely on that crutch before we give up, or dive all in. Learn to rely on people, the ones around you who love you and care about you, instead of on your stage. When you feel you need it, the stage will always be there for you to climb back onto, but try to stay off it when you don't need it. Being an entertainer your entire life but never stopping to watch and take in experiences simply can be a miserable existence. It makes you stop enjoying your life and only allows you to focus on making other people enjoy their experience. It's somehow selfish and selfless as the exact same time. When you're on the stage, remember that you are more of a person outside that stage than you are when you're on it, delivering your best lines and giving the best punchlines. You are not an actor or a performer only.

Try not to become a caricature of yourself, lest you lose your sense of identity and simply melt into that performer identity. Losing your sense of self can be a very scary thing, so make sure you check on it regularly.

To Type 2, the one who gives to receive, you are not liable to the reaction of whomever you aid or give to. You are not obligated to anything when you help another person—that is the concept of helping. You aid someone else out of the goodness and the kindness of your own heart, not so that you can gain something in return.

Whether that something is in the form of a reward or affection, you are in no way entitled to anything in return when you do a good thing for someone else. The other person will likely want to return the favor but learn not to expect it from everyone. Expecting a reward for a good deed will only encourage your selfish temptations and want you to help only out of concern for yourself and your wants, not the wants and needs of others.

In addition, try to stop yourself from accepting any affection that comes your way. It will seem tempting, and the person may have the best of intentions, but try to learn the people around you for affection. The most satisfying love you can have is the love that is given and received by you. Any polite cordiality you receive from someone you have given to is likely not expressing their genuine love for you; they simply want to repay you.

Understanding the difference between the infatuation you feel for people and true, genuine love, will be the thing that saves you from potentially dangerous situations and harmful relationships. Those relationships may seem beneficial to both parties when they begin, but they usually end up becoming something significantly more sinister than what you may have originally thought. They may end up being someone who wants to use you for their own needs, neglects even abuses you, or simply someone who you thought you were going to click with because you wanted to receive affection from them and failed to see that you simply weren't compatible beyond the mutual loneliness shared between the two of you. That aside, you know that to receive affection from others, you have to be upfront about your feelings and why you want affection from them. To have love given to you, you have to make the person you want that love from understanding how, why, and in what you form want that love.

There are people in your life who are more than willing to give you all the love you could ever want or need in the world, but no one is a mind reader; you have to be the person who reaches out and makes the first move so that the other person can exactly understand what you want from them and why. So, in your everyday life, practice the skills you feel you need to accomplish that growth in your confidence by forcing yourself to be upfront about even little things.

If that results in you eventually giving less and helping fewer people, that isn't necessarily a bad thing. It means that when you were giving and helping others in excess, you were predominantly doing so in the hopes that you could receive their love and affection in return, an unhealthy and not specifically moral reason for helping others.

You are not someone who is cruel; however, you have the heart of someone who wants to help others. Don't let that desire to help clash and overlap with your desire to be loved.

For Type 8, or someone who can develop a hero complex, you are not the chivalrous hero you might think you are. No matter how much you help people and "rescue" them from what you perceive perilous situations, don't misread a situation and become involved when you don't need to be, or really shouldn't be in the first place. To be honest, you're often better off taking a back seat to the people you think you're helping. You don't need to help people as often as you might think you do, because people aren't as reliant on you as you think.

Most of the people you surround yourself with can take care of themselves quite aptly, and don't need your help to survive in the world. You aren't a necessity, but the desired companion. The relationships you build with others has to be a relationship in which both parties respect each other equally, or else the relationship will cease to be a friendship, and will instead become a relationship where you treat the other person as someone who needs you to live. Remember that the world goes on without you and that the people you want to protect can live and protect them.

Although your help is usually appreciated, make sure that you aren't becoming overly confident and protecting someone else when you don't need to, lest you just make the scenario worse for both you and the person you want so badly to protect. The people you care for and who care for you understand that you do all of this out of goodwill and the desire to be someone who can help others while asking for nothing in return. The desire to be a hero is universal and relatable to most every one of all walks of life. It's admirable to want to help others selflessly, but don't mistake your desire to help. Just because you are helping others, doesn't mean that they necessarily wanted your help, or really needed it to begin with.

Learn to humanize yourself and treat yourself and your loved ones as total equals. By doing this and empathizing, you become someone who more passionately defends others when it really counts, instead of simply rushing in whenever someone looks like they might not be able to handle a situation on their own. After all, some people may not like being catered to and defended without being consulted—they feel as though you don't trust them to be able to protect and defend themselves, and may feel as though you think of them as someone who is weak and in desperate need of someone else to protect them from the world around them. This can easily result in relationships being strained, something to avoid for a personality such as yours where you depend on the people around you to be there.

You thrive off of the thrill of being able to fight for someone's honor, Type 8, but remember to come back down to earth and recognize the world and the people around you, so you don't accidentally offend and hurt one of the people you so badly want to defend. Although you act purely out of benevolence and courage, that fighting spirit can sometimes be interpreted as malice or something malevolent. Take the time to humanize your perspective and realize you also have things about yourself that you can improve upon throughout your life.

For Type 6, who can become a coward, you are the only person who knows what to do. Who exactly knows what you are thinking at any point in time. The people you rely on now will not always be there to support you and help you and guide you through your indecisiveness. There is a harsh reality in this realization, but it's a realization that must be had if you want to ever improve in your life.

If you dare to live your life constantly using the people around you as a crutch, you will live your life as someone who exists out of their own body. In a sense, it will cease even to be your life at all. You will have, in a sense, lost your identity and your sense of self. After losing this, what will you do when that person who you treat as a crutch abandons you, or you're in a situation where they aren't there to help you? What could you think to do then, when you've been spoiled so much emotionally that you never had to give your own decisions, your own personality, more than a fleeting thought at times? Relying on others is bound to be your downfall, and you know it, Type 6.

You understand that this behavior can be unhealthy for both you and the person you rely so heavily on upon, but you might find yourself in the sense of denial. You don't want to face reality, that you may have already begun to lose a sense of identity and personality that may have once been very clear to you. There are ways you can get it back and keep it for good, but they aren't easy.

The hardest habit to break for you, the loyalist, is going to be the process of letting go of your crutch or crutches. Of course, you don't have actually to let go of those people entirely, but you have to stop relying so heavily on them for everything. Your tendency to latch onto things and not let go is going to bring both you and them down at some point. Someday, you will be faced with a decision, and you will not have had the proper experience you need to deal with making that decision.

Start improving your decision-making skills now by making your own decisions every day. Whether it is your order at a restaurant, or forcing yourself to have a conversation on the phone with someone you may not have spoken to recently, you need to force yourself to make those tiny but meaningful decisions as often as possible.

For Types 5 and 7, who may become obsessed with control, you are, someday, going to be faced with a situation wherein there will be a totally unexpected variable. This is something that, ultimately, is unavoidable. You have to learn that there's simply no way you could ever hope to gain total control over your environment. It isn't the situation which judges your character, but how you react to unprecedented circumstances. Truly, what you do in the face of chaos is what will define your character. Learn to expect the unexpected, and prepare as much as you see fit for whatever you think is necessary to be prepared for. Beyond that, there's little you can do aside from watch and wait. You can predict, of course, but your prediction will only get you so far.

In the face of chaos, understand that to have total mastery of your situation is totally impossible and that the sooner you come to terms with that, the happier you are going to be in the situation where something occurred that was unexpected. In addition, every unknown element is a possible learning opportunity. Whether it takes the form of something you thought you knew about something you were studying that, it turns out, was totally unknown to you after all, or a surprising aspect that ruins your plans for the day, anything that comes up in the way of your everyday life that seems to only be there to ruin your day or your plans, is really a learning opportunity in disguise, is treated the right way. Keep in mind that being flexible and adaptable is more important than being perfect, types 5 and 7!

You have different experiences and different personalities all together, although usually there will be more broad similarities than differences. Keeping that in mind, you are unique to the entire world comparable to everyone else, in your enneagram type or not.

You know different things, and you don't know different things. You are bound to know many things that will help you and be ignorant of other important pieces of advice. This is why humans work best in groups—they can rely on one another to complement each other's' strengths and weaknesses, build each other up, and together form a more perfect example of a human than what one person would have amounted to all on their own. Of course, there are many other things into consideration when moving toward spiritual growth.

CHAPTER 4: ENNEAGRAM AND ANCIENT TEACHINGS

Chances are you've already heard comments from numerous experts on the Enneagram. As you've already gathered, it is a symbol shrouded in mystical significance and the meaning and its different elements are not always clearly understood. This makes it difficult for some to embrace the idea; the lack of a direct explanation of the whole process often leaves some suspicious and wary, feeling that they may be entering a world of occultism.

For many, the occult is exactly what they think of when looking at the Enneagram symbol. Our minds automatically go there because it so closely resembles the pentagram which is directly connected to modern occultism. This makes many pull back out of fear that they are getting involved in something dangerously mysterious and dark. However, by examining the symbol exclusive of any preconceived notions and clearing your mind from those ideas people tend to automatically associate with it, we begin to see some similarities that we can find in other more acceptable beliefs of our society.

It's a natural part of who we are to want to know more about the origins of anything we get involved in, and while the explanation of the symbol itself can sometimes seem vague and obscure, we have been able to uncover enough to unlock the true meaning of the Enneagram symbol.

However, it is very important to point out that the Enneagram we use today has changed a bit from its original purpose. One of the best ways to decipher it is by starting with the human mind. It is a natural tendency for our human brains to view images and break them down into different categories. Nothing fancy, it's just what the human brain is designed for. Since Gurdjieff is considered to be the father of the modern Enneagram, many will automatically associate the modern Enneagram with his symbol. Gurdjieff's teachings leaned heavily on the metaphysical - a means of organizing natural principles and using them to explain how the universe actually works.

There were three basic principles of Gurdjieff's metaphysical theory, all utilizing the Enneagram symbol. The Law of Seven, Unity, and the Law of Three.

The Law of Seven: this law focused on the constant vibrations we all have around us. It is a little different from the Newtonian physics we have come to understand from modern science. Rather than what we've been taught - an object in motion stays in motion, the Law of Seven sees the world as a series of vibrations. According to this law, each object in motion must pass through seven separate stages before it comes to a stop. This means that the energy is not evenly spent but is instead lost at very specific points before it can receive an additional infusion of energy to continue along its path.

His theory was based on the seven note musical octave with the idea that in nature, once something is in motion, that motion cannot be sustained forever. No matter what it is, it must deviate or change at specific intervals. As you go through a musical scale, for example, as the energy vibrations increase or decrease, the consistent rate naturally changes at certain points. With music, the points have been identified as the mi/fa point, and the si/do point. So, in an octave of do re mi fa so la ti do, the intervals where vibrations change would be between the mi and the fa at one point, and the si and the do at another point.

Of course, there is a lot more to the theory of the Law of Seven that we won't go into here.

According to Gurdjieff, the energy that is spent in vibrations does not uniformly dissipate but instead is lost at very precise points where it can receive an extra impulse to keep it going along its path.

Unity: When you first look at the Enneagram symbol, your eyes will automatically recognize the circle first. This is the universal symbol of unity and infinity. It can also signify the oneness and eternal nature of a Supreme Being. To Gurdjieff, the circle represented two different forms of thinking. First, everything in the universe has a place; everything belongs with no exclusions. And secondly, the symbol was used to encourage a panoramic and more receptive awareness of the whole picture. This is done without judgment or labeling of anything as either good or bad. Anyone who can do this is able therefore to see the world in its true state and not be influenced by prejudices and personal preferences.

The Law of Three or the Triangle: This law represents the union of three fundamental things. First and foremost, the Supreme Being of the universe (God) determines its nature and structure. Secondly, its organizing principle, and finally - the power he has to pull it all together. All three of these elements are key to understanding Gurdjieff's teachings of the Law of Three.

It is clear that Gurdjieff's teachings were extremely complex and detailed but understanding just these basic facts is key to being able to grasp the true purpose of the symbol. As human beings, we have always been in a sort of quandary. On the one hand, we are always in search of our own individuality, but on the other hand, we have a powerful, inbred need to belong to something bigger than ourselves. While the western world leaned more towards seeing the individual to the point where nearly everything became disconnected, the eastern world strived for community and connectivity almost to the complete obliteration of the individual.

When you see the world with more importance placed on connections, the price you pay is a loss of human dignity which is sacrificed for the sake of the whole. On the other hand, when too much importance is placed on the individual, the cost is the infringement on the rights of others. Therefore, the ability to create a balance between the two is essential and having the Spiritual Being holding it all together is key. With a Supreme Being, both unity and diversity can have an equal part in our lives, and we learn to live for both ourselves and for others.

While the ancient history of this symbol may seem vague and elusive, our modern understanding can offer us an even clearer meaning. Today, the symbol is used primarily as a schematic on a number of different personalities.

While the symbol we use today is not exactly the same as the symbol that he used (it has been refined over the decades to be more applicable to the world's society of today), it has many practical applications once you begin to break it down. There are many different ideas as to how to use the symbol. With so many different personalities it is difficult at a glance to know where you actually fit on the personality spectrum. However, you will have some very keen insight into the wisdom of the Enneagram so you can know exactly where you fit in the whole scheme of things.

Today's Enneagram

As we've already pointed out, the structure of the Enneagram is simply a circle with numbers and lines contained within it. Each of these numbers, circles, and lines can be analyzed and viewed from totally different aspects.

At first glance, the idea of a circle with numbered lines doesn't mean very much. At least, not until you begin to learn what each of these markings actually means. In the basic Enneagram symbol, the circle is a symbol of unity. The nine personality types are all equidistant from each other showing that they are all equal to one another. No single personality has more influence or power over any other. In essence, we all start on the same equal footing.

An inner triangle formed by connecting the points at the numbers three, six, and nine. This triangle represents a powerful and dynamic interaction of three different forces.

The Circle: You will see that there are nine different points spaced out around the circumference of the circle. We already understand that the circle is a representation of unity and the nine points are all equidistant from one another. This shows that each personality is equal but still connected to the others.

The Triangle: If you look closely, you will see an inner triangle that connects the three points at three, six, and nine. This represents the dynamic interaction of three very powerful forces. If you were to take two opposites, for example, the connecting force between the two would be some form of middle ground or a blend of each of the polar opposites. Here, three Enneagram Clusters are connected together by the triangle.

Hexad: If you were to look even closer, you would also see an irregular figure that connects all of the other six points. This part of the symbol represents the dynamic change we must all go through. As you will learn later, everyone has their own dominant personality, but it is not in control all the time. We are all constantly switching from one personality to another, each one represented by the Hexad, which connects them all together.

The Numbers: The nine numbers around the circumference represent the nine different personality types. Each type comes with its own seed of motivation that is responsible for triggering certain behaviors. While we all have a mixture of different personality types, we still have a primary or a stronger Enneagram type, which is responsible for our personal views on life, the actions we take, and how we respond to the world around us.

The Arrows: What you may not readily see in some Enneagram symbols are the arrows. However, if you see one with arrow tips at the ends of the lines, you'll notice that they follow a very exact structure that shows just how people shift personalities under varying circumstances. When you are under stress, confident, or achieving a personal level of growth, your behaviors will automatically and instinctively shift from one personality to another within your Cluster. We will move along those connecting paths following the directions of the arrows.

Arrows moving backward represent your stress personality which is your automatic way of separating yourself from your usual behavior and protecting yourself from emotional damage. When some people face severe stress, they could switch to this stress point and remain there before they feel safe enough to return to their dominant personality.

On the other hand, forward pointing arrows travel a path to a more secure place that will permit you to perform safer behaviors. When you are at your security point, you are usually in familiar surroundings with people you can trust. When you are healthy, you might make a move to your Integration Point. This is where you blend together qualities that will create a delicate balance between confidence and structure. If you're looking to grow, it is important that you embrace these Security Points and follow those healthy behaviors applying them in your life.

By now, you've probably already begun to identify with a particular personality type. In fact, you've probably narrowed it down to several. If you're interested in pinpointing exactly which personality type you are, there are several resources you can find online that can help you. Some of them are free but those worth their salt will cost you a little bit of money to take the test. However, the benefits you can gain from this knowledge can be very valuable to you and can help you to improve your life in many different ways.

It is easy to see why so many people are intrigued by the Enneagram and what it can mean for them. It is a tool that gives you the ability to look at your own life and see it for what it really is. It provides the right frame for looking inside and identifying specific patterns that have been influencing your every decision since birth.

With this increased knowledge about yourself, you can feel empowered to venture off into different territories that reach outside of your personal comfort zone. As you do, your life's purpose will become clearer and your course in life, your destiny will unfold before you. Learning your Enneagram personality is just as much a spiritual journey as it is a psychological one, but if you take it with an open mind, it is possible for you to achieve greater intelligence about the human mind and discover your personal calling. However, it will require you to look deeper below the surface at what's inside for you to do so.

The Iceberg

Humans are highly complex creatures and are made up of many different elements. While we all have the same components, it is the unique combination of those elements that make us individuals. Your personality is made up of a delicate composite of several elements that reflect not just your inner feelings and experiences but also shows up in how you express yourself and interact with those around you.

It has often been described as an iceberg. While the iceberg is massive in size, what you see above the surface of the water are simply those elements that you are consciously aware of. It is the part of our personality that we allow others to see. Beneath the surface, the part of us that either we are not aware of or the part that we will try desperately to hide from those in our lives.

These hidden elements are the very things that drive us to perform certain behaviors. To put it more simply, those hidden parts of our personality can be described as those things that we feel while those things that are visible to our naked eye could be viewed as the elements that inform us and we consciously react to. Together these all encourage our behavior and give us the motivation to do the things we do.

In order for the Enneagram to be most effective and beneficial for us, we must address what is both above and below the line. The combination is what provides us with the insight and the wisdom to make the changes we may feel we need to improve.

CHAPTER 5: KNOW YOUR ENNEAGRAM TYPE: PERSONALITY TEST

By reading our introduction you are probably raring to find out which your personality type is, and from there you can jump to the page which describes you.

Well, before you come to that conclusion, you need to realise that we all have a basic personality type, but learning about all nine is the best way to truly understand yourself, because everyone has a tiny facet of the other types in them too.

First things first however, how do you find out your core type?

Brutal honesty is the way forward!

Finding out your core personality type in truth is not a short process and it is something which takes time and thought. There are countless Enneagram tests online which will help you gain some insight, and the RHETI (Riso-Hudson Enneagram Type Indicator) is the most commonly used. This particular test has been scientifically validated, and is thought to be around 80% accurate in most cases. On top of this, another credible source is the TAS Questionnaire in The Wisdom of Enneagram. Again, this is scientifically validated, and offers the same high level of accuracy.

There are many shorter online personality tests you can take, if you want to simply start thinking about what type of personality you are, before giving in to self-reflection to truly arrive at the most accurate result for you.

- Think carefully, think about how you react, how you feel, and how you behave on a daily basis

- Be totally and brutally honest, even ask a close friend or family member to list your attributes and behavior patterns if that helps

- Take an online personality test and assess the results – do you agree with them?

- Use a scientifically validated test, such as the TAS Questionnaire, or the RHETI, which we mentioned above

- Think a little more – do you agree with the results? It's important to realise that you might be surprised, so don't discount the results because you simply don't think you display a certain characteristic; you might have it without realizing! Again, ask a close friend or family member for advice

- Once you have gone through this process you should finally come up with a type which reflects you.

We are rarely purely one type

Throughout your decision journey, it's important to note that we are very rarely one type only; we are complicated beings, and therefore we display characteristics of various types – however with that in mind, there should be one type which comes up time and time again, and that is your core personality type.

Whilst we are all born with one particular main type within us, it's likely that this doesn't really show itself too much until the teenage years appear which we all know is a time of experiment and self-discovery in itself. During the 20s, the main personality type will show itself more so, and this is when Enneagram becomes much easier to pinpoint.

Once you realise which personality type you truly are, the journey certainly does not end there
Quite frankly, the whole palava is only just beginning!

The whole point of Enneagram is to use your personality type results to help you understand your inner being in a much more detailed way. Once you figure out which is your main personality type, this is just step one on your journey to self-discovery, self-development, and self-enlightenment.

You can use your results to pinpoint the negative parts of your personality and improve upon them; however it's also worthwhile knowing that everyone has their faults, so Enneagram is never going to make you a 100% perfect person. On top of this, understanding your strengths by pinpointing your personality type can allow you to develop them further, and use them for good, rather than negative causes.

What are Levels of Development?

If you have read anything about Enneagram before, you might have heard of Levels of Development, and you might be wondering what this is all about.
Once you pinpoint your core personality type, you can begin your journey into developing your understanding, using the results to develop as a person. Levels of Development therefore describe how an individual's personality type shifts and changes as they become more familiar with it, and as they develop more a person overall.

Over time, everyone heads upwards and downwards within the line level of their particular personality type, and this changes especially as an individual becomes more au fait with their type, and as a result, their true inner being.

Different personality types

In our coming chapters we will discuss each of the nine personality types in detail. Whilst it is important to truly explore the type you are, e.g. if you are identified as a type four, you should read and re-read that particular chapter; you should also read the others, because as we have discussed, everyone has facets of every type of personality to some degree or another, and to truly understand yourself as a person, and your inner and higher being, you need to see every single facet of it.

Of course, you could also argue that understanding all nine personality types can help you in your social life too, as understanding other people is key to having healthy, functioning relationships, in your personal, work, and social lives.

CHAPTER 6: THE 9 ENNEAGRAM PERSONALITY TYPES DECIPHERED

People vary physically, meaning you can distinguish one person from the other through various features such as their skin complexions, their hair, their height, their weight, and their shapes amongst others. That said, we could classify them further and group those who share these traits together and give those names as we did blonds, blacks, white, and tall.

The same way we classify people with their physical attributes we can classify them with their individual and particular personalities. There is a reason why the world is as it is, why we attain certain achievements in life, why we excel in different areas in life, why we handle situations as we do, why some relationships last and some don't why we handle pain differently and why some people are more social than others. Our personalities, determine a lot in a person because the shape our attitudes towards different stimuli in our environments. This eventually alters our approach and reactions to such circumstances.

Personalities are the people we are or rather the kind of personality we possess. For example, you meet a person covered in tattoos and dreadlocks. One person may assume they are immoral individuals with no respect for religion and therefore dangerous. Another person may think that it's rather impressive, attractive and that he or she has an artistic and creative personality. These different reactions are drawn because of the different personalities within us. This can also apply in our relationships, normally unlike people attract and end up having amazing relationships and this is where people will say "opposites attract". However, imagine a case where no one was different or special? What you stand for is what the next person stands for and the other and the other. Naturally this would bore you to death, listening to the same songs, loving the same things, doing the same careers, having the same opinions and so on. At first this all sounds so interesting and fun but if you contextualize it and put it into perspective, you realize that with time it becomes overwhelming and boring. Then there would be no point of conversing because no different ideologies are being exchanged just the same old things redundantly. This would kill so many relationships as there is no excitement or exploration of different perspectives between people and life. This challenging no purpose and no fulfillment, just reciprocity everywhere, meaning it would be lost in life.

Another area that will be affected by this is our careers because we are moved by the same stimuli pushing us into wanting to achieve the same goals which isn't necessarily a bad thing but can lead to stagnation as there are so many areas in life that need to be tapped into and exploited.

We are pushed by different things and moved by different stimuli leading us to our destined paths, where we are also pushed differently to achieve or reach different levels of our chosen paths. That is the reason why some end up in management, some stagnate, some starts rival businesses and some opt out and choose different paths in life. Our personalities shape our thinking, attitudes, perceptions, beliefs and behaviors. They make us who we are. They make life what it is.

There are various groupings of personalities and they are grouped together because of their strongest traits or the one thing about them that stands out most. We'll look at each of the Nine groupings and how it affects the people towards relations, success, purpose and overall approach what they face in life.

The Perfectionist

The perfectionist, just as their name suggests, they are always keeping it 100. In whatever aspect of life, they do it to the best of their ability, they take life very seriously and whatever tasks the take on they either do it perfectly or don't do it at all. With type Ones, there in no in-between. They are honest, dependable and use common sense. They will make great efforts in straightening the conditions around them. Whatever seems off they would go extra miles to put it back to how it should be even if it is a small change to something.

The challenge comes when their point of view isn't attainable or when what they are trying to change cannot be changed. This drives a hole through them because they are idealistic and believe that everything should be complete and in perfect accuracy. This is a big challenge that affects their perceptions and attitudes towards different aspects of their lives.

For example, in relationships they might try to make their partners see things as they do and try making them have a common point of view with them towards everything. This, in most cases, would make them vulnerable to being prideful and might come off as rude or arrogant possibly lead them to poor relationships and interactions. The ability to take and receive information willingly from different parties is what makes communication and relations what they are and adds meat to the bone. Having a strong minded individual who has strong beliefs about what he knows can be very frustrating at times and can drive away interest or lead to arguments that are pointless, especially if they are wrong.

Their purpose in life in general can also have its fair share of effects from their personality. By this I mean that because they do not accept less than perfect and struggle taking others' opinions they might end up wasting their time, money and energy into trying to prove facts that are nonexistent. Causing them to chase dead causes and since they don't share freely, end up suffering emotionally and psychologically, keeping all of their hurt within themselves and refusing to share.
It isn't all bad though because their perfectionist nature serves them well at most times as they tend to be honest and responsible, meaning they often try and get their facts right. They take full responsibility of their actions, making them reliable people to turn to for advice because they tend to see reality for what it is; right from wrong, good from bad and black from white. Their clarity is essential in life and offers a clear perspective of their journey, allowing them. This is a very important tool in life because life is all about improving and working on your flaws while dropping what doesn't work to attain the end product of being we intend or wish to be.

The Giver or Helper

The second personality is the Giver; I can call them the "fit in" crew, since they like to seek human approval from amongst those they interact with. To them, approval is of utmost importance even if means making personal sacrifices on different things in their life. This personality is cautious of everything they say and can be good individuals to nurture and guide as they try seeing things from your perspective, accommodating or welcoming your thoughts, therefore giving you great advice and opinions on life. This though comes at a cost because having nothing you stand for can make you lose your identity as a person even if it benefits the other parties. The givers are very caring and they like to make sure everyone is 'okay' especially their friends and family. And also this is a very good trait, they can sometimes get stuck in situations where they believe everyone is selfish, however they made need to realize that they themselves need to be a little more selfish.

This affects different aspects of their lives, for example work, friendships and their relationships. They are very loving and accommodating people and the fact that they actually take time to know you and understand things as you see them, means that they are very good people to relate to. Work with and have as friends. As said before this can have a down side where they may depend on people's approval. Lack of approval can then lead them to going into breakdowns and losing self-esteem, lowering their confidence in what they offer or bring to the table.

Independence of thought and having something you stand for brings about purpose and drive in an individual. Lack of that independence would mean someone is easily swayable and gullible, limiting his or her attitude and perception towards people in life. Some would argue that the Givers accommodative and adaptive nature makes them likeable and therefore more opportunities would be presented to them, this making them able to climb the corporate ladder faster than others would. They have a strong ability to welcome other people's ideas and thoughts causing people to view them as the go-to guy or girl. Givers solve anything that is put in front of them. And because of their socializing skills they are able to build a network faster than anyone else causing them to be greater at a lot of tasks, especially team based ones.

The giver may be dependent on other people as a source of

happiness and success and this might lead him into being exploited for approval and taken advantage of. They can find themselves being naïve, thinking they are winning the trust and approval of others but they may be taken advantage of for the gain of others. This has a lot of hypocrisy in it and because of the constant change of personality to suit the situation, the giver might always struggle being appreciated for whom they truly are. Givers love to "give" and overall have an approachable and calming manner that others love to have around. They just need to be careful when being too nice, because some people out their take it for granted!

The Performer

The third personality type is the Performer. He is goal oriented and hugely motivated allowing him or her to achieve great success. Their sole agenda is to make it in life because they are driven by being the odd one out. Most of the time they puts their success before their feelings, opinions and life. To them the best image they can portray of themselves is the revenge they can dish out for being sidelined. They are so obsessed with their image; they don't have time for other things in life which limits their scope and range, lacking to reach people.

They are high achievers mainly because they have dedicated most of their time and life into perfecting their craft. The following their dreams and passion, they can lead towards to developing health and psychological issue like fatigue, depression from possible lack of accomplishment. This may be because minimal time is spent taking care of their health and wellbeing and more on what they need to achieve career wise. The performer and the perfectionist share certain traits, for example, their obsession with achieving goals and doing it in the right way. This meaning that for the performer, nothing less than a hundred percent is accepted and this often leads them being very successful in whatever they do. They can also motivate themselves to overcome hurdles and push others to achieve their dreams and aspirations because they know what it entails. They're very good leaders and this make them exceptional at careers such as sports, acting and taking any entrepreneurial pathway.

The performer should allow life to take place, flow with it and experience all it has to offer. Accept all of its ups and down, and enjoy all experiences that they dive into, so they can draw their own conclusions in anything they tackle in life.

The Romantic

The romantic type is about creativity and using art as a medium to channel their views, opinions and feelings. Different people have different ways in which we channel what is inside us. For some other personalities like the perfectionist they prefer keeping it within them and focusing on other things to stop thinking about their situations. The performer channels it to his work and through the high levels of success he attains.

On the other side the romantic has their own way of channeling his feelings, thoughts and attitudes. They do it through art, music, dance and poetry. Sentimental and elaborate when it comes to expressing their thoughts. They are passionate when moving between expressing what other people feel and what they them self feel. The romantics are emotional individuals who comprehend emotion better than any other personality group, allowing them to reach other individuals who couldn't reach the comprehension point or understand their emotions through art.

Because of their emotional nature they need time to understand and accept whatever it is they are facing before they can welcome the world into their thoughts. They are very fragile and should be handled with care, because they carry so much emotion.

The romantic can be dynamic when it comes to mood in that he or she may be excited at times or dull depending on what he or she has on their plate at the time. They go through life with an open heart, ready for new experiences and they can take that with them on any task or career they want to tackle.

It's best for Romantics to balance between all emotions that occur and understand that they all happen for a reason. Doing this will draw different reactions for them, teaching them different things that help them develop better interactions and problem-solving skills.

The Observer

The fifth personality we are going to look at is the Observer. These people are the introverts in society. They are keen on what takes place around them and do not accept things for what they are. They like to question everything they know and analyze their surroundings to draw meanings and conclusions to everything. The observer tends to dwell alone as he goes about formulating his ideologies. To him, family might be important, but his own interests are of more importance. They don't often indulge in small talk due to their introverted sociological environment and this is because they do not like sharing personal information and tends to keep a lot to them. They like to come up with conclusions and solutions from what they have experienced and from the various analyses they have found in their lives.

The observer does not like indulging in small talk and is more comfortable talking or discussing things that they actually excel at or expert in. This is because they fear what they don't know due to the fact that it makes them feel inferior and unknowledgeable. That said though they don't like sharing all the information the have about a particular topic of interest because they're advanced in it. Making it possible that they may be giving too much 'valuable' information away.

The Observers should drop down the walls they have built and share more, accepting more people in their life. This will help them avoid loneliness and also widen their range of knowledge, towards more things that they may be interested in life. Observers are very smart and are considered highly valuable people.

The Loyal Skeptic

Two main things characterize this group: their ability to judge characters and situations and their ability. This category of people will always be on the lookout for people and situations that bring them harm and hurt to their families or loved ones. The simple reason being to them that people have different attitudes and intentions and it's up to them to figure them out and come up with quick solutions to whatever they might be. They do not trust easily but when they do, they trust very strongly, making them a great close friend because they will most definitely have your back.

The loyal skeptics are quick to come up with solutions and always remain ahead of the competition or situation, allowing them to be in control of their life making it easier for them to make decisions. They are strategic in how they come up with solutions because they either stop a problem or offer remedies to one empirically. They are courageous and selfless acting to ensure the safety and security of those they care about.

They are very attentive to people and situations because they are strategic. Every detail is relevant in coming up with control or preventive measures to whatever they face. They set high walls that others should prove beyond to protect their own emotional wellbeing from wrong people. They are brave; therefore ask serious questions, leading them to aggressive or pushy attitudes.
The Loyal-Skeptic should welcome more opinions and emotions to their lives and become more accommodating to everyone. This will allow them to grow as individuals, developing a sense of purpose holistically other than their careers just solely. Overall Type 6 is obviously very loyal making them a great friend and person to work with. They are very smart and love to protect those in their life who deserve to be protected.

The Dreamer

The seventh personality is the epicure, the dynamic crew. These are the ones that value freedom. They are in it for the experience, and they are driven by exploration. Type 7's wants to visit different places, learn new things, explore different continents and live in the moment. They are never really stagnant.

This group of personalities are therefore always on the go achieving, realizing and exploring. It gives them so much exposure and makes them good people to befriend and talk to because they have a scope of what to talk about and knowledge on the diversified cultures. This is why they should all be appreciated. They are generally very likeable people.

This group though is very uncommitted and undecided on what they want, they hop from one thing to another, and this gives them a sense of purpose and accomplishment, allowing them to draw meaning from their lives. They are all about what works for them and people's opinions don't really faze them. They tend to focus mostly on what they love and go about it whenever and however they see fit. They tend to have an attitude of avoiding their challenges and focus mainly on what's going on correctly. The Epicure group should try to accept that other people hold different opinions and feelings and they do to. Accepting this as a fact and understanding it entirely will help them develop better qualities and become better people all round.

Type 7's like to think as if 'Everything happens for a reason' and this is a powerful mindset to have.

The Challenger

The protectors often come out and speak on behalf of the rest. They have strong standings and beliefs causing them to be very assertive. They air the opinions and thoughts everyone else holds but cannot communicate. They believe that not standing for your rights and defending your opinions leads to exploitation and they term it as weakness.

Protectors are enthusiastic in that they are always on the ready no matter the situation. They await new situations that will come up against what they stand for and defend it fiercely and make sure their opinions are heard and respected by all. Type 8's is powerful people, allowing them to accomplish any task ahead of them. They also put facts as they are, without fear of contradiction.

These individuals, like all the other personalities, have their downfalls, one of them being they are excessive. By this, we mean at times they cross certain lines trying to stand or fight for their rights. It's okay fighting for your rights and enjoying your freedom of expression but all things are done with both sides of the coin flipped. Where one person's rights start is where others end. These people might tend to cross this bridge knowingly or unknowingly from time to time.

The Protector can be quite dominant because their ideals and opinions were not supported. An attitude or perception may have been developed towards themselves if this is the case. Group 8's should try to understand cooperation and mutual understanding, as a means to resolve more issues and make their life easier.

The Peacemaker

The final personalities are the Mediators. The mediator's main aim is to bring peace between two torn parties. This means they are welcoming to all opinions and suggestions as they aim to find a balance between all that is presented before them.

They are characterized positively by balance. They find the perfect balance between the two stories and draw sensible or workable conclusions that are accepted by both parties. Secondly, they are accepting, by this I mean that they consider other people's points of view. Lastly, they are harmonious, meaning that their main aim is to draw a reasonable and acceptable conclusion to issues and phenomenon in the calmest manner possible.

With positives also come negative and type 9's have their downsides like all the rest despite their calm and approachable nature. Firstly, they are stubborn because of their drive to get information for resolution provision, they persist an issue until a situation is fully settled and they are also conflict avoidant. They aim to avoid conflict completely, even if at times it might be the best way to find a resolution and this can be cause due to their fear of the situation escalating and going out of hand.

Mediators offer solutions and are open to ideas and opinions which make them stand out in a group. The mediators should understand that at times conflict management is essential in drawing conclusions and getting solutions to most issues in society right now.

All these different personalities are what give life its essence. The personality of an individual as seen affects almost everything in life from the way we understand things, relate to people the way we solve situations. Ignorance can make one think that someone is rude or someone else is easy going. Understanding that people handle things differently and taking time to appreciate it and understand it puts a lot of perspective into human life and allows us to tap into human potential. It's important to accept the environment, as it is where everyone is given equal chances to be whom he or she is and express themselves in whatever way. Each personality has its own strengths and weakness and understanding that will allow you to drive further action in life and build greater relationships.

CHAPTER 7: PRACTICES FOR EACH
PERSONALITY TYPE

Though this newfound insight into personality is little more than a fun game that lets you compare yourself to other people. However, anyone who makes the mistake of seeing the Enneagram as simply a form of entertainment will lose a valuable opportunity when it comes to making sense of their life and the world around them. Used correctly, the insights offered by the Enneagram can enable you to connect to the core of which you are as a person, recognize and improve on your weaknesses, identify and foster your unique strengths, and develop skills to better understand and relate to the people around you."

Your first dip into the Enneagram can be both comforting and jarring. On one hand, there is an entire group of people who share your core motivations and fears and with whom you can probably relate more than you ever realized. On the other hand, there is a whole world of other "types" out there, and these people operate, in varying degrees, on what seems like an entirely different value system. Be careful, though, not to confuse "type" with the identity of one's "true self." The Enneagram, rather than being prescriptive and static, is descriptive in nature, covering a dynamic range of integration and stress points. On the surface, what the bare bones of the Enneagram types initially describe is not necessarily your true self but rather the fears and motivations that drive your actions and behaviors. Oftentimes, these fears and motivations set up barriers which actually prevent us from connecting with our true selves. A deeper understanding of those barriers can be the first step in breaking those barriers down and discovering the depth with which you can truly know yourself. Once that breakdown has occurred, you have the choice to offer yourself compassion and forgiveness or to begin the process of rebuilding those same familiar walls between your "personality" and your "true self."

By understanding those things which act as barriers to the discovery of our true selves, we begin to identify our points of weakness and our shortcomings. While this isn't fun for anyone, it's helpful. And not only that; it is essential if one is to achieve true integration and self-knowledge. The Enneagram elucidates the various coping mechanisms we use when under pressure. These are the same coping mechanisms which carried us through our childhood and which we are now experts at employing.

With coping mechanisms such as "reaction formation" (One) and "overindulgence" (Eight), and we downplay the harmful effects of these defenses by re-labeling them as valued principals like "virtue" and "courage." In true integration, the One finds real virtue, and the Eight demonstrates actual courage, but by leaning too heavily into our coping mechanisms, we risk experiencing only the shadow of what these principles represent.

The root cause of our fears, coping mechanisms, and motivations, we start to understand the patterns which dominate our decision-making processes. Knowing our "blind spots" and the root of these weaknesses has a two-fold effect: It gives us the knowledge necessary to understand and accept our weaknesses, and it gives us the tools necessary to thrive and utilize our strengths so that we might challenge the perceived limitations of our personality.

While we are in the process of integration, or even before we begin any type of journey toward integration, we need to protect ourselves. In life situations where the stakes are high, we can harness the knowledge of our own weaknesses and use that knowledge to help us avoid failure while also maximizing our chance for success.

Of course, living a life of limitation and avoidance isn't quite the key to growth and integration, but we often need to take a step back before we can start climbing, assess our situation, prepare ourselves, and give ourselves the grace of accepting our imperfections before embarking on the upward journey of connection with our true selves. Once we understand the wounds and insecurities that give birth to our weaknesses, we can begin the work of self-forgiveness and self-compassion, and out of that springs the tools we'll use to work towards true self-knowledge.

When a Five begins the process of becoming self-aware, he may seek to take great care when creating a schedule for the week, choosing not to overbook himself with things that do not add value to his life so that he is able to maintain appropriate energy levels and be present for those things which are truly valuable to him. He may also be sure to schedule in time for solitude in an activity which truly refreshes him, whether it be reading, listening to lectures, or engaging in a specialized hobby. By understanding his limits and moving toward a point where he can thrive within them, he may at some point be able to focus his attention outward and maybe even attempt to push those limits ever so slightly.

Instead of denying our weaknesses or trying to "correct" them by counteracting them and pushing our limits, the Enneagram helps us to understand the root cause of our weaknesses and to develop a sense of self-compassion out of which we can thrive and move towards integration.

Simply put, there are going to be things you're good at, and there are going to be things that make you look like a fish trying to climb a tree. While it's good and healthy to challenge yourself from time to time, you want to avoid the psychological pitfalls that come with perpetually identifying oneself as "the fish that can't climb a tree."

Do people gravitate to you when they want advice (Two)? Do they call you up when they want to forget about their problems and does something fun (Seven)? Do they turn to you for pens, information, Band-Aides, etc., knowing that nine times out of ten, you are prepared for everything (Six)?

The Enneagram can help shed light on those things which just come naturally to you, and better, it can help you understand why this is the case. If you are known as a "charmer" (Three), considers your motivations, and then begins to shift that focus from a point where these motivations serve yourself to where your "charm" actually becomes a practice where you genuinely see and acknowledge the good in others. Instead of "flattery," you offer "loving truths." Instead of "performing," you are "connecting."

Each of the nine types has an innate ability to see the world in a unique way. Each of the nine types offers an essential and indispensable gift to the world. A lot of Enneagram literature talks about the weaknesses each type has, and this is not without good reason. What helps us to identify our type tends to be the hang-ups that keep us from being more like the other types, the things that handicap us from having empathy for those who don't think like us. However, by understanding what our weaknesses are, we can move beyond them.

Once you've mastered self-compassion, it's time to move on to empathy, which, when put into action, translates into having compassion for others. The Enneagram does is that it gives us the tools we need to experience the world through others' eyes. While we all have one dominant type, most of us can find at least one or two ways that we can relate to the other types. Who among us has NEVER felt curious or afraid or self-righteous? Just because your dominant type may experience one of these things more intensely than the others doesn't mean you don't, at some level, have something in common with the other eight types. By studying the fears and motivations of each type, we may find that we can identify a little bit with each number. We can begin to understand what it might be like to experience different aspects of our personality in a more intensified way and to feel overwhelmed by certain thought patterns that our personality may typically repress or avoid.

Once we've gotten in touch with empathy, we can work toward a stance of compassion for others, where we not only understand how others might feel, but we choose to take action by connecting with people. When we understand the various ways that people interpret our behaviors and how our behaviors translate into expressions of value and love, we begin to find creative ways to adjust our stance and the way we communicate. We begin to understand how we can interact with people in a way that communicates value and love as we intend to express it.

By understanding that a Four has a strong need to not only experience each emotion as it comes but also to be understood, you might choose to let him talk through a problem he is having. Instead of offering a quick solution or a distraction, you can challenge yourself to sit in his pain with him, as uncomfortable as that might be, and to connect with him by simply being present.
By understanding that a Nine is likely to deny her own desires for the sake of promoting harmony, you might think to offer choices when deciding on an activity rather than asking "Do you want to [insert what you want to do]?" Along with offering choices, you may also choose to use language which promotes the truth that the

Nine in your life matters and that her voice, her desires, and her ideas matter as well.

As we work towards integration, we can hopefully get to a point where value and love, as we understand it, are not defined by the superficialities attached to our specific "type" or how we interpret another's "type" but simply by the understanding that value is innate in us and that love surrounds us.

Our journey of integration begins when we acknowledge our shortcomings and choose to practice self-compassion. As we continue to grow and shift our focus outward, we allow empathy to color our worldview. The path of integration reaches a critical point when we begin to give action to that empathy and manifest compassion for those around us. This outward focus connects us to others, and, ultimately, it is what helps us to realize and connect with our true selves.

CHAPTER 8: ESSENTIAL ENNEAGRAM TEST FOR BEGINNERS

Please read these instructions carefully before starting the test. This test is designed to assess your personality type according to the Enneagram of Personality theory.

This questionnaire contains 126 statements. Please read carefully each one of them and mark with a circle the answer you believe is the better description of how you stand on each statement.

There is no "right" or "wrong" answers and you don't have to be an expert in order to complete the questionnaire. Describe yourself in a sincere and precise way. Mark your answers in a way that describes you as you are at the present moment and not how you want to be. A failure to answer in an honest way wills most likely compromise the test results and yields an unreliable assessment of your personality.

Please answer ALL the questions. Make sure every answer is marked in the enumerated spot in the answer sheet corresponding to its enumerated statement in this booklet.

Questionnaire

1. I do things according to a plan.

2. I make people feel welcome.

3. I want to be the very best.
4. I think that I'm better than other people.

5. I like to solve complex problems.

6. I try out new things.

7. I do most of the talking.

8. I will agree to anything.

9. I like to plan ahead.

10.I anticipate the needs of others.

11.I want to be in charge.

12.I would like to have more power than other people.

13.I love to read challenging material.

14.I learn things slowly.

15.I am relaxed most of the time.
16. I am open to change.

17. I demand attention.

18. I remain calm under pressure.

19. I pay attention to details.

20. I love to help others.

21. I try to surpass others' accomplishments.

22. I am easily intimidated.

23. I can handle a lot of information.

24. I get overwhelmed by emotions.

25. I Let myself go.

26. I speak loudly.

27. I keep a cool head.

28. I demand quality.

29. I won't take the blame for something that's not my fault.

30. I try to outdo others.

31. I give in to no one.

32. I carry the conversation to a higher level.

33. I fear for the worst.

35. I take the initiative.

36. I am calm even in tense situations

37. I set high standards for myself and others.

39. I never give up.

40. I believe only in myself.

41. I find political discussions interesting.
42. I dislike myself.

43. I like to visit new places.

44. I readily overcome setbacks.

45. I let other people take the credit for my work.

46. I make well-considered decisions.

47. I suffer from others' sorrows.

48. I go straight for the goal.

49. I keep myself well-groomed.

50. I have a rich vocabulary.

51. I get upset easily.

52. I have a vivid imagination.

53. I boss people around.

54. I am not easily bothered by things

55. I detect mistakes.

56. I treat all people equally.

57. I turn plans into actions.

58. I believe that I am important.

59. I enjoy thinking about things.

60. I panic easily.

61. I enjoy hearing new ideas.

63. I accept people as they are.

64. I am careful to avoid making mistakes.

65. I sympathize with others' feelings.

68. I formulate ideas clearly.

69. I feel threatened easily.

70. I like to begin new things.

74. I am concerned about others.

75. I do more than what's expected of me.

76. I don't care what others think.

77. I am quick to understand things.

78. I take offense easily.

79. I would like to live for a while in a different country.

81. I seldom get mad.

84. I carry out my plans.

85. I want to be different from others.

87. I grumble about things.
88. I seek adventure.

90. I don't worry about things that have already happened.

91. I take tasks too lightly.

92. I am out for my own personal gain.

93. I get to work at once.

94. I don't care what people think of me.

95. I avoid philosophical discussions.

96. I am very pleased with myself.

98. I demand to be the center of interest.

99. I yell at people.

100. I leave my work undone.

101. I am not interested in other people's problems.
103. I need the approval of others.

105. I feel comfortable with myself.

106. I dislike changes.

107. I am easily discouraged.

108. I snap at people.

109. I am often late to work.

110. I believe people should fend for themselves

111. I do just enough work to get by.

113. I rarely look for a deeper meaning in things.

114. I rarely get irritated.

115. I prefer to stick with things that I know.

116. I have a low opinion of myself.

117. I lose my temper.

119. I contradict others

120. I put little time and effort into my work

121. I worry about what people think of me

End of the Test
Make sure you have answered to every statement and proceed to the scoring instructions.

CHAPTER 9: CAN ONE ACHIEVE PERFECTION WITH ENNEAGRAM

The first personality type on the Enneagram is often called the "Reformer," the "Perfectionist," or the "One." People with this personality type are idealists by nature. They tend to be very responsible in their actions and often appear more mature than their age. Furthermore, they get consumed with the need to improve everything in their life, sometimes including people as well. While there are many benefits to this personality type, there are also several challenges that arise when interacting with a One. Guilt, anger, depression, and emotional detachment can often hide the fact that Ones love, warm and sensitive souls beneath their perfection-seeking exteriors.

The One in action

Henry has been promoted to department head in his company, making him one of the new bosses for the employees at Café Fresh. Dana and Jane have worked side-by-side as assistant managers at the café for the past four years. They don't interact with higher-ups too often, so they were both initially indifferent when they found out that Henry would be joining the team.

Henry, however, is not like previous bosses. As a One, his approach is very hands-on. He immediately showed an interest in improving the department in every way, including productivity and worker conditions. He met with the supervisors, managers, and baristas at Café Fresh three times in his first week – sometimes sharing new policies that would be implemented and, other times, walking up and down the café while silently scanning for potential areas of improvement.

On one of their lunch breaks, Dana and Jane are surprised to find they have very different views of Henry. Jane has welcomed him with open arms. She is motivated by the enthusiastic vision he brings and admires his self-confidence. Dana chuckles as Jane uses the word "self-confident" and thinks "dominating" is a more appropriate word to describe Henry. She gets more and more fed-up each time Henry starts talking about a new idea.

In the weeks that follow, there is an unhealthy tension in the air that undermines Henry's goal of overall improvement. He senses this and gets disheartened. He thought the team would be excited about the prospect of improving their café and wonders why they seem resistant to progress.

One of the problems here is that Henry does not show respect for Dana's abilities. Having been in her position for several years, Dana feels that she knows what she is doing and doesn't need a new person to tell her how to do her job. Henry, however, has his own vision for what the perfect café looks like. His belief in his own vision is so strong that he forgets to consider whether the rest of the team, including Dana, is in agreement.

Furthermore, Dana feels that Henry's approach questions her abilities, which adds to her stress and frustration. Henry may believe Dana is exceptional at her job — perhaps that is even why he entrusts her with so many important changes. But as a One, Henry's focus is not on what Dana is already doing right; it is on what she could be doing better.

The simple fact is that both Henry and Dana are headstrong perfectionists. This means that they value autonomy in their jobs and have a hard time taking orders from anyone else. Dana may have reacted more positively if Henry clearly explained the vision he was chasing and gave the Café Fresh employees time to buy into the vision and brainstorm their own additions.

You might be wondering: is it possible that this is just a problem with Dana? Some employees wouldn't mind Henry's approach at all. In fact, Jane seemed perfectly happy. Why could that be?

Jane appreciates that Henry shows the tendency to have both a vision of the future and the ability to achieve it. As a Six, she will gladly follow someone with integrity and ability – qualities Ones have in abundance. Therefore, Henry's strong approach is just the thing to inspire the die-hard loyalty that Jane is eager to provide.

Personality profile of the One

Ones are renowned for being reliable and ambitious. Their pursuit for perfection means that they won't rest until the job is, not only done, but done correctly. Subsequently, people can rest assured that any project left in the hands of a One will be done on time and to the highest of standards. They may be the types of people who constantly seek improvement. Rather than seeing the glass as half empty or half full, they want to know why the glass can't be filled all the way. Not willing to settle for how things are, they search for ways to improve on things that other people are perfectly content with accepting. The downside to this, however, is that Ones can tend to be workaholics. Since perfection is rarely achieved, their pursuit for it will consume most of their time, leaving little for relaxation, recreation, and even relationships.

Some Ones believe that if something can be improved, it should be. Therefore, their minds tend to analyze everything — constantly looking for those finishing touches that will turn mediocre into a masterpiece. Other Ones latch onto a particular cause that needs reform. For example, a One might gravitate towards the fight to end social injustices or fervently demand environmental sustainability. However, those Ones may overlook some imperfections in their home when they return from work. Whether or not the one takes action on improving the faults they encounter, the core remains that they, more than anyone else, can identify what is right and wrong. Whether others agree with their beliefs on right and wrong, however, is another story entirely.

Ones are part of the gut center. For them, this manifests as an instinctual feeling of what is right and what is wrong. Henry knew what the 'right' café looked like and could spot deviations from his vision the moment he saw them. Even if he does not know exactly why something is right or wrong, he has a gut feeling that he strongly believes in. Some Ones are perfectly happy to base their actions and decisions on their gut feelings. Others will feel the need to rationalize their feelings with logic and consider all possible outcomes of acting on their instincts. In these cases, the One might spend so much time thinking about their beliefs, actions, and decisions that they mistake themselves for a person who is primarily motivated by reason and logic. The One's driving force, however, is instinct – after that, a logical explanation for that instinct may or may not follow.

Enneatypes in the gut center are most associated with the feeling of anger. For the One, anger might start to arise 1) when others do not understand that something is right or wrong or 2) when others (or themselves) fail to do the right thing. Since their minds are tuned to identify areas they can reform, Ones will find faults more often than not. Rather than accepting imperfection and moving on, a One will not only search for a solution, but will wonder why people have allowed such faults to exist in the first place. Ones may find that they are short tempered when things do not meet their standards. This anger is usually not aimed at other people involved, but rather at the situation itself. Unfortunately, most people won't understand this and will feel as though the One is angry with them personally. The One's search for perfection is not simply for the sake of perfection itself; rather it is to improve the world and the lives of those in it. Often others do not understand or appreciate this, as they find it hard to see that the One is actually a very emotional and compassionate person, even if their exterior seems harsh and serious.

Perhaps you know a One who does not seem short-tempered at all. This is possible because Ones often try to repress the emotion of anger in an attempt to be their own ideal of perfection. Alternatively, anger may be directed internally, which is one reason that Ones are an Enneatype prone to depression. When you consider that depression is also known as "anger directed inward," it begins to make sense why a One's anger might manifest in this way.

While Ones may seem harsh, critical, and/or emotionless, the fact is that they are very warm and caring individuals. They may hold you to the highest of standards, but the truth is that they hold themselves to even higher standards. Any criticism from a One should be taken as a challenge to become your best, not an attack on your character. Additionally, any emotional detachment from a One should not be taken at face value. Ones are very emotional, despite what their appearance might suggest. They simply allow logic to dominate their minds as they search for ways to justify their instinct, which can leave emotions ignored or set aside to be dealt with another time.

If you are a One, you are able to look at a situation and not only see what sits right in front of you, but also what could ideally be sitting right in front of you. You share an Enneatype with several people who have used their power for spreading immense amounts of good, such as Joan of Arc, Nelson Mandela, and Plato. Despite the stereotypes, you are not destined to always be critical and controlling. You may be able to spot flaws a mile away, but you can also spot opportunity. You recognize that regardless of how things are now — they can always get better.

CHAPTER 9 PART 2 : FINDING YOUR UNIQUE PATH TO SPIRITUAL GROWTH

Some people new to the Enneagram mistakenly believe that once they discover their type, they have exhausted the system's usefulness. While it can be tempting to feel like we're "finished" after learning our type, there's more to it than that. Besides, if we learn our own personality type without using that knowledge to work on ourselves, we won't grow. By working on ourselves, we're able to find freedom from our ingrained habits and patterns.

The Enneagram is a uniquely useful tool for growth and change because it delves deeply into our core motivations. While other well-known personality typologies do an excellent job measuring and explaining human behaviors and personality traits, the Enneagram describes us at a deeper level. It explains why we act in certain ways. Seeing what drives our behavior allows us to examine our deeply held beliefs, attitudes, and choices, offering a level of insight that's hard to reach without this kind of road map.

The Enneagram also brings amazing breadth and depth to personal development. When used correctly, as a dynamic system for change rather than as a means of stereotyping and judging, it describes the full range of our behaviors. Along with the insights we get from learning our primary Enneagram type, we gain additional wisdom about ourselves when we learn about our connections to other types through wings, Stress Points, and Security Points.

Regardless of cultural background and life experiences, the core psychological structure of our Enneagram type remains consistent. This makes the Enneagram a growth tool that works for all demographics and can facilitate understanding between them. You can be any race, gender, socioeconomic status, and religion, and still benefit from the Enneagram. All that's needed is a desire to grow.

The Enneagram is a great tool for facilitating change. What's just as important is the fact that the self-awareness Enneagram work brings is a doorway to self-acceptance. Many people describe feeling a sense of relief when they find their Enneagram type. Most of us feel a great sense of reassurance when we finally gain an explanation for why we keep getting caught in the same traps.

Through the Enneagram, not only do we learn that our personality's challenges aren't our fault, we also get glimpses of our greatest possibilities and gifts. We stop blaming ourselves for our shortcomings and see the beauty in our true selves. We begin to love ourselves for exactly who we are.

BREATH AWARENESS MEDITATION: 20 MINUTES OF GUIDED MEDITATION

The idea of meditation may be simultaneously intimidating and boring for those who aren't yet familiar with its myriad benefits. Contrary to popular belief, meditation doesn't require you to possess any particular degree of skill or experience in order for it to be beneficial. You won't need any special props, books, or even guides— though all of these things are widely available, and should be embraced if you find them helpful. All that is needed for a successful meditation session is you: your mind, your focus, your patience, your stillness. It can be done anywhere, for any length of time, and it can be done by anybody, for any purpose. Beginners may want to start with a short practice of five to ten minutes; those who already have some experience can gain a lot more from longer, and regular, meditation sessions.

Let's make it as easy as possible. You can get into a meditation practice by following five simple steps.

First: make yourself comfortable. You can sit or lie down on the floor, a cushion, a chair, a bed, or outside in the grass if you like. Make sure it's a spot and position you can remain in comfortably for several minutes without moving.

Second: Close your eyes. No need to squeeze the eyelids shut. Just let them fall closed and relax.

Third: Breathe naturally. If you wish to incorporate special breathing techniques, such as those learned in yoga, vocal training, or another practice, go ahead— but it's best to avoid any form of distraction. If the breathing pattern requires focus, it can interrupt your meditative experience. Fourth: Focus on your breath. Pay attention to its rhythm and sound; pay attention to the way it feels, flowing in and out of your body. Note the way that it impacts your body, moving your bones and muscles and skin with each inhalation and exhalation. There is no right or wrong thought to have here. There is only mindfulness.

Fifth: Try to stop controlling your thoughts. Often, people advise first-time meditators to "clear the mind," but in truth, the aim isn't to erase or ignore your thoughts; the aim is to detach from them slightly, so that you can observe your own mental patterns from an outsider's perspective. When thoughts pop-up in your first few meditation sessions (and they inevitably will) you can allow them to do so. Recognize that they are only thoughts, not tangible realities; recognize the feelings and emotions they stir up within you; and finally, let these thoughts drift away, back into the æther from which they came.

CHAPTER 10: ENNEAGRAM AT WORK

The Enneagram is a tool for great subtlety though the central premise is based upon what happens to be quite simplistic. That is that the personality was developed in order to protect our higher self and is linked inseparably to it. There is a simple observation which allows the use of this knowledge and it is not unique to the Enneagram. We consist of two people. The first is the soul or the essence. It is neither thought, feeling nor sensation yet it's the person. The other is the personality that identifies itself with thoughts, feelings and sensations. Most of the time, it is confused for the true self but it can be changed.

The difference between the spiritual and psychological nature is only just apparent. Both of them are integral to the people that we are. While being alive, there is not only a need for a personality in order to mediate between the higher selves and the world in order to assist in getting things done but there is also a need to recognize its nature. The personality represents a set of tools which help us through life while other parts do not assist very much. Though you might have adopted them in order to keep you safe, by the time you become an adult, they become part of the negative problems.

In order to change or transcend, the first thing that one has to know is what the problem is. If you want to make a journey, it would be first helpful to create the journey as it helps in having a map of the terrain to know where you are on the map and what obstacles that you may come across. This is a big part towards the value of the Enneagram. It represents a map of the particular terrain. In the same manner that traversing the Sahara would not require one to pack snow climate gear, if your go-to habit is fear, then it will not help to work on anger and pride. Envy is a big issue for some people while anger is for others and so forth.

When it comes to essence, the higher self, and the mystical arts describe the attributes of the soul. The spiritual gifts and the essence of each of the nine types of the enneagrams are variations of being, consciousness and bliss. When you get presents, then you find that all three centers are united and the three gifts avail themselves.

The head center for one corresponds to the visualization center allegedly used in Buddhist meditations and a number of the practices that relate to spirituality. The head center knows what is real and trusts it. That is to say that Christianity is trustworthy. This then relates to faith as it needs no proof because it only knows what is true and discerns the significance of what is in the unique time. This discernment lets us perceive the way that the world works and gives us wisdom in order to act in a courageous manner in harmony with the requirements of the world.

The head is the spiritual heart center opened in the Sufi and Christian practices. The liturgy, devotional prayer and changing all provide access to the spiritual heart. In the west, the heart is associated with love while in the Enneagram the concept of love which is unconditional belongs to the belly. This is a given and it is where people come from or who they are and where they return. The yearning for what is known as love is actually an outward movement for the soil and the urge to unite. The heart types know that it is about the relationships and the unfolding time and space because of the interweaving. The heart wants to reach out and respond and create something new when it comes to hope. The belly center finally has almost been forgotten in the west as an organ of spiritual perceptions. It is correspondent to the concept that is known as hara in Japan and is the focus of all practices that are rooted in Zen. Love exists as a necessary part for creation. The gifts of the belly center would have to do with the nature of reality of being and of presence.

According to Gurdjieff, it is possible to identify the chief features as most of the work has been accomplished and the Enneagram allows for this to happen. The inner self differentiates between essence and personality and that would be the key towards spiritual growth. Through the means of self-observation, it is possible to recognize the automatic reactions of the personality and then use them as the reminders for the qualities that we have. In that way, it then becomes possible to regain the ability to respond to life from a perspective which is not biased and in tune with the true self. If you are skilled, then the inner self may assist in realizing patterns and bring out the unused and hidden potentials. Knowledge of a particular terrain makes the efforts that much easier and accurate. It is not a query for transcending or subduing the personality, but rather befriending it and learning the manner that it points us to. Irrespective of whether people approach the personal growth as spiritual or both, it's completely up to them. People are able to understand their background influences or mediate for long periods of time every day. Unless it increases the humaneness and loving kindness and unless daily actions and thoughts are harmonious and creative, then it is not growth.

Understanding and finding a healthy way to bring out the hidden powers, talents, and aspects of you that would otherwise remain dormant can increase your personal happiness and those of your loved ones.

It's also an empathy enhancer. The more you understand why people behave as they do, the less likely you are to take things personally, get thrown off your own alignment or even misunderstand them. Now that we've become more connected than ever as a global community, there's a greater need for compassion, understanding, and empathy at work, on social media, in public gatherings, and at home. It helps when human behavior isn't such a mystery to you because you can intelligently assess when you have a bearing of the main underlying motives driving human consciousness.

Anything we can do to know more about ourselves and become better humans is worth diving into and investing a little effort. It takes an open mind and heart, but if you're ready to soak in some new healthy perspectives, I promise to deliver the insights that can aid you.

CHAPTER 11: ENNEAGRAM IN RELATIONSHIPS

When couples break up, it is quite common to hear them say, "In the end, we just weren't compatible." What does that mean? Is it just a cop-out? Does compatibility really matter when it comes to love? The answer is yes, it does matter, and though the concept of compatibility seems pretty simple, it can actually mean any of the following things:

We used to annoy each other to the extent that, toward the end, we weren't even fond of each other. We didn't share or respect each other's beliefs. Our expectations didn't match, and our conflicts outweighed our love for each other. We did not know how to deal with our conflicts.

Compatibility has a whole range of meanings which tend to vary from one person to the next. So, what exactly does being compatible mean? According to the dictionary, it means the ability to live in harmony without any conflicts. Think about that though; it is quite impossible to uphold a relationship that is devoid of all conflicts. Conflicts are common in all relationships in life, from that of family and friends to romantic relationships. The closer the relationship, the more jarring the conflict can be. It surprises us when we realize that someone we used to think the world of suddenly doesn't even feel like a friend anymore?

When you enter a relationship, that other person evokes a tremendous sense of connection and understanding, but when that relationship ends, that feeling of understanding seems to disappear altogether. If you want a relationship to last the tests of time, then there needs to be a balance between novelty and comfort. It is ironic when, at times, both familiarity and novelty become quite annoying in a relationship. Everyone knows the story. A couple falls in love. She falls for him because he is fun to be around and caring like her father was, maybe stable and sensitive as well.

Where has her zest for adventure gone? Why has he become hard-hearted? Why don't they share the same interests anymore? She likes to shop and gossip, while he likes to play golf with his friends.

Where did that perfect relationship go? Where did their mutual values go? They seem to be getting on each other's nerves for every little thing.

It's painful when the person you previously turned to for comfort now seems like your persecutor. These frustrations are an indication of the direction in which you and your partner should grow. However, what is quite sad is that instead of working on these problems like a team, most of us make it about our suffering. Therefore, we use the word "incompatible."

There are different types of conflict, and they can be classified into four categories. The four types of conflict are avoidant, validating, hostile, and volatile. The only couples who are in real trouble are the ones that fall into the hostile category. Everything else can be managed with a little mutual understanding.

The first thing you need to understand is that conflicts are predictable. Fights are normal, and they are bound to happen. If you want your relationship to endure, then you should expect a couple of rows now and then. That being said, the more things you have in common with your partner, the less disturbing and insurmountable the conflicts will seem. If you share common views about upbringings, demographics, and even world-views, the conflicts won't look too worrying. That doesn't mean that you won't have any differences of opinions. Everyone has different ideas, and the difference in views is what causes conflicts. Focus on resolving the disputes that come up and know that conflicts don't have to mean the end of your relationship.

They actually offer potential for growth if you expect and learn to embrace them. In fact, they are an opportunity for you to get to know each other better. Even when it seems you no longer like the other person, there might still be some compatibility left. If you can interpret the reason for the dissatisfaction instead of making it about personal suffering, it might help.

When in the midst of conflict, the one question that bothers most of us is "did I choose the right person?" Well, how can we choose someone perfect, when we are flawed? You might be wondering where the Enneagram fits in with all this. Well, have a little patience. There are different types of personalities, and each has its own positive and negative characteristics. You need to know that regardless of the level of compatibility you share, relationships all boil down to how the partners deal with conflict.

There is no such thing as a perfect couple, and you should really let go of that notion if you haven't already. Instead, you should focus on different features of your relationship and try to make it better. According to the Enneagram, there are 45 possible combinations. For instance, relationships can consist of a One with a One, a One with a Two, a One with a Three, a One with a Four, and so on. Some might wonder if one specific pairing works better than the rest, but a type combination cannot predict the success of a relationship.

Every Enneagram type has its own challenges and imbalances in a relationship. A couple of common shortcomings are listed below. Remember that it isn't a full list. If you feel that you and your partner have any of these imbalances, take your time and gradually work through them.

Type Ones are likely to love control. They can be exacting and critical in a relationship to the extent that the other person can feel sad. If you are a Type One, then don't try to dominate your partner or force things to go in a certain direction. Learn to let go a little and trust your partner.
Type Twos are supporters. It is in their nature to help others. However, if you are a Type Two and you ignore your own needs for too long, it will lead to anger. Resentment can sour a relationship quicker than anything else. If you have specific interests or concerns, it is best if you talk about them with your partner.

All Type Threes try to bypass their emotions. As a Type Three person, when you disregard your feelings, it will make you feel lonely and empty, even when there isn't a reason for you to feel so.

Type Fours are individualists. As a Type Four person, it is good to retain your personality in a relationship, and you shouldn't give up your quest for self-discovery. However, too much individualism can make your partner feel left out. Don't expend too much time mulling over what you feel; after all, you aren't the only one that feels things. Be mindful of your partner's interests and desires too.

Type Fives should be cautious of withdrawing too frequently or too extensively from their partners. It can make your partner feel worried. Independence is good, but remembers that you are a team and need to maintain open lines of communication. You cannot have a successful relationship if you both act as individual entities all the time.

Type six personalities have issues with anxiety, so much so that others can feel tested and distrusted. A Sixes doubts and unnecessary fears shouldn't be the reason for their partner's sleepless nights. If you're a Six, it is critical that you tell your partner about the things that worry you.

Type Sevens love to multitask and spend a lot of time thinking about the future. However, Sevens, when you spend all your time thinking about a future that might or might not happen, you often forget to participate in the present and miss out on things. Learn to live in the moment.

Type Eights don't like to feel weak. Whenever they feel a slight vulnerability creeping in, they tend to shut others away. Whatever you do Type Eights, don't push your partner away. If you behave like they aren't wanted, they may believe that you don't need them and decide to leave.

Type Nines love harmony. They love peace more than anything. It means that they try to shy away from conflicts. Nines, you cannot ignore arguments all the time. If you want a strong relationship, you need to learn to discuss things with your partner.

If you want a better relationship, then here are a couple of simple things that will aid you along the way.

Hear

Let down your defenses and open your heart. You must try and understand your lover so that you can meet their needs. It's not just oral communication that you need to watch out for, but non-verbal communication as well. Pay attention to the look in your partner's eyes, as well as body language, hand gestures, and tone of voice. This will assist you in understanding what your partner is feeling.

Your partner should do the same.

Empathize

Once you are certain that you understand what your partner is feeling, you need to pay attention to the feelings you convey in responding to them. It is crucial to search for the tender and softer feelings you have for your partner. Can you connect with your partner on a deeper level and feel pain when your partner is in pain? Can you be kind toward your partner and simply be a shoulder to lean on? When you know that your partner is in distress, your first instinct might be to offer advice or try and solve the problem. Instead, the pure expression of compassion can soothe your partner's distress and calm them down as well. More often than not, your partner needs this more than your advice.

Love

You need to feel and express your total love toward your partner. You need to intentionally make some space in your life if you want to reconnect with your partner. Even if the recent connections that you had with your partner left you feeling angry and distant, you need to make an effort if you want your marriage to survive. Think of all the good qualities that your partner has, the ones that made you love them in the first place. Go through your photo albums or think of those times when you felt that you had everything that you ever wished for and more. You need to find a way to not just forgive the mistakes you made but also the ones that your partner made, the errors that pushed you off track.

Consider how you demonstrate the love that you have for your partner. Maybe you show your affection physically. Perhaps you take your partner to dinner at their favorite restaurant or someplace else you know they enjoy. Regardless of how you express your love, it should be unconditional. It should not be dependent on their reaction or reciprocation. If there's a particular matter that's holding you back from expressing your unconditional love, care, support, and trust toward your partner, then you need to take steps to sort it out.

Act

In resolving your differences, it is imperative that you not only take action to deal with your partner's needs and concerns but also show that you are eager to change. These actions needn't be anything elaborate; they can be something as simple as helping with tasks around the house, calling your partner during the day to affirm that you miss them, or perhaps spending less money if you know your partner has concerns about finances. When your partner can see that you are taking the worries they express seriously, your partner will feel valued and respected. It will initiate a positive cycle where your partner will appreciate you and you will understand your partner. You don't need to be flawless, but you do need to act in a manner that shows that you care and are trying to change.

Empathy

Remember that there is no room for selfishness in a relationship and empathy takes center stage. Empathy refers to understanding your partner's point of view and providing comfort. If you are compassionate and understanding, then chances are your partner will notice, appreciate, and reciprocate.

Respect

In order to maintain a positive, healthy relationship, it is essential that respect flow both ways. You must both work at understanding and respecting each other's interests, even if you don't share them. Asking your partner to give things up can be detrimental to your relationship.

Loyalty

This one goes without saying. It is human nature to be tempted, but it is essential to love and respect your partner and do right by them.

Trust

One of the most critical foundational stones of a strong relationship is trust. Both you and your partner must trust each other and give one another sufficient room to make independent decisions. Interfering in each other's decisions or exhibiting a lack of trust can lead to cracks in the relationship. Though they may start off as small fissures, they can become more pronounced over time.

CHAPTER 12: SPIRITUAL DEVELOPMENT AND ENNEAGRAM

The enneagram is a powerful type of gateway towards the understanding of others and self-awareness. It gives a description of different dynamics and structures concerning the major personality types by creating a path to a life which is more integrated and rewarding.

Your enneagram core functions as a home base from which one can make sense of integration and individuation. The styles are not based solely according to behavior and outward representations can be deceiving.

In order to distinguish between the different enneagrams, one has to access motivation in order to explore and act in a particular manner and why acting in this way is given value by that person.

Determination of an individual's personality type with the use of the enneagram system does not necessarily put one inside a defined box of nine archetypes. It assists people to see the box from where they are able to experience the world. With this in mind, one can step outside their worldview. Ideally speaking, personality is effective in allowing one to express them because they are able to categorize and identify who they really are. At the same time there can be issues when people get stuck in automatic habits. In discovering these unconscious patterns, people are able to lead lives which are more fulfilling and enjoy relationships which are overall healthier. Working within the enneagram model allows people to become successful in their relationships at home and within the working environment. Through understanding automatic reactions and blind spots, people can become more flexible with others in their lives and understand what others are feeling and thinking. This making it easier to tolerate other and be more compassionate. It also helps people to not take the negative reactions or their hostility in such a manner that it is personal. Through the identification of how you are emotionally and psychologically defensive, the enneagram allows you to have a chance at profound growth. At another level it also allows you to develop your relationship with yourself and better this, so that you can become more productive towards yourself and anything within your life.

Simply, the enneagram enables and grows one's capacity when it comes to self-observation. It provides vision for how the healthiest manifestation of people's types can look. Using this detail, it sets a path for the manner in getting to a higher level of awareness. Each type within the enneagram has particular behaviors that satisfy its needs and desires. This is the main strategy of the particular type in life. That would be driving much of what the type does. The enneagram is able to help people spot when they are being run by their passions, allowing people to satisfy their needs in a healthier manner.

For example, the passion for type seven happens to be gluttony. This is the traditional meaning for overeating which extends to over consumption. The people with this type look for experiences in trying to find a sense of fulfillment which they fear may remain elusive. In truth, they may feel that nothing they embark on will bring the fulfillment which they look for to bring happiness and contentment.

CHAPTER 13: ENNEAGRAM AND CHRISTIANITY, JESUS AND PRAYER

When you are reading this book, you are showing something about yourself which is inherently human; your curiosity. As someone who finds the curiosity that is bound to be in all humans and which bind us all together as people in the world, I sincerely hope that by continuing to read, you can find your own path toward the satisfaction of your innate curiosity.
Perhaps it's the or at least, one of the most profound curiosities of man that drives us to read and write books like this, the curiosity of our own souls.

Humans are profoundly selfish, I think, to have such an intense curiosity of self. To have such a truly deeply seated fascination with our own soul, and especially with the idea that souls exist in humans (and furthermore, the idea that if they did, souls would be found to be present in things like humans), shows that we know a truly minuscule amount after all, about ourselves both as individuals and as a simple species.

That is exactly the purpose books like this, and this book to be specific, seeks to serve; the ability and the information to better equip the reader with the ability to analyze them and better understand them as well.

Although many people seem to most often find themselves trying to often without much success analyze themselves through the numerous personality tests they may find online or through other sources or even trying to find the answers to their most internally pressing questions through other means such as mystics or other "professionals" of pseudoscience frankly, these mystics and spiritualists who attempt to persuade the common civilian that their future can be told through a crystal ball, the palm of a hand, tea leaves, or something equally asinine, can be compared to con artists; both people that prey on suspecting people who innocently want to understand themselves and the world around them better.

Although, it should be noted that the Enneagram model is also nothing of an exact science itself; however, personality tests such as ones that assess the Enneagram are ones that ask questions that actually ascertain the personality type or at least, gather something of a rough estimate of the individual who happens to be taking that test. Those who take a test to try and find out more about the Enneagram test, or about what type they themselves fall under, may find that the results they get are ones they don't personally identify with. People that do not identify with the majority are most definitely not broken people or people who answered the test incorrectly. The fault of misevaluation lies not within the participant, but within the examination.

With that in mind, the Enneagram model stems back many, many centuries, by many counts even reaching as far back as the 4th century, when a Christian Mystic developed the concepts of 8 "deadly thoughts," as well as an overarching concept that pertains to the love of self. This is not necessarily one of the many ideas behind the Enneagram model that endured the test of time, and it now remains as an insignificant detail compared to more contemporary ideas that were used and taken into more strong consideration when the Enneagram model used today was being constructed as we now use it today.

Today, the Enneagram model has somewhat faded from popularity among most people, excluding those who are particularly drawn to the spiritual or to personality tests. Replacing the Enneagram in a sense are tests such as the Myer-Briggs test, which identifies the participants' personality type using 4 or 5 letters, depending on the given answers surrounding extraversion, logic, the participant's life priorities, whether they are someone more prone to simply watch or to actively judge another and so on and so forth. Many other tests have also come to replace the Enneagram in a sense, taking its place in the eyes of people, especially young people.

I single out younger people in particular simply because younger generations seem, by and large, to feel more of an affinity with personality tests, no matter how reliable or not so they may actually seem. Why they feel this affinity to the acuity to which many of them do, is beyond me and beyond many. However, the reasoning is not so important as the end result, which is that these young people will be the new generation to take more of an interest, or disinterest, in the Enneagram model and any of its tests available online to these younger people. Whether or not this younger generation actually takes interest may or may not be what sinks or swims the popularity of the Enneagram test or its model.

Although the Enneagram has always been less popular than its comparable "competitors," other sources to determine personality type which simply is more readily available or more easily maneuverable to young people, it has still been a fairly popular source of gauging the persona, or the attributes that make up people.

Though, whether the popularity of the Enneagram models rises or plummets, one has to ask, what makes personality tests so popular in the first place? They love to discover more about themselves; this is, of course, one contributing factor to these tests' popularity.

However, there is another massive affinity that binds most people together—the love of being categorized. Although many people will vocalize about how they find being categorized demeaning, or otherwise unappealing, the vast majority actually find categorization something of a comfort. Being sorted into what we perceive as neat packages, neat boxes or rows under which we exist, lets us release the constant weight hanging over our heads. Neglecting these responsibilities allows us to elect instead to conform to the predetermined path that has often been set before us by our predecessors, the people who came before us and who have walked the same path that is now expected of us as well.

There's a reason that they say, 'to be someone who forges their own path is to be someone with a surplus in will power and in determination'. Once you're determined to exclude yourself from the majority, you're more or less released of the confines that once shackled you to a singular expectation or set of expectations, but you also run a much higher risk of being looked down upon or even ridiculed by your peers, most of which have unwittingly or otherwise chosen to walk their predetermined path. This is perhaps the other most daunting thing about attempting to be totally authentic in the way you live your life; the peer pressure. Most societies, especially ones that are focused of cooperation and social harmony, such as countries in Eastern Asian countries like South Korea and Japan, have in a way engineered their very own cage of lab rats in which the rats are the ones to keep each other from leaving the cage, leaving the actual researchers outside the cage to do as they please without interference.

That's a rather nihilistic way of looking at modern societies, and perhaps one that isn't even particularly accurate, as there are many more optimistic perspectives which offer a much more rational, yet happier, explanation for why most societies function the way they do—such as the theory of structural functionalism, which dictates that all institutions that we have built in society such as educational facilities are all destined to work together like a machine to create the most efficient and content society possible. At any rate, taking the time to consider all of these possible explanations of the philosophical and more is one of the many reasons that we as a species feel so much frustration at having some of our most questions devastatingly unanswered.

As they say, we often come so close, and yet so far, from the answers to man's most pressing questions, ranging from the broad "why are we here?" kinds of questions to the other individual questions which plague some people in particular. Regardless, it may be said that in this day and age where the identity of the individual has often come under scrutiny, and we are forced to take a more rock solid evaluation of our own identities, is at least a contributing factor to the recent boom in popularity of personality tests such as the Myer-Briggs and its predecessors, as well as the Enneagram, of course to a lesser extent than the former.

Keeping all of these things in mind, let's move forward with the intention not only with the intention to learn more about the Enneagram model and its purposes in the world today, but also to learn more about the individual, and what tests like the Enneagram say about us.

CHAPTER 13 PART 2: CONTEMPLATION AND SILENCE: THE NINE TYPES WITH NEW WAYS TO PRAY

WHAT IS CONTEMPLATIVE SPIRITUALITY?

Solitude, silence, and stillness are the quintessential qualities of contemplative prayer and practice. Phileena writes, "By abandoning ourselves regularly to God through prayer in the form of solitude, silence and stillness, we experience more freedom from compulsions and heavy-laden expectations and more liberty in our [T] rue [S] elf with all of our unique gifts to offer the world."

Solitude, silence, and stillness are the corrections to the compulsions that come out of our Intelligence Centers, our head, heart, and gut. Together they make us whole. They bring us home. True contemplatives aren't superspiritual elites or those committed ascetics who completely withdraw from the world. True contemplatives don't simply nurture their inner life in isolation. Contemplative spirituality is critical for everyone. Especially in an age when we are constantly interrupted by digital distractions, contemplation invites us to return to the present moment where God can be encountered.

The true contemplative is any normal person who allows deep soul work to lead to a broad, outward-facing transformation. That's the beauty of contemplative practice: we enter it as individuals, yet emerge enriched and equipped, part of a larger community more capable of serving the needs of a hurting world. Likewise, true activists do not simply throw themselves at a cause for the sake of the cause without first allowing a passion or focus to provide some sort of anchor or grounding point. And so, bringing contemplation and activism together creates a fresh kind of accountability to both efforts, illuminating for us the truth that neither can be isolated from the other if we really want to have an impact.
As I watched her simple commitment to nurturing her own spirituality, it dawned on me that she didn't pray to support her work, but in fact the work was the fruit of her prayers. She led with

contemplative prayer, and goodness came forward.
Solitude
Lots of us are surrounded by people all the time. Many of the people we know, many of the people with whom we interact, and many of the groups we work with are community-oriented, community-based, community-focused. Many of our friends have multiple roommates. Many can't go to the grocery store alone.
Stillness
We live in a cause-driven age. Our neighborhoods are filled with activists, people who care about getting behind the things that they believe will help build a better world. Efforts to establish peace and justice have become part of our social fabric. Just look at people's social media accounts to see how they've branded themselves around their humanitarian concerns. It seems all of us want to do good in the world; we want to help. But in many ways the world is getting worse, not better, despite our best intentions.
In addition to our drive to build a better world, we also live in a time when productivity and impact feed the lies we believe about ourselves. The constant pressure to do more, to fill up our schedules, to work harder. But we have to stop the busyness or we will be stopped by burnout and exhaustion.

The Nine Types with New Ways to Pray

1. Perfectionist

Similarly as the name infers, ones flourish to do everything right. They are effectively basic when things are not done in their manner.
Positive Traits:Honesty, steadfastness, respectability, self-controlled, principled and solid.
Negative qualities:Overly basic, not adaptable, angry.

2. Helper

Twos are known for supporting others and bringing the potential out of others. They will in general give their everything to others in this manner ignoring themselves.
Positive Traits:Generous, mindful, communicator.
Negative Traits:Naïve, People satisfying, subordinate.

3. Achiever

Threes step up and make a solid effort to achieve their objectives. They are profoundly versatile, and they exceed expectations at "getting a handle on" and meeting the desires for others when that will lead them to progress.
Positive Traits:Success situated, Adaptive, Energetic
Negative Traits:Impatient, focused, over worked.

4. individualist

Fours are the inclination based type. They care for the most part about what will profit themselves. They look for significance and profundity in their connections, their work, or in a journey for individual innovativeness.
Positive Traits:Passionate, optimistic, delicate, enthusiastic profundity.
Negative Traits:Temperamental, self consumed, emotional, testy, uncooperative pulled back.

5. Observer

Fives spotlights on scholarly understanding and gathering information. They frequently wish to be separated from everyone else.
Positive Traits:Self dependent, Scholar, creative.
Negative Traits:Secretive, confining, parsimonious.

6. Loyalist

As the name infers, sixes are great at staying faithful to their obligation. They adhere to their promise regardless of whether it requires some penance. They center around guarding the wellbeing of the gathering, undertaking or network. Sixes are great at envisioning issues and concocting arrangements.
Positive Traits:Loyal, submitted, mindful, mindful to other's concern.
Negative Traits:Pessimistic, suspicious, on edge, dicey.

7. Enthusiast

Sevens are normally hopeful and positive. They are keen on a wide range of subjects. They would prefer not to be constrained to doing a certain something and they like to keep their choices and potential outcomes open.

Since their consideration moves so rapidly, it's trying for them to go into things inside and out and to continue through to the end in work and connections.

Positive Traits:Fun-adoring, flexible, speedy reasoning.

Negative Traits:Uncommitted, distractible, not composed.

8. Challenger

Eights are essentially the individuals who are fixated on authority. By attesting power over their condition, they give a valiant effort to secure themselves and any other person who is a piece of their family or gathering. They regularly will in general do things their own specific manner.

Positive Traits:Enthusiastic, liberal, incredible

Negative Traits:Dominating, angry, unreasonable.

9. Peacemaker

Nines are otherwise called middle people. They aren't happy with clashes and differences around. Nines look for amicability in their condition and will put forth an admirable attempt to evade strife. Giving a lot of need to other people, nines now and then think that its difficult to settle on close to home choices.

Above all else the Enneagram will assist you with bringing out the best in one another. It will give you the devices you and your adoration need to make your relationship so secure you will have the option to beat any issue that comes your direction.

CHAPTER 14: RECOGNIZE AND CHANGE BAD HABITS WITH THE HELP OF ENNEAGRAM

Let's get back to the inner observer for a minute. It's a tricky thing to develop because we're used to acting out our habits rather than noticing them. All of us live our daily lives as creatures of our habits, from our morning coffee, to our work schedules, all the way down to our preferred bedtime. Our habits are external, what we do in our daily lives, and internal, as driven by our personalities. Our egos dictate our habitual inner self-talk, driven by our personality type and personal life experiences. This self-talk is largely unconscious, and when we react to this talk instead of cultivating an awareness of the immediate world around us, it's harder to make the right choices to support our own lives.

As you begin paying attention to these daily habits, the things you do when you aren't making deliberate choices, you'll hear self-talk in the back of your mind. As with your habits, this dialogue has probably been following you around all your life without you paying much attention to it. It sounds like the voice of "the way things are." Listen to it without judgment, bringing gentleness and curiosity. While your own personal dialogue will be unique, here are some common themes that appear in the unconscious talk of each type:

- Type One: Ones have strong inner critics, and their internal voice can sound particularly parental. There's a strong sense of responsibility, and of things that they "must" do in order to be a good person. Ones are driven to act in the world largely based on this heavy internal dialogue of inner criticism.

- Type Two: The Two inner voices often speak about other people the Two is in relationship with. Twos will focus on the "other"— what that person needs, and how to provide support. This encourages Twos to provide acts of services, in the hope that true love will come from their efforts.

- Type Three: Threes unconsciously are always looking for ways they can be the best at whatever they're doing. They hear their family's voice: specifically, what they perceived their family wanted them to do to be successful. This causes them to go out and achieve in ways they believe will make them valuable.

- Type Four: After taking action or having intimate conversations, Fours will instantly check in with how they're doing emotionally. The current feelings get absorbed into the Four's internal self-image. Fours will then react based on their most current self-perception, which frequently involves negative comparisons or idealization.

- Type Five: A Five's inner dialogue will always be looking for ways they can learn or know more about a subject or situation, usually in great depth. By continuing to dig deeper and deeper for knowledge, Fives hope that they will finally feel like they know enough to confidently take action in the world.

- Type Six: Russ Hudson describes the six inner voices as being like a pendulum: anxiously swinging from place to place, looking for a true source of safety, security, and guidance. Their anxiety-producing inner dialogue causes them to look outside of themselves for a stable, reassuring place of security.

- Type Seven: A Seven's self-talk is often extremely positive, seeking out the next fun, exciting source of stimulation. A Seven's thoughts commonly move rapidly, looking for satisfaction and fulfillment from a wide variety of sources. They react by going out into the world and looking for new ways to find happiness.

- Type Eight: The habitual dialogue of Eights gets bigger and bigger: looking to sound bolder, stronger, and more confident with each thought. By creating dialogue that's full of confidence and bluster, Eights are trying to drown out the voices of sensitivity and doubt, and the fear they aren't strong enough.

- Type Nine: Nines talk to themselves in a way that's relatively positive ("I'm okay, you're okay"), but can also feel secretly resigned to the way things are. They'll imagine what is nice in their present lives. This kind of talk keeps them in a bubble of internal comfort, stopping them from taking possibly earth-rattling risks.

The first step to changing your inner habits is just being aware of what they are. Through awareness, you can make a conscious effort to introduce different self-talk that slowly changes your internalized beliefs. This kind of change takes time: you've been doing your type's patterns for years, after all, and research shows it typically takes a couple of months to change any habit.

Just like animals, we as human beings have natural instincts hard-wired biologically that help us navigate life. Our evolution has necessitated we develop strategies that will enable us to survive and extend the reign of our species. What the Enneagram of Personality does is facilitate a better understanding of the instinctual strategies we've developed as human beings, and it shows us the various ways it's impacting our behavior. This is more than just getting to know your personality type; it's about pulling back the curtain of the influences that drive you to behave as you do.

The Enneagram teaches that there are three basic human instincts, and out of these three, we see a detailed dissection of how these instincts interact and combine with the nine personality types to form what is generally referred to by some teachers as the 27 subtypes. These are:

• Self-preservation Instinct.

• Social Instinct.

• Sexual Instinct.

All three instincts are within us and are behind our life strategies often ruling unconsciously. While these three are always present, one tends to be more dominant, and we tend to prioritize and develop that particular drive while the others tend to be less dominant. And because we don't make it a priority to improve the least dominant one, it tends to become our blind spot.

Think of these three instincts as you would a layered cake. At the top we have our most controlling one, in the middle we have the second that supports the predominant one, and at the bottom, we have the least developed instinct.

Again, we find some conflict even here with some schools stating they should not be referred to as subtypes while others teach that they are indeed subtypes of the nine-point system. Either way, the label doesn't matter to us. We only concern ourselves with how this can help us better understand who we are and why we behave as we do. The primary instinct that we identify with combined with our Enneagram personality type help shape our path in life and the choices we make.

Since that is our core focus, we'll dive into each of the twenty-seven combinations after a brief understanding of what each instinct entails.

The Sum of Our Parts

So, now, you know about Enneagrams. You know where they come from, what they do, and how they help people. You also probably know by now which Enneagram type you are, what that means for you, and how to best move forward and be a better person. You are not only your own person but also a part of many different groups of people. All of those groups have one thing in common, no matter what basis that group is built upon—they are large numbers of people who are together for a much more cohesive, much more intelligent, much wiser, and much more powerful entity than any of the individual cogs of that large machine on their own.

Although we are strong in our specialization, strong in our diversity, we find a way to make being together and forming a large group more than work. Of course, there are groups who will make much better teams than others. There will always be some people within a group who are more cohesive with one another than any other part of the team. With that said, any team can be great. More than great, they can be impactful upon the world. This is why we form groups, form our own categories. We recognize the sheer power in our own numbers, and we know we would be very foolish indeed to neglect that strength that we rely upon every day.

Going forward, take a minute and stop to recognize how strong you are as one person, how strong you have come to be in your life, how far you've come, and how many trials you have faced and overcome. All of those, you have likely not done on your own. When something is simply too much for only one person to take mentally or physically, they look to their loved ones and to their support systems. They look to those they care about for support, and their loved ones usually and hopefully deliver on that expectation.

From a very young age, our parents, as well as our other guardians, instill in us that we are in a position where we accomplish more when cooperating with our peers than we do on our own. Although, in some parts of the world, our education system teaches us to compete with our peers for the top spot or the highest praise, most parts of the world teach their youngest citizens that the key to success is collaboration and exercising good teamwork and cooperation. We know that the secret to succeeding in most businesses and most places of work, in general, rely on the powers of their employees to depend on one another and cooperate to make the best numbers and the best prototypes and provide the best service and the best product to both their bosses and to their customers.

We all know that the reason we focus too intently on ourselves is that a part of us wants to stray away from that herd. We want to feel as though we have a singular identity, a single voice which is strong enough to be carried throughout the entirety of the night on its own. However, the secret to a good and functional group is that the voice of a group is not one singular voice shouting, it is a mix of all its voices melted together. The secret to a good group is that its cry is many, countless voices crying out altogether. There is still an identity. It is that identity that pushes us forward.

CHAPTER 15: SELF-HEALING WITH ENNEAGRAM

Now that you know more about meanings behind different personality types, you're probably wondering how it can actually help you. The main goal of knowing your personality type is to discover yourself, understand inner mechanisms, and constantly evolve or develop in every aspect of your life.

How can Enneagram help me develop?

Enneagram is your ticket for self-discovery and development through awareness. As mentioned throughout this book, Enneagram personality is identified through inner patterns i.e. those associated with your motivation, thoughts, and ways you respond in different circumstances. Sometimes we aren't aware of these patterns because they seem so natural to us. This is where the Enneagram steps in. It provides a thorough analysis of your personality type and helps you become more aware of your emotions, needs, and thoughts.

Awareness is vital for change. If you're unaware of your automatic predictable behaviors and the effects they have on your life, how would you know what to change and how? By providing a deep insight into your psyche and every aspect of your character. That way, you know what to work on in order to succeed, become happier, or achieve a certain goal. This is how you develop and make a progress consistently.

Your Enneagram personality type shows where you usually get "stuck" or pinpoints common struggles you face as well as your fears. Basically, it reveals all the mechanisms that drive you and it becomes easier to understand your inner patterns. With the Enneagram, it is easier to understand why we experience some hardships, but at the same time, you are more equipped to overcome them. For example, if you can't let go of negative experiences from the past, it could be easier when you understand your Enneagram type. How? That's because it shows why you feel that way and instead of denying your emotions and suppressing them, you develop more compassion towards yourself. Knowing the causes behind emotions, both positive and negative, enables you to process them in a healthy manner. This is yet another way the Enneagram helps you develop.

Probably the greatest advantage of the Enneagram in self-growth is its objectivity. Your personality type has both virtues and flaws. Every person has them, it's impossible to be perfect. That being said, sometimes we aren't objective and tend to criticize ourselves too much. Plus, sometimes you come across as arrogant or bossy even though it's not your intention. Being misunderstood is a common occurrence and it doesn't only depend on other people's perception of us. It also stems from the way you perceive others and yourself. The Enneagram helps you have a detailed insight into your personality in an objective manner. You become more aware of both virtues and flaws, which is a great way to become a more compassionate, successful, loving, person or to achieve any goal you have.

While some people are confident and learned to love themselves, others didn't. The greatest enemy that prevents us from succeeding in life is lack of love for yourself and Enneagram helps you solve this problem too. Only by understanding, you love something, and your own personality is not an exception. The more you understand yourself and the inner patterns implicated with feelings, thoughts, or relationships, the easier it gets to practice self-love.

The Enneagram also encourages you to be active in every aspect of life. What does this mean? Sometimes we are passive and expect things to just happen or we are afraid of failure and it seems logical to just wait and see what's going to happen. Life doesn't work that way. Every individual creates their own success and happiness. Every personality type achieves that success in a different way, depending on those inner patterns, but Enneagram encourages all of you (regardless of the type number) to take action and improve the ability to have a harmonious life. Here, the word harmonious can mean something different for any personality type, but the point is that you won't sit back and wait for things to happen, you become more proactive. With the newfound ability to achieve that, you get an additional opportunity to evolve and reach the perfect image of yourself.

Different ways knowing personality type improves your life

The Enneagram dissects an individual's personality and allows us to take an objective look at inner patterns. Since we're able to identify both strengths and weaknesses, we get an opportunity to develop in all aspects of life. If you're still wondering how it is possible to improve your life with the help of personality type, this will help you. Here are different ways you get to improve your life just by knowing whether you're Type One, Five, Six, or any other:

- embracing your full self – what the Enneagram can teach is that everything about your personality is interconnected. You cannot be confident in your strengths without being aware of your weaknesses. When you know your personality type it gets easier to embrace your full self

- Helps narrow focus – you are drawn to the things that suit your personality the best. Sometimes we are confused and it becomes difficult to find a true passion. A specific personality type defines each individual and allows you to finally understand what you want to do or experience

- You're not alone – there are more than eight billion people in the world and we still feel all alone sometimes. We have both good and bad times, experience success and failures, love and want to be loved, but there always comes the time when you feel like nobody understands you. Just by reading the description of your personality type (or someone else's) you get the sense of belonging and realize you're not alone. There are many other people who are going through the same things

- Becoming less judgmental – although the best thing about our planet is its diversity, we've all judged someone because they didn't think or do things our way. Instead of trying to hide this fact, the healthy thing to do is to acknowledge it. The Enneagram personality helps you accomplish that. Knowing your personality type is a great way to understand yourself and why you judge others. At the same time, reading about other types allows you to understand their motivation and you become less judgmental when you consider some subject from their point of view.

- teaches you to trust yourself – we all hear a wide range of tips and advice for a better life. While there's nothing wrong with those, it is time to admit that one size fits all rule can't apply here.

Different people require a different approach in every aspect of life. That's why it's important to trust yourself and your own ability to do great things in life. Personality type helps you filter people's advice through your set values. That way, you learn what you can from others, but stay true to yourself at the same time.

CHAPTER 16: THE ATTITUDE OF GRATITUDE

Everyone have their different times and seasons with their different experiences at their time ventures. There's a time of planting and a season of harvest. Yours may be that of planting and mine of harvesting but the fact is that no situation is permanent.

Therefore, our reactions due to our present situations can extend the time span or help in the persistence of such situations (either positive or negative). Since no situation is permanent, there is an appointed time for a particular situation to hand over. The matter on ground is our reaction to the situations we find ourselves. Do you know that your attitude in that your situation can extend your span in that situation or vice versa?

Don't you think it's about time we consider our attitude towards our everyday situations and experiences? Yes, it's time. Your attitude is your reaction, gratitude is an attitude that aids positive change in your situations in life. The attitude you propagate can facilitate your experience in life.

INCOMES OF INGRATITUDE

Incomes of ingratitude simply means the gains from ingratitude, what we get as a result of being ungrateful. Some of them are as follows;

* DECREASE IN LIFE:
It is necessary that we all know that decrease in life is an unpleasantry and that it tends to poor living. Decrease in life can be reduction, demotion and deduction in ones standard of living. It is a product of ingratitude, in that; one who is not grateful for what he or she has, will end up losing that which he or she has.

Many unhappy families and homes are inflicted by the product of ingratitude in the sense that lack and want has eaten up their happiness. The surprising thing is that, they never increase but move from bad to worse.

* NEGATIVITY:
Life progression requires a positive impact from every possible aspect of it. A situation where the living isn't grateful, he or she often ends up taking each step backward to negative situations behind time, thereby making his or her life a great misery.

If you do a circle check, you will discover that most people involved in cultism and other societal harmful activities, are there as a result of ingratitude. Do you ask how? Series of stories affirms to the fact that most people join these dangerous groups as to pay back for past lost and also to get swift wealth. Don't you think it's an act of ingratitude that aids their involvement in such groups and their activities? We have ritualist, arm robbers, kidnappers and much more negative personalities causing havoc in our societies, because they have refused to be grateful for what they have and so the best for them is to make life miserable for others, just for them to fit in their desires and aims.

* LACK OF PRODUCTION:
Believe it or not, there will be no production where there is no promotion. Where peoples activities are not appreciated, there's always drifting by the unappreciated. As it is hard to approve what you don't appreciate, the same way it is harder to gain profit from what you don't appreciate. It also amazes me when people who are unappreciative are mostly the expectators of production from what they don't appreciate. How do you expect that young boy or girl to do more or better for you, when you don't even appreciate him or her for the little he or she has done? How do you expect God to do more, when you are not grateful for the ones he had done?
There is no duplicates about this, if you are unwilling to appreciate, then be ready for more lost because what you don't appreciate don't reproduce for you. Reproduction is the product of your appreciation. You don't need to apply force to it, even God is willing and ready to help the grateful to fly higher in life. That's why he is not interested in your origin but your original being.
Who you are from the inside will determine what you get in the outside. I discovered that most young people are choice dormant, because they are forced to do certain things they aren't supposed to. Due to circumstances of life, their alternate choice is being deterred for either one reason or the other. The peoples behind these are never mindful of their actions but on the other hand, are placing a drainage before their products. Before you know, life appears stranding and they begin to accuse another person for their misfortunes.

* INFERTILITY:
For something to be fertile, it must have good qualities and these qualities determines its fertility. Every fertile soil helps to meet the needs of the farmer in due season and according to his or her

commitment to maintain the fertility of the soil. Fertility for humanity is limited to no man but has exited many as a result of Ingratitude, rendering them infertile. No ungrateful man can produce gratuity and every negative thought is bond to produce negative actions or words.

A man of ingratitude cannot give himself nor can he get the required manure or fertilizer to fertilize his life. You may not find this interesting, but this is the main area where productivity is enabled or enhanced. Low quality living most times originates from here, as many people fail to target the foundational aspect of their lives. In all, ingratitude will always end up bringing sorrow, poverty, failure and anti prosperity to everyone practicing it.

Nothing is worth that gratitude compared to the ultimate reason that will be seen in the next chapter. Are you aware of it?

Learn To Be Grateful

Gratitude is not an inborn attitude, it is a practical attitude and so it can be learnt.

Do you know that smiles are contagious? My recent discovery with my mates affirms to the fact that it could be contacted.

As a student, my outlook was never complete without a frown on my face. In line with my uniform, I usually put on a frown on my face but the amazing thing was that I had some beloved friends who were always smiling and when they approached me with smiles, I found myself smiling back at them. With this, I Concord to the fact that smile is contagious but the uniqueness of this is, that I was learning to smile from their smiles.

Even so, it is with gratitude. We were not born grateful, we were born great to be grateful. Take for instance a lawyer, he or she wasn't born a lawyer, he or she was born with the in build capacity to judge.

You were not born grateful, but great to be grateful. The lawyer had to pass through learning strategies for he or she to discover and utilize that inborn ability he or she possessed. Your inborn greatness to be grateful must be discovered through learning and life itself is a great teacher that teaches you on daily basis, to be grateful.

One thing you must know is that you can't graduate in the class of life, if you are not grateful. I must confess that this writing has also taught me to be grateful, what about you?

Learning to be grateful is not a day job, it is a lifetime practical education that we involve in everyday. Do you know that must peoples have failed to be grateful because they refused to learn from life?

Everyday, everywhere, everyone is faced with different things that confront them; either pleasant or unpleasant. These things aim at teaching us either to be grateful or ungrateful. It is in our decision to choose which one to attend to, absorb and apply in our lives, as the result will be revealed on our lives.

Seeing, hearing and experiencing different things at different times, I decisively go for gratitude because it is a way of escape from any unpleasant situation. So, as I watch; I learn, as I hear; I learn and then, I choose what to do depending on the result it has to offer.

In life, I have learnt to understand that, people give bountifully out of gratitude and people receive plentifully due to gratitude. A lady was granted her request to work with a company of her desire, her attitude before the grantor made the grantor grateful to have her work with them, guess what attitude it was? The attitude of gratitude, she was grateful and her gratitude expanded to her grantor.

We need to learn to be grateful, because most breakthroughs don't come from fasting and prayer but from an attitude of gratitude.

Everything and everyone have their good side and bad side, as well as time and seasons. The bad side is one which no one wants to experience and for we to alleviate it, we must appreciate the good side.

With all due respect beloveth, bad times happens to everyone and so we must learn to be grateful at all times and in all things. Learning to be grateful and being grateful afterwards will enhance ones agility and reduce unnecessary stress, as gratitude will aid the solution of certain problems without stress, because gratitude is the force that forces things to happen.

Learn to be grateful and end up being the greatest because gratitude makes greatness an achievement of the great.

CHAPTER 17: UNDERSTANDING MORE ABOUT ENNEAGRAM

1. You are increasingly mindful

The best endowment of the Enneagram is that it encourages you to consider yourself to be others experience you, just as observe your qualities and developing edges (shortcomings) without self-judgment.

With the Enneagram, you find all the defensive dividers you have set up around yourself throughout the years to protect you. While they once may have been required, the Enneagram will assist you with letting go of them.

Fortunately you have a profundity of inward intelligence that is accessible to you in each minute. The Enneagram can assist you with accessing your inward shrewdness through your three cerebrum focuses the body, psyche, and heart.

You get to the intelligence of your body through the sensations you experience. You get to the heart through your feelings. At last, you get to your otherworldly focus through your calm personality.

With training, you can move into nearness. At the point when you are available you are neither living previously or future. You are available to what is happening, at the time. You will just comprehend what you have to do.

2. You comprehend your accomplice

In a relationship, your accomplice will consistently stay a secret and you will to him. Be that as it may, with the assistance of the Enneagram, you can get a look at what it resembles to be from his point of view.

You will start to see how your accomplice sees and encounters the world in various manners. Things which may appear glaringly evident to you won't really be for your mate.

Your accomplice isn't attempting to make you insane. He is acting naturally. He sees the world uniquely in contrast to you do. Nobody is preferable or more regrettable over the other. You are regularly both right.

After some time you will develop in sympathy for your accomplice.

Every one of us has our very own battles. Because we discover something simple doesn't mean our accomplice will.

For instance, you may be outgoing and love to meet new individuals while your accomplice is independent and calm. You will both need to discover approaches to respect one another. You both need to get your needs met.

Every one of the sorts have their qualities and developing edges. As you find out about one another's sorts you gain understanding into both your universes. As you gain bits of knowledge into your accomplice, you are welcomed into increasingly significant empathy for the one you love.

3. You locate a typical language

The Enneagram gives you a typical language to work through your difficulties as a team in a humane manner.

Chipping away at your relationship through the Enneagram can assist you with bringing out your best as people and as a team.

It is an extraordinary instrument to assist you with staying responsible to yourself and your accomplice. Finding your sort can assist your join forces with supporting you in your individual and development as a team.

In the first place, you have to give each other consent give each other criticism. In the wake of giving each other authorization, let each other comprehend what sort of language and activities will bolster you in your self-improvement.

Be cautious: the Enneagram is never to be utilized as a weapon. It is expected to be utilized with tenderness, consideration, and empathy.

Above all, your Enneagram type can assist you with remaining inquisitive about what is happening in yourself and your accomplice.

At the point when you utilize delicate and open language you can welcome your accomplice to go more inside and out into themselves and proceed with the way toward relinquishing apprehension, outrage, and agony that is blocking them.

At the point when you can remain grounded and open, you will have the option to determine any contention with your accomplice since you are carrying on of what is genuine as opposed to fear, silly idea, and control issues.

The Enneagram can upgrade your relationship since it endless supply of you to assemble sound associations with yourself and the one you love.

It encourages you to take 100% obligation regarding yourself in the relationship. You additionally fabricate empathy for the one you love and figure out how to praise every others' qualities and bolster each other in improving the pieces of us that need reinforcing.

The best endowment of the Enneagram is that it encourages you to do your own work without judgment. It encourages us to develop as a team without getting into quarrels over who is correct or wrong.

The first step towards self-transformation is self-discovery. Without self-discovery, we are doomed to keep on repeating and following our old patterns of behavior unconsciously. And as long as we keep this cycle going on and on, we will keep getting the results of the past.

While many of us still have formidable strengths, the weakness of our character seems to slow and delay our progress in life. Thanks to the Enneagram that provides a deep insight into our personality, shows us what went wrong, where the problem lies with our personality, and what is missing in the picture.

When you perform the Enneagram test for the first time and you find your type and wings, you will discover something more than yourself like never before. The Enneagram reveals the unconscious motivations, fears, and desires that drive your everyday actions. You identify your strengthens and weaknesses, and finally know your type.

While knowing your Enneagram type is very important. Taking a closer look at your wing type and analyzing the role it plays in your life is crucial. How are the wing types affecting your everyday life? How does the combined impact of your core and wing-type affect and influence your life?

The Enneagram report is much more revealing. Get the full details about your personality. When you do, don't stop there. The next step is to commit to a personal development and growth program that will move you on the road to the essence. The main goal of the Enneagram is to discover where you fell from essence and then work back to that level. What you want to do is to become the best version of yourself.

And that means working on yourself and transforming your unholy desires to the holy desires. It means converting your vices into virtues by doing the "inner work" of transformation that Ichazo talked about when he first introduced the Enneagram. It is only by discovering our type and doing the inner work that we get to the real essence.

We get closer to the real essence when we discover our unhealthy type and then work through the development stages to make it healthy. The fact is that your unhealthy type negatively affects all aspects of your life: career, finance, marriage, family, organization and everything you do.

Therefore, nothing changes in your life until you transform your personality. The better you get with your personality; the better life gets for you. Just like what Jim Rohn said, "If you change yourself, everything will change for you." When you commit to discovering and developing your personality, your life will transform completely.

According to the Enneagram, there are three centers of intelligence: the head, heart, and body. Our thinking, feeling, and actions influence what we do and affect our personality over time. Whereas in the past, you have been unconsciously programmed by society and the external environment to live in a certain way, you can take complete charge over your centers of intelligence and take control of your life.

Sometimes the journey to a healthy type can be hard and challenging. That means getting a credible Enneagram coach or therapist to help you do the "inner work" to develop yourself. The right Enneagram will analyze your current condition, map out a personal development plan and then help you grow your personality over a period of time.

If you dedicate to learning about the Enneagram, discovering your enneatype and working steadily on growing yourself with the help of an Enneagram coach/therapist, the compound effect will be exhilarating. You'll be amazed at how you will develop your personality over a period of time.

The compound effect will make a profound difference in marriage, career, relationship, family, finances, and social life. People all around you will realize that you are making positive changes in your life that are constantly reflecting in your life. You will find yourself manifesting, exhibiting and showing more of the qualities of the divine nature of true essence.

CONCLUSION

Successful self-development occurs when we understand our inner patterns, determine strengths and weaknesses, but it also depends on fostering healthy and strong relationships with other people. The Enneagram helps us improve relationships in different aspects of our life in more ways than one.

From the very moment of birth, you are in a relationship (parents, siblings, other family members, friends, romantic parents etc.). Most people usually wonder what personality type suits them relationship-wise, but as mentioned earlier in the book, even though some types share similarities all of them are compatible with one another. The Enneagram is not like zodiac and doesn't help you improve relationships by suggesting you should engage with people who belong to the certain type.

When you understand your personality type it means you are aware of the inner patterns, motivations, desires, fears, virtues, and flaws. This means you understand where you're coming from. For example, a person who is Type Five understands what they seek in relationships with other people, but you also get an insight into how they perceive you.

By getting educated about other personality types, one finds it easier to understand their desires and what those people are looking for in different relationships. What can this teach you? Compromise! The key to a healthy relationship is a compromise. After all, the relationship isn't a dictatorship where one person is superior to the other and only they make all the choices. Both people in that relationship, romantic, platonic, family, should be equal and feel free to be open about their desires and what they expect from the other person. The Enneagram teaches you how to be confident, but still, accept other people's opinions and it are a great tool to improve every relationship in your life. The opportunity to understand inner patterns of other people and compare them to yours helps you establish a deeper connection with others. This is the type of connection we are unable to achieve unless we understand ourselves and other people. It's like a domino effect because it's impossible to understand other people without knowing yourself. See, everything is connected, which is why the Enneagram is represented as a circle showing that although all nine personality types are different, they are strongly involved with one another.

Some people are open about their emotions, others aren't. Some of us are easily offended, but others are not. Plus, some people give love and want to be loved while others are confused and don't know how to express themselves the best way. All of us have different approaches to any type of relationship, but you always get puzzled. Why do people react/demand/feel certain things the way they do? Their Enneagram personality type explains it in detail. Learning how they react prevents you from taking them the wrong way or judging them.

MASTER YOUR EMOTIONS

REVISED AND UPDATED

Practical Step by Step Guide to Overcome Negative
Emotions, Stop Anxiety and Depression and to
Live a Positive and Healthy Life

Dr Henry Campbell & Dr Daniel Watson

PREFACE TO EMOTIONAL INTELLIGENCE

If you are currently reading this, it means you are one of the people striving so hard to get rid of anger, stress, and anxiety in order to build a life of positivity for themselves. Well, count yourself lucky because you have just found your one-stop-shop to everything you need to know about anger, stress, and anxiety management; you can now find out everything you need to know about overcoming negativity. The book, "Master your Emotions" contains genuine information, strategies, and techniques that can help you create that happy, negativity-devoid, and quality life you desire and as well, deserve. The book is written in simplified and easy-to-digest language to help you assimilate everything contained within smoothly.

The book will teach you all you need to know about core emotions, meditation exercises, breathing exercise for better management of emotions.

The choice is now left to you to choose a life devoid of stress, anger, anxiety; a life of positivity; and start living life with a de-cluttered and free mind using the strategies, tips, and techniques waiting for you in the book. Add a copy to the cart and get started on the journey to positivity and productivity!

INTRODUCTION

Human emotions are a tremendous force that controls not only our thoughts but also our actions. Emotions push us to good and bad deeds, they cause satisfaction or dissatisfaction, euphoria, and annoyance. In the latter case, a person can break the irritation on others only because, being in the grip of feelings, he was not able to make the only right decision.

In order to be in the right place at the right time, to have a reputation as a reliable and mature person capable of thoughtful actions, you need to be in control of yourself. After all, very often in life, cold-blooded behavior in a given situation helps out more than high intelligence.

The ability to control oneself, one's thoughts and feelings are the main principles of a modern person. Unfortunately, the rhythm of our life does not always allow for a detailed analysis of one's own emotions and their causes.

But knowing the enemy by sight is half the battle. Therefore, we took the liberty to describe the main negative emotions and some ways to overcome them. From this book, you will learn how to cope with anger, fear, irritation, envy and the main enemy of modern man - constant anxiety, which, in fact, is the ancestor of all emotions.

CHAPTER 1 HOW TO OVERCOME BARRIERS ON THE WAY

Every second of our lives, and especially in difficult or contradictory circumstances, we face a choice. Our choice is a reaction to troubles, to conflicts with people, to disturbing situations. It depends only on us whether we will become hostages of negative emotions, whether our actions will be subordinated to feelings, and not to reason, to what extent such emotional slavery will become an obstacle.

But each of us has another alternative. We can calm down, take control of emotions, take a deep breath, and then respond, following sound logic and reason.

Emotional Competence
The term emotional competence, also called EQ, appeared only at the beginning of the XXI century. Since we are past those times, we discuss modern psychology's definition of the words. Breaking it down, it implies:

• emotional intelligence;
• emotional thinking;
• emotional competence.

Emotions are essential components of our life. Analyzing the most effective ways to manage feelings is extremely useful for every person. It is necessary to learn how to control your emotions in difficult life situations. It is especially important for a business person to master the strategy of such self-control. He also needs to be aware of the feelings of his interlocutor in order to find a constructive approach and reach an agreement.

In psychology, it is customary to distinguish the components of emotional competence:
Self-consciousness - the awareness of a person's assessment of

himself as a person - his ethical image and interests, values, character, temperament, emotionality, and motives of behavior.

Understanding your own feelings - the most important element of emotional competence. Without knowing how to listen to their feelings, it is more convenient for a person to assume that he is well aware of what is happening to him at any moment, what state he is in, and what is going through. However, in reality, our understanding of what is happening is superficial. In this regard, we can identify three main functions of awareness of emotions: consolidation of experience, interpersonal communication, and emotional expression.

Awareness of one's own emotions - a step towards control over them. It is important to listen to yourself and understand what you really feel, learn to recognize the nuances of the feelings experienced, their appearance and modification. Perhaps the most important thing on this step is to analyze and find out the reasons: why you feel that way.

Thus, the understanding of one's own feelings promotes sociability, since it allows one to adequately recognize, describe, process, and further express emotions.

Self-control - control over your feelings and actions. To control your emotions is not to suppress them, but to subordinate them to yourself and make you work for the good of the cause. That is, to be able to regulate, at that time, to what extent, and in what form allow yourself anger or joy. Self-control, above all, involves blocking negative feelings. Sometimes people fail to express positive emotions. As a rule, men are more restrained than women.

The gift of emotionally responding to other people's experiences is called empathy. A person capable of such empathy is supremely able to put himself in the place of another person. In a business environment, empathy leads to constructive interaction between the consultant and the client.

Empathy means entering into the personal world of the other and staying in it "at home." It includes a constant sensitivity to the changing emotions of the communication partner. It is like temporarily "getting used to" the other person's inner world, being delicate in it without appreciation and condemnation. This means grasping what the other person is barely aware of. However, there are no attempts to uncover unconscious feelings, as they can be traumatic. It is also necessary to communicate your impressions about the feelings of the other when you calmly observe from the side those elements that excite or frighten your interlocutor. To be empathic means to be responsible, initiative, strong and at the same time thin and sensitive.

A person who is sensitive to the emotions of other people is able to hear, see and take into account the emotionality of another, can understand the point of view of people who think differently. Traditionally it is believed that women are better able to feel the emotional mood of another person than men.

Sociability - implies a person's positive life attitude, the ability to get along with people, smooth out conflict situations, the ability to listen and understand, as well as the talent to manage relationships and adapt to the team.

Tip: Emotions should never be suppressed! Take control of them!

Exercise: Changing the emotional state
What thoughts, images, and actions do you associate with negative emotions? Transform the cause of the negative through your imagination. Imagine what effect such a cause would have under other circumstances. Describe the result in a diary. What thoughts or actions can you call the cause of your depressed state? Could you cheer yourself up? Congratulate yourself if you succeed! Otherwise, do not be discouraged. When you repeat the exercise, you will certainly be able to bring your emotional state in the right direction.

The lack of a modern manager of emotional intelligence (or emotional competence) can be a huge obstacle to prosperity. So, how to overcome this barrier?

CHAPTER 2 EMOTIONAL COMPETENCE. HOW TO DEVELOP IT?

Studies have confirmed that the most successful leaders have a high level of self-awareness, and other personal qualities and social skills that are included in the concept of emotional competence.

Emotional competence begins to develop before mental intelligence. Its components such as self-esteem, appear in a child when he successfully copes with a difficult task, shows independence and achieves a result.

Thus, a characteristic feature that distinguishes outstanding folk was found. Psychologists argue that emotional intelligence, as a technical skill, can be developed and improved. However, unlike technical abilities, the connective channels in our brain that are responsible for social and emotional competence are different from those that govern scientific knowledge and learning.

How to increase personal emotional competence
The emotional world of some people is like a cluttered wardrobe in which memories of the past, unfulfilled hopes and dreams gather dust. Psychologists strongly recommend: do not suppress a violent joy in yourself, cry when you feel like it, at least when no one sees you! And remember that laughter is the best cure for any trouble.

Exercise: Developing personal emotional competence
In order for you to be overwhelmed with constructive emotions, try to regularly do what you like. Immediately remember something that you want to smile.
Man has great potential to rejoice:
• go to the "Children's World," choose the most liked toy and buy it;
• have fun at the marmalade feast (own composition), invite old friends to it and dance to your favorite records. And then pick up a homeless kitten, and under his rumbling eat sweets;
• find the "magic wand," change into a wizard and make wishes;
• inflate balloons and launch them under the clouds;

• periodically skate and swing, attend children's rides and not think about what reaction your behavior causes to others;
• tell tales to children. To you, and them, such a pastime will bring a lot of positive emotions;
• attend circus performances;
• show card tricks in the company. The glory of great magicians may threaten you, but you will gain inner freedom and become more confident in yourself.

Some more tips
1. Listen to yourself. It happens that anger hides resentment, anger - a feeling of fear or insolvency. Listen to your emotional experiences: what do you really experience? The main thing is not to engage in self-deception, and for this, you need to ask yourself questions more often and take time for yourself.

2. Do not say that "I feel bad with this and that ..." Build a phrase differently, for example: "I feel that ..." This is how you assess your attitude, not the situation and people. That is, the difference is that not "this person is not good," but "I feel bad next to him." Do not be afraid to talk about your experiences - this is a sign of strength and emotional maturity.

3. Define your goals and desires. This is an indispensable part of self-awareness. This way will help you decide: take a piece of paper and write answers to two questions: "What do I really want?" And "How do I present myself and my life after a certain period of time?." Record the first thing that comes to mind, relying on intuition. Write down both close and distant goals, both real and seemingly fantastic. Such training will help you find the meaning of your own life, feel your uniqueness and realize your potential.

4. Be confident and independent of the opinions of others.

5. Change "minus" to "plus." If you are fired from your job, start wasting your energy on finding a new, more promising one. This is a successful approach to the use of negative energy. Negative emotions are also good because they serve as a reason for constructive analysis - what should be done so that this experience does not happen again? However, it should be remembered that a person with high emotional competence will not engage in vain "self-digging," he knows the way to get out of depression.

6. Try to put yourself in the shoes of another person. Be sensitive and think about the possible consequences of your actions.

7. Become an active listener. The active listener nods, confirms, asks, and with his whole appearance makes it clear that he is interested in talking to the interlocutor. Naturally, people will communicate with such a person with sincere pleasure.

The ability to listen means more than just silently waiting for an opportunity to speak, nodding from time to time. Active listeners are engaged in only one case, they completely "digest" the information received. They periodically ask again to make sure that they heard exactly what they wanted to say.

8. Listen with your eyes. Perception of gestures - in general, also refers to the ability to listen. For example, during dinner, the most tactful way to hint to the interlocutor that the corners of his mouth are smeared with food is to take a napkin and, looking into the eyes of the interlocutor, wet the corners of his own mouth. It is likely that the other person will do the same, but this will happen unconsciously, and your gesture will not be taken as a hint.

9. Never interrupt the interlocutor and listen to the person to the end, so as not to miss important information.

10. Learn body language. Gestures, facial expressions, intonation. If you are able to recognize this information, you will be able to get the most reliable picture of the person and the situation. This is a business intuition that helps to make the right decisions, to trust to sign a contract with one partner and not to trust another.

Anger. How to curb it?
Anger and irritation are natural, quite adequate human reactions, but their consequences in the form of broken relationships, unsigned contracts, loss of work, and sometimes even judgment can be even worse.

Some people tend to be angrier more than others. This is due mainly to the innate temperament: the natural speed and strength of nervous processes and not bad education. For people who are capable of self-control, strong emotions of irritation, anger, and anger outwardly can be almost imperceptible. Continuing at the same time to tamper with the inside, they deliver a lot of trouble.

Modern psychology offers two solutions to the problem.

The first is that emotions must be kept under control, behave culturally, as befits any civilized person. To solve this problem a lot of psychological techniques and exercises have been developed. The second is to recognize the necessity and expediency of openly manifesting your feelings, both positive and negative. The problem is how to do it in an acceptable way.

Anger under control
You can not own anything without owning yourself first and foremost. These words formulate the illusion that most people completely control their behavior. But in most cases, we act impulsively, and without realizing our true motives. We do not control ourselves and do not want to control, in part, because we are reluctant, in part because we are afraid to take away its unpredictable charm from life. We are satisfied with this situation as long as the emotions do not turn into an uncontrollable beast, with which it will be almost impossible to cope.

Continuous work with anger requires stability, effort and a certain degree of development of the personality. But for a quick fight with momentary anger, there are rapid methods. First, physical activity, which perfectly relieves irritation and aggression. Moreover, it is through anger that your subconscious can tell you a lack of exercise. In this case engage in traditional fitness, shaping, bodybuilding and morning jogging.

We show our feelings openly: several acceptable ways
1. Allow yourself to experience feelings such as irritation, and anger. Assume that you are able to experience these emotions often. By forbidding ourselves to experience "bad" feelings and pushing them out of consciousness, we thereby deprive ourselves of the ability to control them. And vice versa: assuming that we can experience negative feelings, and allowing ourselves to experience them, we gain more opportunities to control our emotions and behavior.

2. Allow yourself to experience negative emotions toward specific people. You know better than anyone else why you treat them that way. It will be easier for you to control your own state if you clearly understand what particular character traits you do not like in people. In addition, you can dislike the person that inexplicably combines several unacceptable qualities to you. In the event that another person associates with an unpleasant person to you, you may unknowingly feel to him the whole range of negative emotions that you are capable of. Therefore, it is important to realize which people are most unpleasant to you, and why.

3. Learn how to diagnose irritation and anger at the initial stages, at the first signs of their appearance. Tension and bad mood are modified in readiness for aggressive reactions, which can take such forms as:
• indifferent, insolent or defiant intonation;
• gloomy, facial expression;
• in speech or in thought coarse expressions arise;
• your humor turns black and transforms into sarcasm;
• you are all unnerving; you throw things.

4. Express your emotions immediately as they arise. Report it to the person who called them. Strong feelings rarely manage to pacify completely. The desire to restrain, repress, suppress them can lead to a stressful state and a sharp deterioration in health. And long-term stress on the background of negative emotions, ultimately, can lead to chronic disease. In addition, suppressed, negative emotions in some people can transform into "explosions." Unable to restrain negative emotions, you, in the end, break into the one who causes you this. Unfortunately, often the "victims" of our anger are people whom we trust and who love us. Therefore, it is important to respond in time to the person who offended you or hurt you.

5. Feeling that you are about to "explode," just warn others about it. This will avoid a possible conflict. You simply notify others about your condition so that they do not fall under your hot hand.

If an annoying colleague
A staff member sitting next door does not look away from your monitor and comments on what he saw or went for tea for the tenth time in the last half-hour, while you didn't get up from the very morning? It is unlikely that there will be at least one seasoned

person who will tolerate such a thing. According to a study conducted by a US company, about 30% of retired office workers say that the main reason for their decision is irritation due to the habits of their colleagues.

Psychologists recommend starting work with any irritation from the most irritable.

Perhaps the person is unconsciously or consciously looking for a reason for irritation. If, on the whole, everything is good, and colleagues are still annoying, it makes sense to find the cause of the annoying habit. Talk to the person who annoys you and finds out more about him. Most likely, there will be no trace of irritation, because you will find a reasonable explanation for his behavior. Perhaps a colleague, annoying you with phone calls, calls his wife every 15 minutes just because she is seriously ill and bedridden.

Advice: In business, in order to succeed, you should think about business, and not about how annoying a colleague is!

Step-by-step recommendations: how to behave with an aggressive boss
1. Show business activity. Speak loudly, quickly and clearly.
2. Do not look away from the eyes of an angry boss. Your fearless look will certainly discourage him.
3. Watch your breath. The air should be inhaled slowly and deeply, and then exhale it as slowly, concentrating on this process. You can silently consider breathing in and out.
4. Do not argue. Only by showing restraint, you can earn respect in the eyes of a furious "chief."
5. Let the boss talk. To interrupt is useless.
6. Use the pauses that the boss needs to take a break and insert the necessary cues.
7. Along the way, try to contact the angry manager more often by name and patronymic. Perhaps this will help bring him to his senses.

If the boss is you
If the boss is you, and for some reason, you are annoyed by a subordinate (he is slow at work, constantly "smokes" and objects to you for any reason). So you have a good reason to doubt your

organizational skills.

Ask yourself a few questions: "Why does the employee allow himself to behave this way? What mistake did I make in my leadership post? Perhaps, I was obliged at the initial stage to let him understand that such frequent and causing mistakes are unforgivable and permissiveness is unacceptable? And, in the end, maybe the company simply does not need such an undisciplined employee?" It often happens that as a result of this understanding, the head comes to the conclusion that, despite all his flaws, the employee is nonetheless valuable to the organization.

What is the use of anger?
Modern psychologists say that it is not the external response that is of particular importance, but the inner self-perception of a person.

The main feature of psychological harmony is the acceptance of oneself entirely, along with all your emotions, both positive and destructive. To cope with anger, sort out its causes. If a person experiences anger, then this makes sense. For example, anger notifies a person that someone or something is violating his rights. He also gives them the strength to defend these rights, because it is an excellent source of energy. Anger can help you hide that you are scared. In any case, he points a person to his vulnerable place: "You are angry, it means that you are wrong"! Because anger is not caused by an event, but only by your attitude to this event. There is no alternative: it is the attitude towards life and people that needs to be changed.

Fear. How to deal with it?
Being an individual is extremely difficult because complexes and fears constantly impose life priorities on us. Well, it's terrible if a person has his whole life subordinated to his complexes and numerous fears.

At the heart of all the complexes is fear. Fear is emotion is a necessary component of our lives and is present in the mind of a person as a signal that signals danger.

Fear often affects not only the psyche but also the entire body: a person moves stiffly, dizziness and weakness appear. Fear activates the work of the endocrine glands, and the release of adrenaline into the blood keeps a person under stress. He can only follow the two primitive instincts - to face danger and attack first or escape. Which option you prefer depends on your self-esteem.

Today, everyone wants to succeed and win. But fears can become an insurmountable obstacle to success. How to deal with this? How to win in life and business?

The manifestation of fear. What is the reason?
One of the most common symptoms of fear is trembling of all muscles of the body. Such a tremor is especially noticeable on a person's lips. When fear grows into horror, we get a new transformation of the emotional state. There are irregularities in the heart. Sometimes a person loses consciousness, his face becomes covered with deathly pallor; breathing becomes difficult, etc.

Fear usually appears on the basis of life experience. The kid is not afraid of heights and can safely, bending down, jump from the bridge. Only after experiencing pain in various circumstances, a person begins to fear what it may cause. Different degrees of fear in a person is detected in different ways: horror, panic, anxiety, fearful expectation, intimidation, downtroddenness, fear of humility and devotion associated with fear. Fear is able to completely subjugate thinking. The idea stops at one thing: to find a way out of a stressful situation. However, fear is a passive-defensive reaction. The first answer to an obstacle in many people - the desire to shrink into a lump and stand still - these are all variants of fear or a passive-defensive reflex.

The main types of fear:
• fear of failure;
• fear of achieving the goal;
• fear of change;
• fear of danger;
• fear of loss (health, work, money, relatives, loved ones ...);
• fear of death.

Thoughts contributing to heightening fear:
1) focusing on the only, often negative, solution to the problem;
2) mental chaos, inability to concentrate;
3) mental failure in a negative future;

4) the world is merciless, dangerous, cunning, we are victims of terrible circumstances.

What threatens fear?
1. Manipulation. A person who is afraid of something or someone is easy to manage.
2. Loss of energy. This is manifested by various psychosomatic diseases, such as sleep disorders (insomnia, nightmares), reduced potency, peptic ulcer, myocardial infarction, high blood pressure, and many skin diseases.
3. Inability to achieve the goal. Fear paralyzes our self-confidence.
4. Hypertrophied sense of self-preservation. Instead of overcoming psychological difficulties, we begin to deliberately avoid certain life circumstances, out of the fear that they may turn into another negative experience for us.

Fear of failure
Cause
The reason for this "frightening factor" is a banal uncertainty in themselves and their abilities. Everyone, without exception, before embarking on his functional duties, asks himself a question: "But can I? ..." But different people answer this question to themselves differently. Most subconsciously answer "no" and never achieve any success. Some have doubts but are ready to test their strength. They have certain chances of success, which are inversely proportional to their uncertainty in themselves, and since this uncertainty disappears with the attainment of certain success, their chances increase uncontrollably. And only a few are sure that they will cope. Such people, sometimes, achieve unprecedented success.

Solution
Evaluating your capabilities should be adequate. Groundless self-confidence is no less pernicious than the fear of failure. It is useless to repeat that you can quickly make huge money if you have not received the relevant professional skills and do not possess the necessary qualities. You need diligence, patience, and hope. It is with the hope that the overcoming of fear and uncertainty begins. Buy the right books to fill in the gaps in your knowledge, carefully study and analyze everything, participate in pieces of training, develop your emotional competency, and then go up to

the next level, not forgetting to analyze your own experience. And you will see how gradually, step by step, uncertainty disappears and gives way to decisiveness, and hope turns into a firm faith in success, which, backed up by quite good initial results, it turns into a half-come true dream. Everything else is completely in your hands.

Fear of needing to act independently
Cause
Unfortunately, most of us are not used to acting independently and making independent decisions. Someone has been pushing us all our lives: parents, management, spouses, etc. Subconsciously, we understand this and fear it. Where is the way out? How to deal with it?

Solution
The technique is as old as the world: self-discipline and self-education. You need to learn to take responsibility and make decisions on your own. You need to become your own chef and demand from yourself in full.

It is necessary to become not only the master of one's destiny and financial well-being but, above all, the master of one's own thoughts, efforts, and decisions.

Fear of instability
Cause
Here we should speak, firstly, of the instability of the functioning of various state and commercial structures (banks, communication providers, etc.), and secondly, of the expected instability of profits.

Solution
Such phenomena should be feared. But here we need to go the following way: provide for various options for activities, use alternative mechanisms, etc. If one thing does not work, the other is sure to be successful. The key to success is variability.

Fear of public opinion
Cause
We are all vain to a certain degree and do not want to seem ridiculous, look worse in the eyes of another person than we would like. So we are afraid, and we are saved from the danger of

"crashing." Interestingly, we ourselves often activate fear in ourselves, going to work with a "success set," with an expectation of praise and applause. And colleagues and management are not always able to love us immediately and unresponsively.

Solution
Do not demand the impossible from others and do not make excessive demands on yourself.

The second reason
Laziness or disorganization. We are not preparing for an active day at work and look forward to "random." As a result - we deprive ourselves of confidence.

Solution
Cultivating yourself by working on yourself daily. Do not put off until tomorrow what you can do today. If the necessary actions are carried out in time, the anxiety will significantly decrease.

Third reason
Excessive suspiciousness. For example, someone does not like their own appearance. But when this person communicates with other people, it seems to him that everyone evaluates him and thinks only of his shortcomings. Naturally, such a person is afraid of any opportunity to be in the center of attention.

Solution
To think more about business and focus on the conversation. Focus on the interlocutor, and do not "dwell on" your beloved self.

Exercise: Victory over fear
Take a comfortable posture with a straightened back, relax, follow your breath, remember the situation that scares you. Go inside it and try to visualize in your mind a "picture" of an intimidating extreme experience. Make it brighter, watch yourself and your body present in this image, and then mentally go inside the body, causing anxiety and fear as brightly as possible. Only in this case do not identify with the experience, but start exploring it from the outside. Try to gradually reduce your dependence on fear, concentrating the muscular pattern of fear and anxiety and slowly

withdrawing fear from you like a dark cloud. You can mentally breathe through this mist, draw energy into the cloud and dissolve it in space. Then remember any circumstances from the past, where you, in similar circumstances, remained calm and behaved correctly, harmoniously and resourcefully. Mentally transfer this program of calm fearlessness to the image of this situation. Repeat the exercise several times until the situation ceases to be extreme.

An, and tigers at my feet ... Or, how to get rid of the fear of the audience
Technique
Let us remember a few rules that will help you cope with fear and prevent the excitement of a public speech or communication in a difficult speech situation.

First of all, remember that for the speaker there is no mood worse than the "installation for success." The higher the mental level is set, the more serious the injuries will be as a result of the fall. The fundamental thing at the moment is not to think about how you look in the eyes of the listeners, but to concentrate on accomplishing the tasks set, on achieving the goal of the performance. A person who is busy thinking about the case forgets to be afraid. It is very important to disconnect attention from the source of fear. Learn to control your attention. Remember that when you worry, your attention is not collected.

Sometimes, already at the moment of performance, a wave of fear suddenly overtakes you. For example, something is forgotten. Do not panic. Gather attention on some object (pen on the table), calm your breath. Hold a theatrical pause. Remember, this is not deadly. Thoughtfully speak your last phrase (perhaps, by slightly changing it). Your brain works in these seconds is activated mode, so the necessary solution will be found without fail. Do not let fear take you. And in general, be aware that the public does not notice your emotion. It only seems to us that everyone is happy watching our panic.

Tension and stiffness make breathing difficult, so you need to learn how to relieve this tension and get rid of it. Only a free person can create. Pay attention to your body and achieve muscle freedom. Imagine that you see yourself from the inside. This skill -

attention to the state of the body and stress relief - should turn into an automatic one.

Relaxing contributes to the right attitude to work. Try to perceive your future public not as a hostile force, but as friends who can help. Before the performance, calm your breathing, take a few shallow even breaths and exhalations. Move-in a quiet rhythm (if space permits).

Who wants to stop being afraid of listeners, should start performing. It is difficult only the first few times. If you do not overcome your fear, you will have to fear all your life.

Some rules for controlling fear
1. "Face fear"
A person who is proud of his "fearlessness" increases the severity of the fear. He is not just afraid of real danger, but fears and show his fear. These additional sources of negativity can be avoided simply by accepting as a fact that you are afraid of something. If you are alarmed, you should think about "where to put the straws." Changing thoughts and behavior in the direction of "safety net" will bring significantly more benefits.

2. Rethinking circumstances
The second rule is a chance to rethink the circumstances. Fear is an emotion, and any emotion is an irritant. But it manifests itself as an irritant depending on your perception and attitude towards it - it is its interpretation that is responsible for the emotional response of the organism. For example, an employee of a company, frightened by the demand to appear to the boss, can get rid of fear, realizing that this demand can be caused not by displeasure, but by working necessity. Rethinking is given with difficulty because it needs objective creative thinking. Sometimes a person needs someone's help to look at their circumstances from a different point of view.

3. Humor instead of fear
In cases where the situation does not allow long-term revaluation, the innate sense of humor can serve an invaluable service. Laughter, even if it seems out of place at the moment, helps relieve emotional tension and keeps people from being overly serious about their own person.

4. Transformation of the energy of fear into the energy of creation
An excellent means of immediately alleviating anxiety is a useful activity. Old ideas about running around the floor of the city or chopping wood to distract, are quite fair from a psychological point of view.

5. Correction of the situation
The best way to get rid of fear is to do exactly that which will directly lead to the correction of a frightening situation. It is easier to attack a problem than to control the emotions that it provoked. For example, instead of trying to control the fear of losing your job, you should try to become an irreplaceable professional. Then such anxiety will be unfounded.

6. Training the ability to cope with problems
The arising emotions depend on a preliminary assessment of the attitude to any frightening situation. A well-prepared student rejoices in the exam as a chance to show his knowledge, and an unprepared student is afraid of verification. A person's feelings, his self-esteem to a very large extent depend on the skills of behavior in society, and they (these skills) can be developed and expanded through the development of emotional intelligence.

Exercise: working with fear at a rational level of consciousness
Write in a notebook what you are afraid of.
Or write those words, phrases, which according to your feelings are connected with fear. For example, "I'm afraid of losing my job, I'm afraid of a divorce from my wife, or I'm afraid of a lawsuit about the division of property." Recorded?

And then you trace the chain of potential events. In the second stage, calculate, and what is the conceivable percentage of failure? At the third stage, for example, the phrase "I am afraid of losing my job" is rewritten as "I am ready to search for a more promising job." Charge yourself with confidence. Imagine as if all the trouble is over.

Envy

So, envy is a strong feeling that motivates a person to a variety of actions, painful and requiring removal.

Its components are:

1) social comparison;
2) your perception of someone's superiority;
3) experiencing annoyance, grief, and even humiliation about it;
4) hostility or even hatred towards someone who is superior;
5) desire to harm to him (or her);
6) the desire or real deprivation of his superiority.

Envy is a comparison and identification. We compare everything and everyone. Just because the comparison is the principle of the functioning of the reason inherent in us by nature. Everything that we see and hear, we compare with what we have seen and heard before.

Envying an adult means living around the clock in a complex comparison system. Yourself with others. The paradox is that Kate can envy Sveta because she has a child. At the same time, Sveta envies Kate because she is married. Or she has more money and a personal bank account. However, they are best friends. And in all of this life. They live in suspense because it is impossible to get ahead of others in all indicators.

The key comparison criterion is "Better-worse." These are unreal concepts invented by man. "Better" or "worse" do not happen by themselves. They are only where there is our comparison. Nevertheless, we think that better and worse are real things that objectively exist.

Envy is comparing yourself to another person, so you experience discomfort. You come to the conclusion that you are worse than him. Envy itself is a very negative emotion. You feel as if something of yours has been taken away from you, which should rightfully belong to you, and given to another person.

Black envy. Where are the roots?

The two extreme measures on the envy scale are called black and white. According to experts in the field of practical psychology, black envy is a negative feeling that leads to anger, devastation, and self-destruction. Those who are gnawing black envy, believe that life treats them unfairly. This kind of envy is very stable. It usually develops in childhood.

"Look, Lena has a neat little skirt, and you are all smeared!" The parent reproaches her daughter. My daughter cannot tell her mother how she feels for Lena now. But if she could, she would say that "she hates her. Firstly, because she was liked by her mother more than her. Secondly, because she does not share her toys. Thirdly, etc, etc. The educational result - the child received a lesson in social comparison, and he had reasons to envy others.

Black envy leads to chronically low self-esteem, which ultimately transforms into destructive hatred, which turns primarily against the envious.

White envy or admiration?
In contrast to black - white envy has a tonic effect. It inspires, as the person who aroused envy, suddenly causes admiration. Such a person does not worry about the fact that another person is more successful than him in his personal life or career, but admires him, and this stimulates him to be active. Thus, white envy can cause a desire for change for the better and provoke creative activity.

You look at the person and joyfully exclaim: "Wow! Well done! "

Envy is a rivalry.
It is hard not to agree that envy is always present where there is competition for something with other people. For example, for the right to consider themselves the most successful, suave, intelligent, professional, in-demand, strong or beautiful. And since we still live "according to the laws of the jungle," we continue to compete in all areas of life. Of course, we are too civilized people to show it, but when a friend has stolen your beloved boyfriend from you, you will most likely give up on convention and will not deny yourself the pleasure of dragging her hair. Exaggerated, of course ... But sometimes this does happen ... By the way, jealousy is a special kind of envy. You are jealous of your competitor because he (or she) gets the love and attention that should rightfully belong to you. Including professional jealousy. For example, in the case when the chief did not appreciate your excellent project, on which you spent the whole night thinking about the "worthless" creation of your colleague.

You compete only on important factors and envy those who by these important factors managed to achieve more than you. Envy is commonly directed towards those who are:
1) more beautiful or stronger than you;
2) luckier than you in your personal life;
3) younger, or look younger;
4) slimmer or smarter than you;
5) earns more (according to popular opinion, those who earn more are happier and happier, and they have fewer problems.).
If you are jealous at work
"Climbing the next rung of the career ladder is an enjoyable event in most cases. If it were not for one "but": gaining a new status, we risk losing friends. The prospect is sad, especially if the experience of friendship is calculated for many years.

In response, sociologists say that strong friendship is nothing more than an attribute of an archaic society. In modern office culture, where the transition from one job to another is perceived as a natural stage of social growth, "friendship for life" loses its former value."

In less radical cases, the transition to a new social level, one way or another, lead to a narrowing circle of contacts. Those who have gone through such situations say that usually everything starts with nothing, but it's almost impossible to get away from it. But even if a successful friend pays for meetings in a good restaurant, buys expensive gifts, detachment in a relationship still appears. And in the end, the friendship ends. Usually, the appearance of remoteness in a friendly circle is explained either by the envy of the "losers" or by the starry disease of the one who reached the top of the career ladder.

Envy is comparing ourselves with others, agreeing that they are winners in life, and we are losers. It hurts the most. At this moment, common-sense changes us, we don't want to live our own lives, refusing to respect ourselves.

Comparing your life with the life of another person demeans and does not allow you to grow to full height, because, envying, it is simply impossible. We have only our potential, we can develop it, and we can refuse it. Other people have other opportunities, money, constitution, abilities, etc. But we should not be perfect. We have to be ourselves. Well, we should not forget about stereotypes - those who work overtime or are creative in fulfilling management tasks will be condemned by their colleagues.

Three ways to avoid the attacks of an envious colleague
Method 1. Under the mask
Marina, a young beautiful married woman who successfully moves up the career ladder, is been envied by her less happy colleague Natasha in her personal and professional life. She does her best to hurt her at work. What should Marina do in this case?

In this case, Marina can begin to complain about family life, to pretend that she alone cannot cope with her functional duties. A complete rejection of cosmetics and the replacement of fashionable clothes for a suit from a grandmother's chest will also work. Surely, in this case, the "gap" between them will decrease and the envy will weaken somewhat. Unfortunately, Marina will feel defeated. This often leads to depression, loss of interest in work and other life joys. Because an important psychological law is being violated: violence against one's personality, as a rule, has negative consequences. In general, this method of protection should be left in the most extreme case. It is never too late to use.

Method 2. "Not for life, but for death"
Marina becomes even more beautiful, shares happy moments of family life with colleagues, shows photos from the Canary Islands. In addition, as often as possible reminds Natasha that normal women do not live with their parents at the age of thirty. Desired result: the envious person begins to experience negative emotions of such strength that his behavior becomes inadequate. Psychological law: the stronger the emotions experienced by a person, the harder it is for him to maintain the chosen tactics of behavior. If we infuriate the enemy, our chances of winning a victory increase significantly.

At the same time, the victim of envy (in this variant, the attacking side) must behave in a balanced and unruffled manner. Her task is to wait for a colleague to make a mistake for real. In addition, Marina can go to the CEO and competently share with him that she is very concerned about the behavior of Natasha. No charges and recriminations. Only friendly care for a colleague and the affairs of the company, to which the unpredictability of Natasha can cause serious damage.

The method of eliminating the envier is quite complicated and ethically dirty, however, it is quite effective.

Method 3. Indifference
We will proceed from the fact that all people live in this world for something creative. Perhaps, such as Natasha meet us in order to teach tolerance or to show others how to take care of loved ones. It is unlikely that we will know for sure about the people around us. However, it is safe to say that there is a positive beginning in every person.

If we choose this method, then we take two steps: first, we are looking for a positive, second, we internally "release" this person. Well, God is with her, miserable. Let it be thrown as rubbish and not get out of the urn in search of compromising the material. We are moving away from her, and, most importantly, we stop living a single life with her.

It no longer has any effect on your emotional state. You do not get involved in discussions with colleagues or with the leader. In fact, cloudless indifference is inside. You are not set up to show, you have an inner personal life. This method has another valuable point. As soon as indifference comes, as soon as we "cut the umbilical cord" and forget about the envious, the psychological law begins to act: we cease to be an attractive victim for the aggressor. The envious leaves us alone.

How to overcome black envy? Proven methods
An American "Journal for Women" makes the following recommendations:
Method 1 - Do not hide from yourself that you feel envy! Not realizing this, you can not overcome the negativity.

Method 2 - Talk to the person you are jealous of. You may know that the flip side of success is stress and a lot of problems, that is, something that does not envy you at all.

Method 3 - Understand that the meaning is that even if we want to compare ourselves with another, then you need to know everything about a person, starting from his birth, and up to the moment when we begin to compare ourselves with him. That is his whole life, all that he acquired, at what price, everything that happens to him. And even in this case, we will not know anything - neither man, nor his life, nor what will happen to him or will happen soon. Today he may be on the crest of a wave, and tomorrow at the very bottom of the social ladder. Life is unpredictable. Therefore, comparing yourself with someone is absolutely a waste of precious time.

Method 4 – Understand that anyone who constantly monitors the success of other people, forgets that he should defend their own interests. In addition, desires will remain unfulfilled, if all the energy goes to complaints and monitoring others.

Method 5 - Find out what you envy: something like that you could have achieved? Think about what you could do for this! Make a list of step-by-step actions and finally take hold of its implementation!

Method 6 - Forget about what you can not afford. Discover your own strengths, which are no less significant than the merits of others.

Envy is like an insult
This is nothing new, much less surprising. This truth is as old as the world. Envy has nothing to do with the fact that the other person is something better, more capable or luckier than you. Just when you notice his progress, you feel unsuccessful, insignificant, incompetent, in general, not a superman. The way you do not like yourself. Envy is a keen experience of your failure. Therefore, envy always arises on the basis of internal complexes: fear, uncertainty, doubt, and anxiety.

The psychologist derives the basic formulas of envy. The main postulates of envy are:
1. "What is in it, I do not have."
2. "Of course, against his background, I look like a nonentity."
3. "How is it that he farts out of the blue?."
4. "Of course, he feels good, he has ... And with my data ...."
5. "Well, why does he have ... but I do not have ...."

6. "Well, how is he doing ..., I'm doing the same thing ...."
7. "I am also worthy ... So why does he get everything?"
8. "What is he able, what can I not?."
9. "Next to him I am ashamed of myself ...."
10. "Everyone knows how much worse I am ...."
11. "I will never succeed as ...."
12. "If I were like ...."

Envy resembles defeat in an important duel for you. You fought for something, hoping for victory, for admiration and applause, but you got it all different. As a rule, the person to whom you envy begins to annoy you. You may not even be aware of this - because from childhood you know that it is embarrassing and bad to envy. And instead of admitting that you are jealous, you begin to look for flaws in another person. And your aim would be only the intention to find them...

The need to curb envy
As you learn not to allow someone else's envy to interfere with your duties and be able to humble your own envy, you will gain more self-confidence, the ability to sympathize and empathize, you will become a more holistic person. Try to remind yourself daily about the destructiveness of envy, but not so that it becomes an obsessive idea, but to confront someone else's envy with your thoughts and actions. Curbing envy is necessary to be able to inspire people to new achievements.

Envy - not a vice? ...
Each medal has a reverse side. And envy, too. Envy is always associated with unfulfilled goals and desires. You envy only what you strive to possess yourself. Therefore, envy can be transformed into a valuable tool for self-development and self-improvement. Admit that you are capable of envy. If you are still doing this, then let it not come as a surprise to you. Let yourself be jealous. Do not suppress this feeling in yourself; it is all the same useless efforts and zero results. Tell yourself: Yes, I envy. And this is neither good nor bad. All people are jealous, only many do not give themselves in this report. Only holy people are not jealous, but I am not one of them. And I am not going to soon become an angel or be canonized. Recognize that the object of your envy is not at fault. This is just your low self-esteem and not yet achieved goals.

Learn not to hide your jealousy. Instead of putting it down, just say, "You know, I even envy ..." Only strong people can be sincere. So your envy will pass quickly. Instead of looking for flaws in a competitor, watch him. Find out what this person is doing and how he is more successful than you.

Ask yourself: is it really necessary for you to have what he (or she) has? After all, we are often attracted to something that does not bring special joy to its owner. If you decide that you also want what you envy, act. And you will have it soon. After all, you feel envy of things that are in principle, real and achievable. After all, you do not envy, for example, the Pope or the President of the United States of America.

Melancholy.
The word "melancholia" has been known since ancient times. Even the priests of Ancient Egypt in the 4th millennium BC treated people suffering from anguish. The priests of ancient India believed that sadness, like other mental illnesses, was caused by obsession, in connection with which specially trained priests expelled evil spirits.

Today, depression is one of the most common diseases in modern society. In successful North America, according to statistics, about 5% of the population is in a state of severe depression, and mild depressive symptoms occur in 50% of Americans. The amount spent on the treatment and prevention of this disease exceeds $ 20 billion a year. More than half the cases of suicide in Americans are due to depressive states.

You are depressed if... Depression is oppression that manifests itself as a chronic feeling of sadness, confusion, apathy, an indifferent attitude to reality, a crushing feeling of guilt and the inability to enjoy life, a penchant for loneliness and peace, a sense of intellectual dullness and weakness. Maintaining emotional tone equally concerns everyone: both those who have made a career and live outwardly prosperous lives, and those who are struggling today for a minimum.

In the East, it is believed that we misunderstand the feelings of sadness and hopelessness, the direct predecessors of depression. Grief and sadness are not always understood exclusively negatively. For a Buddhist, challenging feelings of hopelessness is a positive phenomenon. Without it, no nirvana can be achieved. Eastern psychologists believe that in the West, nervous breakdowns are so frequent because there is no sufficiently precise definition for feelings of sadness. It is not clearly recorded in the Western philosophy of life, and therefore it is convenient to interpret it as a disease. For a person of the East (in this case, a Buddhist), it's quite clear what he feels when he is depressed and then thinks about what needs to be done about it.

The number of people suffering from depression in the East is always less. "In France, the percentage of those who have experienced depression at least once in their lives for more than one year is more than 16% (one of the highest in the world). In Korea, the same figure stood at 2.5%. Interestingly, the divorce rate is also directly interrelated with indicators of long-term depression."

In Europe, starting from ancient Greece, such states were often referred to as madness. In particular, the founder of medicine Hippocrates diagnosed the mental disorder in his patients if he found manifestations of constant sadness in them. "Among the ancient Greeks, the symptoms of melancholy, a distant relative of the modern depression, were considered insomnia and discouragement - the inevitable companions of insanity in that value system.

The Christian Middle Ages interpreted the mental states of hopelessness and anguish as associated with sinful beginnings. Only with the approval of modern psychology at the beginning of the 20th century, depression was given a neutral status of disorder. Representatives of the Orthodox Church continue to insist that the feeling of hopelessness is "sinful gloom." On the other hand, the feeling of sadness is considered by them as necessary in some life situations.

Specialists of the Institute of Psychology of the Russian Academy of Sciences believe that a person of European culture will always suffer from feelings of hopelessness or melancholy. On the contrary, the Buddhist philosophy routinely refers to social failures, therefore, life and career problems mean nothing to it."

Crying at work
None of us are immune to stress. The side effects of this condition are very different - from banal insomnia to serious diseases. Often the cause of depression is a loss of self-control. Young women engaged in their careers are easily stressed. Stress has positive aspects: it increases labor productivity and initiates such qualities as punctuality and accuracy, but chronic stress leads to a weakening of the immune system and causes a specific reaction of stress hormones, which results in an increase in blood sugar levels and heart palpitations.

The open expression of emotions, such as tears, is completely inadmissible in business negotiations. Such behavior undermines the position of women in business. Men by nature are designed so that they rarely show their emotions. They compensate for this with other qualities. Women behave differently because they are socially different from men. For example, they cry four times more often than men. This is confirmed by numerous scientific studies.

Your work is the main place where you should learn to master your emotions. Women's tears, of course, will cause pity among others. But crying is also a sign that a person is not able to control the situation. Tears especially annoy those people who usually hide their emotions. Therefore, they require restraint from others. Men, as a rule, believe that if a woman is prone to tantrums, then she can be manipulated.

Tips for pessimists
Tip 1 - Do not be upset over trifles. Chase away the worries that may come about. Do not look for a cause for concern. And do not build illusions: exaggerated needs underlie many disappointments.

Tip 2 - In order not to suffer from depression, it is important to form a certain psychological attitude towards criticism. If the criticism of your address is tactless or rude, still remain cool. This reaction to criticism can achieve more than unrestrained self-defense.

Tip 3 - It is important to take into account the motives of criticism. Criticism from people who want to show their own erudition, life experience, or emphasize their importance in the eyes of others, is often unfair or one-sided. Because of this criticism, you should not be upset. This, as a disguised compliment, indicates that you have caused jealousy or envy in the critic.

Tip 4 - Reacting to fair criticism, try to be strict with yourself. Tell yourself: "If they knew all about my mistakes, they would have criticized them even more." Self-criticism will rise above criticism and allow you to respect yourself.

Tip 5 - Try not to pay attention to the rumors, do not make attempts to justify. Envious and slanderers people will always be found. And if you will seek revenge on them, this may take your strength, health and years.

Characteristic signs of depression:
• apathy, loss of interest in everything, everything appears in gloomy tones;
• a person lives in the past, constantly returning in thoughts to the memories of work, his wife, friends or money he has lost;
• sleep disturbances: restless sleep, early awakenings or insomnia;
• appetite disturbances: overeating or lack of appetite;
• anxiety, fear;
• a feeling of sadness, hopelessness, discomfort in the chest, thoughts of death are possible.

If there are at least three of these criteria and the condition lasts more than six months, then a diagnosis of depression is made. Depression should be treated with the help of psychotherapists and psychologists.

The salvation of drowning people is the work of drowning people. Depression is a black streak in life. How to survive? Experts say that regardless of whether you are suffering from an attack of melancholy or are in a state of deep depression, you yourself can get out of this state. The whole secret is to stop looking for reasons and start doing something. You can help yourself by using the following tips.

Tip 1 - The most effective way to cope with chronic depression is to seek help from a psychologist and use drugs. The psychologist can teach how to overcome sadness, a sense of hopelessness corrected with low self-esteem.

Tip 2 - Do what raises your spirits. It doesn't matter what you want to do if only something active. Go for a walk, ride a bike, visit friends, read, play chess or play with children. Pamper yourself. The remedy for you can be - a hot bath with foam, an evening at the opera or a disco.

Exercise: Color your senses in pink tones.
The obsessive presence of any negative emotion indicates a lack of joy in your life. And since nature does not tolerate a vacuum, it is important that another positive emotion takes the place of the former feeling. To keep her, you should prepare. Relax. Imagine your emotional state in the form of a canvas. Is it colored?

Then mentally pick up a pink, blue or green felt-tip pen and paint the canvas. If you wish, make the background multicolored. To recharge with joyful emotions, visit art galleries, exhibitions, theaters, go on nature. It will strengthen your cheerful mood.

Tip 3 - Do not make fateful decisions, such as relocation, job change, divorce, without discussing the issue with close friends or relatives from among those whom you trust. Defer decision making on important issues until you get out of depression.

Tip 4 - Do not be alone. Spend time with other people. Try to talk to them about things that are not related to depression. If talking about your problems causes tears, do not seek to restrain them.

Tip 5 - Do not overeat and do not refuse food. Observe a healthy, well-balanced diet.

Tip 6 - Exercise. Studies show that people with depression feel better if they exercise regularly. Such outdoor activities (jogging, walking, swimming, cycling) are especially useful.

Tip 7 - Analyze the facts. Sometimes, when you start to compare your assumptions with reality, it turns out that everything is not as bad as you saw before.

Tip 8 - Do not set yourself difficult tasks and do not charge yourself too much responsibility. If you expect too much from yourself, it may increase the risk of failure, which will worsen your health. Moderate the intensity of your schedule.

CHAPTER 3 CONFIDENCE

You can only say that a person who is confident in himself, realistically assesses his capabilities, strengths, and weaknesses, without detracting or exaggerating them. That is, he has real, not imaginary, grounds for confidence.

If you are shy, unsociable, and the whole problem for you is to call a stranger or meet someone at a presentation, it makes sense to turn to technicians to increase confidence and alleviate anxiety. Thus, having overcome the uncertainty, you will significantly expand the zone of your active life activity.

Confidence is the key to success. Confident people always have a big influence on others. Only calm confidence will allow us to create a zone of attraction around us, which people always unmistakably feel. This is the only internal force that is really able to keep us afloat in all situations.

Self-confident people are more successful than others. They are energetic, less dependent on circumstances because they prefer to organize them themselves. We need doubts in order to part with the prejudices of the past. And confidence in order to build the future. Uncertain people can not analyze the complex situation, are not able to venture a responsible decision. They are not perceived as serious business partners. Their characteristic feature is chronic discontent with life, they are rarely not in a bad mood. They do not know such a thing as fortitude.

Confidence is a state of inner strength.
The fewer people have a culture, the less they are able to think and act, the faster they panic. It is natural that in all sustainable civilizations great importance is attached to the formation of confidence.

Exercise: Defining Prevailing Mood
• Try to recall yesterday.
• Restore in detail the events of the past week.
• What mood did you have? You were confident or tormented by endless doubts?

• Rate your confidence on a five-point scale.

In order to fully understand what constitutes confidence, you first need to find out what insecurity is.

Uncertainty is manifested as:
• apathy;
• weakness in the whole body;
• pallor;
• stiffness of movement;
• unnatural gestures;
• "Closed" poses;
• violation of respiratory rhythm;
• the noticeable change in voice;
• colorless voice intonation;
• inexpressive speech;
• vague wording;
• excessive touchiness;
• sense of inferiority, awkwardness, guilt;
• a feeling of loss of control over the situation.

Doubts about making decisions always lead to loss. The one who makes the right decision, but quickly refuses it, is simply not able to bring it to life. And who can not decide on a decision - never feels the taste of victory? Indecision and procrastination - conjoined twins.

Confidence manifests itself as:
• lightness in the whole body;
 • a feeling of inner strength;
• natural gestures and postures, graceful movements;
• an optimistic perception of the world;
• emotional and figurative speech;
• sense of self-worth, pride;
• a feeling of total control over the circumstances.

Factors contributing to the development of confidence
The development of confidence is contributed to by a variety of factors: self-control, emotional restraint, family environment, type and level of education. The greater our self-confidence, the less we are disturbed by certain circumstances.

Mutual trust

Before analyzing the feeling of confidence from other points of view, we should understand that this feeling has feedback. It is not enough to have confidence in oneself, it is important that others also feel your confidence, both in personal life and at work. Both in large international and small business, wherever a person is busy, creating an atmosphere of confidence is fundamental, as it imposes trust. And most transactions require a certain degree of trust in the partner; and no matter how many contracts are signed, the lack of elementary mutual trust can have a detrimental effect on the negotiations and on the final result.

Tip: First, make an unconditional decision - forget your past along with uncertainty and start a new life. It is necessary, to begin with, the transformation of thoughts. Every time you stop yourself, as soon as thoughts arise in your head: "I am a loser, I'm afraid of everything, I am not succeeding in anything." Even if you are afraid, you still say to yourself: "I am strong, confident, the fear of communication passes, I like to communicate with people." At the same time work on relaxing the muscles of the body. Learn to fully relax and get rid of muscle cramps. At first, relax in quiet solitude, then learn to transfer this state to the atmosphere of your communication. Practice as often as possible, and profound changes will occur in your behavior and well-being.

Confidence in communication

People who are happy to communicate, as a rule, do not have complexes and clamps. A self-confident person who has coped with shyness is able to respect and love himself. At the same time, he also loves other people - this is revealed in the fact that they behave like polite, interested interlocutors who know how to listen. Such people can easily go beyond the limits of their world, open themselves and turn to another person, competently staying in this outer circle.

Exercise: mastering communication skills

1. Observe people who skillfully and competently communicate. Try to determine your shortcomings and mistakes based on your own observations. Perhaps you are too dry, or superficial.

2. Create an image of "pro" communication, what you could become, and start gradually to get used to it.

3. Try to put yourself in circumstances where you need sociable skills and watch how you communicate, orienting yourself in the direction you want. Communication skills come with experience. It is well known how some adolescents worry about complexes, - this is practically not the case with older people.

The expediency of communication
For full communication, it is very important to represent the purpose of a particular conversation. Many empty words, useless phrases to no one appear precisely because people do not ask themselves why they communicate, what is all this necessary for.

Before each contact it is good to formulate for yourself in full what you want to gain from this situation, and in the process of communication you should periodically recall this, especially when the conversation leaves in areas that are not necessary for you or the other person, or goes in a circle or accepts conflict character. The goal should not be understood as something purely practical, it can be a spiritual exchange or pleasure from the conversation, but you should not kill your time. When you think up that any communication can be rational or useless, and also, that in many respects it depends on you and on what level of communication you ask your interlocutor. You can take a seat on the captain's bridge, and not let your ship in free navigation. To do this, when talking, you just need to remember what you are doing: you are making or maintaining contact,

Exercise: Avoiding "empty" communication
1. Learn to make communication full, do not forget about the objectives of the conversation and try to support them.
2. Do not engage in boredom gossip and empty talk.
3. If you feel stagnation in the conversation, try to make it interesting for you, watching yourself and how you manage to manage the situation.

Act confidently!
Be confident. Often we can not perform any action, because they are not sure that we will succeed. Even if you decide to act, but feel insecure, others will feel and take advantage of it. Gaining

confidence is not easy, but possible. You only need to practice. You must learn to give the impression of a confident person both externally and internally.

CHAPTER 4 LAZINESS OR DISEASE?

In the former times, scientists laughed at the capitalists, who wrote down ordinary laziness on the list of serious diseases. In its normal manifestation, fatigue is a signal of the human body that it has overworked and is on the verge of its psychological and physiological capabilities. Usually, an eight-hour night's sleep or a good rest during the weekend is enough to restore the ability to work. In a healthy person, fatigue is always associated with the resulting load and passes quickly enough. But enduring fatigue, which is not a physiological response to the work done, but arises without a reason, is a sure sign of a malfunction in the body. Even physicians of the distant past treated this symptom with great attention. The founder of medicine Hippocrates argued that spontaneous fatigue is a precursor of the disease, and the wise man described this condition as "not healthy, but not sick."

7 ways to alleviate your condition in chronic fatigue:
1. Movement. Your occupation should be favorite sports.
2. Active intellectual activity, stimulating any interests other than career growth.
3. Spiritual or creative activity, meditation.
4. Help your neighbor, or try to.
5. Chat with friends.
6. Pamper yourself and enjoy life.
7. Congratulate yourself with success.

Recipes for fatigue
If doctors have not yet made a diagnosis for you, maybe hyping the issue, you can cope with fatigue on your own. At the same time, it is extremely important to plan your working time correctly. As preventive measures, it is reasonable to observe the correct mode of sleep and wakefulness, a balanced diet, include moderate exercise in the daily routine, get rid of bad habits, temper and the like. First of all, it is recommended to reduce, by as much as possible, the number of stress factors affecting a person: reduce caffeine intake, do not charge yourself with additional optional loads. But the most important thing is to avoid protracted conflicts! Do not participate without the special need in quarrels

and scandals. Do not "digest" trouble for a long time. And remember, you live not only to fly up to the personal or career ladder at any cost.

Recipe 1 - Do not leave important things at the end of the working day, because it can be delayed indefinitely and you might not have enough strength to cope with them.

Recipe 2 - During the day, take a break: walk, work out "industrial gymnastics." If there is such an opportunity, start your working day with a swim in the pool or a workout in the gym.

Recipe 3 - Emotional rest from business problems can be provided by all sorts of trinkets: on the table, in addition to office equipment and documents, experts advise to keep photos of friends and relatives, souvenirs and toys, children's drawings, gifts dear to the heart - this contributes to good mood, causes pleasant emotions and as a result increases performance

It turns out that at a time when many of our doctors still do not believe in the existence of emotionally induced fatigue, enterprising domestic healers are already curing this ailment, and, of course, far from free. For example, according to one very well-known metropolitan healer, this fatigue syndrome is just a scientific name for the long-standing malaise of the people. And he treats it with simple therapy. Like the things you have learned, and will learn in this book.

In the next sub-heading, we discuss stress factors that could pester you to the point of an emotional breakdown and self-induced fatigue. Learning how to overcome these "stress stressors" will help you master positive emotions and help build a better you.

14 rules of a battle against stress

1. Do not pay attention to external irritants.
You can get rid of the standard response, the conditioned reflex, if you learn not to react, keeping cool and imperturbable, for example, in the case of a doorbell. Facing any negative irritant, we must say to ourselves: "The doorbell is ringing, but I do not have to open it. Let it go." And, while uttering this phrase, you will sit quietly, without straining, doing nothing and not responding to the

call, this technique will allow you to keep your composure and spiritual comfort.

2. It is worth worrying about, only tomorrow
The recommendation to count to 10, when you feel that you are about to pick up your irritation on someone, is based on the same principle: delaying the reaction leads to muscle relaxation. And when the muscles are relaxed, the person is not irritated, especially since some problems are contrived. And, first of all, it is required to find out if it is so awful what happened, and, if possible, reduce the level of importance of this event. Analyze the circumstances, determine what really exists, and delete your negative fantasy. Think of the pleasant.

3. Mentally reproduce the place where you will feel protected.
Your nervous system needs rest, it needs to have a "secluded place" to recuperate and protect against stress. Imagine a place where you would feel calm and relaxed: the beach, sauna, family home, forest, etc. As much as possible sounds to reality, smells, paints, etc. - stay there. Relax!

4. Repression of anxiety
To get rid of stress, you should completely forget about work or any other business in order to occupy your brain and thus get away from disturbing thoughts.

5. Do not let trivia crush you
Many of our troubles are based on trifles and trivia. In order not to get stressed or annoyed because of them, we need to form a new installation in our brain aimed at pleasure, for example, to present the disturbing sound of a leaking tap in the next apartment by trilling the spring drip and by the murmur of a streamlet on holidays in the forest, etc.

6. Use probability theory
Calm down, evaluate all "for" and "against" ... The probability of an event that excites you is most likely close to zero. So why bother?

7. Consider the inevitable.
In life, we often find ourselves in various unpleasant circumstances that cannot be changed. They are inevitable. We are faced with a

choice - to accept them and try to adapt to them, or poison our life, bring ourselves to a nervous breakdown, depression or chronic fatigue syndrome.

8. Limit your excitement.
We set a limiter at a meeting, for example, we expect no more than 10–15 minutes. When you wish to continue to participate in a hopeless business, stop, ask yourself the following questions: "How important is this for me?," "To what extent should I worry about this?," "How much am I willing to pay for putting this decision to live?"

9. Do not live memories of negative past
No need to torture yourself with memories of past mistakes. There is only one way to take advantage of the past: to analyze the mistakes made so as not to repeat them in the future, and then to forget.

10. Give if necessary
Stubbornly insisting on our point of view, we make ourselves like naughty children. Listen to the opinion of others, even your opponents, respect him and treat yourself with the necessary degree of self-criticism. Reasonable concessions are not only useful for the cause, but also command the respect of others and, most importantly, prevent stress.

11. It is impossible to be perfection absolutely in everything.
Sometimes people live in the same fear that they are worse than others. And attempts to meet always and in all the highest requirements often lead to painful losses. It is important to remember that the talents and capabilities of each of us are limited. Try, first of all, to strive for the realization of your main life goals, to perfectly fulfill your main work and what you have a calling for. For a sense of satisfaction, it is enough to be successful in one or two areas, and the rest should not be lower than the average.

12. Do not demand too much!
Anyone who expects too much from others is constantly disappointed that colleagues, friends and close people do not meet his exorbitant demands. It is impossible to remake an adult, and you unconsciously strive to "tune" others around you. Accept

416

people as they are because everyone has the right to individuality. Look in the surrounding dignity, and in communication, rely on these qualities.

13. Look for positives.
Whatever happens to you, strive to find the good in everything. This is not about self-deception, but about just learning how to see positive edges, in what seems unpleasant at first glance. For example, you have lost your job, rejoice that you do not have to get to it (the former job) through the whole city, you will have free time, and you will find a job you have dreamed of doing all your life, etc.

14. And as a last resort for stress prevention, we will quote from an ancient Eastern prayer: "Lord, give me the strength to come to terms with what I cannot change, give me the courage to fight what I have to change, and give me the wisdom to be able to distinguish one from the other. "

Relaxation techniques
A more scientific approach, and because of this, differential neuromuscular relaxation is a more effective way of recovery. It allows you to minimize energy costs. Learning to distinguish muscle tension from the relaxation is an important condition for preparing for relaxation techniques. Having coped with this task, you can choose one of the following approaches.

Quick relaxation
Exercise 1
1. Lie so that the clothes do not constrain movements, and the legs are barefoot. You can cover with a light veil.
2. Close your eyes, listen to the thoughts that arise. Do not drive away mental images, release them to freedom.
3. Summon a pleasant impression (remember or imagine) and watch it like a movie. If in the future unpleasant images will crash (for example, memories of such trivial things as a crush on a bus, or something serious), do nothing. Do not attempt to remove them by force of will.
4. Bending the legs in the shape of the letter "L," pat them up and back to relax your muscles.
5. Take a deep breath and hold your breath. Without exhaling, retract the belly and press the prominent lumbar vertebrae against

the bedding on which you lie. Fix yourself in this position until it causes inconvenience. Exhale and completely relax. Lie down a bit in a relaxed state.

Do this exercise three times.

Exercise 2
Inhale and hold the breath in the chest for a long time. After expiration, lie down calmly, without forgetting about breathing, but do not affect it, let the body breathe normally regardless of your desires.

Repeat this three times.

Exercise 3
Inhale, do not breathe and, arms crossed, hug your shoulders, squeezing them as much as possible. Then exhale and relax. Hands can be left in the same position. Lie still.

Keep your hands in the same position. If before you were lying, stretching them along the body, then return to the "embrace" position. When bent at the knees, if it is more convenient, sway in different directions. Then open your arms and, while lying down, feel the relaxation.

Do not rush to complete the relaxation (this is a general rule for all such techniques). Lie until you have such a desire.

Then stretch, as if after waking from a dream, and slowly opening your eyes, gradually sit down.

Anti-stress relaxation
Exercise 1
Comfortably lie down in a quiet, dimly lit place so that the clothes do not hamper your movements.

With your eyes closed, breathe evenly and deeply. Inhale and hold your breath for 10–12 seconds. Exhale slowly, watch the relaxation and mentally repeat: "Inhale and exhale, like ebb and flow." Repeat this exercise 5-6 times. Then take a breather of seconds at 20–30.

Exercise 2

Forcefully reduce individual muscles or their groups. Reduction saves up to ten seconds, then relax your muscles. So do the whole body. At the same time carefully watching what is happening to him. Repeat this exercise 3 times, relax, forget about everything and do not think about anything.

Exercise 3
Try to as realistically as possible imagine a feeling of relaxation that penetrates you from top to bottom: from the toes through the calves, hips, torso to the head. Mentally say: "I calm down, I feel good, nothing excites me."

Imagine that a sense of peace penetrates all parts of your body. You feel the tension leaving you. Feel relaxed your shoulders, neck, facial muscles (mouth can be ajar). Lie calmly like a rag doll. Enjoy the experienced feeling of relaxation for about thirty to forty seconds.

Count to ten, saying to yourself that with each subsequent digit your muscles more and more relax. Now you should only care about how to get the maximum pleasure from the state of rest and relaxation.

There is an "awakening." Count to thirty. Tell yourself: "When I count to thirty, my eyes will open, I will feel cheerful. Unpleasant tension in the limbs will disappear. "

Constructive reaction to a stressful situation
The most optimal and constructive answer to various problems and stressful situations can be found in the question "How can I make the situation better?." It is these reflections that give the surest ways to resolve the conflict and quench it without letting "the flame burn out of a spark."

CHAPTER 5 ANXIETY – REASONS AND CONSEQUENCES

Need an introduction? Forget about worrying!
The problem of liberation from anxiety and causeless anxiety is one of the most important and most serious problems of our time. People are worried for a variety of reasons: troubles at work, strained relations in the family, with relatives ... Anxiety poisons life makes it difficult to focus on the main thing: solving urgent problems. We can single out a common line of behavior that will help. If not get rid of it, then at least tightly control these negative manifestations.

In a number of countries in the WHO European Region, stress-related conditions are the main cause of absenteeism, and the damage to society as a result of sickness benefits and the loss of working days is increasing. The results of studies show that 50–60% of all lost work time in these countries is the result of stress. Fear, anxiety, hatred, irritability, and inability to adapt to reality - this is mainly the cause of many diseases in general. Anxiety can destroy the health of even the strongest person. It can confine you to a wheelchair, making it impossible to move as a result of rheumatism or arthritis.

The most common causes of concern are:
1. Unhappy marriage.
2. Financial disaster or misfortune.
3. Loneliness.
4. Hidden for long time anger or resentment towards anyone.
5. Uncertainty in their own abilities.
6. The habit of digging into the past, instead of living in the present.
7. The desire to listen to the opinions of outsiders.

Rules to overcome anxiety
Do you love life? You do not want to die young? Do you want to

enjoy life? You do not like to hurt? Then start to fulfill your desires right now! The following rules are proposed for this:
Rule 1:
If you want to not worry, live today and do not think about the future. Just live this day, as you wish, and go to bed.

Rule 2:
If you have a problem in your life that puts you in a dead-end, try the following tips:
1. Imagine the worst-case scenario.
2. Prepare to accept it if there is no other possibility.
3. Calmly take steps to improve the situation you mentally reconciled with.

Rule 3:
Do not forget that stress does not improve your well-being.

Concerned? Analyze the situation!
People often in their daily affairs are guided by emotions rather than logic and common sense. At the same time, a huge number of mistakes are made and a lot of stupid things are done. But in most cases, it takes quite a bit to think in order to arrive at the right decision!

No matter how stressful the situation, forget about negative emotions, then calmly analyze the situation. Deal with the worst that can happen, and then begin to improve the situation.

It is necessary to accept that change is impossible. A person can think and act, think and implement their own desires! He can come up creatively to the solution of any problem ... And accordingly, change what does not correspond to his wishes. If you start to get annoyed, anxious, etc., does this mean that you put an end to your own higher human abilities and descend to the animal level? To think, not panic, act, not whine, build and change your life and the lives of others for the better, and not surrender to the power of primitive emotions! Or do you not like it?!

Problem classification
Learn how to classify your problems in the following four groups:
• priority (that is, vital);
• the solution of which may be delayed, and this will not cause

undesirable and irreparable consequences;
• the solution of which can occur without your participation, if, of course, can be delayed;
• that which in principle cannot be resolved by you.

To solve all these problems should be in the order given. The fourth group of problems should not bother you at all. If necessary, do everything in your power, but do not strive for an outcome that cannot be achieved by your own forces. "Do what you must and let be what will be!"

Do not forget that your preference must necessarily coincide with your possibilities. And do not undertake to solve those problems that cannot be resolved in these circumstances, at the given time, and with the forces and means at your disposal. If you find yourself in a situation where an important and urgent problem cannot be solved by you, switch to less significant matters. Give yourself an installation not to worry about what is impossible at this stage.

Consistency in solving problems
In order to protect yourself from a nervous breakdown, try to keep track of unfinished situations. If you feel the pressure of unfinished business, try to reduce their number, for this, follow these four steps:

1) realize that you are held hostage by an unfinished situation, which requires a solution and is wasting your energy, bothering you and preventing you from living;
2) make a decision to put a dot in it;
3) reflect on what you can do and what depends on you, find the best opportunity and rely on yourself;
4) implement your life plan.

If the situation does not come to its logical conclusion the first time, try to find a few more solutions to the problem, but don't leave it unfinished. Do not try to resolve multiple issues at the same time. Remember the golden rule: consistency and comprehensiveness. Things must be dealt with consistently with your full dedication. Concentrate all your strengths on the problem being solved, without splashing on the tasks that can be solved by you later. All your thoughts should relate to the problem being solved, and not the totality of the cases that you need to master.

Tip: Paint all the cases in a chronological sequence: what should be done. Next to mark the deadline. Then take a sheet of blank paper and fasten it over the list with scotch tape or two clips so that from under the white sheet you can see only the first line. Hang the list in a prominent place. Now, having made the intended business, you can delete it from the list and move the white sheet down. So, things will not remain forgotten, and with the upcoming tasks, you will not be frightened by their quantity. The list of victories will grow right before our eyes, giving optimism and confirming that, no matter what the circumstances, you are able to cope with problems.

Incomplete situations
Unfinished situations are always a problem, it is your psychological recipient who pumps out your positive energy. The unfinished situation is as meaningless as an unfinished play. We simply must find our inner peace, and live in peace with ourselves. We must draw a line under all unfinished situations, accepting them, forgiving those who provoked them, feeling responsibility and ceasing to avoid their own guilt.

Unfinished situations make the past topical, turn back time and bring us a lot of suffering and pain. They forbid us to live in the present, return us to the past and force us to re-live in the images that brought us many troubles in due time. The past cannot be changed, but it cannot be allowed to poison our present.

The past is over, with this thought you need to accept. There is only the present and the future that we are shaping now. Therefore, the past must be understood, accepted and forgiven. Let go of your past and stop worrying about it.

Exercise: Sequence of problem-solving
1. Write down in detail what put you off balance. What worries you most at the moment?
2. Describe your possible steps in this situation.
3. Find several solutions to the problem. Stay at the option that, in your opinion, will bring the greatest benefit.
4. Immediately begin to implement this decision.

CHAPTER 6 DO NOT WANT TO DIE YOUNG? LIVE TODAY!

Never rummage in the past and do not regret the decisions made and the actions committed. Then you stop worrying about what cannot be changed and, therefore, turn your attention to the concerns of today.

In addition to the decisions made, circumstances that you cannot argue with can affect every person's life: health, appearance and ability, in other words, potential and heredity. Each person comes to this world with a certain genetic combination, which cannot be changed by anyone. Therefore, it makes no sense to worry about this.

Do not be sad about the past. Past evils are powerless, they can no longer harm you. You will stop worrying as soon as you forget yesterday's insults and defeats. Do not aggravate the wounds, do not remember what can not be returned. Do not frighten yourself with the ghosts of future troubles - only one future, and you can imagine an endless amount of misfortunes, most of which will never happen.

Trouble. Willingness number 1
Waiting for trouble does not diminish disappointment from failures when they happen. The American psychologists came to this conclusion after conducting a series of experiments with students. Most people believe that if you mentally prepare for the worst — for example, failure in an exam or defeat in a competition — then it will be much easier to endure these troubles if they really happen. However, this view is refuted by an experiment conducted by psychologists from the Pacific University of Seattle and the University of Washington.

Unexpectedly, it turned out that the students, who from the very beginning did not believe in a positive result, felt worse than those who were confident of success, but overestimated their strength. But in those cases where the result was good, the degree of positive emotions was approximately equal, according to the journal Nature.

Researchers believe that a person's response to failure is mainly determined by his general attitude towards life, and not by the degree of preparedness for certain circumstances. It turned out that the old advice "to be prepared for the worst" simply does not work, and the pessimistic attitude makes a person a loser. Those who are confident of success, even in case of failure, are convinced that they acted as a whole not so bad.

If you are experiencing a breakdown, if the problems you face seems insoluble, heavy, even overwhelming, use the following exercise, which consists of two stages.

Exercise: Release your desires!
The first stage - Choose a time so that you don't need to rush. If you don't find an interval between cases, make yourself a day off - forget about duties or reassign them to someone. Do not refuse this event only because you cannot allocate time for it, unless, of course, you need to replenish your own forces. So, select the time, ask others not to disturb you, you can turn off the phone and go to bed.

The second phase - Promise yourself to suppress any attempts to start doing something. Lie still, holding back even eye movement. Keep track of emerging goals that require your execution (from the slightest desire to turn in bed on the other side to the need to do some urgent business or think through some projects). Relax as much as possible, immerse yourself in the present, chase any predictions and watch from the sidelines. If the desire to take some action will still appear, and this will certainly happen, "release" your wishes to the will without your own support. Become an indifferent witness of their impulses, look at them from the side, from the position of the third, as something not interesting and completely distant to you. If necessary, strengthen yourself with the thought that you need to gain strength and the only way to achieve this is not to expend them. You also should not think that "here I am now having a rest and will be engaged in what now comes to my mind." You, on the contrary, are obliged to let go of your desires, allow them to do what they want (wander), but without your participation.

Today, we constantly worry about past failures and mistakes and also worry about the future. In addition, because of laziness, we often postpone for "later" what should be done now. And in doing so, we do not pay attention to what is most important - the moment in time.

Full immersion in hope and anxiety leads to a loss of energy and, ultimately, to failure. But the person who gradually, step by step, does what he should do, he achieves the success of his own accord. Fortune herself turns to face him.

It is important to be able to distinguish whether you are planning something for the future, or just worry about it, you should spend every moment of this time only with benefits. The more you think about troubles, the more suffering there will be when you experience them. It treats possible events impartially.

Conditioning your mind to live in the present tense
You can only worry if you are mentally living in the future of which you are dreaming or afraid, or in the past where something has happened that you have been experiencing so far. If you live in the present, you will not be able to worry. For example, are you worried at the moment? Of course no! This is because you are reading this book, and your concentration relieves anxiety. A person cannot think about two things at the same time.

You overcome fear and anxiety if you live for today, and even better for the present moment. Just make a statement that "you will soon...!" Express a positive statement and stick to it for a certain period of time. Do not think about the future that will come later, and your worries will disappear.

Exercise: Coordination of activities in areas of life today
1. Define in detail every area of your life.
2. Describe in detail what you have in each area. This does not mean "wife," "work."
3. Then determine what you are doing in each area. Not what you should do, but what you really would do today.
4. Take the first item in the list of "Coordination of Activities." Find out in each area that you want to put in the first

paragraph. That is, determine the starting intention for each area. Then take the next item, "Desired Goals," and determine what is located here for each sphere. Do this for all items in the "Coordination of Activities" list for all areas.

5. Prefer the most interesting field. Carefully work through the structure of this area throughout the list, until it is agreed.

6. Fully analyze the remaining areas throughout the list until complete agreement.

7. Pay attention to any contradictions between the spheres and deal with them.

Thus, in the events, there is nothing absolute: good or bad. To achieve the goal it is necessary to make serious efforts. And even if you end up with defeat, it can be put at the heart of your future success. But if you are concerned in advance, afraid to make a mistake or lose, then you will fail. We can act only here and now. And because of the anxiety, this present moment is wasted.

CHAPTER 7 ACTIVE EMPLOYMENT - YOUR POTENTIAL WIN

Anxiety often becomes painful for a person when he needs to self-actualize, but fails to do this for good reasons. If you, for example, have a lot of work to do tomorrow, then you can worry much today and tomorrow, fearing to forget something important ... The body "remembers" that it will need to act, and how to act is not exactly clear, because of that you can't keep everything in your head. This explains the concern. In order to get rid of it, in the evenings you should plan for the day to come. Those things that you are going to take should be consistently recorded, depending on the importance. You can even briefly indicate the methodology of a particular case, the details of its implementation. So, knowing that at any time you will be able to see the plan, eliminating the possibility of forgetting something important, you will get rid of this kind of anxiety. Every person has innate spiritual or psychological needs. In other words, each person wishes to self-realize in some way. If self-actualization fails, then the person experiences at best irritation and anxiety, and at worst loses the meaning of life.

The reality is what it is. The very development of the ability to value life, not cursing reality all the time, can be your first step towards complete self-realization.

Full self-realization is possible if the human mind does not cover all sorts of conventional boundaries and forbidden lines. If a person learns to fully use the potential of his intellect and the capabilities of the brain, he will be able to be creative in writing the script of his life and will turn into its director himself.

Action Plan and its implementation
So, to get rid of the anxiety you need:
1. Determine how you can realize yourself.
2. After the goals have been set, collect all possible information on the question of interest to you, then draw up a plan of action and translate what you want into reality.

Suppose that you have something wrong. Instead of worrying, "unplug" the emotions and analyze the situation. Find out what the reason for the failure. Look for new information. Then make a new plan and implement it.

So, the main thing here is not to worry, but to constantly look for ways to remedy the situation or change yourself. It is an action towards the goal that relieves anxiety.

Example:
You have determined that you want to go to work. For this, you need a list of proposed institutions, preferably with working conditions suitable for you ... In order to increase the chances of success, it is necessary, firstly, to review as many of these institutions as possible, and secondly, to make the most favorable impression on employers. Therefore, firstly, collect all the information about more or less suitable and suitable for your jobs. Send information about yourself to all possible agencies or labor exchanges, visit all possible public places, ask all your friends, consult with all possible specialists, read all possible literature on this topic, etc., etc. Secondly, use all possible ways to change for the better your professional qualities and behavior.

If something did not work out for you, do not give way to emotions! Make changes and additions to the action plan and again start its implementation! Anyone must plan their life. Making a plan, you need to pretend it to life. When a person feels any negative emotions, he should immediately stop and find out what exactly caused the negative emotions, and what he can take to get out of this situation. Then you need to start to act in the right direction. Ideally, with this behavior, negative emotions will not arise at all.

In order to better deal with anxiety and more persistently implement the plan, you can use autogenic training. Tell yourself that you control yourself with intelligence. Intellect subdues emotions, etc.

Fill the vacuum. You should not have free time to worry and worry. Do what brings you satisfaction. Set and follow the daily routine. Take care of household chores. Save time ... Try to turn your hobby and your abilities into a source of income. Read books, listen to music, go to visit, meet new people.

To make people want to communicate with you, you need:
1. Search for people who hold the same views as you are experiencing the same feelings as you.
2. Become important to others, and for this to become a self-confident person.
3. Notice the dignity of people. Become open and sympathetic.

Thus, to get rid of anxiety, it is necessary to develop the habit of "turning off" emotions, then finding out the cause of negative emotions, developing a plan of desired actions and putting it into practice.

Trouble is the engine of progress!
Many people are accustomed to always look down, that is, to see what is not going well, what causes sadness, anxiety, grief ... They forget to look up, were light, beauty reign, everything that can encourage their heart to thank fate and find ways to overcome problems.

Whatever we do, there will always be problems and difficulties; it is useless to fight against them, we are more likely to be the losers in this fight. So we must do what we do against bad weather: equip ourselves. Against the rain, we use an umbrella; against the cold - we put on warm clothes or turn on the heating, etc. And there are no other solutions against the difficulties, how to look up to draw light and power because then we will not only overcome the difficulties but also appreciate the lives of the tests that we managed to overcome.

Tough work: planning a day
In some large firms, there is a procedure in which each employee must make at least the smallest improvement in his workplace every day. Why not extend this rule to everyday life. Every day, do at least a minor thing to achieve the goal or improve life. Then you will carry out a huge amount of work between times, effortlessly, leaving a lot of time to solve really important problems.

Today, start making appropriate changes to your daily routine. Only 20 minutes saved a day gives an increase of one year to 70 years. For the year you can do something that can completely transform life. Just not save on vacation, especially maybe go on a dream tour.

Do the hardest work in those hours when the body is capable of maximum activity. During stress, the concentration of certain hormones in the blood increases, and this gives the body a large amount of energy. During the day there are natural fluctuations in the amount of these hormones. The first apogee falls on 9-12 hours, the second on 16-20 hours. Pay attention to the natural cycles of the human body when planning your day.

Tip: You should never worry about single unpleasant events or a black band, and do not doubt for a second that in a month or in a year the situation will definitely change for the better. This allows you to adequately survive difficult times and save health. It should be remembered that "everything passes, passes and that is it. People are so arranged that they always want to get something (benefits, things, money, etc.). However, life often develops so that at a certain point the desired becomes impossible. But people do not want to put up with this state of affairs and are worried about this.

You lost your job. What to do?
You are left without "daily bread." This circumstance is unusual for you, as well as for most people. The main thing - do not panic, do not despair and firmly know that only activity and self-confidence will help in finding a new job.

So that you can better understand the essence of your current state, give yourself the answer to the following questions:
1. Do you think about missed opportunities?
2. Are you trying to find the culprit for what happened?
3. Do you have thoughts about your inferiority?
4. Do you feel insecure and self-reliant?
5. Do you feel the fear of the future?

If you answered "yes" to one of these questions, if you would like to change your life for the better, if you want to find peace and confidence in yourself, then it's time to manage your life yourself.

A few tips: how to change your psychological state
1. You are not a victim of the surrounding reality.

432

Everything that happens in the outside world accepts one or another color depending on your inner state, so watch yourself. Be very sensitive to your condition. Watch your thoughts. Remember that your life is in many ways what you think about it.

It is the negative assessment of what happened, and not the real situation, that is the main source of concern. Do not let anxiety take hold of you. Concentrate on the positive. Tell yourself: "Today I want to see the world differently, modifying the attitude to what I see." Give love and in the world around you, show more positive emotions. Look with optimism at your new professional activities.

2. Repetition - the mother of learning: Live for today
You may fear the past or dream of the future, but you can only live in the present. The present is the only reality that is important to reckon with. What will happen has not happened yet? What you have now is your life. Pay attention only to what actually exists at the moment. Starting today, if you are visited by sad thoughts about the past or the future, remind yourself: "I live today here and now, and I have nothing to fear. For myself, I have to try myself. There are no insurmountable things! "

3. Take care of your health!
A healthy person is much more likely to cope with failures and find a job. If you have not played sports so far, start today. Learn to move, breathe, relax. At the same time try not to overstrain, relax, without waiting for overwork. Walk more often. Gymnastics, good sleep, relaxation and walks are absolutely necessary conditions for health. After all, your self-confidence and performance directly depend on a stable state of the body. This will increase the likelihood of employment.

4. Live and learn!
Take the opportunity to expand your professional horizons. The more you know and be able to do, the greater your professional opportunities will be, the higher the probability of getting a promising job. Improve your skills. Consider retraining.

5. Chat with interesting people!
Be interested in other people, new friends. Rejoice with someone daily. Remember that you always need someone. Share your problems and concerns with friends and family. Consult with those

who were in a similar situation and came out of it with the least loss. Expand your social circle, update old connections, get new ones. Try to make sure that as many people as possible know what kind of job you need.

One of the main conditions for effective job search is to know clearly what you need. Define your life goals, make plans, make adjustments to their implementation, monitor the achievements of each day. Collect detailed information about the work, write down the necessary information, addresses, phone numbers. Job searching needs to be turned into work - lead every day, and not occasionally, considering all possible alternatives to employment. When meeting with the employer, try to make the most favorable impression. And good luck to you will smile! Most likely, your new job will be better paid and promising!

Practical recommendations to expand the circle of communication:
1. Look for soul mates. That is, surround yourself with people with whom you can experience the same emotions People like you more easily accept and reflect information.

2. Increase self-esteem, and this will turn you into a self-confident person. Change in yourself for the better all that can be changed. Throw away from the head about why it is impossible to change. Behave as if you are an attractive person, and others will find you exactly that.

3. Change your communication style. Learn to look at the problem from the point of view of your interlocutor.

To be interesting, you must be interested. Learn to be happy when others are good. Instill others with a sense of their significance.

4. Communicate with people through works of art, any other activity or a common area of interest.

Changing your attitude to what is happening!
A person is as happy as his mind is set to. If there is a setting for a better result, success is more likely. You can find a point in which every experience will have a positive meaning. In any stressful situation, you should ask yourself three questions: "What can this situation changed for the better?" Or at least "What could be good

in it?"; "What else is not perfect, not so bad?" And "What can I do to remedy the situation?"

It is necessary to thank fate and those around them even for the difficulties, considering them as useful lessons that should be learned. Managing consciousness, we manage our happiness. After all, only a negative alignment of thoughts makes a person somewhat disadvantaged.

Dale Carnegie suggests: "If you got a lemon, make lemonade out of it!" That is, take advantage of the trouble. "And if you suffer from the fact that you do not have beautiful shoes, think of the man who has got no legs at all."

Anxiety destroys the body, deprives of energy that can be used for useful things. And, in general, causes suffering. If you want to keep bad thoughts away from yourself, you should think about the ultimate benefit, which will always be as a result of any change. Concentrate on the benefits, not the fears and the alleged deprivation. List the benefits of change and write them on a piece of paper. Every day, read this list and think about the good that awaits you in the near future.

Look at the situation in which you find yourself as a chance to change for the better. If you are transferred to a new job, if your company or department closes, if your workplace is reduced, if your husband or lover left you, if you have to change your place of residence, then instead of despair, think about the possible positive consequences. If you stop resisting, accept changes and begin to master a new, more positive experience, then something good will happen to you. It happens when you are ready for a change.

436

CHAPTER 8 THE HOLIDAY EVERY DAY. WHAT IS THE SECRET OF ALTRUISM?

In order not to think again about anxiety, focus on the main business, the most important one. Think about how to solve it and change, finally, bad thoughts to good ones! Remember relatives and close people, remember the forgotten minutes of a happy childhood, in general, everything that gives the most pleasant sensations. Do not dwell on the bad!

Rules to follow daily:
1. "Do not harm people in thoughts, words, and deeds."
2. "Free yourself from fuss, limit desires."
3. "Do not regret the past, which cannot be corrected, think of the present, which conditions the future."
4. "Accept with gratitude everything that life presents."

Intellectual physical harmony
For spiritual and physical health, an optimistic attitude, a feeling of satisfaction with one's life, the ability to find in it what develops, strengthens and soothes the spirit: favorite activities, communication with good people, nature, learning spiritual practices, philosophical systems and ways of achieving spiritual harmony in this complex, ever-changing world.

If you lead an active lifestyle, play sports, then you will not have time and energy to worry. Spend more time in nature, thus relieving tension. If you overload yourself with intellectual activity and do not keep yourself exercised, you can completely ruin your health.

If you find yourself in nature, take a book with you. Sit back somewhere in a beautiful, quiet place and start reading from any page. Your subconscious will correctly guide you. Take book phrases as a dialogue with a friend. Analyze the words that you had to read, accept their meaning for yourself. Fear begins where there is no balance. This principle is taken into account in physical development but completely forgotten in intellectual development and the achievement of harmony between mind and body.

Try to tell yourself positive news. "I manage a lot, I learn a lot from my own mistakes, I will act and become better." Positive attitude to yourself and life is in itself an effective remedy for stress, emotional or physical!

Ego and Altruism. Any secrets?
Today it is traditionally considered that the thirst for possession as a way of existence is the innate quality of a person and, therefore, practically indestructible. This idea is expressed in the fact that people are essentially lazy, passive, do not want to make any effort if they are not motivated by material gain ... hunger ... or the fear of punishment. This axiom is not questioned by anyone, defining our educational methods and methods of work. However, in reality, this is an expression of the desire to justify human egoism by the fact that it allegedly derives from natural human needs.

You should not take your position as a matter of course while forgetting that the majority of people are not available those privileges and benefits that you have. One way to counter this is to periodically visit places where there are poor or disadvantaged people. The head, no matter how high your position, is sometimes recommended to visit hospitals, nursing homes, correctional institutions, orphanages and other organizations where you can see the suffering of people. Such visits give the determination to help others. In addition, by helping such people, you also help yourself as a leader, since the power of any organization, society or state is determined by the viability of their weakest members.

Statistics
International statistics on the living standards of the poorest sections of society make it something to scream about. Hunger and poverty are progressing and are the most widespread phenomena on earth. Half a billion adults and children are constantly starving, another half billion - and that's 20% of the world's population - do not have an elementary means of subsistence. Imagine how many people live in much worse conditions than you!

Give back to get rid of anxiety!
The truth is that both ways of existence - both altruism and egoism - are potential possibilities of human nature, that the biological need for self-preservation leads to the fact that egoism more often gains the upper hand, but, nevertheless, self-love and laziness are not the only ones intrinsic qualities of man.

A person has a desire to realize his abilities, to be active, to communicate with other people, to escape from the limitations of his loneliness and selfishness.

The need to give, share with others, the willingness to sacrifice themselves for the sake of others, are found among representatives of the medical professions - such as nurses, and doctors. We find the same altruism among donors who voluntarily give their blood; it manifests itself in a variety of circumstances when a person risks his life to save others. People who know how to love truly always strive to devote themselves to another.

Comparison rules
Rule 1
Do not compare yourself with those to whom fate is more supportive - this is a direct road to anxiety. Some people believe that it is necessary to compare themselves with the best samples, and not with the worst. Of course, do not equal those who are lazy, aggressive pessimists. But what will the comparison with those who initially had extremely favorable living conditions lead to?

Separate the aspects of life which are subject to you from those which you cannot influence. And compare your achievements with the success of other people only in the first case. If you are comparing yourself with those who were born in a richer or more prosperous family, who work in a prestigious place, not because you have achieved this on your own, but just so happened "historically," then you are on the right path to anxiety and envy.

Rule 2
It is impossible to make the object of comparison that which does not depend on you, and if it is better to compare with those to whom fate was not favorable. In this case, you learn to appreciate what you have, and not take it for granted. By cultivating a sense of gratitude, you simultaneously get rid of the feeling of anxiety and begin to perceive life as a holiday.

The surest way to happiness
Psychologists have come to the conclusion that those who are sympathetic towards other people live longer and that getting help is not as useful as it seems. Types of assistance may be different, for

example, take a neighbor to the doctor, go shopping for your elderly relative, sit with a friend's child or help a colleague make a report. But these are examples of physical assistance.

At the same time, help can be emotional. Listening to a person who wants to pour out his soul or share his problems with you is sometimes much more difficult than driving someone to the house by car. But it is your patience and responsiveness to the problems of another person that may help him to change his life and overcome difficulties.

Intuitively, we understand that our help will make a person feel better. However, if a person constantly turns to others for help, he may form a feeling of dependence, which will subsequently lead to feelings of guilt and anxiety. Such a person may feel a burden, he may have a suicidal thought. He (or she) needs professional help.

Impact of social contacts
It is experimentally proved that communication has a beneficial effect on the health of each of us. They improve the functioning of the immune system, reduce the likelihood of colds and infectious diseases, and accelerate the healing process. However, today psychologists have come to the conclusion that not all social contacts are equally useful. In any case, understand that by extending a helping hand to other people, you prolong your life, and it does not matter what kind of help you provide, physical or emotional.

By helping others, you also reduce stress, get rid of anxiety, improve physical and mental well-being, heal from depression, and also gain positive emotions, which positively affect the cardiovascular and immune systems.

What can be done without delay for tomorrow?
"Do not postpone for tomorrow what can be done today" - the most important things need to be done on time and immediately, time cannot wait. "Man proposes, and God disposes." Follow the advice of Omar Khayyam: "Do not mourn, mortal, yesterday's losses, Today's affairs do not dare, Do not believe in the past or in the next minute, Believe in the current minute - be happy now!"

Bad habit. Do you treasure the current moment?

One of the classic examples of how a person does not cherish the present day is the habit of postponing for tomorrow what can be done today. It is based on the following thought: "Well, today it is possible for this and not to take it; I think tomorrow it will be easier ...." However, there are no cases to postpone. Bad desires are like drugs: the more you use them, the harder it is to give them up. Therefore, the more you put things off until tomorrow, the more effort it will take to change your life for the better.

Example
Sometimes people put something off because of the fear of finding out the undesirable real state of affairs. In this case, the person does not go to the doctor for fear of finding out that he is ill. Regardless of whether you like the real state of affairs or not, the sooner you start thinking about what measures to take, the better it will be.

This is a vivid example of the fact that the constant postponement to "later" brings you not benefit, but pain, anxiety, and grief.

We can act only here and now ... Let us stop spending such an important moment on anxiety and regret and do not postpone our business for tomorrow.

Today is probably the most precious gift that fate has prepared for you. Do not let it "spoil." Do not let it fill with negative emotions: a feeling of irritation, loneliness, sadness, apathy, etc., charge yourself with enthusiasm. Agree that this day is potentially filled with success, happiness, love, and joy. All this will be today. Do not let this go for anything: go out into today's world, as if in open space, and find on this day success, happiness, love, and joy. You cannot live this day tomorrow, and it will never happen again.

Two reasons forcing you to put things off for "later"
Reason 1
Extreme caution - the ability to see only the reverse side of the coin; thoughts and talk about possible failures instead of fixing the mind on the means of achieving success today. Reduction of all paths to defeat while simultaneously unwilling to look for ways to avoid it; waiting for "his hour," becoming gradually a worldview; memories of losers, forgetting the winners; judgments in style - "oh, all the same, it's no use!"; pessimism leading to

diseases of the stomach, intoxication, respiratory disorders and a general propensity for diseases.

Reason 2
Delay- the habit of postponing for tomorrow what should have been done a year ago; waste all the effort to justify idleness - instead of work. Procrastination, joining over-care, doubt, and anxiety, also means leaving, where possible, responsibility; preference to compromise cruel fight; agreement with life difficulties instead of overcoming them. Refusal from prosperity, and wealth, and abundance, and happiness, and contentment; careful planning of actions in case of failure instead of burning all bridges, all ways of retreat; weakness and often complete lack of self-confidence, certainty of goals, self-control, initiative, enthusiasm, normal self-esteem, ability to think logically; communication with those who accepted the role of a loser in this life, instead of seeking friendship with confident ones.

Winner traits
1. Persistent Labor. There is no better way to succeed than to work hard. But this is hardly feasible if your work is not enjoyable. In this case, "labor" is no longer labor in the generally accepted sense of the word - it's just what people like to do. Artist Pablo Picasso said: "While working, I rest. Doing nothing or visiting guests bore me. "

2. Ideas. Winners should not say that success can be achieved only in one way. They will never believe you and will definitely offer three (or more) ideas that will contribute to the implementation of the same task.

3. Now. The winners do not postpone the case for tomorrow, next week or "for later." They are well aware that on the desk filled with papers, tomorrow, the number of papers will double if you don't deal with them today. Try to distract the winner from work and ask him for some advice, he will tell you: "Let's do it a little later!"

4. The winner does his job today, naturally and with enthusiasm.

Loser traits
1. Postponing "for later." Losers do not tend to perform their work in time, they always postpone it.

2. "Too much work." Losers believe that they have so much work today that it is impossible not to postpone its part to "later."
3. "I beg your pardon!" It is common for losers to forget about the most important matters, about the decisive meetings that are scheduled for this week. Usually, they do not keep it in their head.
4. Excuses. Losers constantly find excuses for their failures and will always find a reason to "shield" themselves, to put everything on the shoulders of another.
5. Rejection. Having come to a loser with a new project, with some new idea, do not expect him to start implementing it. He will always find the reason why this idea cannot be implemented exactly today.
6. Absence of result. Because losers never bring it to the end, postponing it day after day.

So do not become a loser! Be a winner! Everyone loves the winners, especially those who radiate enthusiasm every day.

Daily chores that cannot be put off for "later"
Number 1
One of the main components of a happy "today" is exercise. Physical activity seems to release endorphins, natural antidepressants that are similar in structure and action to some stimulant drugs but are free and not at all dangerous.

Daily exercise or a set of physical exercises should be the rule of every day and get into the habit. And by all means, start today! Make sure that unforeseen situations at work do not take hours of your workouts.

If your life is full of constant travels, business trips and travels around the cities of the world, still plan the main time of your training. Adjust the work schedule for yourself, but do not skip classes. If you have an assistant or secretary, ask him to never include any meetings before 10 am, and you will have enough time for exercise and preparation for the working day.

Number 2
Daily stimulate mental activity. You may miss this component at work, but if this is not the case, then secure yourself some kind of intellectual or spiritual exercise at home. There are many activities that are suitable for this purpose: solve a crossword puzzle, browse

certain newspapers and magazines, read part of a book, talk on an abstract topic with your extremely intelligent friend, write a short article or journal article, in short, do something that will require from you active intellectual work.

Number 3
Daily engage in spiritual or creative stimulation. All that is required of you is to allow your imagination or your soul to work at least 30–40 minutes. Go to a concert, an art gallery, a theater or a cinema, read poems, admire the sunset or sunrise, count the stars in the sky or go to church. Visit an event or venue that can energize you. Have you ever tried to meditate? If not, do not delay for tomorrow what can be done today.

Number 4
Do not skimp on good deeds! Forget about charity, better give someone a random service, for example, help a person who asked you. Even a small altruistic act will lift your spirits.

Number 5
Chat with friends daily. Perfect for half an hour conversation over a cup of coffee and a leisurely walk through the woods. Do not forget to admire the trees!

Number 6
Give yourself a pleasure every day. Making a list of all the pleasures that you can afford is welcome. Make every day have a tick at least about one pleasure, as already received.

Number 7
Every evening, congratulate yourself on being happy. And they did not leave this wonderful feeling on the "later." In general, congratulate yourself on the fact that you have lived this day for good reason.

The reasons why we are afraid to act today
Action leads to consequences. And as a barrier to action, fear arises, this is a kind of instinct of self-preservation in front of the negative side of life. It is much easier to shove it in a "long" box for some time in the future, maybe then everything will be much easier...

We are taught from childhood: to take action - measure seven times, cut once. Before you commit the action, "measure once a hundred times." But, measuring out in his thinking, he spends just that energy and time, which are intended for the action itself, therefore this energy is no longer in action.

Anyway, you will need to choose the only option from the set of those that are proposed. This one variant he realizes, having performed a certain action, but it will already be late, and will not correspond to the current moment, because it is done from "tomorrow," far apart from the current situation.

Action as a real way of dealing with anxiety
The only real way to deal with anxiety is action. It often helps to change diet. During periods of severe stress, when people develop a lot of adrenaline, a healthy diet without salt and carbohydrates is beneficial. Other people who, on the contrary, have lost their immunity and do not produce an action hormone at all, it is useful to include protein foods in the diet. And in any case, all people in the fight against anxiety is useful to laugh as much as possible. Watch only comedies, you can come in the day and several in the evening. It works, oddly enough, and playing solitaire.

Exercises: from neurolinguistic programming
Stay alone. Become face-to-face in the middle of the room, imagining that the problem plaguing you is in a room at some distance from you. Now go in her direction and step on the problem, step over it. Do this several times. At first, you will feel the heartbeat. When you step over the "stress" and return to the place, you will feel that your cheekbones are "burning." Repeat this exercise several times a day. It not only helped people forget about stress but also suggested how to solve the problem.

Some more ways to deal with anxiety
As soon as you decide to act, you "take away" the strength from stress and give it to action. It is important to listen: action and stress can not go together, can not be combined. Meditation or prayer helps very well. You can drink some herbal preparations, teas, or homeopathic remedies. A relaxing bath with a temperature of no more than 38–40 degrees for 8–10 minutes, into which you can pour chamomile, straw, oat, or hypericum, will also have a positive effect. Light candles in the house, create an atmosphere of warmth

and comfort, because the light from the candle from ancient times focuses attention on yourself, calms, and introduces you into a state of rest.

Relieve stress
These exercises help to relax muscles and relieve strong nervous tension.
1.   Put your feet at a distance of 15-20 cm from each other. Reach up to the limit as long as possible. Exhale the air and feel the spine stretching from the waist to the head. Continue to breathe slowly and after each exhalation feel the tension in the shoulders and upper back. Stay in this position for up to 1 minute.

2.   Stand up straight, clasp your fingers with your palms outward and, while inhaling, extend your arms forward at shoulder level. As you exhale, lift them up. Breathe deeply, stretching the spine. Feet firmly press down to the floor, spread your toes, during stretching, feel that you seem to have grown a few centimeters. Hold this position for a couple of seconds. On the exhale, "drop" your arms down, relax your shoulders. Stand straight and take deep breaths and exhalations without straining or stretching.

3.   Get on all fours. Exhale and straighten your knees. Move the pelvis back-up. Then get down on the floor with your entire foot. Hold this position for 30 seconds, then go down on all fours.

4.   Sit on the heels on the rug, knees together. Lowering your shoulders, raise one hand up and the other bent behind your back. On the exhale, clasp your hands behind your back. Do not tilt your head forward, keep it straight. For a few seconds, focus your attention on breathing. Then relax your arms and change their position. Then sit on your heels for a minute or two, keeping your back straight and clasping your arms behind, shoulders relaxed, eyes closed, this helps relax the muscles of the neck and thoracic spine. If you still feel overwhelmed, repeat the exercise 2–3 times.

5.   Lie on your back on a thick blanket spread out on the floor. Bend your knees and put your feet on the floor, close to the buttocks. Press the lower back to the floor, relax the muscles of the buttocks. Without effort, slightly pull the back of the neck, lower

the chin, and close the eyes.

At the exit, relax your shoulders and gently lower them to the floor. Relaxed arms slightly spread apart, palms up, fingers bent. Do not strain your chest. Slowly lower the legs one by one on the floor, pulling them from thigh to heel. Socks divorced to the sides. With each breath, imagine that the body sinks into the floor. Keep breathing evenly. Gradually, you will seize the feeling of calm and stillness. It will not come immediately, be patient.

It is very important that the facial muscles relax. The tip of the tongue behind the lower teeth, the corners of the mouth are relaxed, the eyes are closed and immobile. At the end of each inhalation, hold your breath for a few seconds and, as it were, submerge your back, pelvis, arms, and neck in the floor. Smooth breathing rhythm helps to completely relax. Exhale slowly and slowly, without straining in the shoulders and pelvis. Stay in this position for at least 15–20 minutes.

When you are confident, calm, and your self-esteem does not suffer, you do not need to postpone the problems that have arisen, dodge and hide from them. You do not worry, because you know that you maintain complete control over your feelings and life. You do not need to receive a regular dose of inspiration from others and stimulate your activity, because the impulse comes to you from within. You go through life with the full knowledge that your inner strength can overcome any problem you have.

CHAPTER 9 RECIPE FOR SOLVING "OPERATIONAL PROBLEMS"

There are many factors that can cause stress at work.
Some causes of occupational stress:
• the need to make responsible decisions;
• overload;
• insufficiently clear definition of official duties;
• too vague powers of authority;
• incomprehensible oral directives;
• the need to perform difficult compatible functions;
• vague areas of responsibility;
• incorrect behavior of colleagues, causing stress;
• lack of professional communication;
• the impossibility of advising on complex issues;
• stress policy and management style;
• unavailability of the chief;
• a high degree of stress at the head;
• insufficient illumination of the workplace;
• excessively cramped space;
• poor labor in the organization;
• failure to comply with sanitary and hygienic standards;
• problems with transport;
• impossibility to agree to regular business trips;
• lack of interest in work;
• routine, monotonous work;
• poor job satisfaction;
• an excessively high or an excessively low work rate;
• the futility of the organization;
• schemes of work that conflict with ideological attitudes;
• dissatisfaction with career growth;
• lack of career prospects;
• the threat of dismissal or transfer to less paid work;
• insufficient remuneration;
• unfair labor appraisal;
• lack of tangible incentives;

- conflicts with colleagues, boss, subordinates, other employees;
- failure to adapt to change;
- lack of knowledge of the skills needed to perform a decent job;
- inadequate behavior in problematic situations;
- inability to act in a team, as part of a team;
- introduction of new methods;
- business expansion;
- changing the address of the organization;
- the decrease in income;
- stressful events outside the scope of production activities;
- lack of desire to improve skills and self-improvement;
- incompatibility of professional and personal life;
- low-stress tolerance.

Production extreme situations:
1. Concerns about potential problems:
- being late for work, entailing dissatisfaction with the management and lowering the rating among colleagues;
- poor execution of orders with the same consequences;
- fear of being fined, losing a bonus or being reprimanded;
- Dismissal and related job search issues.

2. Unexpected inspections of their own managers and/or state regulatory bodies.
3. Participation in uninteresting, repetitive, boring, annoying, or otherwise unpleasant and ungrateful work.
4. The imposition of leadership schemes and style of work, as well as image.
5. Difficult interpersonal relationships with management and co-workers.
6. Feeling of chronic time trouble: too much to do in a given period of time.
7. Communication and work with clients with inappropriate behavior.
8. Risk when making a decision.

Dealing with stressful situations in a business environment
Most often, the fight against stress harms passivity. In people with minimal adaptive ability, it is most common. The body can not cope with the load, so stress is born. A state of helplessness, hopelessness, and depression appears. But such a stressful reaction may be temporary. A man can compensate for the stress of alcohol,

women - crying.

In order to adapt to the prevailing extreme conditions, it is necessary to actively fight and, first of all, to correctly use the experience of already experienced stresses. It is necessary to recall and analyze the current situations: the causes and circumstances of their occurrence, to evaluate your own behavior and actions of those around you.

After analyzing the situation, you need to develop an action plan. A person is unable to act successfully if he does not have a specific goal and plan for achieving it.

At first, it may seem to you that you know nothing and can do nothing. But if you divide the task into its components, it turns out that much you can fix yourself. To do this, you need to ask yourself a clear installation of how to act in a possibly stressful situation.

An ideal situation would be when productivity is at the highest possible level and anxiety at the lowest possible level. To achieve this, managers, and other employees of an organization must learn to overcome anxiety in themselves. How to manage to increase productivity and reduce stress?

Professional ways to deal with stress
1. Know how to prioritize your workflow. Something of prime importance must be brought to the forefront and done as soon as possible, which can wait to do later, and also plan for the future.
2. Learn to say "no" when you are already physically or psychologically unable to take on more work. Explain to your boss that you understand the need for the task. Then describe the specific priority work that you are currently working on. If management puzzles you with the performance of a new job assignment, you should ask what kind of work can be tolerated so that the new task is completed on time.
3. Build a productive and reliable relationship with your boss. Understand his problems and help him realize yours. Teach your boss to respect your priorities, your professional workload and to give you sound tasks.
4. Do not agree with your boss or anyone who begins to put conflicting demands. Justify why these requirements are like a double-edged sword. Ask for the opinion of interested people in

order to somehow justify the situation. But in any case, do not show anger, do not choose an aggressive position, even if these requirements lead to huge problems for you.

6. Discuss with your boss why you don't want to work. Remember, do not occupy the position of complaining. Explain that you are a supporter of productive work that requires a commitment of strength and enthusiasm, in connection with which you would like to be able to take part in other activities.

7. Daily find time to rest. Close the door for five minutes, lift and rest on something, completely relax and forget about professional matters. Think of the pleasant, call interesting images to refresh the brain. Leave the office from time to time to change the atmosphere or your train of thought. Do not dine there and do not stay long after the end of the working day.

8. Follow the daily routine, try to adhere to a healthy diet. Get up at least half an hour earlier and do exercises.

Basic stress management strategies:
1. Avoiding problems.
2. Change the problem.
3. Changing the attitude to the problem.

Let's try a simple example to orient how they differ from each other.

An example of a typically stressful situation
Imagine the following situation. You came to the theater and tuned in to watch an interesting performance. It has already begun, but you got a too obscene and restless neighbor in the chair next to you. He whispers something to himself all the time, and sometimes he sends comments to your address that are definitely unpleasant to you. You begin to experience increasing irritation. The grumbling of a neighbor starts to provoke stress. What can you do in this situation?

The easiest option is to leave a stressful situation.

If the theater is half empty, there is enough free space, you can transfer to another place where other sounds will not be heard, and your former neighbor will be able to grumble at your pleasure all alone. But what if you can't get away from the problem? If there are no empty seats in the theater or your neighbor saw you as a grateful listener and follows you everywhere?

Then you have two more strategies in stock: changing the problem and changing the attitude to it.

You can try to change the behavior of a neighbor by asking him to keep himself quiet. If this does not work, you can warn him that you will call the administrator if he continues in the same spirit, etc. The purpose of the listed potential actions is to change the problem (in this case, the behavior of the neighbor). If it didn't help either (the neighbor doesn't respond to requests and warnings, the administrator could not be found) - you can change your attitude to the problem. In the end, the volume of the voice of the grumbling neighbor is not so high compared to the sound level in the modern theater. And if the performance is really interesting and the game of actors at the highest level - you can pay all attention to what is happening on the stage and completely "forget" about the annoying neighbor.

Sequence of strategies
Stress management strategies are specifically indicated in this sequence: care, changing the problem, changing attitudes towards it.

Stress Strategy
Avoiding stressful circumstances is the quickest and easiest option. If you notice increased anxiety and at the same time drink a lot of coffee and smoke a lot (caffeine and nicotine increase anxiety), it will be most logical to reduce coffee consumption and, if possible, stop smoking.

The strategy of avoiding the problem is also good because there is no need for psychological help. It all depends on your own decision. It is not always possible. There are problems from which it is impossible or simply do not want to leave. There are problems from which it is impossible to escape (for example, related to character, attitudes, attitudes to something, etc.). In such cases, the correct strategy will be to change the problem or change the attitude to the problem. Of course, it is better to first try to change the problem.

Problem change strategy

For example, if you suffer from manifestations of social phobia and complain of increased anxiety and difficulty in speaking to an audience, the most appropriate solution would be confidence training or public speaking courses that will help you learn to communicate with the audience in cold blood and confidence.

If the problem is categorized as unchangeable and we can't do anything with it - neither leave it nor change it is impossible - we still have the third strategy, the strategy of changing attitudes.

The strategy of changing attitudes to the problem
Did you observe different reactions to different situations? Many people calmly react to the strong wind, fall asleep without fear of noise. And at another time, they wake up from a knock on the front door and start to act up.

It all depends on the possibility of human influence on this situation. Does the power of man command the wind to die down? Therefore, you will not do anything, you will have to accept ... But influencing the opening and closing of the door, or at least splashing your emotions towards the incoming person, his inhuman power.

When choosing a second or third strategy, a psychologist or psychotherapist can be very effective. There are dozens of different methods of a psychotherapy that allow you to quickly and successfully cope with anxiety.

Criteria for choosing a specialist
One of the main criteria is professionalism. It is based primarily on practical experience. Choosing a psychologist, ask what is his experience, how long has he specialized in this area? A psychologist's own life experience is of paramount importance. It is hard to argue that a middle-aged specialist has more chances to deal with your problem than, for example, a young graduate girl, even with a "glowing" diploma.

Rational problem solving
Problem-solving, like management, is a process that consists of a specific sequence of interrelated steps. Solving a problem requires not a single solution, but a combination of such

solutions. Therefore, the actual number of stages of the solution is determined by the problem itself.

Collecting information to solve the problem
Determining what the problem is is to take a step towards solving it. Identify two kinds of problems:
1) there is a situation, but the intended goals are not achieved;
2) potential opportunity. In this case, you will notice a problem when you realize that something can be done to take advantage of the opportunity.

To give a complete definition of the problem is sometimes difficult since all parts of the organization are interconnected. The activities of a sales manager, for example, affect the work of salespeople, consultants, etc., the research and development department, and any other person in the company. In a large organization, a large number of such interdependencies are possible. In this regard, to correctly define a problem is to solve it in half, but it is difficult to apply in organizational structures.

Identify problems in general
The first phase in defining a complex problem is the awareness and determination of signs of difficulty or potential. Some common signs of failure in the functioning of the organization - low profits, sales, productivity and quality, excessive costs, numerous conflicts in the organization and a large turnover of staff. Usually, several such signs accompany each other. Excessive costs and low profits, for example, are often inseparable.

Identifying destructive traits helps to identify the problem in general. This significantly reduces the factors that are worth paying attention to in the control system. Low profitability also has a rationale for many factors. Therefore, as a rule, it is advisable to avoid immediate action to eliminate this symptom, to which some managers are inclined.

Identify the causes of the problem. Influence of psychological factors on information
To identify the causes of the problem, it is necessary to collect and analyze the required internal and external information. Such information can be collected on the basis of formal methods, using, for example, outside the organization market analysis, and inside it

- computer analysis of financial reports, interviewing, inviting management consultants or employee surveys. The study of the process of communication, psychological factors usually distort information. The fact of the existence of a problem can provoke stresses and anxiety, greatly enhancing distortion.

If employees are confident that the company's management is predisposed to look for the cause of trouble in them, they will consciously or unconsciously present information that more favorably illuminates their positions. If the manager does not encourage honesty, employees can simply communicate what their boss wants to hear. It also emphasizes the importance of maintaining a good psychological microclimate organization.

CHAPTER 10 BE ABLE TO MAKE A DECISION!

In life, we constantly have to face choices and decisions. Many of them are minor, but there are times when you need to make difficult decisions. In this case, the right decision plays an extremely important role.

The decision to become a successful person
Strange as it may seem at first glance, but you have to make your own decision to become a successful person. Nobody will do that for you. And without such a decision you will never succeed and achieve your goal.

The starting point of entering adulthood can be considered the moment when, at a certain age, we begin to decide whether to agree with parental opinion or not. Exactly from this moment, our life path begins. And our future life depends on the concrete choice at the moment. Even if we do not make decisions from ourselves, we go after someone "on occasion," for example, "as my sister asks," it still remains your decision, and not someone else's. You accepted it, you agreed that it is. So life goes on!

Conclusions from the above:
1. All that we have today is our decisions and actions that are in the past. Their decisions and acquisitions are your achievements to date. And after all, not even fate or any rational reasons created it.
2. We cannot change our past. It can bring only its own lessons. But we can change our future. For this, you need to make the right decision in the present.

Decisions need to be made deliberately. Impulsive decisions sometimes lead us to the wrong place. As a result of such decisions, a person often finds himself in difficult situations. It is always necessary to think, but too long meditations often lead us in the wrong direction. People who weigh and calculate for a long time simply miss their chance. And his majesty bypasses such people.

Forced and non-binding decisions

There is a large variety of solutions - from very specific to completely unclear. There are times when it is necessary to make a clear decision to resolve the situation. For example, you must decide whether you will live in the house until the end of the mortgage loan payment period, or whether the decision will be made for you (foreclosure of the mortgaged property). But there are also situations where you have an alternative: to change or not to change your wife, job, place of residence or car. Your decisions are divided into two types - forced and optional.

But on the other hand, by any decision, you usually have the opportunity to choose - which decision to take and how to implement it.

Making decisions in everyday life
All your decisions are limited by life circumstances - financial opportunities, relationships with people, work and other events that you cannot fully and completely control. This affects the decisions you make. Not always there is only one right decision, there is a whole system of the same "right" decisions. But there are also ways to make the most effective and rational decision.

Fear arises as a result of the fear of making a mistake and most often in people with low self-esteem.

Fearing to reassure the expectations of others, a person either postpones business for the future or completely ignores them. He cannot take on such responsibility as making the "right" decision.

Restrictions and criteria for making decisions at work
When a manager identifies a problem in order to make a decision, he must be aware of exactly what can be done. Many possible solutions to an organization's problems will not be realistic since either the manager or the organization does not have enough resources to implement the decisions made. In addition, the cause of the problem may be forces that are outside the organization - such as laws that the head is not able to change. The limitations of corrective actions limit the possibilities for making decisions. Before proceeding to the next stage of the process, the manager must objectively determine the essence of the restrictions and only then look for alternatives. If this is not done, then a lot of time will be wasted or an unrealistic course of action will be chosen. Naturally,

this will exacerbate, rather than solve, the existing problem.

Restrictions depend on the situation and specific managers. Some common limitations are inadequate means; an insufficient number of workers with the required qualifications and experience, the inability to purchase resources at reasonable prices; the need for too expensive technology, intense competition; laws and ethical views. A significant constraint on all management decisions is the reduction of the authority of all members of the organization, determined by the top management when the manager can make or implement a decision only if the top management has given him this right.

Tip: Faced with a problem, do not react to its solution immediately, think over its solution, at least some part and you will come closer to solving the problem as a whole.

Search for alternatives
The next step is to find a solution to the problem. The best thing is to find all possible solutions, thereby contributing to the organization's success and well-being. Although the manual is likely to stop at several options, the most appropriate and most desirable.

Selecting alternatives, you must evaluate them.

Evaluation of alternative solutions
An important factor is the fact that each person calculates and predicts the future. Although it is clear that it is always unclear, but...

Our life is diverse and complex and something can lead to the fact that our plans will not come true. Therefore, an important point in the assessment is to determine the probability of the implementation of each possible decision in reality. The manager includes probability in the assessment, taking into account the degree of uncertainty or risk. Although it is ideal for a person to achieve an optimal solution, the manager, as a rule, does not even dream of such a practice. Due to various constraints, a manager usually chooses a course of action that is acceptable, but not necessarily the best.

Making informed decisions

Consider that many options have consequences that can affect both you and the society that surrounds you.
Consider three factors:

1. Responsibility

Some decisions are mandatory, especially when it involves personal responsibility. For example, if you have children, then you have no alternative — you must take care of their health and safety. Special attention should be paid to who will be affected by your decision, and for whom you will be responsible.

2. Impulsiveness or poise

Sometimes it does not make sense to indulge someone's whims or make a spontaneous decision. Reckless action can be costly. When you make a choice, do it calmly and deliberately.

3. Long-term result

We should not forget that many decisions will influence your life for a long time. Buying a new kitchen set, finding career opportunities, or moving to a rented apartment may take a long time, but it will not have a decisive impact on your life, unlike selling an apartment and moving to another city, dismissing from work and other more significant decisions. Such decisions will be very difficult to change.

Exercise: determine your willingness to make a decision
Before you do something, ask yourself the following questions:
1. Will this act be logical or illogical?
2. Does it satisfy my basic needs?
3. Does this act harm me or anyone else?
4. Does it not contradict the laws of the Universe, as I understand them?
5. What price will I have to pay for it?
6. What happens and can I pay this price and accept the consequences?

Improving bad decisions
Recall how it is usually recommended to solve problems through the following steps.
1. Formulate your problem.
2. Find and come up with several solutions.
3. Find the best solution.

4. Turn the solution into a coherent plan of action.

If at the third stage, when searching for the optimal solution, all the options do not suit you, I recommend adding another stage to improve the "bad" solutions.

Step one - List all the negative aspects of the solution. Treat it as critically as possible.
Step Two - List the desired positive characteristics.
Step Three - Try to combine positive and negative characteristics. Try to replace negative characteristics with positive ones.
Step Four - Modify the solution so as to reduce the negative aspects, taking into account the developments from the previous step.

And now you should again determine the best solution.

Try to implement this approach within 7 days several times in different situations. Invest in it for 10–20 minutes and analyze the results. Do not allow decisions to die just because they have negative sides. You can, if not completely remove all these negatives, then at least significantly weaken them, fill them with additional positive characteristics or replace them with weaker negative ones.

There are other approaches and techniques to improve the solution.

Summarizing all the above, we present several stages of decision making. First of all, it is worth remembering that you are not a passive observer but make your own choice.

Action as a panacea
Are you an active person? Most likely, it depends on what you mean by the word "activity." Maybe you do not always have free time, and therefore you consider yourself an active person?

A huge amount of time and energy is often spent on trifles. But we should not waste our lives. At one point, we will have to choose the most important, because if we try to do everything at the same time, we will not be able to achieve a serious result. The human

461

consciousness is subject to stress, as a result of which too much pressure can lead to a nervous breakdown. Mental fatigue can be just as debilitating as physical.

However, a person embraced by fears and anxiety should strive for action. It is impossible to do something interesting and at the same time worry about something. Some emotions necessarily crowd out others. Constant employment of a favorite thing or hobby does not leave time for excitement and unpleasant thoughts.

Belief in success
How do you rate your activity? How successful or unsuccessful? The predominant number of failures in our lives is the result of our mental attitudes. A person cannot succeed if he does not believe in himself. He is being sought by determined and courageous people who believe in themselves and have high self-esteem. It is the mental attitude to victory, the consciousness of one's own strength and the feeling of inner superiority that creates the impossible in this world. If you do not have such a mental installation, then why not start its creation today?

A person is really able to control his life if he can subordinate his thoughts and actions to his goals. Think again about your cherished wishes.

Weigh again all the arguments that indicate the impossibility of the realization of your dreams. Truly all these excuses are unnatural and false. Forget about them and tune in that your wishes are fulfilled and their realization depends only on you.

Exercise: Elimination of negative reaction to life situations
If you react negatively to life situations, you will involuntarily act and feel in accordance with them. You should control your behavior all the time using the following step-by-step algorithm:

Step 1. Eliminate from life everything that does not contribute to your well-being.
Step 2. Find what works for you and program it in your subconscious.
Step 3. Stably attach something new that you think will benefit you.

Adhere to this algorithm in the future to get a positive

experience. The implementation of this program is best started immediately. It will effectively contribute to gaining self-confidence because you yourself will influence the improvement of the situation.

Motivation
What motivates people to take action? The easiest way to understand their strategies of motivation. Their set is limited, in NLP they are known, studied, but they are poorly individually digested. American scientists have come to the conclusion that a person usually uses the same set of internal strategies in all situations of life.

It is very important to realize what motivation is. It characterizes your attitude to reality in the period when you prefer to do something. For each act, there is a motivation to it. Motivation determines the active search for success in a particular type of activity or your unwillingness to act. If you have no desire, but you start to do something, your actions begin with motivation. Without it, you can not make the slightest action. But you need to understand the difference between positive and negative motivation - the motivation to make constructive actions for your well-being and the motivation to do destructive.

No one can be motivated to action. Motivation arises from within. You will always do what you prefer, and not against your wishes.

Each step you take is a response to an inner need or desire. As a rule, your well-being is the key desire - intellectual, physical, emotional and spiritual. If the needs in any of these areas are not met, anxiety and irritation arise, and you are doing everything necessary to return to a comfortable state, even to the detriment of yourself.

Motivation strategies
Strategy 1
Avoiding discomfort is considered the simplest strategy. There are people who do not feel discomfort, falling asleep on the top shelf in the train, and there are those on whom this strategy operates poorly. This strategy is very powerful! Her strength is explained by the fact that there is always something that you do not want to do

with all your heart. And even for huge money, you will never do this. A strategy that really works. It is vividly illustrated by the question of a boy from a poor German Jewish ghetto - the notorious Rothschild: "Never, never, neither my relatives nor children of my children will be poor boys from the ghettos!"

Strategy constraints
There is a great danger for the leader to subconsciously put himself and his own company, career, family in unbearable conditions, motivating it with the creation of objective prerequisites for qualitative leaps. A kind of adrenaline addiction. It is clearly visible in long-life moments. It requires courage. But, as they say, "only an insecure person counts on luck and success."

Strategy 2
It is considered just perfect for those familiar with NLP techniques. Clearly stated goals, objectives are clear, the incentive is clearly marked. All goals are marked in all known sensory spheres, time management at height, along with management and projects.

Strategy constraint
Its meaning is to choose an opportunity within reason. Who wants to spend 10 years on what subsequently will not come true? And try to achieve something that may become obsolete before it is acquired.

According to the doctors, we involuntarily lay various filters that filter out extremely important information. And it turns out that we do not take into account accidents, and then everything goes against carefully thought-out plans. But dreaming is useful! And about happy occasions too.

Strategy 3
Presence of an example
It is very important to have a living example before our eyes. The psychological rule is triggered: "if someone can, I can! Any learning is based on this motivation. There would be no birds - there would be no planes ... A very inspiring strategy!

Strategy constraints
Innovation. Creation. That which has not yet been an example. Spaceship in dreams. Computer ... What follows next?

Strategy 4
Principle. Do something of the principle. That was! Oddly enough, many people act out of principle. And there have always been people doing exactly the noble principle. For example, much is being done now by virtue of the Development principle, the Ecology principle.

Strategy constraints
Strategy constraints are present everywhere. Sometimes people argue on "weakly," sometimes someone argues that "still can not" or "decide everything on the money" ... and this is also real in our lives. And someone, thoughtfully and slowly, examines the types of motivation.

Strategy 5
State
The condition is a neurophysiological component.
Examples of states:
- creative dissatisfaction;
- state of competence;
- state of comfort and safety;
- consistency, regardless of context.

Limitations of the strategy
Dependencies somehow motivate, stimulate gradually our whole personality. Writers, computer scientists, businessmen ... Thus, the state is serious and almost unexplored.

Strategy 6
The motivation for the future
The motivation for the future is a very beautiful dreamy strategy. We owe her the most numerous achievements. In reality, strategies of motivation, planning, and achievement do not always converge successfully. And sometimes it all ends in motivation. But not always. It is good to have a life goal that goes far beyond borders...

Limitations of the strategy
Danger to miss the beauty of the present.

Practical use

Mark your desires and incentives by which you choose to do something or not. As a rule, there are about 3 leading strategies, one of which is critical and the machine (our brain and body) "includes" the rest.

Define strategies in a specific sequence. Find out if it is difficult to perceive any of the listed motivation strategies. That is, you use it only in the most critical situation? In which?

Be attentive to your own formulations. For example, if the Principle (strategy 4) causes a tough aversion in you and you can't believe it exists in other people - analyze: what if it is your Principle?

Practical task
Motivate your boss (partner, competitor, spouse) when discussing an important problem for you on all the listed points. Be prepared in writing. Suddenly, it will be revealed that we know more about people than we guess, and the result will be predictable.

Solution implementation
The true value of the solution becomes unquestionable only after its implementation. The process of solving the problem is not limited to the choice of alternatives. A simple choice of action vector has almost no practical value. To solve a problem or to benefit from existing potential, a solution must be implemented.

Our habits
Our actions and habits make us who we are. If your life is calm, you live in harmony, happy, full of strength and health, good luck accompanies you, you are independent and satisfied, then you do not need changes. Otherwise, you must get rid of the habits by which you suffer life losses.

Exercise: Getting rid of a negative habit
Use the following tips to eradicate all bad habits that will hinder your future well-being.
Step 1.
Write the following:
A. What negative habit do you want to replace?
B. What positive habit or pattern of behavior do you seek to develop in return for the old?

C. What actions will you take to replace your negative habit?
D. What could be the simplest and most logical way to achieve this goal?

Step 2.
A. Imagine that you have already achieved success. Imagine yourself enjoying the benefits of a new positive habit.
B. Choose and use an optimistic statement that does not go against your imagination.

Step 3.
Watch your actions and mark every occasion when you fail to achieve what you want. Never limit or condemn yourself. Just make an unbiased comment and make the necessary adjustments.

Step 4.
Follow your diary tips for at least one month.

After you consciously choose your new positive habit, these four steps will allow you to program it at the level of your subconscious.

CHAPTER 11 CRITICISM FOR LEADERS

Criticism is a powerful weapon. Any manager knows that it is important to direct the actions of subordinates in the right direction. To achieve this goal, a variety of exposure schemes are applied: order, request, instruction, instruction ... Criticism in this list takes one of the leading places. It seems - there is nothing simpler: he expressed his claims to the subordinate - and the result is obvious.

While most of this chapter is dedicated to heads of various forms – home, as a father, as a husband, as a wife, at work, etc., you as an individual can and will benefit from it. Mastering what kinds of emotions you might bring up in others is vital. Master your natural leadership emotions and influence others to be better, not .., you know…

Criticism. How to respond?
Many live with hatred, criticizing and condemning others. These people have a negative impact on others. They constantly humiliate with disguised sarcasm, making others feel worthless and inferior. Due to such criticism, a person is inclined to withdraw into himself or simply to surrender to the mercy of the winner. People who negatively influence others deliberately block the path to understanding and encouragement. They will always express what they think, without giving importance to the fact that their words have a destructive effect. They justify their negative attitude, calling it "constructive criticism," "honest relationships," or even "objective evaluation." They are well able to recognize human weakness and always use it.

Constructive Criticism Rules
Many studies prove that most people practically do not perceive criticism, they are closed to its perception and do not hear it. Then, how to act so that subordinates listened to criticism from the authorities, and did not ignore remarks in their address? For this, you need to learn a few rules.

Rule 1
The purpose of criticism is not to fix something or to punish a

person who is related to an unpleasant incident. It consists of changing the behavior of a person for his own benefit, as well as for the benefit of his colleagues and the organization as a whole.

Rule 2

You need to criticize not a person, but a specific action, a misdemeanor. Everyone can admit his mistake, especially if the facts are obvious, but no one agrees that he is a bad person.

Rule 3

Remember, discussing the theme of the work of your employee does not strive to splash out ambitions and selfish emotions. If you still made a similar mistake - the interlocutor is unlikely to accept criticism in his address "legally," he will take your remarks as personally as your negative emotions and simply derive dissatisfaction with them.

Rule 4

Some managers use criticism to assert their authority. In this way, they demonstrate to their subordinates their superiority. In fact, sensible comments in themselves provide just such an effect. But to focus your attention on this, to constantly return to the mistakes of the subordinate, thereby downplaying him as a person — this can lead to a "bust," which will bring only the opposite effect. Respect is lost and there is antipathy because no one likes it when they once again emphasize their superiority over others. To aim the criticized at finding a solution to the problem, and not at excuses, help him "save face," that is, do not degrade his dignity.

Rule 5

Do not blame, focus on constructive suggestions.

Rule 6

If you want to express criticism of a subordinate, you should do it alone, without advertising to others.

Rule 7

Try to penetrate and try on the position of the criticized, objectively look at all the arguments, both negative and positive.

Rule 8
If the point of view of the interlocutor does not suit you, do not reject it immediately, try to listen to the partner, let him prove why his opinion is such.

Rule 9
Speak in a friendly, firm and calm tone. Try to start with the topic on which you and the other person have a mutual agreement. Whenever possible, starting with questions on which opinions coincide, can cause an affirmative answer and, thus, set the partner to a compromise. If a person refused from the very beginning, then later he would not dare to agree with you, pride would interfere. Spare self-esteem.

Rule 10
If you want to indicate to a person his miscalculation, start a conversation with praise and sincere recognition of his merits. By drawing people's attention to their mistakes, try to do it in an indirect form. For example, remember a similar case.

Rule 11
Use the technique of "rebound": criticize the actions of an abstract (fictional) person.

Rule 12
You should not impose your opinion, it is better to discuss everything in detail and "sort through."

Rule 13
It is not necessary to strengthen the facts by various methods, like, "I told you so!." If you suddenly feel a keen desire to stab and offend the interlocutor, wait a moment, just a couple of seconds, the opinion should change.

Rule 14
Do not demand immediate, immediate recognition of errors from a partner, agreement with a critical point of view, with your opinion on this matter. Psychologically it is difficult, give a person time to think, do not insist.

Rule 15
Along with criticism, there should be self-criticism, which has good

reasons for its origin. Before expressing criticism of another, admit your own mistakes. Acknowledging your guilt, you soften the perception of criticism by your interlocutor and act as an assistant and friend.

Rule 16
Try to make the error look easily correctable. Often, people are embarrassed by the hopelessness of their situation. Do not "push" on the psyche, and help find a solution.

Rule 17
Speak only about deeds, do not go to the person: criticize actions, not the person. Give him the opportunity to "not fall into the face of the dirt."

Rule 18
It is important to bear in mind that the more a person is excited, the less sensitive he is to logic. The more touched his pride, the more partial and subjective he is. In this case, it especially requires a tactful approach.

Rule 19
If you notice that your interlocutor is too emotional, it is better to transfer the conversation to another time.

What should be constructive criticism?
Criticism is a powerful tool in the relationship between people. Sometimes it is impossible to do without it, but it should be remembered that criticism, especially expressed in harsh form, can hurt the pride of the criticized and even lead to the loss of its performance.

Ideally, criticism should be rational. It should not be much, it should be detailed, and relate not so much to the cause of poor work, but to suggest ways to improve it.

You need to criticize only on the merits and affect only specific facts. Such criticism should be accompanied by practical recommendations for improving the situation.

Forms of constructive criticism
To praise a subordinate is not difficult. It is much harder to correct

and not insult him. Here are some valid options for critical assessments.

• Encouraging criticism: "Nothing. Next time you do better. And now – it did not work.

• Criticism, reproach: "Well, what are you? I hoped so much for you! "

• Criticism, hope: "I hope that next time you better cope with this matter."

• Criticism, praise: "The work is done perfectly well. But not for this case. "

• Impersonal criticism: "In our company, there are managers who do not cope with their duties. We will not name them. "

• Criticism, regret: "I am very sorry, but I must note that the work was not performed at the proper level."

• Criticism, surprise: "How?! Have you not done this work?! Did not expect)...."

• Constructive criticism: "The work was done incorrectly. What are you going to do now? "

All these forms of criticism are suitable, provided that the subordinate respects his supervisor and values his opinion of himself. Wanting to look decent in the eyes of the manager, the employee will make every effort to rectify the situation. Especially if the criticism was constructive and gentle.

If the subordinate is not very benevolent to the manager, it is better to combine negative evaluations with positive ones.

How to respond to criticism?
The reaction to criticism is often inadequate. How to be in the event that you were trying to do everything so that the criticized would avoid, but nothing happened? One should resolutely defend one's point of view, but try to avoid conflict so that the situation does not become uncontrollable.

If the criticized overreacts to your words, it is best to postpone the conversation to a more suitable time so that he can soberly assess what is happening and cope with his emotions. In other words, to give your interlocutor the opportunity to calmly think about the comments made to him.

If they criticize you - your actions...

If someone criticizes you, you need to listen and pay attention to the comments from their side. You should not choose an aggressive position - defense. Quietly clarify the criticism of the interlocutor and make an analysis of everything. In a fit of conversation, you are unlikely to objectively assess the situation.

To begin with, determine how competent this person is in this case, and can he make comments to you? It would be possible to immediately recognize his rightness very wisely. But we must not forget that criticism in your address may be fair. And agree with him or her, or not, it's up to you.

Fear of criticism
This kind of fear occurs as often as the fear of poverty or loneliness, and its consequences are also fatal to the individual because the fear of criticism destroys the initiative and makes any desires and plans meaningless.

Main symptoms
1. Shyness - usually manifests as nervousness, timidity in conversation, when meeting with strangers, in the awkwardness of movements, shifting eyes.
2. Unbalance - inability to control one's voice, nervousness in the presence of outsiders, poor posture and memory.
3. Weakness - uncertainty when making decisions, lack of charm, inability to clearly explain; the habit of "postponing," thoughtless conciliation with the opinions of others.
4. Inferiority complex - self-affirmation in words; the habit of saying "loud words" to make an impression; imitation in the manner of dressing and speaking, the absence of his own style, rapid writing on the subject of his imaginary achievements. Such people often seem overconfident.
5. Extravagance - the desire to ensure that everything was at the highest level, and this inevitably turns life beyond its means.
6. Non-initiative - inability to use opportunities for career growth; fear of expressing their point of view, low self-esteem, evasiveness of answers in conversation with managers; clumsiness in manners and speech; insincerity.
7. Lack of pride - when laziness and apathy, slowness in decisions and actions, suggestibility, inability, and unwillingness to assert oneself are inherent in the soul and body; nonresistance to failure, the habit of easily giving up any undertakings with the slightest

opposition from the side, groundless suspicion; tactlessness in the conversation; unwillingness to admit their mistakes.

How to recover from fear?
If a person does not do something, then he is accused of inertia. If a person is busy with something, then he is accused of this activity. The same people at different times can praise us for our actions or criticize. When we want to please others, we must remember: none of the people who have ever lived could make everyone happy all the time. Yes, so it is.

Are you always happy with yourself? It is unlikely that the answer to this question will be positive. No matter what your goals are, you will always find yourself dissatisfied and ask, why are you doing something else? Therefore, the best way out is to act rationally, in accordance with your own convictions. It must be remembered that we are not immune to mistakes, but hope that others will forgive them.

But if we want people to understand us it is necessary for ourselves, first of all, to be patient. Remember the words of the wise Montaigne that "a person needs strong ears to listen to free judgment about himself"?

• Do not try to please everyone. In this case, you can never become who you really are.
• Go ahead and be yourself, knowing that you will still be criticized.
• Keep doing the best you can. If you live in the real world, you will always be criticized.

Unfair criticism
If you tend to worry about unfair criticism, do not forget that it is often a veiled compliment to you. She signals that for some reason he or she is jealous.

It is useful to ask yourself: perhaps the criticism is fair? An uncertain person falls into a rage over insignificant criticism, but the wise seek to learn from those who condemn and reproach him. An anonymous writer wrote: "The opinion of our enemies is much closer to the truth about us than our own opinion about ourselves."

Tip: Keep a diary and, in order to improve self-esteem, write in it all the good reviews about yourself.

Little about self-criticism
We know that man has two opposite qualities: self-criticism and self-love. It's like two poles, if both properties are balanced, a person behaves most adequately, if one starts to dominate the other, problems arise. Self-criticism in moderate doses is useful because a person, as a rule, cannot rely on his absolute perfection. D. Carnegie also advised the reader to ask for unbiased and constructive criticism for himself.

Self-criticism is often an effective means to reduce the negative reaction of others. In other words, when there is a possibility that certain actions will lead to disciplinary measures, self-criticism may seem the lesser of two evils. And finally, self-criticism, expressed out loud, can be used for the purpose, to hear praise from others. Condemning yourself, you can force other people to give you a compliment. Most likely, you will even be assured that nothing bad will happen to you in the future. Although self-criticism can relieve you from disturbing thoughts, it can also increase personality discomfort.

Extreme forms of self-criticism
Sometimes self-criticism takes extreme forms when a person may need the help of a psychologist.

Self-pity
Self-pity a person begins to experience, due to the inability to manage their own lives. We deliberately allow circumstances and other people to control our destinies. This is because all of us want to be directed towards our attention and sympathy. Often, people rejoice in their illnesses, as others begin to pay attention to a sick person and rush to help him.

Suicide
This is an extreme form of self-criticism. Suiciders do not try to hide from the world, they hide from themselves because they reject and despise themselves as a person. Instead of comprehending the causes of their problems, such people feel unhappy and offended. Therefore, they seek to "put an end to this." Their difficulties, of course, lie in low self-esteem.

CHAPTER 12: THE CORE EMOTIONS

According to research done by Glasgow university, all human behavior can be categorized into four primary emotions, which include; happiness, sadness, fear, and disgust. Initially, it was believed that there are six basic emotions that were listed as surprise, disgust, fear, anger, sadness, and happiness. An arrival at these four primary emotions has been a journey that can be traced back to a first century encyclopedia by a Chinese that dared to break down all the human emotions into seven major ones which included; liking, disliking, love, fear, sadness, joy, and anger.

Happiness is the general feeling that we have of a moment, event, or person that gives us pleasure. Research has attributed happiness to have been contributed by a variety of factors such as; the individual personality type, individuals' physical health, wealth and the social class of a person, personal goals and self-efficacy, time, place, seasons and in general, other positive emotions. A recent study on happiness has also gone out of the way to redefine happiness and its causes. Unlike what all religions and grandmothers around the world have led us into believing, this study has shown that being kind to yourself, and putting your needs first causes us to be happy. Well, I know this is a hard nut to crack, since we all grew up in environments that insisted on the need of putting others' welfare first. In addition to focusing on yourself as someone who is worth your time and attention, the study also suggests that prosocial focus is likely to increase the overall happiness of an individual. When someone engages themselves in acts of kindness and helps other people out, their overall happiness is said to increase significantly.

Happiness is something that has been pursued globally, with different governments doing different things to ensure that its citizens are happy. A classic phrase by Easterlin revolutionized the way global economies would look at happiness. He suggested that money couldn't buy happiness, something that led a small country, Bhutan, to channel its focus on the happiness of the citizens other than the wealth of the country which was measurable by an increase in the gross domestic product. As a result, that small country has been rated among the happiest nations of the world, and not only that, her economy registered an enormous growth. More organizations and nations are becoming increasingly vibrant on their push for happiness; an example is the United Nations, which has set March 20th as the world's happiness day.

Measuring individual happiness is a highly subjective act and therefore, this necessitates the need for individuals to report their own happiness. Psychologists, however, have deduced specific measures around which questionnaires are formulated to measure individual happiness. The three parameters include: the presence of positive emotions, individuals' satisfaction with life, and the absence of negative emotions. Various instruments have been developed to measure happiness. Ruut Veenhoven, in the recent past, developed another way to look at happiness. He came up with a model, popularly known as, the four qualities of life, which gives us a glimpse of happiness based on a variety of factors. In all the four ways to look at happiness, personal satisfaction was the subjective aspect that was used to measure happiness, as we view life as a whole. Ruut's model was divided into two major components, the outer and the inner qualities. He further subdivided this into what was availed by chances in life and what availed results in life. The four factors that resulted from these constructs included; the livability of the environment, the utility of life, satisfaction and life- the ability of an individual.

Happiness, however, is not an all externally stimulated feeling, psychologists have suggested that it is actually possible to train yourself to be happier. It has been suggested that only up to 40% of our happiness is inborn and at least 10% is contributed by having the basic needs. That totaling up to 50%, the remaining 50% is ours to work out. Psychologists have said that individuals can train their brains to be more optimistic about life, to think in a happier and resilient way. This is done by making ourselves more aware of the positivity that hangs in the air and exercising our brain to do this regularly. By improving our physical health and exercising regularly, we are also likely to improve our overall happiness.

Sadness is a negative emotion that we experience when faced with a situation that is not pleasurable to us. It is a live emotion that usually, the almost immediate human response to it is, avoidance. Unlike happiness which is pursued globally, sadness is avoided from an early age due to the misconception that it is a bad emotion. Some of the reasons why it has been seen this way is its close association with more complex health disorders like depression. When kids are growing up, there is a conventional tendency to shush them when they are wailing and to bomber, them with positive words like you are going to be alright, please don't be sad and the like. Without knowing, we pass on the information that sadness is a bad feeling that shouldn't be experienced. Sadness is a natural part of our day to day lives, which often results from experiences that are painful, or at times, some moments that are meaningful and of deep connection with our souls. It acts as a reminder of what we value most in our lives, and often when embraced and put into good use, it can center us. It is not meant to be stuffed somewhere at the back of our minds but rather, it should be felt.

Sadness builds up from our painful experiences that probably, we couldn't put into words either growing up, or we were too young and dependent to express ourselves. This buildup of sadness has seen most people frantically try to look for ways to put away any feeling of sadness as they fear that any of it would trigger and unearth the well of sadness inside them. In addition, people all across the globe have built up walls and defenses to shield themselves from the pain of sadness. At the very beginning, these defenses work but as we grow into adulthood, they become either destructive for example, substance abuse or limiting, for example, keep a safe distance from people to avoid being hurt. Trying to suppress our negative emotions also numbs our ability to experience positive emotions such as joy, love, and passion. Allowing ourselves to go through our sadness is the only effective way to use our emotions. This allows the emotion to boil to its peak, wash all over us and then subside. This doesn't remove or reduce the pain caused by our sadness but instead, it helps us navigate through it, obtain balance and be truthful to ourselves. Feeling our sadness should be done without exaggerating, dramatizing or without feeling victimized about it.

Disgust, this is a withdrawal response from the object of disgust. Its signature is usually, nausea. Primarily this emotion is meant for rejecting food that is ideally not good for consumption either it is bitter, or, it is contaminated. The word disgust in itself means bad taste. Disgust is not only a way of rejecting bad food but also, it is an emotion that communicates to the other members of the species that the food is not good for their consumption. In human beings, disgust evolves into sensitivity to contamination and the drivers of disgust vary across different cultures. For example, if a fly floats on someone's drink that was otherwise consumable, it renders the drink not consumable due to the perception that the fly has contaminated the drink. With time, disgust grows and is resulted in some offenses such as a human being engaging in sexual activities with an animal. With increased moral sensitivity, disgust grows from an emotional response for protecting the body to an emotional response that shields one soul.

Fear is both an emotional and a biochemical response towards a dangerous occurrence. It is a response mechanism when we are threatened by a highly life-threatening situation and on the other hand, it can be a really subjective emotion that is experienced differently in different people. Fear could be a result of a traumatic experience that we have gone through in the past or, just our perception of a certain situation. One of the ways that we can reduce fear is by familiarizing ourselves with a certain fearful situation. For example, if one is fearful of animals, maybe a regular visit to the national park could substantially reduce the fear. The complexity of fear has left everyone in a dilemma of whether to classify it as an observable behavior or something that is hardwired in our brains.

CHAPTER 13: OBSERVE YOURSELF

By understanding how having emotions ties into the many aspects of emotional intelligence, we can healthily approach the subject. Some of the stigmas that come from so-called emotional people are that people that have been labeled as emotional may not engage in the associated steps of understanding other people's emotions, self-regulation, and empathy. This was touched on in the discussion of narcissism, but those who healthily embrace their emotions also embrace the emotions of others and know how to regulate their emotions if they begin to get in the way of social interactions.

This perception has to do with the idea that thinking about emotions too much is something negative. These dysfunctional perceptions have led to some people eschewing in any emotion, while others have taken the opposite side and have become advocates for emotion and emotional thinking. But this is a downward spiral that results from terminology not being used appropriately in the case of emotion. Showing compassion for someone is a sign that you feel emotion. All religions are infused with emotional feeling, and people become better friends, better family members, and better lovers because they care.

Emotion is the basis for meaningful social relationships. Having emotions does not mean that you are bogged down by them, which is how some characterize the term. By rejecting emotion or mischaracterizing emotion, we create a society where people either have distorted emotions because they do not understand them correctly or they feel no emotion at all because they have been taught to be wary of emotion based on misconceptions about emotion.

Coping with destructive emotions is rarely simple and rarely easy. You can begin to identify your repressed emotions by listening to the body. When dealing with repressed emotions, especially anger and rage, the body is often as affected as the mind. Repressed anger can cause chronic pain as well as other emotional turmoil like high anxiety and depression.

Overall wellbeing isn't just about emotional and mental health; it's about physical health, as well. Your physical and psychological selves do not exist separately. They are constantly interacting with one another. Keep reading to discover how your poor emotional health may be negatively affecting your body and your physical wellbeing.

Knowing how our minds work is part of the greatest mysteries we are yet to solve. A lot of individuals have dedicated their entire lives to understanding the mind, sadly to no avail. Understanding the roles of our mind and emotion to our well-being is paramount as it puts us in the driving seat in controlling our lives. This is simply a little part in our quest to use the mind in controlling our feelings but is one that must not be neglected. Similar to the relationship held by every part of our entire make-up, ignoring the interactions between our minds, emotions, thoughts, and feelings means we will be ignoring their roles. On a more serious note, this might be an aspect that we need to get fixed before taking further steps.

The mind and body do not function independently. They are not separate systems, and this can be observed when we are tensed. An instance of a moment of nervousness is a job interview or a first date with our long-time crush. Regardless of how calm and confident, we would like to appear in such instances; we discover that we are both tensed and self-conscious at the same time. The muscles of our buttocks will be tightened as a result of the self-conscious feeling we are experiencing. We sweat more than usual, and might even feel nauseous in such events, not forgetting those periods we would fluff our lines when we desire or attempt to be confident.

Our emotions which are constructed by the subconscious and highly influenced by the unconscious layer of our mind is what adds value to our thoughts. For instance, let us say you were raised to believe that tipping a salt shaker over is a sign of bad luck. When you observe someone tipping a salt shaker unintentionally or do so yourself, your mind sends thoughts which project emotions.
Our feelings are expressions of our emotional and mental state of existence. Normally tied to our physical and social sensory feeling, they are used to react to joy, fear, love, disgust, sadness, hate, pleasure, and a host of other emotions. In other to prevent extreme behaviors which usually comes at high costs, we must control and suppress some emotions and feelings.

Managing your emotions can be likened to developing a skill. It involves learning a better way of doing something. It requires change on our part. In reality, we struggle to accept change as humans. This is largely due to many factors, but the working of the mind is highly influential in this regard as we have discussed earlier in part one of this book. Controlling your feelings will get you mentally stronger. The good thing is, everyone can benefit it from controlling their feelings. Here is why you should keep your feelings in check.

Keeping your feelings in check is not the same thing as managing them. Ignoring how you feel about a certain situation will not make these feelings go away. Rather, such feelings will get worse when they are not addressed properly with time. Also, there is a likelihood of turning to coping skills that are unhealthy for support. These include the abuse of drugs and alcohol. Experts think that medical attention is needed to help persons who cannot keep their feelings in check to regain control.

CHAPTER 14: OPEN-AWARENESS MEDITATION: 20 MINUTES OF GUIDED MEDITATION

Start by getting in a comfortable seated position. It's best to sit cross-legged on the floor. If this is uncomfortable for you, try sitting upright in a chair with your back straight and your shoulders relaxed. You can also do this laying flat on the floor, but there is a risk of you going to sleep.

Once comfortable, take a deep, long breath in through your nose, and as you exhale, take your attention to the middle of your forehead, between your brows and slightly above the brow line. Imagine that there is an indigo-blue chakra sitting there. The dark glow of this indigo light begins to illuminate your mind and then spreads out through the rest of your body.

Create a door to your mind with your third eye. Imagine yourself opening this new door and walking through it into an empty room. Take a moment to decorate this room however you would like. Pick colors, looks, and décor that makes you feel calm and happy.
Make sure your room suits your tastes perfectly so that this area is now your new personal sanctuary.

Locate an area of the room that is the most comfortable and takes a seat.
From this position take a look out onto the world. Bring into your mind that same ideas, situations, issues, and thoughts that plague your everyday life. Take a few moments to contemplate these things silently.

Now image your sixth chakra spinning and gaining strength. The faster it spins, its indigo light washes over your body and invades all of your cells, and every pore of your body.
Take a deep breath in and feel all the energy bursting out your third eye as rays of dazzling indigo light.

Rest in this sensation for a few moments.
Still, in your mind, stand up for your peaceful place and walk back to the door you created earlier. Walk out of the room and look back into your new sanctuary and notice how you feel one with it.

Once you are ready, bring your attention back to the present and slowly open your eyes.

CHAPTER 15: 5 MINUTES TO LEARN TO BREATHE: BREATHING EXERCISES

To live a happier, calmer life, you should begin doing simple breathing exercises. Focusing on your breathing is an important factor in the practice yoga, meditation, or mindfulness therapy.
It is inevitable for tension build-up, especially if you have a lot of things on your mind – keeping the household, excelling in a career, nurturing relationships, or juggling work and school. But through all these, all you can do is breathe your way out of negativity and you'll be living a happy and stress-free life.

If You're Always Worried or Anxious
Anxiety, if left untreated, can lead to more serious medical conditions, like heart problems. Any variation of breathing exercises can help aid in the treatment of anxiety. However, there is one breathing technique that may help soothe not just your muscles and your body, but also your brainwaves.

Lie down in a comfortable position, with your back straight on the mat (or bed).

Now begin to bend both of your knees towards your upper body. When your knees are almost near your chin, hug your legs gently, then relax both your feet, and ankles. Gently soften your stance and release your shoulders on the floor. Your back should stay relaxed. Then slowly lower your chin to lengthen the back of your neck. Keep your eyes closed.

While you're hugging your legs, focus on your breathing. Feel the slow rise and fall of your body as you gently inhale and exhale deeply. While you're inhaling, allow your stomach and ribs to rise towards the direction of thighs, before sinking back down as you exhale. Hold this position for a few seconds.

Now, gently roll your body slightly to your right, and then to your left. You are using the floor to gently massage your back. Don't force your movements, keep your motions as relaxed, soft, and rhythmic as possible.

Next, start to coordinate the rhythm of your rocking motion with your breathing. When you inhale, slowly roll to your right; and when you exhale, roll your body back to the center. Inhale, and now slowly roll your body to your left, then exhale as you go back to starting position.

Continue with this rolling and rocking movements for 5 to 10 minutes, or until you feel your body and mind are starting to calm down. Be aware of your breathing and don't force your movements.

If You Want to Get Rid of Any Negative Emotion
When your thoughts are full of negativity, it affects how your attitude and behavior will go. However, it is quite difficult to maintain your positivity 24 hours a day, 7 days a week, as there will always be distractions, situations, and experiences that initiate negative thinking.

Initially, it will be hard to replace negative thoughts (and emotions) with positive ones, but it is possible.
Negative thoughts can only consume you when you begin to believe them. The key is finding a balance between positive and negative emotions.

This powerful technique called the Qigong practice, will help release any negativity in your life and welcome more positivity.

Stand with your feet firmly planted on the floor, a little wider than hip-width distance. Position your legs parallel to your feet, with your toes pointing forward. Keep your abdomen relaxed. Place your arms by your sides.
When you inhale, breathe through the length of your spine, then release down your arms and shoulders, as both your palms are turned up. Then, take several steady breaths.
When you inhale next, gently raise your arms, and gather all the negative thoughts, emotions, feelings, and beliefs that you have long been holding back.
On your next exhalation, turn your palms down, while lowering your arms in front, and gently bending your knees. As you do this, release all the negative feelings you gathered.
Make two repetitions more.
Now, inhale and gently raise your arms and gather all the positive

emotions, feelings, and beliefs that you can find.

Exhale and gently lower your arms, and let those positivity flow into your whole being. Feel the sensation deep into your inner core.

Make 3 repetitions more.

End by breathing and standing still for a few seconds.

If You are Feeling Extreme Anger

Suppressing anger is not a healthy way of handling this intense negative emotion. When you leave it unresolved, it can escalate to more serious conditions, like depression, anxiety, and high blood pressure.

You can learn to control your anger when you practice this simple breathing technique.

Find a quiet place to perform this. Lie down and make sure you are comfortable in your position.

Now, close your eyes, feel your body begin to relax, and settle on that position.

Focus on your breathing.

Begin to inhale slowly, through your nostrils. Feel your lungs gently filling up with air from your lower lungs, all the way to the top. The moment you feel your lungs is full of air, pause, and hold your breath for about 1 to 2 seconds

Then slowly exhale with your mouth, as you "release" the full weight of your body. Feel your body lighten and soften its stance.

Inhale slowly, then pause, and hold your breath a second longer.

Now, relax. Exhale slowly with your mouth, in a long and steady release, as if releasing all tension that you feel in your body.

As you inhale again, feel your stomach rising, while your chest is slowly opening, and your lungs are expanding.

As you slowly and fully exhale with your mouth, let out a deep sigh and let go of your body weight and let yourself "melt" to the ground, thereby releasing tension from your body.

Repeat 3 more times. However, rather than letting out a big sigh from the mouth, purse your lips and just blow air through your mouth – it's like blowing a feather to keep it flying. Be aware as your body sinks into the floor whenever you exhale.

Perform another cycle, 3 more times. But this time, when you exhale, let some hisssss sound flow from your mouth as if mimicking the hissing sound of a snake. Consciously feel irritation, frustration, and extreme anger being released while you exhale. Repeat any of the above to release tension. Free your mind with any form of negativity. Maintain your relaxed state.

When You've Just Got into of an Argument with Another Person
If you become enmeshed in an argument with your partner, or with your sibling, or any of your co-workers, you battle an inner conflict that you alone can "correct".

Here is an effective technique to try:
Find a comfortable position on a mat and lie on your back.
Don't rush the process. Take your time breathing slowly.
Take 5 deep breathes – breathing through the nostril has its benefits

As you breathe in, feel the sense of coolness in the air.
Gently guide your breathing, from the right nostril to the left side.
Slowly breathe in through your left nostril, feel the air entering through your nose. Inhale at equal length through your right and left nostrils, and then exhale. Make another 5 repetitions and focus on the flow of air, in and out of your nostrils.

Focus on the balance between the length as you take in air, and out again. Let the breathing come easy and become more relaxed.
Now, focus your attention on the strength of your breathing, in and then out. Feel air flowing into your lungs and out again. Repeat a few more times.

Next, be aware of your torso. Breathe slowly, gently, and evenly.
Now, focus on your body. Continue with your breathing exercises. Breathe evenly, while you feel the floor underneath you, and the space above.
Lastly, cultivate the smoothness from the beginning to the end of each inhaling and exhaling motions.
Make a few more repetitions. Savor the balance and the renewed strength of your breath, body, and mind.

CHAPTER 16: SELF- AWARENESS STRATEGIES

Self-awareness is about self-knowledge, about getting mindful of what is happening in your life, and about having an idea how you see your daily life or career developing. To be self-aware you need a certain degree of maturity and at least a vague idea of what you'd like to do with your existence. When you know what you want, it becomes easier to find a method of getting it. If you don't, you are left drifting aimlessly, with neither a goal nor a plan.

So, how can you develop self-awareness? Begin by increasing your sensitivity to your very own gut and emotions emotions, as they are generally the most trusted close friends you'll ever have. Make an effort to set aside a while for self-reflection, and think about your behavior, thoughts, emotions, frustrations, goals, etc.
Those who are used to self-analysis will find this easy probably, but if you're not used to this type or sort of thinking, this may be hard, even unsettling. In that full case, start by setting aside 30 minutes each night, once you're finished with the work for the day and may relax a bit, and think about the day or week behind you. If you had a difficult day/week particularly, ask yourself everything you can find out from the experience.

The purpose of this exercise is to truly get you used to considering how you feel and why.
Or, you may start journaling, and this is not about keeping a diary and covering your day-to-day thoughts and activities. Journaling is about recording any unusual or frustrating experiences, thoughts or emotions you might have had. Some things are not easy to go over with others, and anyway, not really everything is for posting, so why not get it off your chest by authoring it. The great thing about journaling is normally that to write something down, you need to believe about what to write; in fact it is often this technique of thinking about a problem that helps you see what's at the root of it. Therefore, if feeling upset, angry or disappointed, write it out and move on.

CHAPTER 17: RELATIONSHIP MANAGEMENT STRATEGIES

By understanding your emotions, how to manage them, and express them, you can build stronger relationships with your friends. This is because you are able to express your feelings positively to the other party. Emotions also help you to communicate effectively without fear both at work and in personal lives, which aids in building strong relationships with other people. One should try to figure out other individuals' emotions. This helps to avoid hurting them, which significantly destroys relationships. Without strong relationships, success becomes hard to achieve. World-leading business entrepreneurs and leaders associate their success to healthy relationships that emanate from understanding their clients' emotions. For you to survive and thrive in the modern world, it is therefore vital to understand the role of emotions.

For emphasis, improving your emotion can help in relationship management when one has to be assertive. There are a lot of misconceptions about assertiveness as some people think it projects one as domineering, selfish, or rigid. Assertiveness is important as it helps communicate boundaries and your position. Assertiveness does not imply not listening to others or being inflexible. In this manner, assertiveness in a relationship can be a source of friction when one or both of the parties does not acknowledge the idea of assertiveness. An example is where an individual is trying to assert her opinion and the other person misconstruing that to mean that the former's opinion has to prevail at the expense of others. However, with emotional intelligence, one can perceive the reactions of the other person and take into consideration when asserting personal views.

Furthermore, improving your emotions is likely to make it easier for you to resolve conflicts with others with success. In life and especially at the workplace, conflicts are unavoidable due to the unique nature of human behavior. Most contemporary workplaces are diverse, and this increases the risk of conflicts. Diverse workplaces may see conflicts arising from cultural insensitivity, stereotypes against sexes, race, religion, and socioeconomic aspects of other workers. All of these contribute to making a workplace a depressing sight. If each employee could recognize their emotions, it becomes easier to make others aware of how they feel and this can make it easier to prevent a conflict.

CHAPTER 18: EMOTIONAL INTELLIGENCE QUIZ

How to Measure My Emotional Intelligence?
You probably know that you can measure your IQ by taking a test online or offline (you can find tests in various books). It's completely the same when it comes to measuring your emotional intelligence – there are different tests on the web that will show you how you handle and express your own emotions and how you assess and understand what other people are experiencing. However, you should keep in mind that the test you choose should be from a reliable source and not just a random online test. That is why it might be a better idea to buy a book and find a test within it. It might give you a better idea of your EQ and the areas you should work on.

Why Is Emotional Intelligence Important?
Hundreds of studies were conducted during the last decade to determine which factors play a role in whether you will succeed in your life or not. The core focus of those studies was the role of IQ and EQ. The results were extremely revealing – the researchers discovered that the success in someone's life depends only 10-25% (depending on a study you read) on your IQ. Everything else, so at least 75% of success is comprised of all the other things, including emotional intelligence.

So, emotional intelligence plays a crucial role in the success in your career and personal life. The great news is that everyone can work on their EQ and work on reaching their potential. If you are still wondering why you would do that, let's take a look at some reasons why emotional intelligence is important:
Is It Easy to Develop Emotional Intelligence?

The good news is that we can all improve our EQ and successfully work on our emotional intelligence skills. The bad one is that it will take time. Working on your EQ is not an easy job, and it will require investment from your side, both in time and effort.

The first thing you need to know is that you will have to be completely honest with yourself. Yes, that means facing your fears and habits and being ready to change them, as well as all other emotions you consider inappropriate of negative. You have to be willing to go deep and have an inside look into yourself. It's the only way that you will be able to work on your emotional intelligence and adapt the emotions to the things that are happening in the environment.

How to Improve Emotional Intelligence?
Self-awareness, as we mentioned in the first chapter of the book, is the skill of recognizing your emotions and acknowledging them as they occur. It can help you know your strengths and weaknesses, and it is considered to be one of the main elements of emotional intelligence.

There are several techniques to develop self-awareness, but there is one important question to ask before we start:
Do You Know Yourself?
I advise you to be cautious and not to ask yes immediately. The important thing to do before you can start making changes is to understand yourself and see where your starting point is.
Self-awareness is nothing else than the process of being able to know yourself, which is exactly what you need to focus on. That includes recognizing the emotions as they occur, as well as feelings that come with them, and realizing what your thoughts and actions based on them are.

Top athletes often have psychologists working with them on how to assess and deal with emotions during an important match. They certainly don't need to be overwhelmed by anger or frustration because it can affect their performance. It's the same with life – if you can recognize your emotions, you can deal with them in a better way.

Knowing yourself also means knowing your strengths and weaknesses. This has to do a lot with confidence, but we will move towards confidence tips a bit later. Your goal should be to be assertive or, to explain that better, confidently communicate your ideas and thoughts and be able to justify them with good arguments.
How do you Properly Know Your Values and Assumptions?
We are all proud of at least some of our values, such as our morals,

principles, ideals, ethics, or standards. Furthermore, we often emphasize that they are what guides us in our lives. In case you are not completely sure of your line of values, it's about time to properly get to know them. That way, you will feel like you are on a well-secured road full of signs. You will feel more secure because you will be aware that you are on the right track and relaxed and confident because you know where you are headed.

Aside from values, there are always certain assumptions that we have of both others and ourselves. Developing self-awareness also means that you shouldn't neglect them. There are positive and negative assumptions. Unfortunately, it seems that the latter ones dominate when it comes to people with average EQ. One of the most often negative assumptions is "I believe that bad things happen to me all the time." On the other hand, there are positive assumptions such as "I believe that all people are good."

CONCLUSION

From time to time we are all overwhelmed by emotions, both positive and negative. And no matter what kind of emotions a person experiences, they can interfere and usually prevent him from making the right decisions. It is no secret that people are manipulated mainly through the emotional sphere because emotions cloud the mind of a person and do not allow him to think about his decisions. Therefore, acting on emotions - people often make mistakes. And if we talk about extremely negative emotions, they seriously undermine our physical and mental health. Therefore, it is necessary to be able to cope with any emotions, when it is necessary, both with positive and negative.

Having learned to cope with your emotions, dear reader, you will significantly improve your life. I promise you that. You will not only reduce the number of mistakes you make because of strong and often inappropriate emotions but also improve your relationships with many people, even those who are overly emotional and unable to control themselves. You will gain clarity of thinking and confidence in your abilities since you will know that you control yourself. And learning to control yourself - you can control and own much more in your life.

Well, that's it for now, about everything in order.

SOCIAL ANXIETY SOLUTION

REVISED AND UPDATED

Proven Techniques and Strategies Reprogramming Your Mind to Stop Living in Fear and Stress, Overcome Panic Attacks, Shyness, Low Self-Esteem, Negative Emotions and Thoughts.

Dr Henry Campbell & Dr Daniel Watson

PREFACE

The pages in this book were developed through years of experiences that I have gone through, as well as what has proven to work for others that I have talked to and have researched. I also want to congratulate you for taking the time to understand your own fears and how you can overcome them.

After experiencing many different types of fears throughout my life and struggling to overcome them, I decided that I wanted to write a detailed book to help other people who are in a similar situation as I was. I also wanted to help people understand how fears form and why we experience them, because many of us have friends or relatives who struggle with fears and we have trouble understanding what is going on in their heads.

I can guarantee that you will find this book useful if you make sure to implement what you learn in the following pages. The important thing is that you IMPLEMENT what you learn. Fears are not conquered overnight but the important thing to remember is that it is definitely possible for you to overcome them. What I am giving you is the information so that you can better understand your own mind and body, as well as some steps you will need to make that journey.

Every person will experience fear in his or her life. A small amount of fear within you can be helpful in stirring up some motivation when faced with frightening situations, but hanging on to it for too long and with no good reason, can be nothing short of crippling.

As you go through these pages, you'll get a better understanding of what fear really is, where it comes from, and you'll learn several ways that you can overcome it. We will dive into what is going on in your brain, how your body reacts to your triggers, how your early childhood can influence the rest of your life, as well as what work is required of you to get past the roadblocks that you have.

INTRODUCTION

I would like to thank you for purchasing a copy of my book. Congratulations on taking the first steps toward overcoming your social anxiety and becoming a much more comfortable and confident person in your own skin. By the time you finish this book, you will be able to have a complete understanding of social anxiety disorder and the different forms that it can take, as well as the symptoms that it can cause, how you can prepare yourself and prevent these kinds of symptoms, and even how to handle them on the fly. This book will go over a number of different concepts that relate to the topic of social anxiety and social anxiety disorder, including different kinds of tools that you can use to handle its symptoms on your own, like breathing techniques and other ways to calm yourself during extreme periods of anxiety. Some of the later chapters of this book will also explain several methods of preventing these symptoms, like techniques for visualization and becoming a much more optimistic and positive person, as well as the benefits to adopting a more positive personality or outlook. These can be important things to consider with regards to handling and overcoming your social anxiety because of the nature of the disorder and how it can affect your everyday.

A significant portion of this book will be dedicated to describing the different kinds of treatment that are accessible to people who suffer from social anxiety disorder, and how you can go about seeking those treatment methods. Some of the later chapters of this book will be dedicated to different ways that you can handle your anxiety and ways that you can begin to move past and overcome this very difficult disorder on your own if you do not have access to or prefer not to see professional treatment from a licensed mental health care professional. Through reading this book you will be advised about the meanings of the symptoms that you might experience because of your social anxiety. The earlier chapters in this book, however, will be largely devoted to advising you on the basic concepts of what social anxiety is, as well as social anxiety disorder. We'll also talk about a number of different related concepts that are similar to or relevant to social anxiety, and that will be beneficial to understand for a person who suffers from this disorder.

By the time you finish reading through the chapters in this book, you should have a clear understanding of the different symptoms of social anxiety and how to handle them, whether that be by seeking out professional treatment methods, or by practicing visualization and breathing techniques to help you to overcome your anxiety. You should have all of the tools that you will need to begin to progress and grow, moving past your social anxiety and becoming a much more emotionally and mentally healthy and stable person.

CHAPTER 1:WHAT IS SOCIAL ANXIETY?

Social anxiety can often be a very confusing issue for people who
do not experience it, to understand. Many are unaware that they
suffer from a form of this disorder and would greatly benefit from
an understanding of it. Social anxiety can be one of the most
difficult to cope with and one of the most common issues in the
mental health world, affecting about seven percent of the human
people at any particular time. The average chance of a person
developing social anxiety during the course of their life is reported
at about 13 percent. However, these numbers are very likely to be
inaccurate, as they only represent cases of social anxiety that have
been diagnosed. Many people choose not to seek help for personal
issues such as social anxiety, perceiving these kinds of problems as a
sign of weakness. Some people might even believe that their issues
are trivial or unimportant, as well. A lot of people will compare
themselves to other people, especially those who they believe to be
"stronger" than themselves, or who have gone through more
difficult times. A very common phrase that might come up is "well,
it could be worse," which is used as a justification for a person to
ignore the problems that they face. This can be harmful, however,
and it will often also make that person's problem or problems worse
in the long run. Some people might also fail to understand that
they have social anxiety, whether that is because they simply are
not aware, or because they might be in denial about their mental
health problems.

Social anxiety is a very commonly ignored and misunderstood
mental illness. It is most often described as an excessive or
unnatural fear of all or some particular kinds of social situations,
or of any kind of interaction with other people. Most often, social
anxiety will come from a sense of fear or dissatisfaction that comes
from being judged negatively by other people, especially by people

who they are close to and whose opinions they care a lot about. Social anxiety is a very significant problem for people who experience it, and it can cause issues like anxiety or fear that invades almost all of the different parts of an individual's personal life, even affecting things like their friendships or other kinds of interpersonal relationships, or holding them back from succeeding at work or in enjoying their hobbies. Social anxiety can sometimes also be extremely uncomfortable and difficult for people to cope with, since it is a "chronic" disease that will not be cured with time, it will take active work in order to cure.

These kinds of disorders are also usually too complex for the person who suffers from them to handle themselves. Reaching out to friends and communicating openly and honestly about the things that are bothering you can help a lot when dealing with mental disorders like social anxiety. However, professional mental health care, such as cognitive behavioral therapy, is the only method that can be advised to help you to understand and overcome mental disorders such as social anxiety. This can be thought of as similar to a medical condition; it is always best to go to a licensed medical practitioner to diagnose and treat physical conditions, just in the same way that the best method of handling mental illnesses and conditions is to have your problems diagnosed and treated by a licensed mental health care practitioner.

Social anxiety can also be a very discordant and paradoxical disease, causing a lot of conflict and turmoil within a person who suffers from it. It can cause a lot of dissonance between people who are close to someone who is suffering from social anxiety. People who suffer from social anxiety are usually perceived by others in a way that is very different from their own reality. For example, the friends or family of a socially anxious person will often perceive that person as distant in some way. They might describe that person as awkward, unfriendly, nervous, quiet, inhibited, withdrawn, or even aloof, disinterested, or hostile. In truth, however, people who suffer from social anxiety are usually prevented by their anxiety from doing the things that they want to do like enjoy their hobbies or make new friends. More often than not, a socially anxious person will want to act more friendly or communicate with other people and be more social, but their anxiety keeps them from feeling comfortable in those kinds of situations, causing them to "overthink" the situation.

Social anxiety is very commonly triggered by a large number of various situations. These can include situations such as being introduced to new or unfamiliar people or being in a space with a lot of unfamiliar people. When you are not familiar with someone, it can be difficult to understand their attitudes and intentions, and that can be daunting, making you feel judged or even on the spot. You might perceive yourself as uninteresting or worry that you make the other person uncomfortable. It can also just be difficult to "open up" and feel comfortable in a conversation with someone who is outside of your typical group of friends who you have already formed relationships with.

Being criticized, teased, or "made fun of" can also be very common triggers for social anxiety. A lot of people will be made uncomfortable by criticism or by being the "butt" of a joke, taking these things as insults or attacks on their character. In a similar way, being at the center of attention or being watched while they are doing something, especially something that they are not normally comfortable doing, can sometimes trigger feelings of stress or anxiety. When someone is watching you while you are performing a task, even one that you are comfortable with or normally enjoy, it can ramp the pressure and make you feel judged as well. This observation of a socially anxious person can also apply in situations when you have to make any kind of public statement or performance in front of a group of people. This particular kind of social anxiety is often referred to as "stage fright," and is one of the most common kinds of social anxiety. It can be seen as a common trope in film and television. Of course, this is not a complete list of triggers and causes for social anxiety or the development of social anxiety. There are a number of different situations that can trigger it, including things as simple as making eye contact with someone or being in any kind of social encounter with another person or group of people, that can cause feelings of anxiety and that can manifest in ways that will vary from person to person.

These symptoms which are either caused as a result of or which can sometimes worsen a person's social anxiety can include things like nervousness or anxiety or even excessive amounts of fear, increasing high heart rate, trembling, muscle twitches or tics, as well as other kinds of symptoms such as an abnormally dry mouth and throat, blushing, unusual or excessive production of sweat, or general feelings of discomfort or unease. These symptoms will vary from person to person in both the ways that they manifest and the levels of intensity in the symptoms that they experience.

Additionally, people who experience social anxiety will usually understand that their anxiety is irrational and that their concerns are not based on fact or reality, at least on a logical level. However, this will usually not prevent a person from experiencing thoughts and feelings of anxiety when they are placed in social situations. This can be frustrating because even if we logically understand that we are not actively being judged by other people or that our concerns are not based in reality, that does not make our anxiety go away. In most cases, we will be aware that any perceived issues are very likely to be caused by our feelings of separation or discomfort, and if we simply dismiss or ignore those feelings and try to be more confident, then the problems that we perceive in ourselves or that are created by our feelings of anxiety will simply go away. That doesn't change the circumstances or the causes of our anxiety, and will not "cure" us.

Social anxiety and social anxiety disorder are conditions which can be successfully treated with time, patience, and professional therapy. It is important to understand that these things all take time and that you will not be able to overcome your social anxiety in one day. The best way to go about this is to first begin by actively seeking assistance and treatment from a licensed mental health care professional. Social anxiety disorder and other kinds of anxiety disorders and mental health issues can be successfully treated today through cognitive behavioral therapy. It is usually recommended that you search for a specialist in anxiety disorders, who will be able to fully understand the problems that you are experiencing and will be equipped to treat them. Cognitive behavioral therapy is a very reliable and proven method of talk therapy which, if performed properly, can be incredibly helpful to people who suffer from social anxiety disorder and other similar kinds of problems. Studies have told us that talk therapy that is used for the treatment of social anxiety and social anxiety disorders can help people who suffer from these mental disorders, and they're often able to live a much happier and much more comfortable life which is no longer hindered by their anxiety or by their fear of social encounters. Cognitive behavioral therapy can be incredibly helpful in allowing people to change their thoughts, feelings, and beliefs, as well as the ways that they behave, in a very positive way. A person with social anxiety disorder who is being treated, however, must be willing and able to actively work toward bettering themselves and invest in their own growth, in order to overcome their anxiety and their fears of social situations.

Usually, this therapy will be paired with other forms of treatment like medication in order to help with the regulation of the moods and stress levels of the person who suffers from this disorder. Socially anxious people will often be given prescribed doses of drugs that have been created to ease the effects of their anxiety and stress, such as certain kinds of antidepressants. However, these drugs are usually seen as more of a temporary solution, similar to a crutch. They should not be used as the primary method of treatment, instead being used in tandem with more permanent and reliable forms of treatment, such as cognitive behavioral therapy.

Additionally, it is important to remember that every individual person will be different, and there are not any universal methods that will always work to treat complicated issues like social anxiety. Medication can usually be fairly effective as a method of helping with the treatment of social anxiety or its symptoms, specifically for people who do not have extreme amounts of anxiety. It should also be noted that the person should not have a history of substance abuse, as these kinds of drugs and medications can be very addictive. For this reason, mental health and medical professionals will be hesitant to prescribe some of these drugs, and will usually only do so for short amounts of time in order to prevent the development of any sort of addiction or dependence on them from potentially developing. Additionally, the specific kind of medication should be important to consider. In the past, many kinds of antidepressants were promoted (usually by the drug companies that produced them) and were claimed to be very helpful in the treatment of anxiety and anxiety-related issues. This is not true, however, since antidepressants usually work by increasing the amounts of specific chemicals that are produced by the body of the person who consumes them. This can make the anxiety that a person experiences worse than they would be even without the drug, producing the opposite effect of what was intended. Medications that are more commonly and much more successfully used for and during the treatment of social anxiety and other kinds of anxiety disorders usually include depressants and other kinds of drugs that can provide a soothing effect or inhibit the production of chemicals within the body. However, not all people even need or want to use drugs to help themselves to overcome their anxiety.

One very significant change that has been made in the last decade is that the use of these kinds of medications for the use in the treatment of anxiety disorders has been decreasing gradually by the people who undergo active therapy for these disorders as well as the mental health professionals who treat those people. A large majority of these people choose to forego the use of these kinds of drugs during their treatment, focusing primarily on CBT instead.

Regardless, these kinds of medications can only help on a temporary basis and should really only be used in extreme situations to reduce the symptoms of anxiety for the person who is experiencing them. Consuming them can be dangerous in the long run, as they will encourage the user to rely on them and focus on their symptoms as opposed to primarily treating the causes with active therapy. If drugs are used in this way for an extended period of time, they can also cause the user to form a physical dependence on them. This is very broad, blanket advice that might not be as true or applicable for every individual. You should try to talk to your psychiatrist about this topic in order to make the best decision for yourself that will allow you to overcome your anxiety as effectively as possible. You should try to find a mental health care professional who is aware of the negative effects of these drugs as well as their benefits and will be able to make an informed decision about the best kind of treatment for you and your level of comfort. You should also feel comfortable talking with your psychiatrist about the dosage and expressing whether a particular dose seems to be helping. Often, people will take the wrong dosage of prescribed drugs, which can have negative effects on your mental state and ability to overcome your mental health problems.

It is incredibly important to be aware of all of the factors that might influence your therapy and your ability to overcome your condition or conditions. However, it is also important to understand that the prognosis for these kinds of disorders is generally good. Individuals who are completing active therapy and cognitive behavioral therapy situation in overcoming their anxiety or other kinds of mental health disorders.

CHAPTER 2: SOCIAL ANXIETY DISORDERS

The official definition of social anxiety disorder has changed over the years as our understanding of it has changed and evolved, but there is a fairly consistent and reliable source of information regarding the diagnosis of mental and psychological disorders like social anxiety disorder, called the Diagnostic and Statistical Manual of Mental Disorders, sometimes abbreviated simply to "DSM". The most current edition of this manual is the fifth and is referred to as the DSM-5. The DSM and its most recent versions have begun to change the definition of many of the diagnoses over the years. The DSM used to define the diagnostic criteria for social anxiety disorder simply as a condition that occurs for an extended period of time, which was required to have been "at least 6 months". This portion of the definition of social anxiety disorder has been changed, however, and is now a little bit more specific, stating that "The fear, anxiety, or avoidance is persistent, typically lasting 6 or more months." This new definition doesn't seem to change much of the definition of this disorder for the people who experience social anxiety, but it does allow for more clarity to those who refer to the DSM-5 for guidelines on diagnostic criteria regarding mental disorders. The definition of social anxiety disorder has been made a little bit more specific in order to prevent a lot of potential misunderstandings that come as a result of ambiguous wording. The rest of the definition for the diagnostic criteria for this disorder have stayed the same.

The full DSM-5 definition for social anxiety disorder from the 2014 edition is as follows:

- The first criterion is that the individual in question will experience anxiety related to specific kinds of situations that require the person in question to interact with other people in a social context, or that will expose the individual in question to possible scrutiny or judgment from other people around them, either real or perceived. This can include things such as being watched while they perform normal tasks such as drinking or eating food, or performing in the presence of others. This will usually apply to things like singing or speaking publicly but can be applied to any kind of performance. If the individual in question is a child, their interactions with other children will usually be slightly different from their interactions with adults, so it is also important to evaluate this criterion in the context of the individual's interactions with friends and other peers.

- The second criterion required that the person in question will experience a fear of being judged or otherwise perceived negatively by the people around them if they act in specific ways that reveal that they have some form of social anxiety. This can include excessive fear of embarrassment or humiliation, as the person will often believe that these things will lead to them being rejected by their friends or families. In children, specifically, a common method of expressing this kind of fear or anxiety is through things like crying or throwing tantrums, or even some quieter reactions such as being unable to act or "freezing", hiding themselves behind an adult or someone who they are comfortable with, or being unable to speak in some cases.

- The third criterion is simply a sense of anxiety that persists during social encounters. A lot of people will avoid these situations or tolerate them for their duration, attempting to hide the feelings of anxiety that they experience. This is usually expressed in media with the common trope of hiding in the bathroom during a party or other kind of social gathering, which is not entirely untrue. A lot of people will find that quiet, private spaces like that can allow them to breathe and recover during stressful social encounters.

- The fourth criterion is that the anxious or fearful responses that a person experiences as a reaction to social situations is excessive, or disproportionate to the actual situation or threat. Sometimes, there is no real threat, and the person in question is simply perceiving a threat that they have fabricated out of their fear or is anticipating a threat in their future which causes them to become fearful or otherwise anxious.

- The fifth criterion is that the anxiety that the person in question experiences lasts for an extended period of time. Usually, this will require the condition to persist for at least six months before it can be considered social anxiety disorder. The sixth criterion also requires the anxiety that the person will feel to cause a significant amount of stress for that person. For the condition to officially be considered as social anxiety disorder, the person in question will need to be very significantly impaired by their social anxiety in a number of different areas of their life.

- The seventh and eighth criteria each refer to the sources of the symptoms of this disorder. The seventh criterion will require the person in question to be experiencing symptoms that can not be attributed to the consumption of specific substances such as recreational drugs or different kinds of medications. Their symptoms can not be caused by a physical illness if it is to be considered as social anxiety disorder, as well.

- The eighth, and final criterion requires that the sense of anxiety or fear cannot be attributed to another mental illness that has overlapping symptoms with social anxiety disorder that the person already suffers from. This is similar to the previous criterion in that it refers to the source of the symptoms that are being experienced, but is specific to mental health instead of physical health. Some of the common mental disorders are things like autism spectrum disorder or panic disorder, which both alter the ways that a person will be able to socialize and connect with the people around them, as well as things like body dysmorphic disorder. Of course, there are a large number of other kinds of disorders that share symptoms with social anxiety disorder, and which are commonly mistaken for social anxiety disorder. This is one of the most important points, as misdiagnosing these kinds of disorders can result in the wrong kind of treatment being applied, which can sometimes cause your symptoms to worsen, in some cases.

There are a few issues with this definition, as it represents a flawed understanding of social anxiety disorder which has since been changed. It can be incredibly helpful when you are trying to understand the nature of these kinds of disorders that the definitions of different kinds of mental disorders such as social anxiety have been revised over time. Social anxiety disorder, much like many other kinds of mental disorders, have only been

517

recognized as an officially listed and valid mental disorder for a short period of dime, only having been officially recognized for the first time in the year 1980, and this disorder was also only added to the DSM in the version that was published in the year 1987, which was also the first time that social anxiety disorder would be explained adequately. The ways that we are able to understand these kinds of disorders changes over time, and social anxiety disorder is a relatively new term which we are still learning more about. Because of this, the disorder's definition also changes with our improved understanding of it, and it is able to be much more clearly and accurately defined in each new edition of the DSM. The specific criteria will also very likely be changed and altered more over time as our understanding of these kinds of disorders also changes and evolves. There are also a few specific changes to the DSM definitions that have been suggested, such as some more specific language and wording that could prevent potential misunderstandings due to ambiguous wording. Another version of the DSM, for example, references "panic attacks" that fails to clearly define the event that it refers to. It is especially important to understand the differences between anxiety, which is typically a response to a specific situation or external stimulus, and a panic attack, which is typically understood to be a warning sign, precipitating some sort of perceived oncoming medical issue or emergency of some sort, such as a heart attack, the fear of losing control in some way, or even death. Whether these fears are legitimate or warranted or not is obviously based on the specific circumstances; sometimes, the stress that one experiences during a panic attack can cause the body to experience some sort of strain, even pushing someone to a heart attack under the wrong circumstances, but they are not always omens of thee kinds of events. This can be confusing for a lot of people, and a clear definition here would be incredibly helpful.

As was mentioned briefly in the first chapter of this book, every person is different and the specific nature of the particular disorder or disorders in question and of the individual person who is suffering from these disorders can very likely affect their symptoms and can cause them to manifest very differently. There are, however, a number of more common signs and symptoms that can help you figure out if you are suffering from this disorder or even from a similar one. Some of these more common symptoms might be things like physical reactions to stress or struggle such as blushing, excessive or unusual sweating, trembling, increased heart rate, nausea or physical feelings of illness, and rigidity or "freezing up." There are also mental and emotional symptoms that can be seen, as this is a mental disorder. These symptoms include things like the mind going blank, as can be seen in cases like stage fright or if the person is put on the spot and find themselves in a situation that they are not expecting or are not familiar with. They might also tend to speak more softly or less confidently than usual, or they might avoid making eye contact with other people or avoid interacting with other people in general, especially with people who they are not familiar with or who they might be afraid or worried about being judged by. Feeling self-conscious, awkward, or embarrassed are also common, and can sometimes cause a person who is suffering from these kinds of symptoms to have a difficult time in making conversation with or interacting with other people.

Social anxiety disorder can also sometimes run in families, but the method by which it is actually passed down is still mostly unclear. In a lot of cases, some of the family members of someone with this disorder will have it while others will not. Some people might not even have any family members who share this disorder with them. Researchers who specialize in mental disorders like social anxiety have found that there are a number of different parts of the brain which are involved in emotional and instinctual responses like fear and anxiety in humans. Some researchers even believe that conditions such as social anxiety are largely caused by, or are worsened by, misunderstandings and the misinterpretation of the thoughts or intentions of other people. For example, a person who suffers from social anxiety will usually be triggered by situations when they perceive the words or actions of another person as hostile or malicious. When in reality, their intentions were simply not made clear, or they might not be particularly good at portraying their thoughts and opinions accurately. Underdeveloped social skills could be another likely contributor to issues like social anxiety. For example, if your social skills are particularly underdeveloped, you might sometimes be discouraged or feel negative about your own words and actions after talking to or interacting with other people, causing you to be apprehensive or hesitant in future interactions with those people or even with others. As our understanding of the origins of these issues evolves and becomes more clear, we can develop more reliable and effective treatments for them. Researchers also try to look for other contributors to social anxiety and other similar kinds of disorders, such as stress and other similar situations.

Social anxiety disorder is a very difficult issue to cope with. It is often the cause of a lot of unwanted and unnecessary stress in people who suffer from it, and it can even begin to cause harm to or damage the personal life of people who suffer from it or who are close to socially anxious people, like their friends, families, and even their coworkers. The DSM has a specific set of criteria for the definitions of these kinds of disorders of the mind, which are used for purposes such as forming clinical diagnoses of these disorders, and they use these criteria in order to understand whether something will fit the description of a mental disorder or if it might be caused by medical issues or other factors. The DSM specifies that the criteria for the qualification of these illnesses include things such as a pattern of behavior or psychological syndrome in a specific individual, which is not typical for that person. This means that usually, there will need to be some sort of change in the person's behaviors or mental states that are not normal for that person. These kinds of behaviors or mental states also need to be related to sources of stress that the person encounters, such as pain or trauma.

Sometimes, physical disabilities will also be considered in this context, as well. The symptoms that the person is experiencing should not be typical responses to specific events, such as the loss of a friend or family member. If the symptoms are culturally appropriate and typical for a person to experience for a period of time in response to specific events which the person in question has encountered, it can not be considered. They will also not be considered if the symptoms are revealed to simply be caused by other kinds of dysfunctions within the person, such as previously diagnosed mental disorders or physical illnesses.

These criteria apply to all mental disorders, and this includes those like social anxiety disorder. A person who suffers from this kind of mental disorder will see significant and usually harmful effects in almost all areas of their life, including all of the areas that have been mentioned above. The first area of a person's life that social anxiety will affect, of course, is their social life. They will have trouble forming relationships with other people, and they might even begin to have trouble maintaining their relationships with their current friends or family, becoming distant, awkward, or evasive.

This can cause people to isolate themselves, which can also lead to other kinds of issues like depression or a number of other illnesses, both mental and physical. They might end up suffering at work or expiring a feeling of dissatisfaction with their life. Social anxiety and other chronic mental disorders like it can permeate all aspects of that individual's lives and experiences, and if continues to be left untreated, this disorder can eventually begin to alter a person's life completely., causing them to break their connections with their loved ones or leave a job that they otherwise would have liked. The longer these problems persist, the worse they seem to get, and avoiding seeking help with these problems can be incredibly harmful, almost as much as the original illness itself.

If you decide to seek treatment, an examination will usually be performed by your doctor where they will question you about your history of mental health issues and even with medical issues before they do anything else in order to be certain that your symptoms are not caused by an undiagnosed medical health condition. If your symptoms are not caused by physical illnesses, then your doctor might refer you to a mental health care specialist, such as a counselor, psychiatrist, psychologist, or a social worker. The first step toward receiving effective treatment is to have your illness or your condition diagnosed and to work with your doctor in order to create a treatment plan that will work well for you.

Cognitive behavioral therapy (often shortened to just the acronym "CBT") is a specific kind of talk therapy that is often found to be incredibly helpful for people who suffer from social anxiety and will allow their treatment to be much more effective and helpful. CBT is intended to help a person to learn about different methods of thinking, behaving, and acting in situations that can help them to overcome their mental illnesses, and in the case of social anxiety, can help them to feel much less anxious about being in social situations. It can also help people to be able to learn and practice social skills. CBT that is conducted in a group context with multiple people can also be incredibly helpful, especially to people who struggle with social anxiety or other kinds of disorders that can affect a person's social life. A lot of people with social anxiety can also find benefits to support groups and other similar communities of people who struggle with the same kinds of disorders. In a group of people who all have social anxiety disorder or some other illness that can affect their social life, people with the illness can be a little bit more comfortable knowing that the other people in the group understand their anxiety and can relate to the struggles that they face. In this kind of therapy, it is often much easier for people struggling from mental disorders to be able to recognize that their thoughts and their fears related to their disorder are untrue and not based in reality or that they might be distorted in some way. It can also help you to understand how other people who suffer from the same or similar issues as yourself will tend to manage their issues and overcome their fears and disorders.

The most common kinds of medications that are prescribed to help with the treatment of illnesses like social anxiety disorder have also been proven to be helpful in short term uses and in smaller doses. Some professionals will use other kinds of medications, but the three that are seen most commonly are known as antidepressants, anti anxieties, and beta-blockers.
The medications that are developed specifically to treat the symptoms of anxiety, also commonly referred to as anti-anxieties, anxiolytics or antipanics, are medications that treat the symptoms of or inhibit the symptoms of anxiety. These kinds of drugs can be relatively strong and will usually start to take effect almost immediately after they are consumed to help lessen the symptoms of anxiety. Unfortunately, though, these kinds of drugs can also be very addictive if the user begins to rely on them more heavily. Many people will eventually develop a dependence on these drugs if they are taken for longer periods of time and in high dosages, which can cause that person to require increasingly higher dosages over periods of time in order to achieve the same relief from the symptoms of their anxiety. Because of this potential addictive quality in these drugs, they are typically not meant to be prescribed in high dosages or for extended periods of time, and should only be used in emergencies or as prescribed in order to avoid developing a dependence. A lot of doctors will also try to avoid prescribing these kinds of drugs for patients who have not reached adulthood yet for similar reasons. Antidepressants can be defined as anything, especially a drug, that is used to prevent or treat depression. These kinds of drugs are most common and will be the most helpful for the treatment of the symptoms of depression or of similar issues. Antidepressants work very differently from anti-anxiety

medications, and because of this, are not usually very helpful for the symptoms of anxiety. Antidepressants can sometimes take several weeks before they begin to take effect, which is not helpful for immediate relief, which is usually necessary during stressful events such as panic attacks or periods of extreme anxiety. These kinds of drugs also act as stimulants, whereas anti-anxiety medications will usually be depressants, working by limiting the production of certain chemicals or by providing a calming effect to the person who consumes them, lessening the effects of that [person's anxiety and similar extreme responses to external stimuli. Antidepressants, on the other hand, will usually work by increasing the amount of certain kinds of chemicals which are produced by the body, lessening the symptoms of issues like depression. Additionally, these kinds of antidepressants can sometimes have some side effects or other problems like insomnia or trouble with sleep and altered or unstable sleeping patterns, nausea, or headaches. The side effects that people will usually experience from the use of these kinds of drugs are not usually too severe, especially if they are consumed in lower dosages. However, if the dosage amounts for these drugs are increased over a period of time, the person might end up developing a dependence on them. The third kind of drugs which are commonly used to help with the treatment of social anxiety is beta-blockers. Beta-blockers are drugs which are used to prevent or lessen the effect of many of the symptoms of anxiety by regulating the body's responses to the chemicals which cause these kinds of symptoms. Beta-blockers have been shown to be incredibly helpful for more mild kinds of anxiety such as "stage fright" or social anxiety because of this and can be very effective for these kinds of issues. They also have fewer side effects, which can be helpful for people who are trying to recover from and move past a mental disorder.

You can work with your doctor or mental health care professional in order to determine what the best medication or treatment plan might be for you, as well as the correct dosage and length of time that you should be on that medication in your treatment. A lot of individuals who suffer from anxiety and anxiety related disorders will often receive the most effective tools for their recovery and to overcome their illness through a combination of psychotherapies like CBT and medication.

Each person and case will be different, however, so it is important to find the correct dosage that works best for you. You should try to communicate with your doctor and discuss any side effects that you might be experiencing as a result of the consumption of these kinds of drugs, as well. They will be able to address your concerns and potentially change the kind of medication that you receive in order to prevent some potentially negative side effects. It is important to remember that both psychotherapy and medication methods can take time to work. A healthy lifestyle can also help fight symptoms of anxiety. Things like exercise, sleep, and a healthy diet can also be much more helpful than you might think, and you should always try to reach out to your friends and family for support as well when dealing with these kinds of issues. One of the most significant issues for people with these disorders is effective communication.

CHAPTER 2 PART 2: THE SKILL OF OVERCOMING ANXIETY

To overcome low self-esteem, it is important to evaluate your logic and rationale. This way, the mistakes you make in your thinking that are driving you to make exaggerated, negative, assumptions, and conclusions. This process is called cognitive restructuring and can be used as an individual treatment, as a part of a wholesome CBT treatment plan, and as an additional treatment to exposure. Exposure is, as you learned, the ultimate way to improve your self-esteem and overcome anxiety (Antony, 2000).

Exposure is in theory, a simple concept. It requires you to face a situation that you fear and learn positive lessons from experience. This is easier said than done, as you're about to learn. It is a lesson that I learned through my efforts to support my recovering sibling. What I learned during my studies was that exposure needs to be carefully designed to be effective. If not, it can be counterproductive. As it turned out, exposure requires meticulous planning, constant self-reflection, and open-mindedness to question your beliefs. This is yet another demanding task since most of us are inclined to hold on to what we believe. We believe what we perceive to be accurate and right, and challenging that leaves us feeling confused, and often lost.

Here's a simple depiction:
If you believe that your abilities are low, you have an idea about what your life and activities should look like to live and survive with that truth. But what if you're wrong? What if you're talented and smart? What if you're even above that? Considering this idea means stepping into a headspace where you no longer understand who you are. Because your life and self-perception are made on the grounds of core beliefs, shaking those can also cause turbulence in the way you see yourself and your life. In this chapter, we'll review the process of performing and applying exposures so that they indeed teach you lessons of self-worth.

How to Plan Exposure
Exposure is also a treatment in which you purposely create a situation that tests your fears. This can be an effective way to test

and overcome negative evaluations and assumptions. However, to ensure the beneficial effect of the exposure exercises, one must first create a plan. Planning exposure is necessary to identify the problem, set goals, and define evaluation standards. With that in mind, the three main parts of planning exposure treatment include (Hope, 2004):

Identify the Problem

First, you'll need to examine your thought process to identify what situations trigger anxiety, which thoughts preceded it, and what core beliefs are driving your logic. The mindset needs to be scrutinized to determine and successfully challenge fears and review the perceived risks from social events. People with SAD tend to have a perception of low emotional control, meaning that they feel powerless to manage their emotions. One of the ways to correct this is by creating a distance between the perception of your emotional state and the objective view on yourself from an observer's point of view. This helps you understand that others can't see that you are shivering and that your hands are sweating, relieving the fear that everyone notices your symptoms.

Prevent Safety Behaviors

Next, alongside your therapist, you'll review inadequate coping mechanisms that you use to cope with social anxiety. Safety behaviors are successfully treated during exposures and usually eliminated after a certain number of repetitions. You will detect and review the actions you take to relieve your anxiety, identifying those that shouldn't be used in exposures. Next, you'll work on planning to prevent or reduce, post-event rumination. Post-event rumination treatment is done by learning how to process events using rational reasoning, such as whether your recollection of the event is factually accurate, what is the evidence of the (in)accuracy, and whether or not potential mishaps have any true impact on you and your life.

Design Exposures

To design exposures, you will plan out actions, like going to places and planning events that challenge your false beliefs. This means that the situations need to be specifically designed to target core beliefs, such as:

- That you don't know how to act in a situation
- That other people will be overly critical and negative towards

you

- That a social situation will have a catastrophic outcome due to your inadequacy
- These exercises are also great for you to learn that you can cope with the symptoms of anxiety and that the other people aren't noticing them as much as you think they are

For example, you might notice that you don't have to present yourself as perfectly as you thought to be accepted in a group. Another form of exercise includes engaging in a situation while making sure that no safety behaviors are being used. These behaviors make you think that you are somehow relieving the symptoms and protecting yourself from the negative outcome, but this isn't true. These behaviors are preventing you from facing the situation in the way in which you should. This way, you not only survive a situation but also feel good about yourself. These situations may include anything from spilling a drink on purpose or revealing information about yourself that you used to believe people will judge you on.

Relaxation Training

A significant portion of exposure therapy is to learn how to manage physical symptoms of social anxiety. Relaxation training helps you not only relax and feel better but also learn to control mental oversensitivity. Mental oversensitivity becomes high in social situations, and learning how to relax will help you go through the situation a lot easier. Multiple exercises can be used in relaxation training. Some of them target relaxing specific muscles, creating an exposure ladder, and doing the so-called homework, which requires you to write down thoughts and observations on the exercise you perform without a therapist.

With muscle relaxation, you are encouraged to focus on specific muscle groups within your body, noticing the difference in how they feel when they are tight and relaxed. This form of body scanning helps you notice the muscle tension and record how it feels to be relaxed. Relaxation training can also be used in the form of cue-controlled relaxation, which means that you use the word "relax" over and over while you are in a relaxed state. Then you move on to use this approach in your everyday activities.

For example, once you notice that you feel anxious, you then take a couple of deep breaths and repeat yourself to relax. As a result, you learn how to manage your symptoms better and get a hold of yourself when you start to feel like your symptoms are getting out of control.

This technique seems simple, but it needs to be exercised frequently to be effective. It will help you learn how to manage the physical sensations when you are distressed, and eventually, learn how to relax very quickly during everyday activities. After that, you may apply this exercise to the situations that provoke anxiety. As a result, you learn to manage feelings in anxiety-provoking situations.

GIVE UP YOUR SAFE ZONE

Anxiety is constantly telling us that we have to change our external environment to soothe an internal problem. However, the opposite is true, when we heal ourselves internally, and meet our fears and traumas with authenticity, the energy that our mind has been using to shield us from those fears can now be used for actual productivity and creation of the life that you want. Change your internal world, and you will manifest the in the physical world what you truly desire.

Step One: Recognize that you are overwhelmed and that it's okay and perfectly understandable to be so. Absolutely everyone experiences being stressed out at one point or another in your life. You are definitely not alone in your experience. Admitting that you have stress is the first priority, if you can't come to the realization that you need help, you'll never get out of the thought patterns that are disrupting your life. These thoughts can have significant damage to your mental health and getting out of the maze of thought patterns has infinite benefit.

Step Two: Think of the stress reaction as preparation for the circumstance that is arising, rather than stress and anxiety being inherently bad and uncomfortable feelings, stress is necessary and valuable to our survival, and should be appreciated as the tool it is. Ask how you can use this energy to overcome the situation.

Step Three: recognize that having to constantly think about and monitor yourself to avoid the judgments of others is exhausting and that it's time for a change of pace. The impossible task we give our minds of having to shield us from perceived threats-questioning if we said the right thing, thinking about what other people think of us, our minds are on hyper-alert because of trauma, even acute trauma will keep us feeling as though we have to prepare for a catastrophe constantly. Our perception of someone else's perception.

Step Four: Get outside of your own mind. I don't mean to push away or ignore any feelings, but to consider all the lives, perspectives and experiences that are occurring right now. We have no way of knowing all that other people are going through. Stress and anxiety can make us feel isolated, feeling like everyone around us don't understand the discomfort we are experiencing.

HOW TO FEEL SAFE WHEREVER YOU ARE

Safe attachment, which is considered necessary for a healthy state of mind, is nurtured by unconditional love, responsiveness, and support from the main caregivers.

Usually, people who have anxiety fall in one of the three remaining categories that represent insecure attachment: Avoidant, anxious, and disorganized attachment share a different degree of disconnecting oneself from their own sensations, suppressing. This happens when, for different reasons, you start to withdraw from asking love, support, and company when you need it.

SAD links to insecure attachment styles because you form an ambivalent relationship with people: On the one hand, you want to be close to friends, family, and coworkers, because you need love, friendship, and company. You shy away from making these connections because you feel unworthy of acceptance. Feeling unworthy of acceptance goes back to early infancy, when crying for consolation or shouting out of confusion and insecurity brought you shame and criticism. However, as a conscious person, you can practice making connections to overcome emotional blockages due to feeling unworthy. You can do this in following ways:

- Socialize, even when you don't feel like it. The only way for the anxiety to go away is to persist socializing despite feeling awkward.

- Practice seeking emotional support. Overly self-critical people tend to deny themselves help and support when they need it the most, further worsening the feeling of detachment from the outside world. Commit to contacting at least one person when you feel upset. Choose a friend or a family member who can understand your condition and is capable of giving rational feedback, but still cares about you and can offer understanding and consolation.

- Don't refuse help. Chances are that you rarely, if ever, ask for help at work or at home, and delay seeking medical help until your symptoms become critical. Refusing help is typical for all forms of anxiety and depression. The desire to do everything by yourself arises from feeling incompetent and from having an exaggerated perception of standards for competence and success. Learning how to ask for and accept help will help you normalize your social standards, and bring you closer with people around you.

CHAPTER 2 PART 3: HOW TO DEAL WITH A FEAR OF FAILURE

Fear is one of the basic human emotions. It is run and controlled by the part of your brain in charge of the most primitive physiological responses, called the limbic system. This system causes your mind and body to activate the "fight or flight" response, designed to save a primitive human from imminent danger. While fear is a response to a present threat, anxiety is oriented towards a future threat that can't be prevented or stopped. In other words, when you're anxious, you feel a sense of danger, and you feel like there's nothing you can do to stop it. You fear negative events coming your way that are beyond your control, and you feel defenseless.

Anxiety goes hand-in-hand with rumination, which is the habit of obsessively thinking about unpleasant scenarios and picturing situations that can occur. This puts you in a state of constant worry, which combines with physical symptoms like pain, headaches, muscle tightness, and increased pulse.

Severe anxiety can cause a lot of emotional pain and interfere with one's quality of life and performance. However, that doesn't mean fear is always harmful. To a certain degree, it helps you act responsibly and take good care of yourself, as you're aware of risks that might come from certain behaviors. To a certain degree, anxiety helps you protect yourself from threats and meet the challenges of daily life prepared.

Anxiety and fear are all normal emotions that everyone faces. Typically, they decrease with time — however, people with SAD face chronic physiological responses that intervene in their daily life. They have the purpose of keeping you prepared for future events and are helping you protect yourself from threats. Getting rid of anxiety and fear ultimately shouldn't be your goal; you should aim to reduce the responses so that they don't interfere with your life.

HOW TO NO LONGER CARE WHAT PEOPLE THINK OF YOU

Everyone makes mistakes. However, the majority of people are able to recover and bounce back. If you have low self-esteem, it may seem like the way you feel in a particular situation determines the way you think of yourself in general. The way you feel about yourself and what you believe about yourself depends on the situation. So it's very easy for you to spiral into negativity. Those who have healthy self-esteem can evaluate themselves accurately and estimate their strengths, weaknesses, and they also believe they are worthy people, regardless of those.

Self-esteem is a personality trait that reflects your sense of self-worth. If you have high levels of self-esteem, you have a healthy sense of your worth. You understand that you deserve good things in life, such as happiness, love, satisfaction, and success. You don't expect or feel entitled to the good things in life, but you profoundly believe that you are worthy of them. People with healthy self-esteem are usually the happiest and most successful, as they tend to measure and evaluate their performance and actions accurately. However, this sense of self-worth isn't grandiose. You don't believe that you're better than other people in any way; you think that you are good enough, capable of doing both right and wrong.

People with a grandiose self or sense of self-worth are often called narcissists, while those with a deficient feeling of self-worth tend to suffer from depression and anxiety. If you have SAD that means your self worth is most likely compromised. You should be working towards improving self-esteem and self-confidence. As you can see, neither extremely high nor extremely low sense of confidence is healthy. You should work towards developing a healthy sense of self-worth that is a balanced measure of understanding your good traits and personal strengths, as well as limitations and challenges.

FEAR OF DRIVING AND FLYING

Each and every person, at some point, becomes afraid. People get scared of different things such as heights, death, driving, ghosts, being alone, and even a fear of the future. Fear is normal. It is a reaction or instinctual response when you feel like there may be a physical and emotional threat and/or danger coming your way. Fears are essential to our survival as a human race. Besides, you wouldn't be able to protect yourself from any kind of threat if you didn't feel the emotion of fear.

However, fears can become a problem when people fear circumstances that are far from any real danger and are just imaginary scenarios of the future playing out in their mind. Through years of research, we've learned that there are certain experiences, sometimes called traumas, which can happen in a person's life to generate a fear response much later in that person's life.

Pinpointing these events can range from being very obvious to extremely difficult. The good news is that the way to overcome these fear responses is within our own power. It comes down to pinpointing the events and then slowly exposing yourself to similar situations. This is often what psychologists, psychiatrists, and psychotherapists do when you visit them.

Scientists have also learned that fear of the unknown is a natural and basic human emotion that is meant to keep us safe as individuals and as a species. For example, historically, you would benefit greatly from having the fear of being lost in an unknown village. This kind of a fear would help us hundreds and thousands of years ago because societies were much less safe and had little to no connection to one another.

If you got lost back then, you might not be able to communicate with the other societies because of a language barrier or even worse, you may die of a disease because you are not immune to the diseases of this mysterious village. However, our world is much more connected today, and now that we're in a time where almost everything can be tracked or translated between cultures, this fear of being lost in an unknown village may still be there, but it has no real benefit to us anymore. In our current world, you can go into most countries and as long as you have some form of currency, you can survive.

Another example of this would be the fear of approaching a member of the opposite sex that we are interested in. This one here often holds many people back from living the kind of life they want. It is important to remember that when we lived in much smaller societies of 50-100 members, it would benefit us to have a fear of approaching an unknown member of the opposite sex because we could be risking our safety or even our chance of reproducing. In those days it was very important to be aware of these things because inbreeding and social hierarchies were key to our individual survival, as well as the survival of our tribe.

This also had a huge impact on our social status, if we were to mess up with a certain member of the opposite sex that we were interested in. Could you imagine how the other members of the opposite sex would judge you if you developed a bad reputation with another? All of your potential mates could reject you, just because you made a few mistakes or were not mature enough at the time. But in the world we live in today, you could live in New York City and not see someone you dated for months or years!!

So how does that fear of approaching the opposite sex benefit us in today's society? It doesn't. In fact, as long as you are respectful to that person and the environment you are in, you can approach whoever you are interested in with really no consequences at all! So this fear doesn't really have a use in our current overcrowded society. Unfortunately, many people haven't been able to live fulfilling dating lives because they allow their fear of approaching a member of the opposite sex to override their own desires of happiness.

Depending on your point of view, you may consider these kinds of fears as a hindrance towards your own personal growth. As a human being, you will undoubtedly begin to feel fear at times, but you have to be cautious not to allow it to negatively influence any of your actions or decisions in life. Unfounded fear can usually jeopardize your chances of success, for it can be a controlling and manipulating factor in life.

Fear can also be deemed "real" or "imaginary" and is felt due to the interpretation of a situation. It can make you feel anxious and pessimistic and incapable of thinking rationally. You'll tend to procrastinate or become doubtful and let it set some limitations in terms of your own abilities. It is also important to note, two different individuals can view the same situation completely differently.

If person A and person B have both never been in a plane before, they are both completely new to the phenomena of flying on a plane. However, if person A views the action of flying in a plane to be a new experience that will expand their view of the world and person B views this action as an extremely risky situation that he/she should avoid because of the movies they've seen, person A will feel little to no fear when the plane is starting up while person B could be terrified the entire trip. By keeping this in mind, you will be more in control of how you feel in a new or different situation.

One key is to never let your mind settle on negative thoughts that can lead to fear. Instead, fill it with courageous thoughts and your fears will eventually fade away. Courage is not really the absence of fear, but instead it is being able to prevail over the fears that are there. If you allow your mind to keep on anticipating that something horrible is bound to happen, your mind will only be clouded with daunting thoughts. The same can be said with positive thoughts.

CHAPTER 3: PHYSICAL, EMOTIONAL, AND BEHAVIORAL SYMPTOMS

Social anxiety disorder can manifest in a lot of different ways depending on the specific person who is suffering from the disorder, but there are different symptoms that can be more common in people who suffer from social anxiety. Some of these common symptoms and traits can even be things that the official definition that is used in clinical settings might not consider. These kinds of qualities can include a number of different things such as a sense of inferiority for the person, an excessive sensitivity to criticism, having some sort of difficulty or otherwise struggling with assertiveness or the lack of ability to assert one's thoughts or opinions, or even a sense of difficulty with or a lack of good judgement. Many who struggle with social anxiety will also experience some sort of fear of the judgment of other people who they meet or interact with. Because of this, social anxiety disorder might cause a person to have difficulty with pressure of any kind, and they might even go as far as to actively refuse to participate in things that they feel like might cause them to be put under some sort of social pressure.

Because of a lot of these common issues with social anxiety, this disorder, and the limitations that it can impose on the person with the disorder, can cause them to have a lot of trouble in forming relationships with other people. A person with social anxiety will have issues not only in their social life, struggling to form close bonds with people and to maintain their friendships, but also with their romantic lives because this kind of anxiety related to social situations can make it very difficult to form meaningful long term relationships with people.

In a lot of cases, social anxiety disorder and avoidant personality disorder will tend to exist comorbidly with one another, making it much more likely for a person who suffers from one of these disorders to actually have another disorder they are fighting, as well. The DSM 5 defines social anxiety disorder and avoidant personality disorder as their own distinct conditions, however they both share many of the same diagnostic criteria, meaning that they share a lot of the same traits, symptoms, and causes, and many specialists of these kinds of mental disorders will argue that the two conditions should be officially recognized as one disorder. Additionally, many mental health care professionals will also argue that avoidant personality disorder is not actually its own condition; it is simply a worsened or more extreme and progressed evolution of social anxiety disorder. They will argue that since social anxiety disorder is characterized by an inability to perform comfortably in social situations, it can lead to the avoidance of these kinds of social situations altogether, in especially extreme cases, and can progress to become avoidant personality disorder, which is characterized by the lack of the ability to relate to other people. It is unclear, however, whether these two disorders are directly connected or not.

Social anxiety disorder's symptoms are also generally split between two slightly different categories. The first of these is commonly referred to as the nongeneralized symptoms, which only present themselves in very specific social situations, or specific kinds of social situations. The second group of symptoms that accompany this disorder is called generalized symptoms, which are not necessarily triggered or worsened by specific events. Instead, these kinds of symptoms are usually present in most or all kinds of social encounters and situations. These kinds of symptoms cause a sense of dread or fear of all different kinds of social situations. Usually, people who suffer from nongeneralized social anxiety will have a specific list of the kinds of situations that make them uncomfortable or that they might have a fear of. This list might be short or long and can range from as general as stagefright or performance anxiety, to much more specific triggers, such as performing in front of certain people or types of people. A lot of people might not even be aware of the "full list" of triggers for their nongeneralized social anxiety, and might still be discovering new triggers. The symptoms of these kinds of disorders and the severity of the symptoms that you might experience can also vary depending on a number of different factors in your environment or a number of other things. Your symptoms might be especially strong and noticeable in one place and time, and might be completely gone or diminished in another, even disappearing for extended periods of time or worsening for long periods as a response to certain stressful or difficult situations that you have a lot of trouble being able to cope with. Regardless, the symptoms of these kinds of mental disorders will usually persist over the course of a person's life, and the only way to be able to move past these kinds of issues is to learn and understand how to handle the symptoms when they come up and prevent.

CHAPTER4: ISOLATION, SHYNESS, AND SOCIAL RELATIONSHIPS

This chapter will be about isolation, shyness, and the relationships that you form and keep with other people, and how they are each related to social anxiety. The first topic that will be covered is isolation. Social anxiety has a very direct and a very strong relationship with isolation , with each of the two worsening the other's effects for the person who suffers from them.

The troubling relationship that exists between the concepts of isolation and anxiety can be a very hard thing to unpack and to heal. Isolation and social anxiety seem to come hand in hand, in most cases. For someone with social anxiety, their isolation, and the habits that they form because of that anxiety regarding social situations can tend to follow them and even grow stronger as time goes on. During a social interaction, whether that social situation is something like a party where there are unfamiliar people, or something simple and seemingly insignificant like a quick trip to a grocery store, they might tend to avoid these kinds of situations because of their anxiety or because of the perceived judgement that they are afraid will come to them during that task. If they do manage to convince themselves to participate in social situations and open up to the people around them, the stress that they experience because of those kinds of situations can be extremely crippling. And after they have been removed from that situation, they might even carry that stress away with them and experience a strong, growing sense of dread regarding the actions that they have taken and how they behaved during the social encounter in question, often demonizing their own actions and perceiving them as wrong for some reason or another. These kinds of fears and concerns regarding social situations can cause the person to begin to avoid these kinds of social situations, and can also begin to impact the ways that that person is able to connect with others, even damaging the relationships that they have with their friends and families. You might even begin to view social encounters as a burden or as a "hassle," perceiving them as negative experiences and preferring to spend time in isolation instead and avoiding others instead of communicating and engaging with other people.

Your avoidance of situations and social encounters, however, will not get rid of the anxiety that you might be experiencing, as social interactions are necessary for everyday life and you will continue to dread any future social situations that you might encounter.

However, while social anxiety can often lead to isolation from the outside world or from social situations, the reverse can also be true. Being isolated or experiencing feelings of isolation can often be a very significant cause of social anxiety, and can cause you to want to be alone out of a sense of insecurity. Many people will do this out of a desire to avoid feeling the anxiety and the stress that can come with social situations. If this is the case, then the anxiety that comes with social situations can be much more difficult to work with, because of a sort of disinterest in the situations at the root of your anxiety.

CHAPTER 5: DAILY PLANS FOR MANAGING YOUR SOCIAL ANXIETY

Keeping a journal that you write in daily can also help you to overcome social anxiety over time. Writing about the things that you experience in your day to day life can help you to logically work through fears that you might have about social situations. Recording your thoughts about the different kinds of situations and experiences that you encounter can help you to gain a new perspective about those experiences, and might even allow you to understand your habits a little bit more effectively, allowing you to know when you might be starting to slip back into old, negative habits or patterns of thought, and possibly even preventing yourself from falling back on them and halting your progress. Similarly, you can try writing down simple and attainable goals for yourself that you can use to measure your growth and understand what kinds of situations make you anxious and where you need to "improve," socially speaking.

Additionally, the kinds of goals that you set for yourself and what you would like to reach can be incredibly important for your growth as a person. Whether those goals are smaller or more mundane things such as being able to overcome your social anxiety and move past your illness, or if they are a little bit larger, like long term career or relationship goals, it can be very helpful for you to write them down and have concrete goals for yourself to work towards. This can make it much easier to motivate yourself, as well as making them a little bit more real and easier to measure objectively. You will be able to set multiple smaller goals for yourself to reach within the larger target that you are aiming for which can be a helpful motivational tool as well. You will be able to reach these smaller checkpoints much more easily, and they will seem much less daunting and intimidating than the large overarching goal alone, which can begin to seem pointless or impossible if you simply keep working away at it with little reward. Another very important part of setting goals for yourself is to understand where you are along that path of growth and self-improvement in order to better know how far you still need to go.

Working toward a concrete goal is often much easier than mindlessly churning away at an impossible and endless task.

CHAPTER 6: FOCUSING ON YOURSELF

This chapter will be all about focusing on yourself and your own personal growth, instead of comparing yourself to others. Additionally, when you are working toward improving yourself, and toward overcoming your mental illnesses that you might be suffering from like social anxiety, it is important to be doing that work for yourself, so that you can be more comfortable and can grow as a person. Your motivation can be incredibly important for any goal, and external goals like impressing other people can be sort of empty, and will not usually be able to serve as adequate means of motivating yourself to move forward.

You should take care to understand your motivations and the reasons that you are seeking to better yourself in this way. Maybe your daily life is difficult or stressful, and you would like to be a little bit more comfortable around the people around you, such as friends or family members.

Physical health can often be a very significant contributor to social anxiety. Improving your physical health and maintaining your body will not only allow you to feel more confident in social situations, but it can also be incredibly fulfilling! Maintaining good health can also improve your mood in a number of different ways. A healthy body can lead to a healthy mind. If your body is able to function effectively, then your mental states will also improve as your body is able to regulate itself better, and you will begin to see a lot of improvements with regards to your mental health and the illnesses that you might be suffering from. You should try to get a lot of regular exercise, mixing up the different kinds of exercise that you get, balancing a good amount of things like cardio and weight lifting or other kinds of workouts depending on your own health and the things that you might need or want to work on a little bit more. Other things can also be very helpful, like making sure that you are receiving a balanced diet, drinking enough water and staying away from alcohol or sodas. You might even want to begin to drink a little bit more tea or even small amounts of coffee. Caffeine is technically a toxic substance, and it can cause a lot of problems, such as skin irritation and the slightly more scary nerve receptor blockage that people who are against the usage of caffeinated drinks such as coffee will often cite. This is true, that coffee can cause some loss of sensitivity because the caffeine particles can become attached to your nerve receptors, after a long period of regular consumption, and you can begin to develop a dependence on it, and if you stop drinking coffee or stop consuming coffee very abruptly, then you might go through some withdrawal effects, like headaches, or your blood vessels might begin to open up more freely because the brain's adenosine receptors will not be blocked by the caffeine that you are consuming as much, which can lead to headaches. However, there are also a lot of benefits to drinking coffee, if you are able to make sure to consume it in moderation. Because coffee and the caffeine that it contains can trick the adenosine receptors in the brain, a lot of people will consume coffee if they have a headache or migraine in order to receive some slight relief. Caffeine consumption will trick your body into constricting its blood vessels, which can lessen the symptoms of headaches and migraines a little bit, as well as a number of other health benefits such as a decreased risk of things like Alzheimer's and Parkinson's diseases, higher rate of metabolism, and even a lower risk of depression. However, if you consume a lot of coffee, it is also important to remember that caffeine is mildly toxic, and that it can cause some negative effects if it is consumed in excess, so it is also very important to remember to drink a lot of water in order to flush those toxic substances out of your body in order to prevent a lot of those negative health effects.

Coffee has also been found to reduce a lot of pain after intensive workouts considerably, which can be helpful in allowing you to stay motivated to continue to exercise regularly, which can also help people who suffer from social anxiety by allowing their bodies to function as they are meant to, which can help to lessen the symptoms that you might be experiencing. If you are going to the gym more frequently, you will also be spending more time around other people without necessarily having to engage or interact with those people, which can allow you to become a little bit more comfortable with others over time! The gym is a nice neutral space to allow yourself to become comfortable with other people, because most of the other people there will also be more focused on their own workouts and won't necessarily be paying attention to you, so if you struggle with issues like social anxiety, then you can allow yourself to spend time around other people without feeling like you are obligated to socialize. Even if you are not going to the gym, you might try hiking or jogging outside, or even practicing yoga and working up that way.

Another very helpful thing that you can do is to keep regular, healthy sleeping patterns. If you are keeping a very irregular sleep schedule or staying up until the sun rises every day, that can lead to a lot of health issues, or can even cause you to feel a little off-center, which can lead to higher levels of anxiety as well.

In order to prevent this kind of anxiety, even if you are still unable to sleep at night, you should try to simply enjoy yourself in moments when you are alone. This might seem a little bit counterproductive to the goal of overcoming social anxiety, but a lot of people who suffer from social anxiety are also simply introverted people, and if they spend too much time surrounding themselves with people and throwing themselves into uncomfortable social situations without realizing their introversion, this can lead them to believe that they simply do not enjoy social situations, even if that might not necessarily be true! Sometimes, you might just need to take a little bit of "me time." You might want to spend a calm weekend by yourself every so often in order to allow yourself to recharge. You might not want to be alone, finding that you become bored or don't know what to do with your free time. If this is the case, then you can also spend your quiet weekend with one or a couple of really close friends who also understand that you just need some time to unwind. You can sit down with friends or family and watch a movie instead of going out, and this can still be an incredibly effective way to relax and unwind for an introverted person.

One of the most important things that you should remember is to simply allow yourself to be comfortable, and that you should do whatever is best for you and your own personal growth. Overcoming your social anxiety does not mean that you need to become a "social butterfly" or to always be at a party or going out. The only thing that this entails is being comfortable in social situations, at least to a reasonable degree. You can be a social person while still maintaining an introverted nature.

Additionally, you should try to remember to recognize your mental growth and reward yourself for the improvements that you have made in your recovery. Being able to move past complicated and difficult issues like social anxiety is not easy, but it can become much easier to stay motivated and continue to grow and develop, moving past your social anxiety if you are able to treat yourself every so often! You should allow yourself to be proud of your development every so often and recognize the progress that you have made by cooking a special meal for yourself, buying a new book or movie, or even by taking a little vacation if you are able to.

In that same way, it is also important to have real goals that you can work toward as well. You should be aware of what you want in your life and have concrete goals for yourself and your progress. A lot of people will actually write lists of these kinds of goals and put them up on their door or above a desk as a source of motivation or as a reminder of the kinds of steps that they need to make. You should be able to visualize what you really want and use that to continue to push forward because overcoming complicated issues like these can sometimes be difficult. You should be trying to keep your strengths and weaknesses in mind during this process as well, building on your strengths and improving on weak points where you might be lacking. You might want to start by working on the areas that will be easier to improve on, starting by working with your strengths and sticking to what you already know and eventually moving forward to the other qualities that you know you aren't as good with. Challenging yourself can be difficult (or challenging), but it will be necessary in order to overcome this kind of disorder.

CHAPTER 7:SOCIAL CONFIDENCE

A big part of social anxiety is the way that it can affect the friendships and other relationships that you form and maintain with other people. This can be difficult for people who are uncomfortable in social situations, but the key to long-lasting and meaningful relationships is effective communication. If you do not express why you are hesitant to go out every weekend or why you fail to respond to text messages every so often, then your friends might begin to think that you do not want to talk to them specifically or that you are pushing them away as opposed to simply needing to spend some time alone to help yourself to recharge. This can cause a lot of harm to your relationships and can be even worse for new friendships or ones that you are trying to form with new people. You should try to communicate effectively with other people in order to prevent your friends from misinterpreting your words and actions, as well as preventing you from being able to form new relationships. You should try to take initiative and extend invitations first sometimes, as well. You can suggest something to do to a friend, instead of relying on them to plan everything and make the first move every time. This will tell them that you want to spend time with them as well, if they might be thinking that you're avoiding them for some reason.

This can even include people who you do not necessarily consider to be friends already, who you typically view as simply acquaintances such as your neighbor or a coworker. You should try to communicate more effectively for the sake of the relationships that you already have with people you know, as well as people who you don't already know. You should try to form new bonds and relationships as often as you can. You might try to find a hobby or join some sort of cause that you believe in that can allow you to immerse yourself in social situations and meet new people. You can try taking a class of some sort or volunteering at a shelter. Getting out and doing these things can allow you to do something that you enjoy or that you believe in, as well as allowing you to meet new people who are probably interested in some of the same things that you are. This is similar to the example of going to the gym because these kinds of things can also allow you to get out and be around with people without feeling too obligated to engage or socialize with a lot of people, and you can move out of your comfort zone when you are ready to do so.

Another very important thing to understand for people who struggle from mental disorders like social anxiety is how to assert yourself. Being able to recognize and understand your boundaries and being able to say no or to express your thoughts and opinions is a very important skill and a very important part of being able to communicate well with other people. If you do not express your needs and the things that you want, then other people have no way of knowing that information and you will very likely be unhappy with the situations that you find yourself in because your interests are not being taken into account, especially if the people around you think you are already satisfied. If you think that you would prefer if things were different than how they are or if you have an opinion that simply goes unsaid, simply being a yes man can be very harmful as well. If you have a bad habit of allowing yourself to be pushed around by other people, then you should try to say "no" a little bit more often. If other people tend to make somewhat unrealistic requests of you or you simply don't feel comfortable with something, then it is completely okay for you to say no if you need to. However, you should also try to keep the opposite kind of situation in mind, as well. If you have a problem with not going outside of your comfort zone as much as you should or would like to, then you might want to start employing the "yes, and…" technique a little bit more often, or being a little bit more of a yes man. You should try to agree more often in situations that might put you a little bit outside of your comfort zone. Of course, if you are not ready to do something that is a little bit too far outside of your comfort zone then you can still say no, but this is a very important part of being able to handle your social anxiety effectively, and you should try to step outside of your comfort zone as much as you are able to.

CHAPTER 8: BOOSTING SELF ESTEEM

Being able to move outside of your comfort zone, as was mentioned in the previous chapter, is an incredibly important part of allowing yourself to move beyond the limitations that social anxiety can put on you. As you are able to do this more often and take larger and larger steps toward self-improvement and progressing toward the goal of eliminating or minimizing your social anxiety, you will be able to improve your self-esteem as well, and you will begin to find yourself feeling much more confident and comfortable as well.

One very important aspect of being able to be confident in yourself and your abilities is to have reasonable expectations and to understand yourself accurately. A lot of people will place unrealistic expectations on themselves and will strive for perfection in all aspects of their lives. This will only cause unnecessary stress and can serve to cripple yourself and hold you back from actual growth and progress. You don't need to be the absolute best at everything you do; sometimes it is perfectly okay to simply be okay. This is not to say that you should stop caring about the things that you do, or that you should simply give up at the first sign of difficulty, but it takes time to grow and develop skills, and nobody can be perfect. You should try to allow yourself to be okay with how things are, and to have realistic goals and expectations of yourself, because worrying about the things that you do will often be harmful to your growth and will halt your progress toward overcoming your social anxiety.

Surrounding yourself with positive people can also be very helpful in this way. If the people around you are understanding and patient, then you will probably be able to perform tasks without feeling pressured or uncomfortable because of a fear of being judged. You should try to understand the kind of people who you enjoy spending time with, and who will be positive and understanding of you and your boundaries. Having a strong support system can be very helpful to people who are struggling with mental health disorders like social anxiety, and might even help you to be a little bit more positive and confident in yourself if you are surrounded in other people who are the same way.

CHAPTER 9: PRACTICING GRATITUDE

Being able to be a more positive person yourself can also be a very important skill to learn, and one of the easiest ways to learn how to do this is to begin by taking note of negativity that exists in your life and replacing it with positivity instead. Positivity can be an almost "contagious" quality and can allow other people to both, directly and indirectly, gain a much more positive and light outlook on life by being around a person with a positive attitude. Adopting an optimistic personality can be difficult, but will help you a lot on your path to overcoming this incredibly difficult and complicated disorder.

One very easy way to begin to replace one very big source of negativity in your life with positivity instead is to simply stop apologizing for the things that you do. Everyone makes mistakes, and if you are always focused on what you are doing wrong, then your self-esteem will begin to plummet. Constantly apologizing like this can seem almost like a habit as well, and will almost begin to lose its meaning after a while. Additionally, most apologies are primarily about the person who is apologizing; you are saying that YOU are sorry or that YOU regret what you have done, and this essentially does nothing for the person who you are apologizing to. If you must, you can try to help the situation by fixing it or dealing with the consequences of what has happened. If you feel that you absolutely need to say something about the situation, then you should try to thank the other person who you would be apologizing to. This puts the emphasis on them, instead of on yourself, which can be much more effective, and is also much more genuine and meaningful. For example, if you accidentally bump into someone walking down a narrow hallway, then your first instinct might be to say "oh, I'm sorry." And to try to let them pass, leading to an awkward interaction wherein both people will try to let the other pass first. If you instead react to the other person letting you pass and express your gratitude toward that person for allowing you to go first, then this will allow them to understand that their politeness has been noticed and appreciated. This will allow them to feel a little bit better about themselves instead of simply having an awkward and uncomfortable experience with a stranger in the hallway. If you feel like you have inconvenienced someone or that they have gone out of their way to help you, then you should not apologize; instead, you should thank them for the kindness that they have given to you.

You should also try to stop complaining about minor inconveniences in your day to day life, and blaming other people for unpleasant or uncomfortable things that happen, especially events that occurred in the past that have caused you some unpleasantness. If you dwell on the past in this way, then you will not be able to move forward in the present. Additionally, you will not be able to take ownership of those events and take the agency that will allow you to move past them completely.

CHAPTER 10: COGNITIVE BEHAVIORAL THERAPY

One of the most common methods of treatment that is used with patients who suffer from a social anxiety disorder is a form of talk therapy which is called cognitive behavioral therapy (or CBT). CBT will usually have you working with a licensed mental health care professional in order to allow yourself to better understand the way that you think and perceive different things and be able to handle different or unfamiliar situations a little bit more effectively. Most of the time, cognitive behavioral therapy will be structured in a very specific kind of way with a more limited number of sessions which have been decided beforehand.

This kind of psychotherapy can be a very effective tool to allow you to develop better methods of handling yourself in uncomfortable or unfamiliar social situations. Sometimes, CBT will sometimes be performed on its own, and sometimes it will be used alongside other kinds of therapy, depending on the person and the kind of care that they and their illnesses might require. It can also be very effective for the treatment of complicated mental disorders like depression, anxiety, eating disorders, personality disorders, and even things like post traumatic stress. Some people who use CBT to help themselves to be able to grow and improve their mental health might not eve have a specific mental health disorder; they might be relatively mentally healthy people who simply wish to improve their general mental health and be able to handle unfamiliar or stressful kinds of situations a little bit more effectively.

The different kinds of things that people will use cognitive behavioral therapy for are to treat or manage their existing mental illness or illnesses and the symptoms of those illnesses (especially if they do not have access to- or prefer to avoid the use of- medications to help them with their mental illnesses), to be able to understand and manage their emotional and mental states more effectively, and to cope with their mental illnesses more effectively as well as the kinds of events that cause those illnesses to develop. Some of the common mental health disorders that people commonly use CBT to help to treat are depression, eating disorders, substance abuse, obsessive-compulsive disorder, bipolar disorder, and schizophrenia, as well as things such as anxiety disorders like social anxiety.

In a lot of cases, this kind of treatment is the most helpful when it is used along with other kinds of treatment methods like the use of medications or other therapy. Luckily, this kind of talk therapy has very few risks outside of a possible feeling of discomfort or unease when discussing particularly stressful events or topics. CBT will try to encourage you to explore a lot of stressful or painful kinds of emotions or memories, in some cases. Some people might even feel physically drained after leaving a particularly difficult session wherein they had to confront a lot of uncomfortable topics.

If you want to get started with cognitive behavioral therapy, then it can be an incredibly effective method of treatment. You should first start by finding a good therapist. If you are not sure where to look, then you might want to try to ask your doctor or find out if there re any doctors or particular kinds of services that your health care plan covers. A lot of people will have access to a number of different kinds of counseling services or suggestions for effective services through their employer, through an employee assistance program of some sort. If you do not have access to these kinds of services or if you might prefer to do your own research, then you can go that route too. You can look into different kinds of treatment and different doctors online or through a local psychological association in order to find out about the kind of doctors that you feel might be able to help you the most effectively.

Part of determining the specific kinds of services and the specific doctors that you will want is to consider the costs as well. Some health care plans might only provide coverage for a certain number of sessions within a specific period of time, or up to a certain cost amount per year.

Once you have found a doctor and scheduled an appointment, you should prepare for that first appointment with this new doctor. Before you go in, you should try to think about what specific topics or problems that you would like to discuss, and if there are any concerns that you might have about the kind of help that you would be receiving from this doctor. This can include things like the qualifications of the doctor that you are seeing or if they specialize in any particular area, among a number of other topics. A lot of people will usually advise people new to this kind of therapy to write a list of topics that they want to discuss with their doctor, on the first session as well as future sessions, because it can be very easy to forget these things once you enter the room. The most important thing to consider is that you are able to find a therapist who is able to meet your needs and provide the kind of care that you will require.

CHAPTER 11: PANIC ATTACKS

Another symptom of high levels of anxiety that you might experience are panic attacks. On a yearly basis, it is estimated that somewhere between one-tenth to one-third of the entirety of the human population will suffer from at least one panic attack. Panic attacks can be defined as very sudden or unexpected fits of stress that usually take the form of an unusually high level of fear or anxiety. These experiences are usually unwarranted or disproportionate to the external stimulus that led to it, often being much more than the actual situation calls for. Most people who experience these kinds of panic attacks will experience an unexplained or unreasonable amount of stress or anxiety, usually accompanied by things like trembling, sweating, trouble to breathe, and increased heart rate, as well as a number of other similar symptoms. Many people will even feel things like a tightness or pain in their chest, or a feeling of disorientation or detachment from the world around them, which is referred to ad dissociation. This is the "out of body" experience that people will sometimes talk about during stressful or traumatic events. Some people have even claimed to feel sensations that have led them to believe that they might have been experiencing things like heart attacks or strokes, in extreme cases.

The terms anxiety and panic are commonly used as if they were synonymous, but the two terms actually describe distinct and different kinds of experiences. Usually anxiety, especially more general forms of anxiety that are triggered by many different kinds of events as opposed to non-generalized forms of anxiety which are triggered by much more specific events, will usually last for a little bit longer. On the other hand, fits of panic will usually be much shorter, but they will also usually be much more intense. Most panic attacks will only last for approximately ten minutes, since the human body is not particularly well equipped to handle these kinds of intense and heightened states of arousal or stimulation for extended periods of time. Panic attacks will usually trigger the "fight or flight" response, which is normally a survival instinct which is triggered as a response to dangerous or hazardous events or experiences. However, a panic attack can be considered to be harmful in this way, since they do not always require a real threat to have occurred in the moments when they occur, because many of them are sparked by flashbacks to previous events, whereas anxiety will typically be a response to things that are happening around you. A lot of different kinds of things can trigger a panic attack, such as the act of exercising too intensely or too much, drinking too much coffee or consuming an excessive amount of caffeine, or even simply watching a scary movie, in some cases. However, anxiety is a much more future- or present-oriented emotional response which usually comes as a result of the anticipation of a negative occurrence in the future or the experience of one in the present. Feelings of anxiousness will usually last a little bit longer and will cause a little bit less stress on your body when compared to something like a panic attack.

Only about 3 percent of the people who might be prone to experiencing panic attacks will actually be diagnosed with the panic disorder because of its similarities with other kinds of mental disorders, and especially with anxiety disorders. Panic disorder is known for causing repeated anxiety or panic responses such as panic attacks. A person who suffered from the mental illness, which is referred to as panic disorder will be likely worried about any potential panic attacks that they might experience in the future. A lot of people will consider panic disorder to be characterized by a fear of panic attacks that the person who suffers from the disorder might anticipate. A lot of the time, this anticipation of future panic attacks will often cause a lot of fear and stress about the possibility of experiencing another attack at a particularly inopportune time, which can severely impact that person's life, often holding them back and preventing them from reaching their full potential, or even pulling them down from it in some cases. Even just the anxiety about possible panic attacks that might come in the future can sometimes cause a lot of stress on both the mind and the body, and can often lead to a panic attack a lot of the time. Usually, these kinds of experiences will be characterized by symptoms that are common with strong fear, such as an increase in your heart rate, trembling or general nervousness that can sometimes grow to become a panic attack.

When people have a high level of sensitivity to anxiety and the symptoms of it, they might sometimes interpret normal physical feelings as if they were a little bit more serious than they are in reality. These kinds of misunderstandings and misinterpretations can sometimes cause increased levels of stress as well, which can also lead to panic attacks. If you suddenly begin to feel a sharp increase in your heart rate, this can be scary, especially if you are not sure why this is happening. In these cases, you might begin to worry that you are about to or having a heart attack, which can sometimes lead to panic or general anxiety. Similarly, the feeling that a person is beginning to lose control of their life can also lead to panic attacks in some cases. These symptoms and their causes will vary from person to person, but most people will usually find these kinds of situations very uncomfortable and will usually become anxious or begin to panic.

A lot of people will believe that these issues are inherited from the parents of the person who suffers from then. While this is true in a sense, these kinds of mental health issues are very rarely inherited genetically. Issues like these kinds of mental disorders are usually developed as learned traits as a result of past experiences that a person has had, a lot of which happen with or because of family members during adolescence. Sometimes, a person might develop a fear of a particular kind of internal response, like the symptoms of panic attacks or anxiety, which is often referred to as "interceptive conditioning", and can cause some people to "teach" their bodies to force them into an excessive fear or panic state as a response to normal changed in their physical states that can occur throughout the day like increased or decreased heart rate or other kinds of things. This is the reason for a lot of habits that people might develop which are related to their mental illnesses. Some people can experience nocturnal panic attacks for this reason, even without having a nightmare. It appears as if there's no trigger, but the trigger is these slight body changes. Luckily, this kind of sensitivity and the conditioning that can cause anxiety and panic in people who have developed these kinds of habits can be treated and handled very effectively with specific kinds of talk therapy like cognitive behavioral therapy.

There are a number of different kinds of things that can lead to a person being a little bit more likely to develop these kinds of habits through interceptive conditioning. If you are able to understand these factors, then you will probably be a little bit more likely to help yourself or other people around you to avoid developing habits like these, which an be very helpful for people who suffer from anxiety, and especially social anxiety and social anxiety disorder. Traits that are inherited biologically from your parents or families can make a person a little bit more likely, or even a little bit less likely to develop specific kinds of personality traits and styles that might lead to these kinds of habits or the development of anxiety disorders later on in their lives.

In a similar way, you can also develop these kinds of traits as a result of learned behaviors that you might have picked up throughout your life as well. This is especially true for traumatic events or experiences, or ones that happened during the adolescent or developmental stages of your life. These experiences can lead to an increased likelihood that a person will end up developing negative habits like the ones that have been discussed in this book or to develop harmful mental disorders. People who grew up in isolated environments and who were not exposed to situations that allowed them to explore the world and become familiar with the kinds of interactions that they might need throughout their lives will probably be a little bit more likely to react poorly to these unfamiliar situations and develop mental disorders like social anxiety disorder as a result of stressful or traumatic experiences. This leads to the third kind of triggered event for the development of these kinds of psychological disorders. A particularly negative experience with specific symptoms or manifestations of mental illness might cause an irrational fear of those symptoms or of that illness. This might take the form of some sort of traumatic event that the person in question experienced themselves or even as a negative event that they might have experienced witnessing a friend or a family member in their own struggles with that disorder. Usually, these kinds of things will cause an initial panic attack that will typically catch the person off guard. Not understanding how to handle their panic attack, they will usually have a particularly stressful time which will likely cause them to develop an intense fear of panic attacks that they might experience in the future. These initial panic attacks can be especially frightening if the person happens to be a difficult activity during this time, or one that requires concentration and can be made very unpleasant by the sudden appearance of a panic attack, such as driving or performing in front of other people in a social situation.

A lot of people who suffer from these kinds of mental disorders will also very likely only realize that they suffer from them after a panic attack. Usually their first panic attack- catches them off guard and they end up going to the emergency room because they do not understand what is happening to them and what might be causing their symptoms. One popular reference in recent media is from a movie, but can be a very apt comparison for the purposes of understanding this kind of experience is tony stark in the third iron man movie, rushing out of a restaurant during a panic attack, thinking that he had been poisoned. Panic attacks are very intense experiences, and thinking that you might have been poisoned is absolutely a legitimate response to experiencing one for the first time. However, most emergency rooms are not very well equipped to help to ease the symptoms of anxiety and panic disorders. Most medical facilities should have some drugs that can provide immediate, short term relief, but they will not be able to provide counseling or other kinds of mental health care. If you are worried that you might be suffering from a mental illness or are experiencing some significant psychological symptoms, it is recommended that you consult with your primary care provider and ask them what the best course of treatment may be.

Luckily, a lot of anxiety disorders are very easily treatable and can be "cured" very reliably with a number of different techniques. One of the most successful and effective methods of treatment for these disorders is referred to as CBT, or cognitive behavioral therapy. There are other certain kinds of treatment as well, like acceptance and commitment therapy, or ACT, which have been developed as effective methods of treating specific kinds of mental disorders, such as panic disorder and social anxiety disorder.

A lot of doctor will aso prescribe certain kinds of drugs to aid in the treatment of these kinds of conditions as well. Some of the most effective and most common of these drugs are called SSRI's, or Selective Serotonin Reuptake Inhibitors. These SSRI's are types of medications which are commonly used to prevent the symptoms of anxiety, panic attacks, and other kinds of emotional and mental symptoms caused by mental disorders by regulating the amounts of certain chemicals which are produced by the body. These drugs can be somewhat helpful, but CBT (as well as other kinds of talk therapy) is usually a lot more effective in treating these kinds of issues than simply taking medication.

While panic attacks will be most common in people who suffer from anxiety disorders like panic disorder or social anxiety disorder, they can also happen in people who do not, and can happen for people who don't necessarily meet the criteria for these kinds of illnesses, especially in trauma survivors and people with other similar kinds of histories. There is also a very common misconception about the ways that a lot of people can or should try to go about dealing with them. The most common advice people will give to others who are experiencing a panic attack is to take deep breaths, think positively, and try to calm down. However, trying to control your anxiety in these ways can backfire or even be completely counterproductive. Struggling to prevent a panic attack can have a very negative effect and will actually very likely trigger or worsen a panic attack. During a panic attack, a person should try instead to do something that might seem a little bit counterproductive; let go of control and allow the panic attack to run its course. It can also be useful to remind yourself that you can't die from a panic attack, and that it's your body's normal, natural reaction, which is not dangerous.

If it is possible, you should try not to remove yourself from the situation that you are in when your panic attack begins until the anxiety has subsided, instead choosing to confront your fears. If you absolutely need to, you can remove yourself if the symptoms are too difficult to deal with, and let the symptoms subside on their own over time as you relax and calm yourself a little bit. Regardless of how you handle it, you should try to pay attention to the situation that triggered your panic attack so you will be able to better understand how to handle it in the future. This is similar to the reason why you should try not to completely remove yourself from the triggering situation if you can handle the symptoms on your own; If you don't run away from the triggering event, you will be able to immerse yourself in it more, and you will eventually be able to familiarize yourself with that situation and become more comfortable over time. There are some ways that can help you to handle panic attacks and lessen the symptoms or effects of the attack until it passes, however.

One of these methods is to try to practice breathing a little bit more mindfully. If you are having trouble breathing, this can be especially helpful. This can be very helpful during panic attacks, since one of the most common symptoms is a tightening or pain in the chest which is caused by constricting muscles, and can tighten on the lungs or airways, causing that "wheezing" effect that some people will experience. When this happens, you should try to practice a special kind of breathing based on the diaphragm. This will essentially mean that you should be breathing with your belly instead of your chest. This allows you to breathe a little bit more deeply, as well as forcing you to focus on your breathing and take a little bit longer to inhale and exhale, which can help to slow your heart rate and allow you to calm your nerves a little bit more easily. Visualizing a balloon in your belly can be very helpful in helping you to breathe in this way as well as serving as an effective distraction in some cases, from the triggering event that caused your panic attack. You should also try to exhale a little bit more slowly than you will be inhaling, as well, in order to allow the air to flow more smoothly. A lot of people will spend about three seconds on the inhale and four seconds on the exhale.

Another kind of strategy that you can use to handle your panic attacks is commonly referred to as "progressive muscle relaxation." Progressive muscle relaxation is a technique for relaxing groups of your muscles individually. In order to do this, you will need to try to do a short examination of your body and the muscles on your body, tightening and releasing each of the different groups of muscles one by one. You can try to clench your fists hard, tensing your muscles a little bit, and let go slowly, and doing the same for your forearms, and then the shoulders and back, moving through the different groups one by one. This is very similar to when you might get a leg cramp and have to tighten your leg in order to move it to a better position and loosen the muscles, allowing the cramp to disappear.

You should also try to remember that the panic attack is temporary and that you will eventually be fine, once the sense of fear that you are experiencing subsides. At the moment, you might forget that you are experiencing a panic attack, or you might be aware but still unable to keep yourself from experiencing it. Either way, it will be very important for you to remind yourself that it is a panic attack and that this sensation and the symptoms, and the feeling of dread that you are experiencing will go away soon. You will only need to focus on your breathing and ride it out.

You might also try to use some kind of grounding techniques like coloring in a book or looking at your surroundings. A lot of people will gain a sense of comfort from coloring, as on a page in a coloring book. It can be very easy to become immersed in simple activities like this, which will make it a little bit easier for you to distract yourself, causing your panic attack to disappear. A lot of other people will say that listing the things in your surroundings can be effective. This can include things like saying the names of the things in the room with you out loud or noticing all of the individual sounds that you can hear can be an effective technique for grounding yourself during a panic attack.

CHAPTER 12: FACING YOUR FEARS

A topic that has been brushed upon in the previous chapters in this book is being able to "face your fears", immersing yourself slowly in the situations that might trigger your social anxiety or other mental disorder in order to overcome that condition more effectively than if you were to simply remove yourself from the situation and avoid it altogether. This is a concept of "exposure therapy" which works in much the same way as this technique; You place yourself in situations or in proximity to objects that trigger an anxiety response from you in order to become better acquainted with it and lessen the amount of discomfort that you experience by being around that thing more often. For a person who suffers from an issue like social anxiety, this usually means social situations and other kinds of gatherings or interactions with other people. Ordinarily, these kinds of events would be overall pleasant experiences, but to a person who suffers from social anxiety, they will be much more negative and stressful kind of experiences. Entering into social situations like these can trigger feelings of discomfort or unpleasantness, and can lead to many of the symptoms that accompany anxiety, and can create a much more negative experience. This can cause you to begin to avoid social situations and other kinds of events wherein you might be around other people in large or small numbers. This can be very harmful to your development, and can negatively impact a number of different areas of your life.

However, there is a very effective way to allow yourself to become more comfortable in these kinds of more stressful situations. Exposing yourself to the kinds of things that make you uncomfortable, if you intend to try to move past that fear, can allow you to acclimate yourself to those things much more easily as well. This is a very large part of treating social anxiety and will be important to get used to doing. Stepping outside of your comfort zone is helpful for people who might not necessarily even be suffering from social anxiety disorder or any other mental disorder. You should always try to experience new things as often as you can.

CHAPTER 13: HOW TO STOP WORRYING AND SLEEP BETTER

Social anxiety and social anxiety disorder can also cause a lot of damage to your sleep schedule, as can most of the different kinds of anxiety disorders. You might find yourself lying awake at night unable to sleep because you are lost in thought, and unable to clear your head and relax. The National Sleep Foundation most often refers to this kind of late-night restlessness as "maintenance insomnia," and characterizes it as an inability to fall asleep, or stay asleep, as well as the inability to go back to sleep once you have woken up. This is usually caused by a chemical imbalance or by a sense of "confusion" within the body, which is why a lot of people will take things like melatonin capsules in order to help them to maintain a more regular sleep schedule. These capsules will allow the body to regulate the rates and the times at which it will produce serotonin and melatonin, which can help you to keep a much more consistent sleep schedule and get much more calm periods of rest.

However, these do not treat the underlying cause of your late night restlessness or maintenance insomnia. This can be a very dangerous pattern to develop and can cause a lot of damage to your emotional and mental states as well as simply causing you to feel poorly in general. You might end up sleeping poorly or uncomfortably, which can lead to much higher levels of anxiety as well.

There a number of very helpful things that you can do to help yourself to get o sleep much sooner and prevent yourself from having to stay up all night trying to get to sleep, stressing out about the sun coming up in so many minutes. The first thing you should try to do is to limit the amount of usage of your computers, televisions, and other electronic devices for about two hours before you plan on going to sleep. This is also true for phones. You should try not to have your phone next to you while you are trying to sleep if you are tempted to pick it up and begin scrolling on facebook or Instagram when you are bored. These kinds of devices emit a kind of light that generally exists in the lower end of the color spectrum, closer to the blues that you will see in the sky during the day time. This can trick your body into thinking that it should be awake, which is a very significant cause of a lot of those sleepless nights. You should also try to keep your bedroom light off, or only use red light bulbs during the night. The light that is emitted through those red bulbs will allow you to still be able to see while preventing your body from thinking that it is the middle of the day and that it should be awake and active, which will allow you to be able to sleep much better than otherwise. A lot of people will also wear sleep masks in order to completely cover their eyes as well, but eliminating the use of electronic devices for a few hours before you plan to go to sleep is probably one of the most important parts of a good night's rest, especially with the accessibility of our mobile phones and laptops. It might be tempting to kill your idle time with a few episodes of your favorite TV show, but this is actually hurting your sleep patterns more than anything else. Sometimes, even the noise that these shows produce can disrupt your sleeping patterns, so it is usually best to simply eliminate these external stimuli altogether.

Another good strategy is to try to eliminate any potential cause for concern before you go to bed. If you are cutting out your phones, computers, or TVs a couple of hours before you go to sleep, then that two hour period before you actually lay down can be a great time to get rid of all of the issues that you might think about when you are trying to sleep. The key with these strategies is to keep it light and avoid sources of heavy stimulation that will make you think that it is midday at that time. While you are preparing to go to bed, you might try writing down your experiences in a journal. This can help to pass the few hours before you actually lay down, and it can also be incredibly useful for people who suffer from social anxiety to write down their experiences and the things that they might be worried about. This kind of practice can help you to understand the situations that you are stressed out about and to be able to stop worrying about them a little bit easier. You can get all of the worries out while you are writing, which can be helpful for calming your nerves and assuaging any potential sources of fear or anxiety, as well as simply being a very nice and calm activity that can even be somewhat therapeutic at times. This can help you to unwind and allow you to clear your head BEFORE you lay down so that you don't have to have any of those moments when you realize that you have to take care of one last thing before you forget.

If you do these things, cutting out the use of electronic devices that emit blue light (or really any light if possible) and getting out all of your concerns by listing the events of the day to yourself or writing in a daily journal that you keep, they will almost certainly allow you to be able to get to sleep much more quickly. There is another method that you can use as well, which isn't its own method so much as just something that you should be doing; you should be allowing yourself to unwind and relax before you begin to go to sleep. You might take a shower or try to draw, or do whatever can help you to unwind. If you are anxious when you get into bed every night, then your brain will form that connection and will make you much more anxious in bed. Stop stressing over getting to sleep. Of course, this is not as easy to do as it is to say, but nothing is worse than realizing that you are struggling too much and that the fact that you are trying to go to sleep is preventing you from actually falling asleep. This can create a sort of feedback loop, wherein you just become more and more irritated and then when you finally do get to sleep, you won't be properly rested anyway because you are still anxious and tense. A lot of the grounding techniques that people will use for dealing with panic attacks and other forms of anxiety will usually work very well to help you to distract yourself and relax yourself enough to be able to sleep in most cases. In addition to this technique, cognitive behavior therapy can be very helpful in dealing with worry, anxiety, and associated sleep difficulties.

Some other different kinds of techniques that can also be very helpful are meditation, as well as other kinds of relaxation techniques. These kinds of practices can allow a person to be able to calm themselves and reduce the symptoms of their anxiety or their panic attacks. Of course, they will usually be most effective if you are already familiar with these techniques and can remember how to use them during these episodes of panic and anxiety. If you are trying to use these techniques for the first time during a panic attack if you do not already understand how they work and how to perform them effectively can be very difficult, and will very likely not work at all. Trying to do this will probably only cause you to be more stressed than before, and might potentially worsen your symptoms. If you attempt these techniques in this way, they might even end up convincing you that the technique is not helpful, even if it might be once you learn how to use it effectively.
Another very important thing to remember is to simply get enough

sleep. Starting with the basics can be helpful in any situation. One should never underestimate the powers of rest, water, and exercise. A lot of people will be tempted to stay up later into the night and to sleep in later during the day, but this can be harmful to your body, causing it to be less effective in the regulation of certain chemicals, which can worsen a lot of the symptoms of anxiety and will make it a little bit more difficult to manage your disorder. Additionally, keeping an irregular sleep schedule can also make it more difficult for the body to manage itself and recover from stress, like wounds, and you will probably notice that cuts take longer to heal or that you feel very strong hangovers after nights of drinking. Being able to keep a consistent sleep schedule is very important for any person, but especially to people with mental illnesses like social anxiety disorder that can be made worse by chemical imbalances in the body.

CHAPTER 14: STRATEGIES FOR CREATING A POSITIVE MENTAL ATTITUDE

Being able to manage your mental and emotional states can be very important for your growth and your ability to overcome your social anxiety. There are a number of different methods that you can use to be able to manage these mental states as effectively as possible, which is what this chapter will be about. Several of these strategies will be detailed here.

One very popular strategy that a lot of people use to help them to manage their emotional and mental states more effectively is a very simple one; You can try putting a rubber band around your wrist, like a bracelet, in order to serve as a reminder to notice your thoughts. A lot of people will actually snap the rubber band in order to give their bodies a little bit of a shock as a punishment for negative or otherwise harmful thoughts, but in this case, simply having the band on your wrist should work just fine. You might be tempted to fidget with the rubber band every so often, as well, stretching and pulling it when your hands are not busy. This will be very helpful for the purpose of the band. Whenever you look at your rubber band (a regular bracelet can also work) you should try to take note of it and remember to pay attention to your feelings and thoughts. Often, you might catch yourself fidgeting with the rubber band out of nervousness or anxiety, in which case you can take a moment to remind yourself to try to avoid unnecessary stress or worrying too much. If you are sad, irritated, or uncomfortable and you aren't particularly good at noticing these emotional states, you might find yourself fidgeting with the bracelet in a lot of these situations, out of stress or anxiety. Try to notice whether you are uncomfortable and if you are usually uncomfortable when you fidget with your rubber band, taking note of the habits that you form around this simple tool that you now have on your wrist.

When you can begin to pay attention to the habits that you begin to form with this rubber band or bracelet. You can understand the emotional states that cause those habits and any fidgeting that you might do when you are uncomfortable or irritated. When you are able to catch yourself in these negative states of mind, then you can also begin to work through those and replace them with more positive mental and emotional states instead. The rubber band is a very simple and inconspicuous tool.

Once you have spent a few days with this new rubber band or bracelet on your wrist, and you have allowed yourself to begin to understand when you mess with the band or look at it every so often and note your emotional and mental states, you can then start to actually take action with regards to these emotional responses to your surroundings. This is when you might want to pull on the rubber band and give it a little snap when you notice yourself having some sort of negative thought or feeling. If you do this, you should only snap it lightly. Of course, you are not trying to hurt yourself. You only want to draw attention to it and allow yourself to be aware of the situation by lightly snapping the band. If you do not want to actually snap that band, then you can instead switch it to the other hand or perform some other unusual action with it that you will take note of. The important thing that you need here is the actual physical pattern that you use to break the "loop" of unpleasant thoughts or feelings.

After you perform that action to break the situation, you will want to think about the situation and what led you to feel uncomfortable or unhappy, or what you might have been doing when you began to feel unpleasant. You should actively take note of this situation, and if you are alone, you might even try to say out loud what has happened. You might say to yourself, "Oh, this thing made me feel this way," or "that situation leads to these kinds of thoughts or feelings." You should be paying attention to these thoughts, allowing yourself to better understand your emotional states and your emotional responses to certain external stimuli.

If you are able to understand the specific kinds of situations and external stimuli that lead to which kinds of emotional and mental responses from you, you will be able to understand your own boundaries and where you are comfortable much more effectively. If you keep this rubber band or bracelet on your wrist every day for a longer period of time, and you begin to form habits around the use of it as a tool to help you to recognize and understand your emotional states in this way, then you can begin to use that information to develop some more positive emotional habits and being able to replace your negative emotions with some positive ones when they come up. If you practice this for multiple days, then eventually you will be able to keep these much more positive and pleasant emotions at the front of your mind instead of other harmful or negative ones.

CHAPTER 15: BECOMING AN OPTIMIST

Finding a positive state of mind can also be helpful to your growth and your ability to overcome your social anxiety. Adopting an optimistic attitude can be very helpful in accomplishing this goal. A lot of different researchers in this topic will define it slightly differently, and this definition is usually be based on the different mentalities and the different specific areas of research that they operate within. Some of the different definitions of the term "optimism" will be listed below in this chapter for you to better be able to understand them.

One of these different kinds of definitions that people use to explain the concept of optimism is referred to as dispositional optimism. This kind of optimism is usually used to explain the degree to which a person will usually expect a lot of events that will occur in the future, or at least a majority of those events, to turn out to be positive or negative in nature. For example, if they encounter an unfamiliar object, will that person believe that the object will be inherently helpful to them or more harmful to them. Of course, a person who leans more toward the optimistic or positive end of that scale will usually anticipate more positive outcomes, where a person who tends more toward the pessimistic side of the scale will be much more negative and will perceive unfamiliar things as threats or anticipate that future events will be much more likely to bring them hard than good. Most of the time, a person who has a more positive or optimistic kind of attitude or personality will also have a much lower level of risk for things like the development of mental disorders, because they will be able to handle a lot of different kinds of situations much more effectively and will be able to maintain a much more happy and healthy kind of mental state. It can also be very commonly connected to much more healthy behaviors before and during stressful or traumatic situations as well, whereas a much more pessimistic personality will lead to or even cause much more unhealthy behaviors that end up causing a significant portion of the negative results or consequences that a pessimistic person will typically anticipate.

As is the case with a lot of the traits that can help to determine an individual's outlook and mental states, dispositional optimism and pessimism are also considered to be heritable traits in many cases. Optimism, as well as pessimism, are both very heavily impacted by factors within your environment, such as family or friends who you grow up with or the people around you. A lot of people will also believe that an optimistic attitude can be inherited in an indirect way because of influence from other kinds of heritable traits like alcoholism, personality type, or intelligence. A lot of studies conducted on this topic have shown that it can also be directly inherited from parents or family members in about one-fourth of cases of people with a very optimistic kind of personality and that it is a stable personality dimension and a predictor of life outcomes. Things like subtle chemical shifts and biological factors can impact the kind of outlook that a person will carry with regards to a pessimistic, or an optimistic personality can impact these traits as well as environmental factors that will impact the outlook that a person will have during their life. Most people will usually argue that these traits are based mostly on these kinds of environmental factors, but can be influenced by genetic factors as well, to a slightly smaller degree. A lot of people will develop changes in their outlooks during the course of their life, possibly flipping from an optimistic outlook to a pessimistic one or vice versa. This can increase the risk of a person developing mental conditions such as depression or anxiety later in life. Optimism and pessimism are often considered to be learnable traits, which can be helpful if you need to get yourself out of a more pessimistic state of mind and become a more positive and optimistic person.

There is also a test that is used to measure where a person might fall on the scale of optimism and pessimism, which is referred to as the life orientation test, or the LOT. This test was designed to help people to be able to assess and evaluate dispositional optimism and pessimism in 1985 and has since become one of the most popular tests that is used to measure the prevalence of traits. This test is usually made up of eight different sections, with four sections that are made up of filler. The sections of the life orientation test are also split up into positive and negative ones as well, with four of them being more positive, and four of them being more negative. These different splits of the test are meant to create a more significant sense of diversity and a more accurate result from it. There are two primary revisions that have been made to the life orientation test, which are referred to as the extended LOT and the revised LOT. The revised LOT is made up of six sections instead of the original eight, which are scored on a more specific scale with five points which range from "strongly agree" to "strongly disagree," with the middle point being a neutral response. There are also four sections which are made up of filler as well, and each of the coded sections is also phrased similarly to the original, with half of the coded sections being phrased in a positive manner, and the other half being phrased much more negatively for the same reason as with the original test. The LOT-R is intended to produce slightly more consistent results than the original LOT test.

There is also another kind of test that is commonly used to measure a person and find out where they fall between optimistic and pessimistic outlooks, which is referred to as the attributional style questionnaire, or the ASQ. The ASQ will have the subject read off a list of six events, each of them coded in a specific way, with three of the six events being phrased in a positive way and three of them being phrased much more negatively. After each of the situations has been read off, the subject will be asked to come up with a possible cause for that specific event. These explanations will also be measured on a number of different scales such as whether the explanation of the event in question is external or internal, if it is changeable or stable, or if it is local to the event or a more global one. The ASQ has been modified a number of times, and different versions of the test are used by different people in different areas and have been changed out at various points in time, but most of the variations of this test are relatively similar, serving the same purpose and having the same general structure.
Optimism has been found to be connected to a person's well being, as well as pessimism, in positive and negative ways, respectively. People with optimistic personalities have been found to be a little bit less likely to develop different kinds of health conditions, varying from about 5 to 10 percent in the difference in likelihood of developing a number of different kinds of health conditions ranging from physical diseases and conditions like cardiovascular diseases to even mental ones like depression or anxiety. On the other end of the spectrum, people who have a more pessimistic kind of mentality will be a little bit more likely to develop these conditions when compared to positive or optimistic people.

Optimism and pessimism have been found to be connected to allow a person to be able to develop much more effective and healthy methods of handling and coping with different kinds of negative symptoms like pain or negative emotional states caused by specific events. An optimistic person will usually be much more likely to handle their problems and issues in a more direct way, taking more active steps and solving their problems, whereas a pessimistic person will be much more likely to give up or to avoid their problems. This response is largely influenced by the higher levels of cortisol that a pessimistic person will produce, which leads to higher levels of stress in your daily life. Pessimistic people might also have a lot more trouble with the regulation of these reactions, causing their cortisol receptors to be overloaded, leading to a lot of issues and a higher level of stress in general. Optimism can also improve the rate at which a person is able to recover from physical or mental stress, as well, because of the different kinds of ways that they will use to handle these kinds of events. However, the most significant and obvious thing that will come as a result of a more optimistic kind of personality will be much more generally happy in their day to day life.

There is another definition of the term optimism which is slightly different from dispositional optimism, called philosophical optimism. Where dispositional optimism focuses on a belief that things will usually work out for the best and the disposition that a person has, the philosophical view of optimism is more primarily focused on the perception that the present moment is the "most optimal" or the "best" state that can be, and that things are working out in the best way that they can in the present moment as well as future moments that will come. This philosophical optimism is very commonly referred to as "optimalism", and focuses on a belief that all of the events that occur at any given moment are governed by the laws of "optimization", and can also be thought of in terms of different "timelines", and that the one that we are currently on is the
most optimal" timeline, and that all of the events that occur within it are and will be the best combinations of those events that can possibly be. This can be thought of and explained with the common phrase "everything happens for a reason," which is typically used in a religious context, but can also be applicable with regards to philosophical optimism as well. This will usually be countered by pessimistic views related to realism that people with pessimistic personalities will have.

Philosophical optimalism is usually defined with this "everything happens for a reason" explanation, or with the timeline explanation that is similar to the many-worlds interpretation's theory in that there are "different timelines" that exist side by side and that our timeline is the most optimal or best version of the different combinations of events that occur and can occur in our timeline. Of course, this kind of outlook can be compatible with religion as well, by attributing the path of the timeline that we are on to choices that have been made by a god or gods, but it does not require one to stand up on its own. This kind of philosophy is simply a way that can be used to explain the natural laws of the world around us.

Psychological optimism is representative of an acceptance of failure that you might experience and can be explained by connecting its opposite philosophical standpoint of pessimism to perfectionism, which can hold you back in a lot of cases. Perfectionism is often explained as a consistent and almost compulsive drive to try to reach unattainable goals of perfection which will almost always lead to a sense of failure and defeat. Perfectionism is usually driven by a drive to reach these goals and focusing on the overall accomplishments that you might be striving to reach, or some other kind of unrealistic goal. A perfectionist will usually ignore the limitations of human ability and still struggle to achieve perfection regardless of the reality of the situation. Optimism can allow for a lot more failure in pursuit of a specific goal and expects that while the trend of activity is towards the positive, it is not necessary to always succeed while striving towards goals. This basis, in reality, prevents the optimist from being overwhelmed in the face of failure.

CHAPTER 16: THE POWER OF VISUALIZATION

It should be no surprise by this point, but social anxiety can be very difficult to live with and to cope with. Visualization can be a very helpful tool to allow you to be able top cope with and handle your anxiety and maybe even alleviate some of the symptoms that come with it much more effectively as well. If you are suffering from social anxiety disorder, then your ability to enjoy the things that you encounter can be severely impacted, and it can become much more difficult for you to be able to enjoy yourself in your day to day life, including things that you wouldn't even notice if you didn't suffer from this very difficult disorder and that you might even have taken for granted without it. Social anxiety can cause you to miss out on a lot of things and have a lot of regrets.

A lot of the biggest parts of finding good opportunities in your life can come from networking and knowing people who can open up certain doors for you or who can suggest certain paths. Of course, if you suffer from social anxiety, you will have more trouble with the networking and building new bridges or forming connections with new people, which can have negative effects on your career, especially if you choose a path that requires a lot of networking, as well. Luckily, there are a few methods that you can use to help yourself in building these kinds of connections and forming new professional relationships with people, to allow yourself to gain higher levels of confidence in your professional life as well as all other aspects of your life too. One of the most effective methods that you can use in order to do this is by using a technique referred to as visualization. If you suffer from social anxiety, you will probably be familiar with this concept, whether that is by name or because social anxiety will often involve a high level of negative visualization in anticipation of future events. However, the kind of visualization that you will need to be doing here is much more positive and will be used to help you to to become much more confident and improve your self-esteem. Instead of imagining yourself performing negatively or having a lot of negative things happening to you, you will instead need to begin to imagine (or visualize) positive things coming your way in order to begin to replace those negative expectations with positive ones, which can improve your self-esteem significantly.

This kind of visualization can actually be very easy to do and can be incredibly helpful to improve your self-esteem. It can also be used in a lot of different ways, for a number of different things including managing emotional pain. A lot of doctors will even use things like television or even virtual reality to help people to manage physical pain because those are both simple, light activities that are very easy to immerse yourself in and to use as a distraction from the real world. Visualization is very similar, only it is performed in your own mind as opposed to with the use of an external tool to help you with this visualization.

This kind of visualization will also usually take two slightly different forms. The first of these two forms is to imagine yourself in a different place from where you are actually at. Usually, you might be doing something you enjoy, or something that gives you more pleasure than what you are actually doing. This is sometimes referred to as the "happy place" technique and involves imagining yourself going to your "happy place," visualizing yourself in a pleasant situation, especially if you are actually in a more unpleasant or less enjoyable one. This kind of visualization can be very helpful for preventing yourself from feeling very negative emotions or thoughts, and for getting rid of high levels of anxiety by picturing yourself in a situation where these things are not a concern.

This method of visualization can be very effective for lessening the effects of symptoms that you are experiencing in the present moment, alleviating these symptoms much more effectively than you would otherwise be able to. This kind of visualization will have you try to imagine yourself in a different place from where you are, mentally removing yourself from the situation without necessarily needing to physically leave. You might try closing your eyes for a moment or simply stopping to think about your "happy place." After a few moments, you will very likely notice your symptoms becoming a little bit lighter, and before son, you will be much calmer and you can continue through the interaction, probably feeling refreshed. Doing this will help reduce your anxiety and will stop the snowball effect where your fear would just keep increasing.

The second method of visualization that you can use is to imagine events that you will be picturing soon in the near feature. This technique will usually involve stopping before an interview and mentally preparing for that by imagining it going very well, which can help you to improve your self-esteem and go into that interview more confidently than you otherwise would. You can be vague or specific, and it can work differently from person to person. This can be similar to maybe having conversations with yourself while you are in the shower, practicing and anticipating how you will react to certain situations. Some people, especially if they are on TV a lot, or they perform a lot of interviews or other kinds of similar "performances", where they might need to be able to be a little bit more socially adept than normally might stand in front of the mirror and practice responding to questions that they might be anticipating to themselves. This can be very effective for preparation and for improving your level of self-esteem and confidence before you enter the situation or situations that you are preparing for.

This method is slightly different from the "happy place" method, in that it is a very preemptive strategy that you can employ and will allow you to prevent the symptoms of your anxiety before you enter the situation, and can sometimes be much more effective for anxiety disorders such as social anxiety than the happy place strategy. This will also probably be able to come much more naturally to you if you suffer from social anxiety because you will probably be much more used to imagining these events in a negative way, and in order to do this, you will only need to do the same thing in a more positive context. You might even have no trouble at all flipping that switch. You might also, however, have a little bit of trouble switching from negative to positive visualization techniques. Regardless, once you pick it up and begin to become better at using this technique, you will find yourself becoming a little bit more comfortable in social situations as you become more adept at visualizing future situations in positive ways and conditioning yourself to become a more naturally confident person though these techniques.

You might even eventually find yourself reaching a point where you are able to look forward to social events because you will imagine much more pleasant situations and conversations with people at those events. If you can picture an interview going very well, then you will naturally be much more confident, and you will be much more comfortable when you enter those situations as well. When you are able to visualize future events in this way, then you will be able to give yourself a much higher chance of being confident when you are actually in these situations, and this can allow you to progress in your growth much more quickly, and you will very soon begin to be able to move beyond your social anxiety as well.

When you are trying to visualize these kinds of situations, you should try to start in a very calm mood, as relaxed as you can be. You should begin in a very calm state. If you need to, you should try to do some breathing exercises, because a lot of people will usually struggle with breathing difficulties when they become anxious or have panic attacks, because of the tightening of their chests and the airways. You might try to close your eyes and focus on the rate of your breathing, practicing some of the techniques that have been mentioned earlier in this book. You might try to notice particular sounds or other sensations that you are able to experience, taking in all of the different external stimuli around you. You should try to breathe slowly and pay attention to the way that you are breathing, taking more time on the exhale than on the inhale, breathing a little bit more slowly on both when compared to the way that you breathe normally. You should also try to breathe from your diaphragm, instead of from your chest, as was mentioned before as well. Continue to practice breathing in this way, and visualize the event that you are about to enter while making sure to be as specific as you can.

You should try to account for all of the different senses, like the smells, sounds, and sights, as well as the physical sensations that you might experience. Make sure to imagine positive things more than anything else. This is one the most important aspects of this kind of visualization. Be very specific and be very positive. You should try to start from the beginning, as well, picturing all of the things that you are participating in chronological order. For example, if you are out buying clothes, you might try to visualize yourself in your new outfit and thinking about how good you will look in that new outfit. You should try to exaggerate a little bit maybe even going a little bit overboard and picturing this hypothetical situation very vividly and being maybe more positive than the reality can be, even in a best-case scenario. You should try to indulge this exaggerated positivity as much as you can allow yourself to be, even if it seems a little bit ridiculous at first. This kind of excessive positivity can be very helpful in boosting your mood, which is the whole point of this exercise!

You should try to continue to anticipate these hypothetical positive events up until the actual thing happens, and even maybe during it. If something doesn't go your way, you might try to lean on your visualizations and get yourself back up. Try to recover quickly and move onward as well as you can. Try to visualize yourself after you have finished with the situation in question and reveling in your successes. You should try to imagine all of the sensations that you will feel during this event as well, accounting for all of the physical sensations like sights, smells, and touch as well as you can. You should try to enjoy smelling and tasting the food if you are preparing for dinner (this might also help you to decide on what you might like if you are the kind of person who struggles with deciding on menu items at restaurants!).

If you know that someone at a party or other kind of social gathering might like to wear a lot of perfume or cologne, imagine that as well, or the kind of vibe that you might feel during this event, remembering to imagine those things in a positive context. This will serve two purposes. The first is possibly boosting your self-esteem, and the second thing that this can do for you is that you might begin to view these things like an excessive amount of perfume that a person wears in positive contexts similar to the way that you imagined during your visualization. If you repeat this over and over, and as you continue to do this for everyday things, especially new or unfamiliar experiences, then you will begin to be able to do this naturally and form a habit out of it. It will eventually become natural for you and will allow you to more effectively and easily remove any doubts or fears you may have by reinforcing the positive outcome. Try to imagine this situation as many times as you can or as frequently as you can, but in a much more positive context than you might initially be anticipating before the actual event happens. Make sure to visualize the event one last time right before you go in and actually experience the event, and make sure that you are continuing to maintain a positive attitude because this is often when these kinds of things can begin to fall apart. You will need to practice the primary way where you can mentally remove yourself from an anxious situation. Repeat this time after time until you are able to visualize yourself somewhere else that you consider safe and free of stress or discomfort. Of course, this can take a lot of time and practice in order to master effectively, but once you do master this you will be able to go in, and your self-esteem will be passively increased over time, almost automatically.

CHAPTER 17: VISUALIZATION TECHNIQUES

The visualization techniques that are explained in this book are very similar to the law of attraction in the way that they work and the ways that you are able to use them to improve your confidence and allow yourself to find more opportunities. The basic concept behind both of these ideas is that you will change your way of thinking by imagining positive situations that are relevant to something that you might normally picture going poorly. Replacing this kind of negativity with positivity will allow you to have a much easier time, as well a preparing you for things that are coming up in the future. If you imagine things going well, you will be preparing yourself to go into that situation much more confidently and much more comfortably. This is one of the simplest and one of the most useful tools that you can use to help yourself to overcome things like social anxiety or other kinds of stress that is caused by mental disorders or worsened by them.

When you are able to passively visualize these kinds of situations more easily, you will also be much more likely to be able to confidently handle these situations in reality. You will also be more comfortable in unfamiliar situations, being able to anticipate them much more positively, and you will be able to recondition yourself to be able to have a much more positive attitude than you would otherwise be able to.

There are a few things that you should make sure to do as well, when you are visualizing events coming up in the future, in order to begin to excite yourself for these events. The first of these methods is to try to "fall in love with" the things that you want and the situations that you are anticipating. If you can try to artificially excite yourself about something, then that interest will eventually become real. This is similar to things like smiling to try to make yourself a little bit happier, or like taking an ironic interest or forming a real habit out of an ironic gesture or a comedic bit that just becomes a thing that you do out of habit. Your emotions and your thoughts are a very important part of your interests and desires, and they will be one of the biggest parts of being able to "reprogram" your mentality to be more positive and optimistic. However, you should also remember to be open to new possibilities and avoid becoming too attached to a particular course of events.

You should also try to visualize this fantastical situation as often as you can, but not necessarily as much as you can. This sentence might seem to contradict itself, but it essentially means that you should try to practice this technique and perform this kind of visualization in a lot of short, small bursts. If you are able to perform this kind of visualization in small sections, then you will be able to train yourself to become a little bit better at this kind of visualization, as well as being able to prevent yourself from possibly dwelling on one specific moment or getting stuck on one kind of interaction that you might be anticipating. If you can picture small, discrete moments in this way then you will also be able to anticipate a lot of different kind of scenarios with a lot more variation, and you will also eventually be able to perform this visualization on the fly, as well.

One of the most important parts of this kind of visualization is to explore different possibilities as much as you can and to try to have fun with your visualizations by exaggerating the positive imagery situations that might occur. The point of this is to form positive associations with social interactions that you are anticipating in order to build up your own confidence. You should try to imagine the best case scenario, or even a ridiculously good outcome, as long as it is a positive situation that you can enjoy and immerse yourself in. It doesn't necessarily need to be 100 percent based in reality, it just needs to be positive and allow you to enter the situation comfortably and confidently.

CHAPTER 18: MEDITATION AND BREATHING EXERCISES

Imagining your breaths carrying negative and upsetting thoughts and energy away from you or picturing waves of calmness wash through you as you exhale can also be very helpful. If you get distracted, gently bring your attention back to your breath and your words.

CONCLUSION

Congratulations! By this point you should have finished all of the different chapters in this book, and you should have a complete understanding of social anxiety disorder and the different forms that it can take, as well as the symptoms that it can cause and how you can prepare yourself from and prevent these kinds of symptoms or even how to handle them on the fly. After you have finished reading through all of the chapters in this book, you should be able to understand the symptoms and the different signs that come with social anxiety or that you might be experiencing a high level of anxiety or a panic attack. When you begin to notice these signs and symptoms, you should also be able to remember the different steps that you need to take and have a plan for how to handle your social anxiety in an effective way that you have practiced and can perform almost instinctively and without thinking. You should be able to remember the different techniques and tools that have been explained within this book as well as how to use them to help you with the symptoms that are caused y your anxiety and how to determine the undetrlying causes of these symptoms in oder to be able to handle them on a more long term basis as well as how to alleviate these symptoms for more immediate relief so that you can continue on and be able to lead a much more successful social life even if you might be suffering from a more severe case of social anxiety. With the use of these kinds of tools, you will be able to continue to maintain a normal social life and you will be able to continue to work toward moving forward and overcoming your social anxiety disorder, eventually becoming a much more   mentally and emotionally stable and comfortable person, with a little bit of work.

MENTAL TOUGHNESS

REVISED AND UPDATED

Trains the Abilities of Brain and Mental Skills with Powerful Habits and Self Esteem, Control Your Own Thoughts and Feelings, Develop a Strong and Unbeatable Mind of High Performance.

Dr Henry Campbell & Dr Daniel Watson

INTRODUCTION

Do you have the desire to be successful in life? Do you envision yourself leading a different life that does not conform to societal norms? Have you set life goals and failed to achieve them? How did you feel? How did you recover from the failure? Did you have the mental toughness and resilience to pick yourself up and fight another day? The truth is, no matter the nature of your ambitions, achieving success is never easy. The road to success is marred by adversities and some demotivating challenges that can easily bring you down if you are not mentally tough. Moreover, the daily grind, effort, and energy required to work towards success can easily take a toll on your mental, emotion and physical well-being. When that happens, how do you stay afloat?

High performers and achievers from different walks of life also face ups and downs during their journey to success. They have to concur discouragement, stress, self-doubt when things do not turn out as they imagined, fatigue, burn out, failure, and demotivation just like everyone else. Their zeal to fight and their desire to win helps to continue striving to achieve their personal goals. Above all, they have mastered the art of mental toughness that ensures they do not get distracted by the numerous adversities life throws at them. They are able to remain strong as well as persevere at the height of failure and discouragement.

Mental toughness is an important success element that can no longer be overlooked or brushed off. It is common to set goals oblivious of the mental and physical dedication you require to hit your target only to get discouraged halfway through your journey. In such a case, your goals will wear you down; you will be exhausted and discouraged to carry on with your plans because success seems impossible. At this point, the desire to quit burns hot. Though most people would normally quit, high achievers and performers stick and find alternative solutions that will lead them to achieve their initial goals. This is because they are mentally resilient enough to understand that challenges are normal and are just a learning opportunity that prepares you for other challenges ahead. As such, they easily push beyond life adversities and often forge a new path to success when an original plan fails as opposed to quitting. They only quit when quitting is the only available option.

So, if you aspire to achieve success in life or be the best version of yourself, you must learn how to be mentally tough and resilient. To some people, mental toughness develops naturally while others must work towards developing it and mastering how to use it to their advantage. No matter where you come from, who you are, the nature of failure you have experienced before, and the goals you would wish to achieve, you can develop the level of mental toughness you need to succeed in life. Al that you have to do is have a positive mindset, focus on addressing the why and seek assistance from the people around you who believe in your vision.

Conversely, mental toughness is a quality that all parents, teachers, coaches, business people, and performers must hold in high regard. This is because developing psychological toughness through studying mental skills is the key to better performance and achievement of goals. To build and uphold the level of mental toughness that success requires you must learn how to maintain positive thoughts even when the world seems to be against you and indulge in positive self-talk as a way of encouraging yourself to keep on fighting for what you believe in. above all, you must avoid negative habits and unhealthy behavior that derails your efforts to succeed. As a matter of fact, strong people are not only those who show strength public but also those who win battles that we never see them fight. These are the people who possess grit, determination, resilience and a never give up attitude all of which describe the intangible mental toughness qualities. However, you need mental strength and the necessary skills required to work towards achieving your goals. For example, most coaches want their athletes to possess an unshakable ability to remain motivated and focused under pressure; this is a special factor that drives success in sports. In light of this, here is a guide on how to develop, master and tap into mental toughness in a bid to perform optimally in all life aspects.

CHAPTER 1: MENTAL TOUGHNESS AND EMOTIONAL RESILIENCE

Mental toughness originates from sports where it has been applied effectively for over 30 years. The term was popularized by a top sports psychologist known as Jim Loehr. He went ahead to define mental toughness as the ability to remain consistent as you utilize your upper range capabilities even when working under highly competitive circumstances. Jim Loehr worked with a wide range of elite athletes who become renowned champions globally under his watch. He believed that mental toughness is a skill that can be learned with determination and the will to a better life.

Though mental toughness retained its recognition as an elite sports concept, continuous publications and research by Peter Clough; a psychology professor, changed the perception by redefining mental toughness as a personality trait that affects how people react to stress, pressure, and challenge irrespective of changing circumstances. It is through Peter Clough's research that additional mental toughness concepts such as hardiness and resilience were discovered. The concepts are referred to as the 4 Cs of mental toughness that explain the term mental toughness as a crucial life concept applicable to everyone and not just elite athletes as was portrayed.

The 4 Cs of Mental Toughness

The 4 Cs of mental toughness are; confidence, commitment, challenge, and control further explained below;

Control
Control entails having a sense of self-worthiness and defining the extent to which you feel you are in control of your life and the changing circumstances. Most importantly, it defines the extent to which you can control the public display of your changing emotions. Control holds that a mentally strong individual possesses high control and can easily just get on with it irrespective of the challenges they face or how they feel. They work through emotionally challenging and charged situations without being

derailed or distracted.

In light of this, it is important for parents to train their children on self-esteem so that they are able to manage their emotions better and become comfortable in their skin. How can parents achieve this? Each day after school, ask your children what happened, find a few positives and explain to your children why they were good experiences even if they do not view them as positive. Also, identify a few setbacks like losing in sports or not being able to accomplish something and remind your children that challenges are normal and there is also a chance to try again after failure. Discuss the daily school events that they do not like and evaluate how they react to them. Based on their explanation, empower them on how they can choose to react better to events, how they can set school and life goals and work towards achieving them.

Commitment

Commitment entails stickability and goal orientation. It defines the extent to which a person is willing to set reasonable goals, make measurable promises and work hard towards achieving the goals and promises. Mentally tough individuals with high levels of commitment can be relied upon to set reasonable targets and goals as well as do what must be done to achieve them. Sticking to the parent and child example given above, parents should also teach their children how to set reasonable goals and achieve them. Start small with daily goals like brushing their teeth after every meal or arranging the living room and commend them once they achieve their goals in a bid to keep them motivated. Such, habits develop and become inclined in children as they grow. Therefore, they are able to make good and achievable goals when they become adults. It encourages them to accept that every skill requires time and practice to master.

Challenge

Challenge is the extent to which a person can push back boundaries, accept risks, and embrace change. This also depends on how you view different outcomes whether good or bad. You must challenge yourself mentally prior to taking serious and life-changing tasks. This ensures that you are mentally prepared to deal with challenges that arise along the way until you achieve your ultimate goal. With the right mental preparation, no challenge can be too big to stop you from implementing all your plans. Notably, a person with a higher challenge score tends to enjoy being around new people, being in new places, creativity, innovation, and are quickly bored by following routines. Conversely, parents should help children embrace challenges and view them as opportunities to learn and thrive under unusual circumstances. Every failure and challenge offers a unique lesson and encourages individuals to try something new that will most likely offer better results or what they seek to achieve.

Confidence
Confidence completes the mental toughness picture by describing the self-belief a person possesses in their abilities and their interpersonal confidence that influence others as well as help them deal with challenges and conflicts. Mentally tough and confident people possess self-motivation to deal with the situation as they arise and inner strength to stand their ground as required. Confidence enables a person to boldly represent their views and handle rejection positively. It is important to develop confidence and self-belief at a tender age. For instance, children should be made to understand that it is okay to have fears and be scared of certain situations and accepting such feelings is the first step towards overcoming them. It is important to never forget the power of YET. If you feel like you cannot do something, tell yourself, "I cannot do it YET." This reminds you that you still have another chance to try and accomplish failed goals and that you are special in terms of how you think. Learn to make your mind and disagree with people positively without compromising on what you believe in.
Mental toughness is well-defined by qualities such as; grit, perseverance, and resilience but at a broader concept. Resilience, on the other hand, is the ability to get back on your feet after experiencing setbacks or challenges that hinder you from growing and achieve your desired life goals. Mental toughness is proactive while resilience is reactive. When mental toughness and resilience are mastered, they help in seeking challenges, changes, and identifying opportunities with self-esteem and confidence. Mental toughness allows you to thrive while resilience helps you survive.

But do not get confused; mental toughness is not characterized by being self-centered, uncaring, or winning. Rather, it is about being confident in your skin and having self-awareness. You require inner strength and toughness to remain put and positive that you will triumph even when all odds are not in your favor.

Building mental toughness is important because of mentally tough people leader healthier lives physically and mentally. Meaning that they perform better in their daily jobs and activities that propel them towards achieving their desired life goals. People who have mastered the art of mental toughness perform consistently even when under pressure and are better at addressing challenges and stressful situations. Studies have proven that mentally tough students perform up to 25% better in their studies. They are quite engaged in class, have higher life aspirations, show better attendance and sleep better. As such, they tend to have smoother transitions from junior school to secondary schools and are rarely prone to falling for peer pressure or assuming anti-social characters.

Emotional Resilience

The term resilience is derived from a Latin word 'resilio' that means to bounce back. Emotional resilience is the ability to withstand adversities and bounce back on track after experiencing challenges that incapacitate your efforts to achieve life goals. Emotional resilience is an important skill for everyone who wishes to handle inevitable ups and downs more effectively. Though some people are born with high levels of emotional resilience, it is a skill that can be developed where a person is willing and dedicated to work at it. Mastering mental toughness and emotional resilience require patience and time.

Emotionally resilient people view life adversities as temporary challenges and tough life experiences as rare opportunities to learn and become better at handling different life outcomes. They do not allow themselves to feel or be viewed as victims of circumstances. Among other traits, they are responsible, better at relating with others and themselves, persistent, self-confident, mindful about others and possess high levels of emotional intelligence. Mastering mental toughness and emotional resilience require continuous practice with situations that you face daily. This way, it becomes easier for you to deal with stressful life situations as they arise. Nobody is protected from experiencing life adversities. So, why do some people seem unperturbed by the challenges they encounter and tend to bounce back while others get stuck and remain in stagnation?

Developing and mastering mental toughness and emotional resilience should be a personal journey. The main aim is identifying different ways of building emotional resilience that works well for you as part of your personal strategy to foster resilience and address future life challenges much better. All that is required is deliberate and continuous practice as well as self-awareness and confidence. Emotional resilience tools are ways to develop the art that works similarly to body muscles that need to be worked on to get stronger. Through resilience activities, you are able to develop mental toughness and emotional resilience skills.

Resilience Building Activities

Purpose exercises

Purpose exercises help in finding meaning in your environment as a way of building resilience. People who possess a strong sense of well-being and purpose are more resilient and display better cognitive functionalities. Having a purpose in life fosters resilience in the sense that, you will be determined to protect your brain against negative stress effects that may deter you from achieving your set life goals. Moreover, according to psychologists, purpose strengthens the brain and makes it more resilient to the influence of diseases like Alzheimer's. Further studies prove that having a strong life purpose that you are dedicated to achieving predicts longevity and better health; people who have a strong life purpose live longer than people who lack a clear life purpose. This is because the key to building resilience is finding meaning in different life experiences especially when working to overcome challenges.

A study was done in Japan on women of Okinawa that sort to determine the reasons behind their life longevity which was attributed to their strong life purpose and sense of well-being. Women of Okinawa pursue their ikigai which is a concept that means the reason for being and waking up every morning. Conversely, individuals can conduct ikigai activities in a bid to discover, exercise, and foster their unique life purpose. It works best at helping people determine their purpose, mission, and meaning in life in the midst of practical life concerns like maintaining a certain lifestyle and earning a decent living. To achieve this, you must conduct purpose reflection activities.

Purpose reflection activities entail answering questions like;

- Why you are

- Why you get up every morning

- Why you stay awake at night

- Determining when you feel alive

- Defining what success means to you

- What you can do to make a difference in a person living at your current situation

- Would you summarize our life purpose in one sentence?

- If you are for living a purposeful life, what are you against?

- What advice can you give to yourself?

Strength activities
Identifying and leveraging personal strengths enhances mental toughness and emotional resilience. As a matter of fact, strength building is an activity that is used to help people recovering from trauma. It entails identifying your personal talents and strengths and determining how you use then=m to make a difference in your life. You could ask people who are close to you and know you well to note down the strengths they see in you and compare with what you believe are your strengths. Identify the positive character traits like creativity, persistence, leadership, bravery, and self-regulation among others that you can use to address your current life challenges and build resilience.

Performing acts of kindness

Research has proven that one of the ideal ways to boost personal happiness and emotional resilience is by performing acts of kindness, mentoring others, expressing gratitude, and volunteering. It is common for people to get lost in their daily jobs and forget that they need to experience life differently. But, where there is will there is away. So, if you are looking to change your daily routine and develop mental toughness and emotional resilience, create time for volunteering programs or simply display random acts of kindness to people you do not know. The fact that you are giving and making a person's life easier or simply making them smile, you get a unique level of emotional satisfaction and self-worthiness. At your lowest moment when life adversities are pulling you down, it motivates to know that you are still strong and valuable enough to make a difference in another person's life. Additionally, acts of kindness exude joy and happiness to you as well.

Silver lining activities

This entails looking at the bright side of things in a bid to boost mental toughness and resilience. People who undertake silver lining activities tend to increase their resilience levels, become more engaged and have less negative thoughts. For instance, think about any upsetting experience you have had lately. It could be anything like your child waking up late and missing the school bus. It can be upsetting given the fact that you would have to drop them to school on your way to work which may be inconveniencing. But, rather than focusing on the inconveniences caused, it would be wiser and less frustrating to reflect on a few positive things about it. For example, you have time to have that special talk as you drop your child to school, you get to meet that subject teacher whom you always wanted to talk to about your child's performs in the subject, and you get to change your morning routine. The idea is to always remain positive and attract positive energy despite the challenges that may arise. That is how you build resilience and have the motivation to fight another day because hope makes you believe that better days lie ahead.

Why you Need Mental Toughness and Emotional Resilience

Though resilience is used to describe mental toughness, they are technically not the same. Mental toughness refers to mental hardiness while emotional resilience refers to adaptation to adversity exposure. However, the two terms are used to define each other because they go hand in hand at ensuring that a person achieves their goals and remain sane through challenges. Emotional resilience is a developmental process that builds and enhances existing personal strengths. It embodies external and protective factors. Mental toughness applies to positive situations and is more geared towards personal attributes that impact how a person approaches and appraises difficulties.

For instance, the US Army designed a resilience program known as the Master Resilience Training with the aim of preventing depression among soldiers. Later, the program was availed not only to soldiers but also their families in a bid to develop a proactive approach towards readiness and emotional resilience. MRT participants learn what emotional resilience means theoretically and practically and learn different skills they can use to deal with challenges and bounce back as though nothing happened. The program aims at equipping participants with the necessary toolkit for overcoming daily adversities and reassessing challenges as they arise. Participants are taught to view daily adversities as localized, transient and manageable with the right dedication and personal efforts.

Further, the program covers three components; preparation, sustainment, and enhancement. Preparation focuses on the nature of resilience, its mental factors and how to develop them. The resilience mental factors include; mental agility, self-awareness, self-regulation, connections, character strengths, and optimism. Preparation educates learners on how to identify the strengths internally and among other people. Sustainment applies and reinforces the resilience skills that are covered during the preparation stage. Participants are taught how to be psychologically resilient and how to nurture the same in others. Enhancement simply focuses on confidence building, goals setting and energy management.

Evidently, the MRT program not only seeks to build emotional resilience among participants but also mental toughness. It teaches skills such as; problem-solving, through activation, goal setting, detection of icebergs, management of energy, avoiding thinking traps, real-time resilience, identification of character strengths, mental games, events, and consequences. These are skills that characterize mental toughness and emotional resilience. For example, avoiding thinking traps entails recognition and identification of negative self-talk and cognitive distortions that are achieved through critical thinking. Individuals learn how to replace maladaptive thoughts with realistic, rational and proactive thinking patterns. Mental games are exercises that are designed to shift the focus of irrational and unhelpful thoughts by stimulating the mind. Real-time resilience focuses on enhancing concentration on tasks by shutting down counterproductive thoughts.

Mental toughness and emotional resilience prevent motivation lapses that deter people from achieving life goals. Each time a motivation lapse occurs, a person is left in doubt on whether or not they are capable of achieving their goals despite the fact that they had already taken the right direction. Challenges trigger motivation lapses; emotional resilience helps in addressing the challenges effectively to deter negative thoughts. Mental toughness keeps an individual focused on the end goal despite the adversities they face. The mental hardiness reduces stress and frustration through the belief that all challenges can be solved to pave way for what lies ahead in this case, personal goals. Upon mastering mental toughness and emotional resilience, you are able to decentralize situations. Instead of reacting instantly to events, you take a mental pause, examine the situation objectively and come up with a rational solution to the challenge or problem at hand. Therefore, you achieve a high level of satisfaction and happiness since you are able to deal with adversities calmly and positively. You easily adapt to the dynamic and complex life demands that we must all face at one point of the other. Build mental toughness and emotional resilience by learning to accept what you cannot change, viewing things perceptively, remaining hopeful, viewing the crisis as learning opportunities, nurturing your positive attributes, upholding decisive actions and embracing self-discovery opportunities.

CHAPTER 2: FEAR OF FAILURE AND CONTROLLING FEAR

Has fear of failure subconsciously led you to undermine your efforts in a bid to avoid a larger failure? Have you been too afraid to fail at something that you opted not to attempt it completely? The truth is, most people have experienced one or both of this at some point. Unfortunately, the fear of failure is immobilizing and it leads you to do nothing and ultimately resist forward progression in life. When you lead a life where you speculate, contemplate, and work effortlessly to avoid pain, you automatically rod yourself the chance to thrive and become the best version of yourself. Failure is an inevitable and crucial component that helps people achieve their full potential.

Fear is what causes you to avoid potentially harmful encounters despite the fact that they could lead you to a better life. Fear of failure stops you from attempting, it triggers self-doubt, derails progression and in some cases, causes people to go against their morals and principles. In order to understand what fear of failure is and how to overcome it, you must understand why it exists or what triggers the fear of failure.

Childhood patterns: unknowingly, hyper-critical parents, guardians, and caregivers make children internalize negative and damaging mindsets that are hard to change. This is because they establish fear-based rules and ultimatums that make children believe that they constantly require to seek reassurance or permission prior to attempting something lest they do it wrong and end up being punished. Unfortunately, children carry fear into adulthood where they always feel the need for validation before trying something.
Perfectionism: Perfectionism is classified at the root of fear. Perfectionists view failure as highly humiliating and terrible that they would not dare try something they deem would lead to failure. They are afraid of stepping outside their comfort zones.
Over-personalization: ego causes people to over-identify with

failure where it becomes hard to look beyond failure for positive things like growth opportunities, the effort made and mitigating circumstances.

False self-confidence: truly confident people know that they are bound to fail at one point or the other. On the other hand, people with a false sense of self-confidence tend to avoid risks in order to avoid failure. They prefer to play safe and retain their self-confidence.

How Fear of Failure Demeans Success

Unhealthy societal cultures: Too many people today have become slaves to the perfection cultures. Perfection cultures are a set of societal beliefs that failures are unacceptable. The society praises "untainted success" where individuals conform to societal expectations whether or not they make them happy. In light of this, people constantly find themselves covering up for small personal blemishes and end up blaming each other for any wrongdoings because they are caught up in unhealthy societal cultures. For instance, it is a societal culture that you should join college at a certain age, get employed at a good or top firm, earn a good salary, start a family by a certain age, and so much more. People who are caught in such societal cultures tend to avoid exploiting their inner strengths if they would end up swaying them away from fulfilling societal expectations. Only the mentally tough individuals will embrace non-conformity in a bid to exploit what the world has to offer or be the best versions of themselves. Such people tend to be mentally strong enough to get through the societal ridicule and misunderstanding due to opting for a different path altogether. Ultimately, they end up leading better and more satisfying lifestyles as compared to people who choose to conform to unhealthy societal cultures.

Missing valuable opportunities: many people fail because they have ego-driven commitments to things that turned out well in the past. This mainly affects seniors who might have become popular by introducing critical changes years back. Such people tend to shy away from making further innovations due to the fear that current innovations may not be as good as their previous achievements. Moreover, they believe that the success of something new may portray that their previous achievements were not as great as people made them appear. As such, they ride on past glory for way too long. Such people are deeply invested in their previous glories and egos that they would rather watch opportunities for future glories disappear.

High performers become losers: successful people and high performers like to win always and work towards achieving high standards. Unfortunately, this can be a huge setback because such people will so afraid of failure to the extent where the fear ends up ruining their lives. When a strong and positive trait like achievement and high performance becomes part of a person's life, it ends up becoming a major handicap to their future success. High performance and achievement is a powerful value for successful people. They build their lives on it and get accustomed to thriving at everything they do in school, at home, at work, sports and hobbies. Every new achievement or high performance adds to the power of value they hold in their lives.

At the height of glory, failure becomes unthinkable because maybe, they have never failed yet in all their undertakings and such, they have no experience of rising and bouncing back after encountering failure. To them, failure is a nightmare that they must avoid at all costs. The simplest way to avoid failure is by never taking huge or challenging risks and sticking rigidly to what they are sure they can do and succeed. This may be characterized by factors like; being too conservative, conscientious, working long hours and having to counter check everything to ensure that it is in order.

Lack of creativity: when the fear of failure becomes dominant, you are unable to accept that mistakes are inevitable. Therefore, you overlook the importance of trial and error in trying to find the most creative and best solutions. The more creativity you have, the higher the number of errors you are bound to make in the process of achieving the best creation or solution. Making a decision to avoid errors because you are afraid of failure destroys your creativity and ability to come up with better and more effective solutions. It is important to recognize and accept the negative parts of life because they also have a crucial role to play in determining our success in life, work, and relationships.

Signs that You Have Fear of Failure

Everyone loves success and hates failure. To some people, failure triggers a huge psychological threat that shifts their motivation top avoiding failure as opposed to achieving success. The strong fear of failure triggers them to sabotage their success in different ways. This is because, failing at something elicits strong feeling like anger, disappointment, frustration, confusion, and regrets. To such people, the fear of failure is the fear of shame and public ridicule. They are highly motivated to avoid failure because they cannot handle the negative emotions that accompany failure like shame. Shame, on the other hand, is a toxic psychological emotion that triggers you to feel bad about yourself instead of feeling bad about your efforts and actions. Shame attacks your ego, self-esteem and personal identity to affect your entire well-being. Therefore, it creates a false urgency among people with the fear of failure to prevent the psychological effects associated with failure by coming up with unconscious ways of mitigating the implications of failure. For instance, a person may have the time to shop new clothes for an interview and lack time to go through the company details in order to have the excuse that they lacked enough time to prepare for the interview. So, how do you know you have the fear of failure?

- You worry about what other people will think of you if you fail.

- Failing makes you doubt your ability to achieve future goals.

- You are afraid that people will lose interest in you if you fail.

- Failure makes you doubt your capabilities.

- You are afraid of disappointing people whose opinion you hold dear by failing.

- You announce beforehand that you do not expect to succeed in something in a bid to reduce their expectations of you.

- Upon experiencing failure you have trouble re-evaluating what you could have done differently to achieve better results.

- You experience last-minute tension, stomach pains, headaches, and other physical symptoms that prevent you from adequately preparing for a task.

- You are prone to procrastination that causes you to run out of time required to prepare for or complete a task that would propel you to greater heights.

The main problem people encounter with addressing the fear of failure is that; it operates on an unconscious level. However, there are two things that a person can adopt to conquer their fear of failure. They include; owning the fear and focusing on aspects that are within their control.

Owning fear: owning fear is all about accepting that you will experience failure at one point or the other and that you will feel shameful and fearful when it happens. Accepting that you will experience such feeling helps you in preventing negative expressions that may include unconscious efforts to sabotage your success and your capabilities to achieve better in the future. Notably, reassurance and empathy from people you trust or people whose opinions matter a lot to you go a long way to boost your feeling of self-worthiness and reduce the fear of failure.

Focus on aspects that are within your control: it is important to identify task aspects that are within your control or that you can perform with much easy and focus on them. However, this does not mean that you should not attempt to complete tasks that are not within your control. Brainstorm ways you can reframe different aspects of the task that you deem to be beyond your control to ensure that you gain control over them. For instance, you can fail to secure your dream job because you do not know the right people who can push the job connections for you. Instead of feeling blue about it, you can purpose to expand your network and social media contacts in a bid to connect with the right people as you reach out to people you know can help you secure the job. Do not be afraid of approaching things differently when your predetermined approach fails to work in your favor. Focus on an aspect that is within your control but at the same time, be open to learning how to take control of aspects that would otherwise freak you out. Conquering personal challenges is one way of developing mental toughness and emotional resilience.

How to Control and Overcome Fear

The fear of failure is an intense and overwhelming worry that occurs when you imagine the negative things that may arise should you fail to achieve a certain goal. The intense and overwhelming worry increases a person's odds of giving up on a goal or holding back. Hence, it is an obstacle that stands between a person and their ultimate life goals. As such, being successful in life, work or relationships relies heavily on a person's ability to control and overcome the fear of failure. Here is what you can do to control and overcome the fear of failure.

Redefine failure

What is your personal definition of failure? Not achieving set out goals? Giving up? Not achieving your desired results within a predetermined period? You may think that the definition of failure is obvious until you are prompted to define it in your own understanding. Failure is an object of fear and an obstacle to personal success. Therefore, it is important to have a clear understanding of what you consider it to be. Once you achieve that, make all your goals fail-proof in that, you stop thinking about the results of failure in achieving the goals and think about the discrepancies between what you may achieve versus what you wish to achieve. Discrepancies offer crucial information that you can use to learn so that you can plan your future goals better. As long as you keep trying and making an effort to achieve your goals, there is no room for fear of failure.

Differentiate between real and imagined threats

Fear is a response to imagined and real threats where real threats pose survival risks while imagined threats are hypothetical. For instance, delivering a presentation in front of a huge crowd is an imagined threat because it does not pose a risk to your survival. On the other hand, standing in front of a pride of lions reading out a speech is a real threat because lions are interested in eating you and not hearing what you have to say. By definition, fear of failure entails imagined threats because the fear may be real but the threat is not real. In such a scenario, the threat is a product of imagination and a prediction that you formulate. However, this does not mean that your fear is irrational or unfounded; it is only termed as unnecessary and premature. Therefore, instead of allowing imagined fear to stop you from achieving your goals, it is advisable to study it and come up with different ways of dealing with the consequences that freak you out.

Design promotion goals

People follow two types of goal setting approaches; avoidance and approach or prevention and promotion. Promotion goals focus on attaining positive and elevating outcomes such as; expecting a salary raise, wanting to get a job promotion. On the other hand, prevention goals entail avoiding negative outcomes like saying that you would not want to lose your current job or I hope the client does not give negative feedback. In light of this, prevention goals are characterized by lower engagements, disorganized goal achievement approaches, anxiety, and poor self-esteem. In addition, prevention goals trigger the creation of more prevention goals when planning for your future. The fear of failure is what triggers people to develop prevention goals that end up blurring their focus, make future plans difficult and undermine your efforts towards achieving your life goals. Therefore, it is important to reframe prevention goals as promotion goals in order to eliminate the fear of failure. Though most people set promotion goals and prevention goals at different occasions, it is prudent to understand that how you set your goals can either delay their implementation, obscure your good intentions, make giving up easy or make achieving your goals a bliss.

Always expect positive outcomes but do not get over-attached to them

The more attached a person becomes to the outcome they envision, the more likely they will view any discrepancies from the outcomes as a failure. As you work towards achieving your set out goals, circumstances are bound to change and the experience you encounter along the way may change you and your view of the initially envisioned outcomes. What you thought of as the ideal outcome may no longer be appropriate, meaningful or attainable. In such an eventuality, if you choose to retain your initial outcome and fail to re-evaluate it, you will end up getting stuck in discrepancies and believe that you are failing. People who reappraise their goals to accommodate changes and current circumstances can easily adjust their expectations and approach to ensure that they enjoy better mental and physical health. There are personal goals that require persistence and focus while others require more flexibility and openness. Having the ability and goodwill to reevaluate your expected outcomes is the best buffer against the fear of failure. You should evaluate your success based on the amount of effort and thought you put forth as opposed to the outcome achieved.

Believe that you are strong enough to prevail

The fear of failure is triggered by the imagination of consequences you may suffer should you fail. People are never afraid of the amount of work they have to put in towards achieving their goals but are afraid of the rare chance that their effort may not be good enough to yield their expected results. According to researchers, people with the fear of failure expect different negative consequences such as; embarrassment, blow to their high self-esteem, feeling of shame, loss of the public influence they hold, and disappointing other people who look up to them. Such people hold the psychological cost of failure to be higher than the monetary loss it may incur. As such, they tend to be more worried about losing friends, faith or face as opposed to losing money. Therefore, it is advisable to identify the consequences of failure that scare you most and develop the confidence to deal with them.

For instance, you can try to answer questions like; what consequences scare you most? What is their impact? Are they life-threatening or unpleasant? Will they hurt or just make you uncomfortable? How fast can you move on from the consequences? Are the consequences reversible or permanent? Can you handle the consequences? Or will; you hide and avoid damage control measures? In the end, your confidence to deal with the different consequences and challenges is what you fearless, mentally tough and emotionally resilient.

This chapter has defined the fear of failure and how it causes crippling effects on a person's ability to achieve their goals. As explained, the fear of failure originates from childhood events, lack of confidence, perfectionism, and over-personalization. Luckily, there are numerous ways of dealing with the fear of failure. Start by determining where the fear of failure originated from and re-frame how you think and feel about it. When you view failure as a chance to learn and grow, it becomes easy to overcome the fear and embrace all possible outcomes whether positive or negative. Therefore, the trick is to stay positive, have an ideal back up plan to your original goals and focus on learning from every situation that arises.

This way, your failures will no longer be a source of sorrow and embarrassment but a source of inspiration and education on how to deal with future events.

CHAPTER 3: FORGE RESILIENCE WITH INSIGHT MEDITATION

How do you manage your life in a manner that you are aware of who you are and what you want to achieve at every moment? Do you always feel the ground supporting you? How do you respond to the different joys of life and adversities while staying true to yourself and your heart's desires? It all boils down to how you connect with yourself and slow down long enough to experience the space between different events and life occurrences. This is achieved through insight meditation that benefits the body both physically and mentally. Healthwise, meditation reduces heart rate, blood pressure, respiration rate, stress levels and boosts a person's overall well-being. Mentally, meditation has been found to enhance problem-solving, concentration and compassion. Therefore, it is now applied to help people enhance mental toughness and emotional resilience required to deal with day to day challenges.

One of the best benefits of practicing insight meditation is that you build more resilience and mental flexibility. This occurs because insight meditation focuses on the breath that in turn keeps the brain focused on the present to develop an awareness level that allows you to clearly visualize your mental patterns and let go of what does not build you positively. You are able to let go of whatever takes away your concentration form experiencing current moments and events. You let go of whatever that distracts you from achieving your goals in life.

You are never aware of what can happen in your present moment but it is always a delightful surprise when you are open to discovering the available possibilities. Through practicing insight meditation, you are inspired to pursue relaxation more often and be open to embracing every outcome as opposed to having to think about everything and control the outcome of every situation. Meditation for building resilience helps you to evaluate different possibilities and options prior to undertaking certain tasks that would have otherwise deemed difficult and unattainable. This happens thanks to insight meditation and mental awareness practices. Insight meditation teaches you to relax and enjoy the present whether or not you are faced with some challenges. You gain the required energy and motivation to bounce back; which is emotional resilience.

Emotional resilience is the quality that eliminates the feeling of giving up no matter the adversities you face or the number of times you fall back on your plans. Conversely, insight meditation helps in seeing the gap that exists in your thinking by recognizing your mental patterns. It is easy to get tense, forget your required practices and get lost in thoughts that pull you down instead of building you. Meditation gets you from the lost thoughts into the present where you believe that everything is possible and can be done no matter the nature of adversities insight. Whatever happens in the current moment, you should enjoy it.

Concentration through breath

The key to mind and body transformation is correct breathing. This is because breath links the body and mind. Breathing is a psychological process that occurs voluntarily and involuntarily. Meaning that a person can control their breathing patterns when they want to and it also occurs automatically when they do not take note. Notably, all emotional shifts are reflected in a person's breathing patterns. When excited, you breathe fast, you sigh when depressed and breathe regularly or deep when calm. Similarly to how the state of mind alters the breathing pattern, you can shift your mental state by consciously changing your breathing pattern. Meaning that you can learn to control and regulate your mind through adapting correct breathing techniques. On the other hand, you can easily eradicate some of the mental and emotional sufferings you encounter when in a state of loneliness, depression, fear, rage, and anxiety by mastering the correct breathing techniques. Dysfunctional behavior and negative emotions often hinder personal development and growth. Therefore, if you want to improve the way you live you must learn how to avoid emotional pain and adopt a rare state of inner clarity and peace. When the mind is clear and calm, you are able to view things objectively and make rational decisions wisely as well as work more diligently. For instance, monks have long relied on breath counting techniques to boost their concentration power. It entails abdominal breathing and other core breathing techniques as explained below.

Abdominal breathing

Sit upright in a strong chair that is not pillowy; do not lean. Keep your feet shoulder-width apart, parallel and off the floor. Place the right-hand palm edge up and against the lower belly and allow it to rest on your lap naturally. Place the left-hand palm up and on top of the right hand. Join the thumb tips lightly to form a rainbow arc and tuck your chin slightly in. Press the tip of the tongue lightly against the roof of your mouth behind the upper teeth row. Keeping your eyes open, look ahead without staring at any object; just maintain relaxation. Slowly inhale through the nose as you push the lower belly out gently to appear as though it is slowly filling up with the air you are inhaling. When the belly feels almost full, pause for 3 seconds then exhale the air slowly through the nose and you pull the lower tummy back in gently. The inhalation should take 3 seconds, pause for 3 seconds and exhale for at least 4 seconds. Repeat the process at least 5 times. Abdominal breathing may feel awkward for beginners but it gets better with time.

Next is the breath counting meditation that is applied by monks for better concentration.

Start by engaging in abdominal breathing, inhale and pause then exhale and as you release the last bit of air, count one mentally. Repeat the same process as you count mentally to ten then start reverse counting from ten to one. If for whatever reason you are distracted and forget the number you are on, you must start from the beginning. The aim is you count to ten and backward without making any mistakes or forgetting the number you are on.

Breath Counting Meditation is an exercise designed to strengthen the mind. It purifies and builds concentration energy from distracting ideas. You will understand that it develops your mental power because you can achieve 10 easily and return to 1 again. If you can do it easily, boost the number to 20. Increase to 30 when that becomes simple. And that's it. Son Buddhist masters argue that you know you have developed intense mental strength when you are able to go up to a hundred and go back down again regularly. At that stage, you can achieve anything you set out do in life without getting distracted by challenges.

To function correctly, all the cells in our bodies need oxygen. Meaning that periodic breathing practices can reduce the impacts of stress on the body and improve general physical and mental health. It makes at least as much sense to give your mind regular workout as the way you train your body to harden with physical exercises. Breath Counting Meditation requires only a little over 3 minutes to count to 10 if you do not make any error. If you are a full beginner, then perhaps every morning you can begin your breath counting five minutes. You can boost the count accordingly to how you building mental toughness and resilience. Surprisingly, our way of life does not take much to change entirely. You can simply alter your life by incorporating this breath counting meditation to your daily routine. Why not give it a trial and experience the results yourself?

Those who meditate tend to be happier than those who do not. The flow of constructive ideas and positive emotion is well-known for meditation. It can create a large difference even for some minutes spent frequently meditating. This assertion is confirmed by scientific proof: comprehensive studies were performed in meditation on a group of Buddhist monks. The pre-frontal cortex (part of happiness) of the monk's brains was more active. The transformative potential of meditation should not be underestimated. Meditation helps you manage anxiety, stress, and depression. Meditation affects the brain physiologically. Researchers, for instance, discovered that when meditation is continuously practiced, the part of the brain that controls stress and anxiety declines. Through concentrating on the experiences of each instant, meditators train the mind in stressful circumstances to stay calm. In addition, because of uncertainty about the future, they also face much less anxiety.

A further big reason for the exercise is the many health advantages that arise from meditation. After individuals begin sitting, certain advantages can begin to take effect very fast. A feeling of relaxation and peace of mind is quite common although it can be fleeting and subtle. Some individuals care about the reverse impact of meditation because their minds appear to be busier than ever. We advise: maintain your sessions brief. Stick with them.

Meditation isn't about cleaning your mind's slate, it's about realizing what it looks like. And you are a step forward: you already realize how busy your mind can be. Besides improving your joy and your well-being overall, meditation also enables to keep your memory sharp and to keep your focus steady. You train yourself in non-judgmental awareness of the present moment through consciousness meditation. As a result, distractions tend to sweep you away from less. Just another reason for meditating.

By raising the consciousness of what is going on inside and outside, insight meditation enables you to create mental toughness and emotional resilience qualities. Many studies have shown that nonjudgmental awareness activates the portion of the brain that keeps you happy, up-to-date and hopeful, and implementing thought and sentiment sensitivity generates an internal space that enables you to live with your experience without thinking that your mind is stressful. Moreover, mental awareness allows you to view life rationally and ideally rather than react to situations without a second thought. It teaches you to maintain growth and forward progression even when faced with the inevitable difficulties of life. A recent study indicates that attention is the best method you can use if the situation becomes tougher and the core of resilience continues to be balanced.

In either case, the resilient is not disturbed by the adversity, but become stronger when facing and learning from it. In difficult circumstances, they tend to keep positive attitudes and mental states (especially accepting themselves), to remain open to benefit and meaningful lessons, to embrace emotional intelligence without being overwhelmed by hard sentiments, to draw on greater internal resources, and to continue moving towards their aims despite their setbacks.

You can be a master of your brain to construct resilience so that after stressful occurrences you bounce back quicker and stronger. Resilience even promises to recover quickly following a disease or retrogression. The challenge is, that our brains are often deprived of adverse mental conditions and behavior. These "negative villains" perpetuate pressure and chaos, rob us of vitality and make us feel susceptible and helpless. Fortunately, we can overcome the negative villains, decrease our amount of stress in times and increase our ability to increase our health. Decades of resilience study show that you and I can nurture beneficial mental toughness and emotional resilience traits. All we have to do is learn and practice daily until will are able to tap into our full potential.

In conclusion, Steve Jobs, 2011 noted that "if you just sit and observe, you note how restless your mind can be. If you attempt to calm it, you only make things worse, but it calms down with time, and when it does, it creates room for you to hear and experience more subtle things. That is when your intuition blossoms and you begin to view things clearly and be in the current more. Your mind slows down for you to see tremendous expanse at that particular moment. You view so much than what you could see before. It is a discipline that must be practiced."

CHAPTER 4: HOW STRONG PEOPLE THINK

Despite the goals you aim at achieving or the adversities that may crop up in your path to success, mentally strong people understand that the toughest success battles are fought between in the brain. This is because a person's actions and behavior must travel through the thinking gateway and the pathway of failure and success is held in the brain. Hence the famous saying that "when you rule your mind, you rule your world." Meaning that, when to take control of your thoughts, you determine your results. Be it emotional reactions to an event, mentally tough people always take responsibility for their thoughts prior to reacting with emotional intelligence.

Mental strength and emotional resilience are determined by the choices a person makes every day. Moreover, it has a lot to do with good and positive habits that propel a person towards achieving their life goals and being the best they can be when dealing with challenges. This entails adopting habits such as; maintaining healthy relationships and showing gratitude more often. Notably, mentally strong people tend to avoid negative habits that are likely to diminish their success and mental hardiness. For instance, they do not give up after failing, they do not doubt their capabilities, and neither do they shy away from adopting change. All in all, here is a description of how mentally strong people think.

Thinking habits of mentally strong people

You know what needs to be done: mentally strong people know and understand the path they need to take from the start to the end. They never generalize their actions and intentions. This is because they are dead set in their minds about what they need to achieve and formulate a clear picture of how they are going to achieve their goals. They act with absolute clarity every step of the way.

No over-dramatizing reality: ever heard of the saying that your perception is your reality? There are people who have a knack of explaining things in the worst way possible especially when they are experiencing adversities when in reality, things may not be as bad as they portray them to be. They speak with a lot of negativity that activates an over-blown crisis mode that makes everyone believe that no solution can be found. In reality, mentally tough people avoid by all cost getting carried away by their own drama vortex. In similar scenarios, they put in energy and time to come up with possible solutions for the problems they made encountering while acting on the right decisions with a lot of confidence.

No regrets about past decisions: mentally tough people may regret bad decisions when they happen and may even dwell on the decisions for some time. However, they do not over-analyze what they should have done differently or when could have happened if they made different decisions. It is prudent to focus on self-care and healing your wounds as well as recovering from the consequences of bad decisions. Whatever happened already happened and cannot be undone; you have no power over it so, the best you can do is learn and move on.

You are not a lone ranger: when facing challenges that they must overcome in order to make the next step, mentally strong people will seek to answer the question, "who can I contact for advice?" This is because high achievers network and connect with the right people and advisors they can count on for guidance when faced by daunting challenges. They are keen to retain connections because they know that they will be of use one day.
Set out to achieve one realistic goal per day: mentally tough and emotionally resilient people plan well and ahead. In addition, they are committed to a morning routine where they map out their daily tasks and determine that one main goal that they must achieve before the day ends. This ensures that they remain focused throughout the day and avoid unnecessary distraction or time wastage as they try to decide on what to do next after one task is successfully completed. For this reason, mentally string people protect their daily schedules fiercely because they know that they must complete their day's goals before sunset or retiring to bed.

Focus time and energy on what really matters: in the words of Warren Buffett, "the difference between really successful people and successful people is that really successful people decline almost everything." This is because they do just what matters and are not open to receive new surprises along the way that may end up compromising their goals. To avoid spreading yourself thin, simply determine what matters the most in your life at each particular moment. That is where all your time and energy should be invested in to ensure that you lead a better life and achieve what your heart desires. This way, you end feeling more productive and fulfilled in life.

Have the courage to move forward: it is common for people to be paralyzed by the fear of failure and fear of the unknown. Unfortunately, it can cause stagnation and deter success. For instance, a person might have the fear of changing careers, fear that if they try something new they will fail, and fear that they will not have the financial means to support their family. All these are mental barriers that hold a person back and prevent them from experiencing the challenges that make them better people and propel them towards achieving more success in life. It is important to gather the courage required to beat the fear and take the first step in the right direction. That is all it takes!

Beliefs influence your habits: unhealthy and negative thinking habits like; thinking you are a loser, doubting your capabilities and believing that the world is against you are things that prevent people from tapping into their mental toughness and emotional resilience they require to reach their greatest potential. Strong people beat such habits by talking out of their core beliefs and embracing what the world throws at them. As the saying goes, "when life gives you lemons, find someone with vodka and throw a party!" For instance, each time you fail, you should push harder to make sure that brain adapts to being persistent at all scenarios. Developing mental toughness and emotional resilience is a lifelong process that begins with changing your beliefs and habits that are self-limiting.

Visualize success: you were born to win

Visualizing success helps people achieve higher levels of success in their career fields. Notably, most people who have successfully and gained global recognition like; Jim Carey, Oprah and Tiger Woods have openly confessed that success visualization has been an important tool in propelling their careers to the next level. The power of visualization is extremely effective when applied correctly and harnessed.

Here is how to achieve it

Overcome fear and develop self-confidence: studies have revealed that, the brain does not differentiate between imagined and real memories. Meaning that, when you visualize success so emotionally and vividly, the brains chemistry changes to act as though the experience is real and in the end, the mind records it as an actual memory. This brain characteristic makes it possible for individuals to visualize overcoming fear and building self-confidence and esteem through making the unknown known.

Anxiety and fear develop from a negative intuition of future occurrences of the unknown. If you are able to visualize a future situation vividly in your mind, it is recorded as an actual memory and becomes known like something you have already experienced in the past. This way, feelings of insecurity are reduced and you end feeling more confident in your capabilities to experience different situations because the mind has recorded it as a past experience.

Developing new skills faster: different studies have proven that exercising the mind through visualization tends to be highly effective at refining skills as real practice would. Therefore, you can develop and reinforce new mental toughness and emotional resilience skills by visualizing yourself practicing them. Once you visualize an action, same brain regions are triggered as they would when performing it in real life. This explains why visualization is a part of world-class athlete training programs. It works to help them win their race and matches. For instance, Muhammad Ali the boxing legend always stressed on the importance of visualizing himself as a winner before he took on big matches.

Program our inner GPS: visualization communicates what the mind should focus on. It is important to determine what the mind should focus on because the objective of your brain's focus determines your perception of reality. There is a biological explanation behind this phenomenon referred to as; reticular activating system (RAS).

This is a network of neurons that are found in the brain and function to ensure that the brain deals with just as enough information as it can handle. It determines the sensory information that is perceived by the surrounding environment and determines what remains noticed and unnoticed. It acts as a filter for all the information that is presented to the brain from the environment.

Without RAS, the brain can be overwhelmed by information and data. RAS notices and prioritizes everything concerning personal safety and survival as well as events and thoughts that match the content in the mind like beliefs, emotions, and thoughts. Therefore, it records information from your environment that rhymes with your belief and thoughts system. RAS is the inner GPS that you must program so that it works in your advantage. The best way to achieve this is by visualizing your success.

Overriding limit beliefs: visualizing under deep relaxation mode is known as self-hypnosis. During deep relaxation, the brainwaves shift from Beta to Alpha and sometimes Theta. The Alpha and Theta are mental states where it becomes easier for a person to reprogram beliefs and patterns at the subconscious level.

Therefore, if you visualize yourself accomplishing a goal while at either of the two mental states and do it repeatedly, you override limiting beliefs that deter you from adopting new beliefs. But, you must relax the mind and body in order to reach the suggestible mental states.

Stop laziness

There are moments in life when we become overwhelmed by the tasks at hand and it is during such times that we tend to procrastinate on a number of tasks. In most cases, this results from the fact that we are ready to deal with the challenges facing us at a particular moment or we are simply not ready to make certain decisions.

However, when laziness and idleness become habitual, it becomes a cornerstone form of failure and no success at all. If you struggling with constant laziness and feeling unmotivated, there are things you can do to change that and do what needs to be done in a smart way.

Be king to yourself: when you realize that you have been too lazy, you may get tempted to beat yourself up with the hope that it will lead you to make better decisions and stop being lazy. Though it may work sometimes, beating yourself up causes you to feel like a failure and guilty. As such, you end up feeling demotivated and procrastinate tasks because you do not see the point of even attempting to do anything, after all, you are a failure. Instead of sucking up your self-esteem, it is advisable to be gentle on yourself and encourage yourself that you can do better with just a little effort.

Take a small step forward: getting started is always the hardest thing. Therefore, it would help to reduce inner resistance and take action despite the current situation. Start with taking baby steps towards your goals. For instance, you can spare at least 10 minutes every morning to write that college application essay you have procrastinated on for long. The point is, push yourself daily to achieve small milestones towards achieving the ultimate goal.

Dedicate mornings to do a small bit of what matters most: to make you feel like you can enjoy your lazy times without feeling guilty, it is advisable to do what needs to be achieved in the long run every day and first thing in the morning lest you get distracted or lazy. To avoid feeling overwhelmed by the amount of work you need to put in, it is recommended to break down the mega task into the smaller task that you can accomplish within the shortest time possible and without putting too much effort. This way, you get motivated to complete the mini-tasks every6 morning because they take up less time and energy. Additionally, starting your mornings with a goal-oriented task keeps your mind focused and effective at doing what needs to be done throughout the day. You get a morning win that triggers you to be active all day as you seek more wins.

Have small rest/ lazy breaks: to lighten your work routine, have small breaks between short but highly focused work bursts. Like you can do 30 minutes of serious work and take a 10 minutes break. The lazy breaks make work seem less daunting and you feel more energetic to take on tasks after the break.

Shut down escape routes: it is common to get bored during work or before starting a task you deem difficult. In such cases, a person seeks to escape routes that trigger procrastination. It could be logging on Facebook or Twitter for the days' highlights or playing your favorite video game. If you shut down such escape routes, you minimize your chances of procrastinating and being last in the long run.

CHAPTER 5: DETERMINATION, RESPONSIBILITY, AND PERSEVERANCE

Everyone thrives on being successful and in so doing, people forget or overlook the difficulties that could crop along the success path. It is common to set realistic targets and have the thrill to achieve them within the shortest time possible. But, it is also common for humans to fall short of their goals despite having planned and visualized them actualize. Failure at the beginning is always frustrating to the point where it dents your self-confidence and self-esteem. As a matter of fact, some people even consider giving up their dreams because they no longer believe in themselves or their capabilities to achieve what they set out to achieve at the beginning.

Success is not a straight line or a one-way path; you have to get through the muddled road and overcome challenges here and there before achieving the level of success you envision. Falling and getting lost along the success path is quite common but it all depends on how a person handles the failure and destructions. You must keep moving towards the right direction no matter what comes your way. Do you ever wonder how some of the most successful people achieved their high levels of success? What did they do that was so unique? Did they encounter challenges along the way? If so, how did they overcome and remain positive until they achieved their heights of success? Successful people have a few characteristics that help them throughout their success journey beyond. The secret ingredients to success are; determination, responsibility, and perseverance.

Adversities and failure are inherent parts of life that everybody encounters. You can plan and strive for success only to encounter a dark despair abyss of falling short of your goals. The truth is, everyone has failed at some point in their lives but what matters most is their attitude towards failure and success. You either choose to be fatalistic and self-demotivating or remain resilient and optimistic. This where the three qualities: determination, responsibility, and perseverance come in handy.

Determination is what gives you the drive to keep going and to work towards achieving your goals. Responsibility entails working on what needs to be done without supervisions because you are accountable for your actions. Perseverance is the ability to get back on your feet after going through failure and find a new path towards being productive and accomplishing the initial plans despite the unintended obstacles you encountered. As such, having determination, being responsible and having perseverance is the immunity a person needs to beat disappointment and humiliation that comes with failure to ensure that they not only bounce back but also remain focused on the ultimate goal. The three traits give you a unique sense of control that drives you to work responsibly and remain motivated to carry on. Successful people uphold 5 core factors that make up their determination, responsibility, and perseverance; they help them to take on difficult and intractable situations and turn them in growth and success opportunities.

Positive attitude: a positive attitude is rare to come by yet it is always the main driving force that triggers a person to get up in the morning and take a step towards the right direction. It keeps the desire to move forward burning such that a person upholds a unique level of responsibility and perseverance in the face of hardship and changes. This is a self-fulfilling mandate that foreshadows personal success when combined with conclusive decisions.

Conclusive choices: in order to succeed, you must choose one course and stick to it till the end. Decisive and conclusive actions require the mettle to make hard decisions when faced by the convenience of making an easier decision. This is because it is always advisable to make decisions that are guided by the ethical compass.

Ethical compass: use the values you deem to be imperative as the guiding star when making serious decisions that determine your success because they fill you with the belief and moral certainty conviction. Once you make a decision and begin to work towards it, you must stick to it no matter what; this is something that requires uncompromising determination, responsibility, and perseverance.

Uncompromising resolve: persistence and determination are compared to omnipotence for mortals. This is because, a person is required to persist until they realize that the best option is to quit and venture into something else; as much as it is advisable to keep on keeping on despite facing challenges, there are times when quitting is your only option. The point is to ensure that a person realizes when quitting is rational as opposed to being the easy way out.

The power of positivity

A positive attitude is a belief that good things lie ahead despite the adversities a person encounters. This is also referred to as optimism which can either be active or passive. Passive optimism holds that the world runs on the brighter side and that positive effects follow negative situations despite the timing. The passive optimist believes in their benevolence and that of other people. On the other hand, active optimism holds more resilience where a person becomes emboldened against negative events. Such people are able to make decisions with much confidence by merely assuming that they are bound to triumph and prevail despite any apparent difficulty they may encounter. This aptly defined as personal success expectation.

The active optimist sets the bar for self-fulfilling prophecy by expecting the personal success that is vindicated and bolstered by successful moments to determine real outcomes. Mental attitude towards and event or cause of action correlates with the consequences of the actual outcome. Some people refer to this as manifestation or destiny. But, it is more of the self-fulfilling prophecy that is present in the mental attitude of an active optimist. This is because they are less likely to accept failure and give up after failing. As such, they easily accept failure and rejection and remain determined to work towards achieving what they set out to accomplish before failure set in.

The mental attitude of an active optimist towards failure and challenges is the key to their success. However, that alone does not guarantee success. There are different ways of harnessing optimism and using it to gain actual results. They include;
Incremental planning: this entails breaking down large tasks into small and more manageable tasks. Breaking down a large task into manageable steps makes it less daunting and more achievable.
Vicarious optimism building: this requires a person to observe as others succeed and ultimately analyze their trajectory in order to understand that there are no differences between them and

successful people they know. You can also acquire their level of success by remaining actively optimistic and determined.

Collective optimism: connectedness and interpersonal success are key success determinants. For instance, unit cohesion is key for military success.

Self-control: this is the ability to control all your actions, reactions and thoughts. It not only cultivates active optimism but also exudes self-confidence. This is because you do not become a victim of your temptations and whims making it easier for you to conjure the mental attitude towards success. Note that, decisive actions not only require optimism but also determination, responsibility, and perseverance.

It's not simple to make decisions. It is difficult, at any given time, to choose from one of the countless alternatives before us. Often, we have inadequate data at our disposal to provide assurance about any specific result, so we work mainly in the dark. Hence, we must be decisive in order to remain in the right course of action. Being decisive does not necessarily originate from being right or sure about something. You behave confidently when you are sure of a specific result. This alone can improve your likelihood of achievement considerably. Timeliness is an important part of decisive actions. Chances occur and every second disappear. Some of them are bigger than others. Some people are fortunate. They are often grabbed faster. Recognition of a viable opportunity is always the fast step towards success and grabbing it as fast as possible is the second and most important step.

Interestingly, it has been shown that decisive action has reduced stress and enabled individuals to rebound. Steve Jobs is an example of this active optimistic function. When others might have succeeded, he resisted prevention and paralysis. Take his removal from Apple as an illustrative instance. This is an irrecoverable blow for some. But Steve Jobs defined it as a chance. "The difficulty of succeeding was substituted by the lightness of again becoming a beginner, less certain of all," he said. "It liberated me in one of my life's most creative phases." Jobs also continued to say he was not sure if I hadn't been fired from Apple, none of his achievements would have occurred. It was awful medication, but I think it was necessary for the patient. "Steve Jobs was not extra-human here. He was actively hopeful, decided, determined, responsible and resilient to his fortune-telling turn. He rebuilt this failure, turning it into a growth chance. This brought Apple a turning point and took a huge private responsibility.

Simply said, if you do not own your actions, you will feel detached from them and never fully invested. Otherwise, you and nobody else needs perseverance, active optimism, decisiveness, and determination in all the things you want to do. Responsibility, particularly if things get difficult, is naturally shifted. In these instances, our natural inclinations should be stagnated and self-reflective. The circumstances are fertile for self-reflection, failure, and adversity. You cannot do that if you feel not accountable personally for your behavior. You're not going to think about yourself and develop. It needs to be very brave, but it must be achieved.

Your private characteristics determine your success, but they also depend on others. Without the confidence of others, the interpersonal support that is essential to achievement is less likely to construct. Honesty, integrity, faithfulness and ethical conduct generate trust. These are the four components of your moral box. The moral compass tends to eliminate risks and predictability in corporate and personal interactions, thus guaranteeing security and fostering confidence. If the situation is right, other people's confidence and support can be crucial to success, because life offers opportunities that you can't address alone. This is particularly true because so many results and possibilities depend on other people's choices, which usually have no impact on our accomplishments. It helps decision-making and at the same time gains you more responsibilities and confidence from your environment, the amazing thing is to have a clear moral compass. Both of these factors contribute to success. Success fosters achievement.

We've been talking so far about the central importance of active optimism, decision-making, determination, responsibility, perseverance and achievement ethics. It is clear that the concept that continuing persistence, despite problems, adversity or discouragement, is essential for a purposeful course of action. The stability of your continuity depends mainly on your motivations for the action you have selected. It is also clear that the activities that are motivated and harmonized with your moral compass create the greatest confidence levels and thus, found success. Therefore, when we talk of persistence, it is not only a mental, emotional and moral state but also a mental approach to face challenges. This is important because we have to remember our motivations sometimes. The nearer you are to our values, the more bravery you can draw from them.

Learn to live under pressure by strengthening your character

Do you find yourself with so much work to do that you do not know where to start? Or overburden by other people's expectations of you? Or disappointed with your progress on a certain task? It is common to feel this way when working under pressure. Unfortunately, the pressure is a part of our daily lives and we must learn how to work under duress otherwise we may not accomplish much in life. There are two types of pressure; internal and external pressure.

Internal pressures are caused by pressing yourself too hard or when extremely concerned about your capacity to fulfill your duties and your expectations. For instance, you could lead yourself to be your company's number one distributor or doubt your capacity to speak. External pressure originates from the circumstances or from the people around you for example, a micromanager who makes you work in a particular way, or who gives you an enormous amount of work to deal with. There is a little link to your job with some external pressures, but how you respond to them could negatively affect how you function. You can all be seriously affected and act by lengthy journeys, diseases, financial difficulties, family duties, deprivation or hazardous jobs. You may even feel compelled in extreme cases to take risks, act against your values or to engage in illegal operations, such as "massage" of the tax bill in your company.

The concept that pressure encourages individuals to improve their performance until they reach an optimal point goes back to 1908. When the stress exceeds that optimum, psychologists Robert Yerkes and John Dodson discovered that it has the reverse impact and that people's output begins to suffer. The adverse effect of pressure shows, first of all, a mild discontent and a minor impairment of an individual's job quality. If the pressure is excessive, stress, anxiety, and unhappiness can be subjected to it. If the situation does not enhance rapidly and there is extended and excessive pressure, the danger is that workers will burn out.

How to thrive under pressure

Find an outlet for frustrations

It is widely recognized that an excellent workout activity at the exercise facility blows off steam. Exercise calms and dissipates stress, according to studies. For instance, rats on a running scheme have generated a big amount of new neurons intended specifically for freeing GABA, a neurotransmitter that inhibits brain activity and readily prevents other neurons from firing. These fresh, calming neurons are called "nanny," because they are intended to shock and quiet brain activity. It is not an enormous extent to indicate, according to scientists, that comparable rehabilitation occurs in the brains of individuals who worry. Hence, it is advisable to find a workout activity like cycling, walking, running, gardening or swimming and purpose to do it long term.

Enhance your self-awareness

Research involving over a million individuals shows that 90% of top artists are calm and controlled in moments of pressure because they have mastered how to manage their feelings. The capacity to avoid feelings from blowing over and stay cool under fire is directly linked with success. You need to understand your warm buttons; those circumstances and individuals that make you lose your patience and composure to handle your feelings. Often you mostly react to recurring catalysts or triggers that raise your adrenaline. So, begin by increasing self-confidence and self-awareness to master self-management. You can train your brain in order to master your response to these occurrences if you plan ahead of time. Tell yourself, for instance, that you will treat anything that occurs with equanimity especially when dealing with a certain individual or problem. To do this, you can choose from a repertoire of behaviors. These include listening, being patient, not interrupting, breathing, taking notes, not making a choice right now and altering your stance, sitting down if you are standing, sitting down, standing up, walking around the room and bringing in a coffee or water glass. Do anything to purchase time before you react so that you prevent adverse reactions. The more you do, the more you will be in control of your emotions and end up performing better when under pressure.

Body language

Studies indicate that not only does our body language reflect, but it can trigger our feelings. An article in Scientific American,' Smile! It could make you happier,' demonstrates that Botox recipients with a compromised ability to frown are happier and less concerned than those who can frown on average. Physically showing adverse emotional expressions such as anxiety or anger is like a feedback loop, which in turn increases this emotion. We do not have Botox operations to maintain our faces smooth, but we can all be aware of our facial expressions when we are in heated talks or when significant meetings are held, where it is vital to have a calm attitude. It is important to be cautious about your facial expressions because some can be habitual and portray the wrong message during a conversation or heated debate. Always relax your facial muscles and remain calm.

Note down your negative thoughts

A research conducted in Chicago demonstrates that it is calming and can enhance efficiency to write down our adverse ideas or concerns about a major forthcoming case. By writing down our thoughts, we are forced to give coherence to stressful thinking that not only reduces but can even negate the intensity of these thinking. This research showed that situations of pressure can deplete some of the working memory of your brain and make us less efficient to stay calm and reason clearly. Develop the habit of noting your worrying ideas in order to avoid worries, stress, and anxiety from undermining your brain strength when you need it most. You may do this at any time of the day, but before a high stakes event, it's most important. Another nice exercise is to carve out everything that worries you for about 20 minutes during the evening.

Listen to the music that helps you relax

Everyone has their unique musical preference and what appeals to one person may not appeal to another. Songs use musical principles that ooze out a calming effect. Therefore, experts advise on sparing a few minutes or about 10 minutes per day to listen to that music collection that calms you down and helps you relax. You could this before attending a crucial office meeting that you know might require a lot of input or in the morning before you leave the house as a way of setting the mood.

Some people are blessed with calm personalities; a factor that gives them a competitive edge over others. However, this does not mean that anyone cannot master the art of remaining calm and collected when working under pressure. All that is required is practice, determination, and dedication to master how to remain calm.

CHAPTER 6: EMOTIONAL INTELLIGENCE AND MASTERY OF YOUR THOUGHTS

Your emotions are a sacred and natural part of you. This is because your feelings correlate directly with the responses derived from your perceptions. They are a sign of whether you are having awful or pleasurable experiences. Acknowledging your feelings helps you get in touch with your unique personality, humanity and you are able to honor them better, demonstrate emotional intelligence and self-respect. You are able to take wise actions that help in minimizing troubled feelings. In fact, embracing your vulnerability is a good sign of emotional intelligence and a step towards achieving wholeness. Often, people suppress, avoid, and devalue disturbing feelings because they are not aware of how to address them. The good news is that emotional intelligence and mastery can be achieved at home, in your workplace, and in relationships to ensure that you lead a more fulfilling life characterized by mental toughness and emotional resilience. Emotions serve the inner compass and keep on tabs whether your actions and thoughts are in harmony with your core humanity. Sometimes they communicate with a whisper and when you fail to take note of the message, they increase the volume until you pay attention and take the right actions. For instance, painful feelings are a sign that your actions and thoughts are bad for your well-being and you should make the right changes that are in sync with your soul's calling. You experience the best feelings and life events when you are in charge of your humanity and your crucial needs are satisfied. In order to effectively understand and interpret your emotions more effectively, it is paramount to understand the different emotions that we experience daily.

They include:

Discomfort
Discomfort is an unpleasant emotion which often leads to lurking, annoyance, impatience or disquiet. You experience discomfort because you interpret a situation or a number of conditions in a particular manner that naturally leads to a sense of discomfort. This interpretation actually gives rise to discomfort. This thus

implies you have power over your emotional experience when you convert or alter your understanding of the environment. If you ever feel discomfort, it is important first of all to see what you do, and secondly, to see how exactly you understand reality. If you don't get the outcomes you're looking for, then just attempt taking a distinct strategy. However, if you cannot address the scenario in a distinct light, attempt to modify your point of view. In any case, you should discover a solution that helps you get out of this unpleasant emotional state. If you are bored, for instance, then try to do something else at that particular moment. Or you can just attempt to interpret your situation differently. Any strategy can work when you are flexible with your approaches.

Fear

Fear is often an emotion that is very weak, leading to anxiety and indecision. You are afraid because you interpret a circumstance or a certain amount of conditions in a manner that leads you naturally to a sense of terror. This fear is often the result of an emotional reaction to what can happen in the future if you decide or take particular measures. All of this is fine if it is based on tough facts and proof that safeguard you from damage. But our fears are often overwhelmed by inaccuracies which confuse and mislead us. You therefore always have to take the first step to deal with fear by determining what is real and what is imagined. Naturally, fear is a very precious emotion, because it protects us from damage. Most of the moment, however, it truly harms us in this contemporary day because it prevents us from attaining our objectives and goals. There are two fast things you have to do that can be more effective in managing your concerns. First of all, you want to explain what it is. The second is to carefully prepare your activities to accomplish your required results. The overwhelming majority of our fears are based on the lack of understanding and preparations. If both are mastered effectively, you will have what it takes to overcome any type of fear.

Hurt

The hurt emotion tends to make us feel helpless and causes us often to a sense of loss and jealousy. You are hurt because you interpret a situation or a number of conditions in a particular manner, which naturally leads to your feeling hurt. Similarly, feeling hurt may not efficiently communicate your requirements to others. As such, today you must communicate clearly and without threat what you need from your relationships. If it does not work to communicate your needs, take the expectations into account. You might not have sensible expectations, perhaps they will change over time or may simply stop applying to your existing relationship, which might mean that you will have to reassess. Finally, the hurt is sometimes due to the incomprehension of our relationships or conditions. In these cases, it helps to fascinate and remain curious in a bid to avoid getting hurt. You start to ask questions, which increase the way you believe and lead to responses and opportunities you might not have previously taken into account, by becoming curious.

Anger

Anger tends to spin us out of control and often leads to resentment. You feel the anger because you interpret a situation or a certain number of conditions in a particular manner which naturally causes you to rage. However, if we can comprehend the fundamental significance, anger can truly serve us. It is essential to realize before you are ready to adopt the emotion of anger that anger often occurs because another violates one or more of our laws. As such, we are upset because of the scenario, individuals or situations that are out of our control.

In such cases, in fact, we can rapidly get rid of frustration by re-evaluating our laws over time. They might not be reasonable, they might be out of date or perhaps in such circumstances they should not be applied. Anger can also arise because conditions or intentions are wrongly interpreted. You must ask if you have misinterpreted the situation or have simply misunderstood the intentions of people in such situations. Be open to opportunities and look for alternative meanings in this situation passionately. You will only find answers with an open and flexible approach.

Guilt

Guilt tends to make us feel slightly deflated and can often lead to regretful feelings. You are guilty of having a situation or a number of circumstances interpreted in a particular way, which naturally leads you into guilt. And the longer that guilt is maintained, the worse it is, as it continues to grow and grow in your head. If we experience guilt we should remember that we simply interpret what we did or didn't do and what its effect it had on others. The time you choose a fresh and distinctive interpretation of occurrences and situations in your life is when fault changes suddenly and becomes something that can possibly motivate and empower you to act positively. Know that your activities may not have an effect on others as they appear. In such cases, therefore, your guidelines for feeling guilty may have to be examined. Perhaps these rules must be re-evaluated. Guilt can only be resolved once a person makes peace with themselves and the people they hurt.

Frustration

Frustration is one of the feelings we love to hate only because it makes us feel like we are so near, yet so far from the result, we want. You are frustrated because you interpret a circumstance or certain situations in a manner that obviously frustrates you. Yet your responses lie within this sensation. However, you don't appear to get the outcomes you're after, because you're attempting to do something. It's like some external force that you can't seem to regulate, holds you back from your objective. Instead of attempting to regulate the environment, it is important to start thinking outside the box, to start thinking about fresh options, thoughts and possible solutions that might assist you to fix this issue. And sometimes all you need is to seek fresh data that will give you insight into the situation from a slightly distinct point of view. Finally, frustration occurs often because you don't get the results. In such situations you need only change your approach to resolve your frustrations; try something different and new that you haven't regarded before. Curiosity, determination, and flexibility.

Inadequacy

Inadequacy can cause you to feel miserable, insignificant and lacking incompetency. It's an emotion that makes you feel that you don't have a way out of the heap. You experience inadequacy because you just don't have your high expectations and experience, abilities or understanding. You can either change your expectations and skills or try to gain the required knowledge, skills and experience to achieve the results you would like in your life. You may also feel inadequate because you simply undermine your own strengths and abilities. It is always essential to have a second opinion in such situations. So go out and ask for feedback from anyone. Please ask them to make honest comments. You may have some very surprising perspectives and insights. Inadequacy can often be caused by a lack of trust. If you have low self-esteem, then it seems quite fine to feel insufficient. However, if you take the time to construct your trust, your self-belief and opportunities will also increase. You will feel better.

Overwhelm

Overwhelm is one of those feelings that get to you over time and that takes over your life before you understand them, sometimes leading to very weakening feelings of sorrow and depression. You're overwhelmed, because you're not able to handle or regulate different elements of your lives, or merely have too much to deal with. You are unable to react in these circumstances and feel out of control. The alternative is to take control of tiny parts of your lives, a step at a time. It implies taking part in your life and splitting it into smaller and manageable pieces with which you can work effectively. It also implies letting go of any unnecessarily daunting obligations and commitments, or simply reprogramming them in such a manner, as to give you more room to do what is most essential. It is easy to overcome overwhelm if you are aware of what to do and dedicated to taking the required measures to reset and reprioritize your life. All it requires is a little productivity lesson sometimes.

Disappointment

Disappointment is triggered by the feeling that you don't get what you want and may also be caused by a sense of defeat. You're disappointed because you interpret a circumstance or a number of conditions in a manner that makes you feel disappointed. You are stuck in an unsuccessful pit of unfulfilled objectives, goals, and dreams, which have never come true instead of seeking alternatives and responses. Whenever we feel disappointed, we always want things to turn out differently. But we cannot change the past, though we can change our experiences of the past in a beneficial manner. Instead, choose to learn from your experiences in order to improve yourself in the future, instead of being deceived. In other occasions, the opportunity that you have just had is even worthwhile looking for as a consequence of the disappointment. Disappointment can often be caused by unrealistic and high expectations that can hardly ever be realized. In this situation, you can alter your expectations by reducing them to a realistic level. This could well grab you out of the fearful pit of disappointment. Disappointment is merely the outcome of an unfulfilled objective. Therefore, it is important to have realistic goals that you can achieve.

Loneliness

Loneliness can lead to sorrow and stagnation and can be a very debilitating emotion. You live in solitude because you see your life through a lens that distinguishes you from all others outside of you. There are so many ways to communicate with each other every day. The key to overcoming solitude is reconnecting, reconnecting with people and reconnecting with your surroundings and with a greater cause that allows you to feel fulfilled and enthusiastic. Loneliness develops in the heart when a person forgets all the things they should be grateful for. Gratitude helps a person in restoring the life balance they may be missing and it encourages you to be accommodative to other people.

How to master emotional intelligence and your thoughts
When you are caught up in a moment, your initial reaction is always emotional and in most cases, it works against you. Hence, the need to be aware of the different emotions and how to manage them in order to react in a rational and effective manner. Understanding how to control your emotional state allows you to respond to emotions in a habitual manner that requires less thought and conscious efforts. Here is how to do that.

Identify your emotions
The first step to master your thoughts and emotional intelligence is to understand the emotions you could be experiencing at a particular moment. If you are unsure about the emotions you are experiencing, then it could be hard for you to act or respond to situations accordingly. To determine your emotions, you need to answer questions like; what are you feeling? Is it all you are feeling or there is an underlying state? The better understating you have of your emotions the easier it becomes for you to master your thoughts.

Appreciate the emotions you experience
It is important not to resist whatever emotions you could be experiencing whether good or bad. This is because resistance only brews uncertainty and tension as well as prevents you from turning your emotions into something meaningful and you can use to build emotional intelligence for future encounters. Therefore, it is prudent to openly acknowledge your emotions and understand its inner meaning and significance in your life and the situation you are in. for example, if something makes you angry, acknowledge that you are angry and that something triggered your anger.

Analyze your emotions

Curiosity opens doors for new opportunities and perspectives that help you to gain more insight into the circumstance you are facing and the emotions they trigger. To spark the curiosity about your emotions, it is important to address questions like; what does your emotion offer you? What is the value of the emotion? What can you do to make things better? What do you really feel and desire? How does emotion serve you? What should you believe in order to get your preferred outcome? What do you learn from your current emotion that can make you better?

Note that, every emotion you experience serves you in one or the other to teach you pricey lessons about yourself, life and the circumstances you encounter daily. Therefore, you must be open to finding the right answers that will help you in gaining insight and overcome the emotion roadblock.

Be confident that you can handle your emotions

Being confident about your emotions allows you to consciously choose an effective emotional response that you can utilize moving forward. It also helps in obtaining the necessary knowledge and support you need to manage your emotional responses better. It would help to recall a time in the past where you dealt with a similar emotion effectively and things favored you. The memory can serve as a foundation for paving way for a better future where you are able to master your thoughts and build on emotional intelligence.

Take action

Once you have gathered all the knowledge, information and support you require to react to your emotions in a healthy and effective manner, you should take proactive actions to transform your emotional state and achieve emotional intelligence.

In conclusion, it is important to take things seriously and remind yourself that it is not what happens to you that matters most but how you respond to circumstances and events in your life that makes all the difference. You should always be in control of your emotions despite how things may appear. Emotions come from inside out and not outside-in.

CHAPTER 7: STRATEGIES TO BE QUIET AND STRONG IN EVERY SITUATION

When you are faced by a serious life situation, the first reaction is always to panic not knowing that severe stress and anxiety can cause a complete mental meltdown. As a result, you can end developing long term health damage as well as reduce your ability to perform optimally when required to. Most of the world's top achievers, athletes, artists, and entrepreneurs could not have achieved their heights of success without mastering how to remain calm and collected when under pressure be it work or life-related. As a matter of fact, they have developed and maintain a certain psychological state of readiness and mental preparedness that helps them to accept situations much faster and address them calmly because they understand that situations van change abruptly but they do not define who they are or what the future holds for them. Circumstances and the people around you will often break you down. But if you keep your heart open to receive and give love, the mind focused and continue to move towards the right direction, it will always be easier for you to recover from the break downs and come back as a much stronger and more knowledgeable person. Here are tips on how to remain calm and collected at the height of pressure.

Accept the reality of the situation at hand

Through life, you can't discover peace. Instead of avoiding it, life spins every hour with unexpected modifications and takes every shift and experience as a growth challenge. Either it will offer you what you want, or the next stage will educate you. It does not guarantee any challenges and no hard work or noise before you find peace and good fortune in life. It implies to be in the midst and stay calm in your core. It's about letting your thoughts know how things should be. This isn't simple, of course; it's going to be a continuous fight. It's nevertheless infinitely simpler than fighting to adapt your life to some old delusion. It is also a trip that is endlessly more pleasing. There is peace, beauty and there is happiness when it works if you can separate from ancient beliefs. Honestly, life is too brief for you to go to war. Misappropriate expectations often lead to the greatest disappointments in our life. The first step towards happiness is to let go of unnecessary expectations. Come from a spirit of peace and acceptability and you can cope with and develop beyond virtually anything.

Understand that everything is temporary

Even when the storms are heavy, it eventually stops to rain. You also get a cure whenever you get hurt. Additionally, you are reminded every morning that light always comes after darkness, but choose to think that the night (dark moments in life) will continue forever. That's not going to happen because nothing lasts forever.
So if it's nice, appreciate it right now. It's not ever going to last. Don't care if things are bad, as it will never last. It doesn't just mean you can't laugh because life isn't simple at the time. It does not mean that you can't smile just because you're bothered by something. You get a fresh start and a fresh end at every time. Every second, you get a second opportunity. All you need is do the best you can.
Always push yourself to take another step forward no matter what you are going through
I am confident that about half the difference between good individuals and everybody else is sheer perseverance, this is after studying the lives of many successful individuals. We need to know the beauty of effort, patience, and perseverance in a society that wants fast outcomes. Be powerful, current and unwavering. Usually, the most beautiful smiles are those which have fought through tears. Because failures often ultimately lead to breakthroughs. Each error, heartbreak, and loss has its own answer, a subtle lesson for your performance and result from next time around. So it is you that is the most credible to predict your own future.
Enjoy life today, rather than just looking over it as it passes. Do not allow the few things out of control to interfere with the endless array of things you can control. The reality is that sometimes we all lose. The bigger reality is that we never have a single loss. Learn from your experiences and become wiser. Good things don't finally happen for those who wait: nice things come for those who remain patient as they work hard for what they most want in life, in good times and bad. This is about bravery. It is about being extremely

scared and still proceeding to take the next step regardless.

Use positivity and do not let negativity bring you down

There might be no apparent reason today to be positive, but there is no need for a reason. Being always positive is a life strategy and not a response to something nice that might have happened. In fact, the ideal time to overly positive in life is when everything around seems negative and the world seems to be against you in every aspect. It is hard but achievable. Long-term happiness is not lack of issues, but the capacity to address them. Bring your consciousness to your own internal strength and positive position. You are responsible for how you respond in your lives to individuals and activities. You can either offer your life negative energy or choose to be positive by concentrating on the good things that really matter. So speak more about your blessings than today's issues. In other words, don't expect a favorable reason. Choose to be positive about your position, your opportunities and what you can do to get from one point to another. Look for ways to convey your favorable view rather than seeking reasons for being positive. Work to bring this vision to your lives and to enjoy the rewarding results you achieve.

Focus on achieving small fixes
Do not envision mountains in your mind. Don't attempt all at once to conquer the world. You unnecessarily make life difficult and frustrating if you look for instant gratification (large, fast fixes). Instead of making a small, beneficial investment in yourself at every time and the prizes will naturally follow. It's simple to discover a lot of small stuff when all is broken. Even the most important beneficial effort can create a major difference when nothing seems to be correct. Understand those times, when you are faced by the greatest adversity, are times when you encounter the greatest opportunities in life. If issues arise in every direction, it means that there is some great value somewhere waiting to be discovered and created. It's simple to get lulled into an indulgence routine when everything's well. How unbelievably capable and resourceful you maybe is simple to forget. Resolve to continue with small fixes daily. These little tweaks bring you to where you want to be in the long run. Every day, dense and thin, small steps, short leaps, and small fixes (small repetitive modifications) will take you places.

Look for something to appreciate no matter how small it may be
You may not have what you want and you may be very sad, but you can still enjoy more than enough at this time. Do not spoil what you have by wanting what you don't have; remember that what you got now was once just one of your desires. It is a sign of management and strength to remember that being positive in an adverse position is not naive. If you have so much to cry about and complain about, it is okay to mourn, but it is also important to smile and enjoy your life. So don't pray for the great miracles and forget to give thanks for the usual gifts in your life, simple but not that small. It may seem strange to be grateful for those ordinary events in your life, but it is precisely by being grateful that you can turn the ordinary into the uncommon and remain calm amidst pressure. Think of all the beauty around you, see it and smile. It is not gladness that makes us grateful at the end of the day, but gratitude that makes us happy. The most strong happiness activity here is to show gratitude for the excellent stuff you have.

Accord yourself the attention you deserve
It does not serve you to resist and ignore your own emotions and feelings. This leads to stress, disease, confusion, broken friendships, anger, and depression. Anyone who has had any of the above knows that those mental statements are terribly unhealthy and it is nearly impossible to escape them if you have the habit of self-disregard. You must confess to having spent too much of your life attempting to diminish yourself to a certain extent. Trying to be smaller in size, less sensitive, quieter, and less needy, have fewer opinions, and just be less of you simply because you were avoiding to push people away or to make feel like you are too much of a burden. You just wanted to fit in and make people like you by creating a certain good impression. You wanted to be needed.
For years, therefore, in order to please others, you have sacrificed yourself. You've endured for years. But you're tired of the pain and shrinking yourself. Good! It's not your job to make someone else's idea about a valuable human being shift who you are. You're valuable. Not because others believe you are, but because you breathe your own air, so you matter. Your ideas are important. Your emotions are important and your voice counts. And you must be who you are, and live your reality, with or without anybody's approval or authorization. Even if it turns the heads of individuals. Even though it does not make them easy. Even if they decide to

quit, refuse to shrink your personality. Choose to give yourself the best in life, pursue your dreams and goals, and spare enough time for yourself. Above all, honor your emotions and feelings because self-care defines you. Once you take care of yourself and focus on being the best you can be, it will be easier for you to deal with people and situation under stressful conditions.

Always remember that everyone suffers and experience pain in life. But it is how people deal with adversities at the height of pressure that defines their level of success. Remaining calm during stressful situations helps you to make rational decisions and tap into your mental strength to ensure that you are not swayed by emotions. The key is to use your past life experiences to grow and move towards your achieve your goals a step at a time. When you remain calm and collected when under pressure you only give yourself the power to come up with the ideal solutions but also get to learn how to deal with future situations like the one you experienced. When you apply what you learn now in future plans, actions, and choices, you move forward and certain challenges also become easy to deal with. This is because, you took advantage of a stressful situation to learn, become stronger and wiser. It is not easy to remain calm under pressure because we are all humans and we are bound to react when our emotions are altered by situations. However, it is achievable and totally worth it in the end. Find what calms you down when stressed or under pressure and use it to remain motivated and positive to carry on with work.

CHAPTER 8: CHANGING YOUR MENTAL STATE AND IMPROVING MENTAL SKILLS FOR PERSONAL SUCCESS

Though most people do not realize it, a person's perception of the world greatly depends on their inner state of mind. For instance, we all know how alienating and disturbing things become when we are in a bad or frustrated mood. On the other hand, there is another state where everything we wish for seems to flow just right and everything you do feels effortless. These two states define your mental state. Therefore, it would be great to understand how to have full control over your mental state in order to control your moods, feelings, and actions that eventually lead to success. Having the power to change your mental state proactively means that you can control how you feel and how you perceive things around you. You get to be in control of how you function and most importantly how to feel about different circumstances. Every emotion is triggered by something and if you have the power to choose your reactions carefully, your mental and emotional state would not be determined by what happens in your life whether good or bad.

People grow up with a certain expectation of how their adult life will be and no one envisions a life full of challenges and failure. But unfortunately, life rarely turns out as envisioned or as planned. In most cases, the milestones that people long to achieve are derived from other people's perceptions of what a good and satisfying life should be. In reality, you only have one life and therefore, you should live it as you imagine by doing the things that make you happy and give you satisfaction as opposed to living by other people's rules. To achieve this, start by forgetting all the opportunities you missed and all the failures you might have encountered in the past. Regret does not change your life the bad choices you made before; instead, it wastes your valuable energy and time that you would have used to build yourself. Give yourself a break from everything and refuse to heed to outside expectations of what life should be. Focus on working out what truly makes you happy and propels you to achieve your life goals. If you get to this point, you will have mastered how to control your mental state. The next step would be learning how to improve mental skills for success as explained below.

Mini habits for great goals every day

Take control
You have to know how to be in control of yourself if you are to be mentally hard. Mental toughness and overall achievement rely mainly on your ability to control the mind. Mental skills and state control are some of the most significant things that a person should learn. This is because many other things flow quite smoothly when you can control your thoughts. Life itself ensures that it is not simple to be in control of your thoughts. This is because of the many uncertainties that make up life. Yet something you can regulate will always be there. And you can find most of the factors. For instance, there could be predictions of an economic downturn. Many individuals automatically become afraid, stressed, and possibly take actions such as the sale of some of their assets. But did you know there's a different alternative? Other alternatives are always available. You can simply decrease your expenditure and retain your property until things get better. You can contact a family and all of you agree on cost reduction policies. Thus, while many are stressed and glued to their TV screens to updates on when the economy is eventually crashing, you plan for those difficult moments ahead. This plan will keep you in control because you thought about the scenario before it actualized.

Quit thinking about things you cannot change

When you are in control of your thoughts and mental state, you will understand that your van only changes matters that affect you. Other things that affect your life may be changed but it is never a guarantee. This is because most situations occur as problems that require solutions in the form of changing how the situation occurred. However, there are a few situations that cannot be changed no matter how hard you try. When you overthink such situations, they become a source of stress and demotivation and end up hindering your success. To avoid this, it is important that you change your perception towards particular situations that you cannot change. To save your precious time and energy, it is advisable to always change your view about situations you cannot change. Evaluate them from a different perspective and you will definitely get an idea of how to tackle them effectively.

View failure as a learning opportunity

Failure is inevitable if you are going to accomplish anything tangible in life. You must fail before you succeed. As soon as you know this reality, life will be better for you. It is therefore very important with this understanding that you learn how to look at mistakes in a different and positive perspective. It is essential that you realize that if you fail, it is not a sign that you are headed for total failure. It's a sign that you're trying to achieve an objective instead. View failure as an opportunity to learn, become mentally tough and emotionally resilient. Avoid the view of many that failure is bad and should not occur. This is a lie based on how people misunderstand failure. Such lines of thought tend to somehow pursue perfectionism. Even in tiny quantities and practically undetectable the spirit of perfectionism will always get you frustrated. This is because you will never be in a position to view failure as a life lesson. But if you fail to realize that it isn't the end, it's easy for you to rebound and play on the field again. Failure is thus a friendly stepping-stone, not an enemy. Just view it at the right angle.

Celebrate other people's achievements

How do you feel when you see other people succeed when you are failing? If you are like most people you will develop resentment towards them. Unfortunately, you get back what you give out. So, the resentment you give to others will get back to you and affect you negatively. You become jealous when you resent those who do better than you are. Moreover, you lose a lot of sleep because you worry they're better than you are. You overlook your strengths and distinctive skills and underestimate them. You just don't think you're good enough. This creates adverse thoughts that directly and adversely affect your chances of success. On the other side, you are motivated if you celebrate successful people and respect mentally tight people. You are motivated to work harder and to succeed. This inspiration will lead you to research and to discover everything you need to know in order to accomplish your objective. It is also feasible to celebrate the achievement of other people. This is essential because you may have a very large objective to accomplish. At some stage you or your colleagues may have been afraid of the magnitude of this objective and doubt might cripple you. However, when you see other individuals attain their objectives, you are motivated to move forward, too. You reason if they could do it, then you could too and you are actually going to do.

Give solutions instead of complaining

Weak-minded individuals always complain about it all. They detect and reveal mistakes quickly. But it's just an effort at showing how bad things are at the core of their speech. Such people exaggerate situations and this is one reason why these individuals rarely succeed. You must refrain from being a complainant to be mentally hard. And the best way to do this is to cultivate a custom of working towards alternatives. Search for and work with buddies who have the same mind. If you are unable to discover anybody, prepare yourself to find solutions on your own. This will truly distinguish you and may even cause conflict among others. However, that should not worry you because your aim is to develop mental toughness and emotional resilience to deal with the challenges life throws at you.

Stop trying to impress others

Don't attempt to create a fan base if you want to be mentally tough. You cannot stand firm on your own if you want to have many fans and people who love you. Those supporters will determine how far you can go, always or at least very largely. Believe in yourself and your capabilities because the world around you always tries to bring you to its mediocrity. Although it is unfortunate, there are a lot more mediocre individuals than excellent individuals. Of course, we all want and need consent. But the issue is that everyone does their own stuff and has no time to go over what you want to achieve. Parents have no time for kids; spouses have no time for each other, etc. so people tend to seek attention and consent from the wrong places. The issue, though, is that you have to do what that individual wants you to do if you need someone's approval. And as he wishes, you have to do it. Then he's going to say that you're ok. You'll have to exceed his expectations if you want him to praise you. The issue is: when are you going to live your life if you always try to please someone else? When are you going to evolve enough to become a professional advisor? Where are you going to introduce, grow, employ many and assist relieve poverty? The individual or individuals who demand something from you, simply seek glory without having to work for it. They are the ones that have been labeled successful. Yet, you will be busy building their vision. If you have a vision or goal you would like to accomplish, be sure to follow it without being swayed.

Take responsibility
This is important if you want to be or do anything in life. As long as you feel like the world owes you something, you will be driven down. For instance, you have lost it if you decide that because you pay taxes, that your state owes you a decent life. Keep on with this and quickly you'll believe someone should clean your backyard and you live alone. You will develop a very hazardous characteristic, called laziness, as much as you can employ someone. This characteristic continues to deter you from developing mental toughness. You acknowledge that your achievements depend on your actions when you are taking responsibility. Taking responsibility to assist you to rescue a certain amount of time, energy and situations. People could be busy discussing an issue that arises as the shifting blame while you are looking for solutions and different ways to change the situation. And certainly you will come up with one to carry it forward. You are still going to do so even if you do it alone. Responsibility begins gradually and increases with time. You will have to evolve and make it a habit. You could start by keeping your office space clean and organized. If the ability to find saved files on your computer can impair your efficiency. Why not generate and save folders in the corresponding folders? The simple assumption of accountability implies you know it is your duty to do something. You will understand that it is your task to find a solution if you are faced with a challenging scenario. You will share and work to achieve it with others. You will go on to enforce it even if you are alone. Others will soon see the feeling of what you do and join you. This is the development of excellent management. Great rulers see an issue and choose to solve it. You commit to it, then others celebrate it, knowing little about the struggles you had to endure to achieve that much.

Overcome fear

Fear could be a sensation or emotion. But as far as science is concerned, you will understand that fear is a severe impediment, especially when pursuing your vision. It's not just a sensation that attacks and disappears. Fear gets ahead of you and says, "you cannot make it beyond this point," and remains put. If you attempt to challenge it hard enough, it will change to "You're not going past this stage." Some people reach the second point. However, given the effort engaged, few people still push the second declaration to the point of passing by. You have to decide to be one of the very few who move further to be mentally tough.

It is not an event but an on-going process to fight and overcome fear. And, as with many other ways to construct mental toughness, you are best at starting tiny and gradually building the ability. Identify your little fears every day. Are you scared you'll waste a lot of time making lunch? Is your home cleaning going to leave your back dull? Will you lose a lot of sleep for an additional hour? Will you lose your friendship by fighting between two staff? No matter what you are afraid of, remember that it is a barrier which proudly says that the established position cannot be removed. You don't want to be a winner? You want to be a winner, don't you? Resolve to challenge fear and overcome it to ensure that you gather the courage and mental toughness required to fight the obstacles that lie ahead. Overcoming fear also boosts confidence in a big way.

Focus on winning your goals

Only two results can be achieved: to win or to lose. Gaining and losing are absolute, so scales from 1 to 10 or other comparable methods of looking at them are not available. Naturally, the achievement is progressive and construction implies some things will be lost and others won. The loss of which we are speaking is the loss that comes out of surrender and you stop working for your objectives. To achieve your objective is to set an objective in the first place. For instance, you may decide that in two months you want to make 100 bucks. Then you think you will not settle for less. It's never simple to win. So you must wake up at dawn and earlier than you used to before. Prepare yourself and get down to work. Work carefully on your plans. Make sure you remove any distractions from your mind irrespective of how much fun you have. This is the same recommendation: begin low. You need a hundred dollars once two months when calculating the construction of a large house, then check whether it is really in sync with your lifestyle or your present practices. If you will need to alter your life too much, it means that you need to alter your goals otherwise you will end being frustrated after failing to achieve them. If your idea of building a big house cannot change, it would be better to increase the timeframe in which you need to accomplish that goal. Breaking things down rationally ensures that you retain realistic goals that are within your current capabilities and highly achievable. After breaking things down, set daily and weekly goals that you must evaluate and do not overthink.

Choose your company

As the saying goes, you are what you eat; it also implies that you are who your friends are. Since not many people are mentally strong and this capacity requires a great deal of effort, you can rest assured you will stand out. However, this is only the lovely consequence of the fight. Are you conscious of future setbacks? Don't always underestimate your friends. They determine a lot about who you become. Your level of understanding, patterns of reasoning, speech and dressing styles, etc. Your friends are in reality greatly affected by your life's achievement. Do you hang around the same individuals and expect to be hard on your mind? That can never happen. You have to invest time and energy to achieve mental toughness in the midst of your friends who do not recognize its importance. When you start your journey, some of your colleagues will arouse jealousy. Some will get upset because you can feel better than them. You definitely understand that not all your friends will help you get to where you wish to be. You'll quickly have no time for your buddies if you begin this process. Can you live with that? Would you like in the meantime to have fewer friends or none at all in order to achieve mental toughness and emotional resilience? You make them uneasy mainly because they prefer to maintain the company as a console that mediocrity affects all. But you are doomed if you give in to their demands and opposed to fighting for the opportunity to master mental toughness. Make a choice between mental weakness (your current friends) or mental toughness (new friends).

Delayed gratification

You will seldom succeed if you fulfill all your wishes instantly. Delayed satisfaction is needed to ensure that you keep focused on what you want to accomplish. There is a well-known children's experiment to demonstrate late gratitude. These kids had to eat a marshmallow, or wait for a few minutes and get another so that they could have two. You can refer to the things that come to you as distractions from your path to achievement. You could even call it temptations. They must be ignored or deleted, regardless of how that is achieved. Mental toughness requires you to hold on for whatever period is needed to appreciate the outcome. This doesn't imply life is boring and unprecedented. Developing mental toughness implies that you can judge correctly. When you have a scenario, you can better evaluate it and decide what you want. All the fun you wish you can have. Actually, you'll never feel guilty if you've developed mental toughness and have decided to indulge. What is the reason? You understand you control the situation, not the other way around. We understand you could have said' no' if you wanted to. Furthermore, the present indulgence can also be a reward for the achievement of your objectives. Go forward in that case and don't lose control while at it because losing is always easier than developing.

Uphold optimism

Do you mainly work with possibilities or impossibilities? In the case of both, which occurs regularly? If you are to achieve mental toughness, optimism is essential. If you're hopeful, it just implies you can handle the scenario you face. You can come up with a solution as soon as possible. But you do not even have to attempt if you see this as an impossible thing. You're disappointed that you face an impossibility, and moreover, you feel stuck. If you feel and think you're stuck shortly thereafter, you will give up. Mentally tough people do not give up no matter what. Your mental toughness journey will be like climbing a steep hill. First and foremost, it is a hill and not a mountain, because you should start small. Secondly, you must be hopeful. Whether it's a hill, see it as a large hill or a high hill. It's very important how you see it. Tell a friend that you'll be climbing mountains and he can join you enthusiastically. Tell him you will climb a mountain and the answer will be quite distinct. You may be asked how good you are, if you have any knowledge, have a first aid kit, etc. Such factors are just as essential, but rarely are extremely crucial. Do you believe it's possible to climb the mountain? You are good to go if your reply is "Yes."

Be in control of your emotions

We all experience emotions. You don't have to be a lady to be emotional. People who say people should not be emotional plot the ruin of men ignorantly. Men should not be crybabies, of course, but certainly should not conceal their feelings. These emotions assist link them with others. It's a fundamental component of humanity. It's essential to remember that you first need to be conscious of feelings. Then you understand how to monitor them. It will also be important to be aware that it may not be possible for others to do the same. And these are society's bulk. People who are angry because somebody has done something wrong, for example, don't regulate their feelings. This control is so crucial that it is one of the key components of management. Emotional intelligence is more frequently referred to. You know what you feel and can say what other individuals feel when you are emotionally smart. You can restrict your reactions so that a bad situation doesn't get worse. You can work on something, for instance, and suddenly you have a discussion with a friend or colleague. Your colleague utters some demeaning phrases and clearly, you get angry which is okay because anger is a normal emotion.

But your answer is the most important thing. You may get physical and lose productivity for the whole day or you can react in kind. You may incur hospital bills if you lose a few teeth. Worse still you may end up losing your job. What if you restricted and even excused yourself? The findings are incredible. Of course, you will prevent this and, above all, you will have time to continue with your job. That will make it more likely that you will complete your job and celebrate your win. See how the better answer has succeeded you? Your mind had been powerful enough to withstand an emotional explosion that might have created many unexpected issues. Acting with emotional intelligence may also get your colleague to realize their mistake and apologize. In such a case, it becomes a win-win scenario and you end up gaining some form of respect from other colleagues who may have witnessed the ordeal.

Exercise the mind

Just like the muscles of your body grow, so does the brain only that it grows slightly differently. The brain grows by multiplying the number of neurons. This is particularly true when you learn fresh stuff. You enhance your capacity to do more by exercising your mind. These include having a clearer recollection of past events. Brain exercises assist you to fix issues in different ways for mental toughness. Your mind teaches you fundamentally how to take into consideration distinct angles, how to anticipate unforeseen turns, etc. In this manner, you are more ready to deal with the unforeseen circumstances that are an ordinary component of your lives. These brain workouts enhance your brain's key function. Therefore, you can focus without coffee for longer, remember more obviously, calculate without a calculator, etc. These apparently tiny advantages enable you, once everybody else has given up to handle more challenging duties. You stay the only one standing when the power of others is gone. This is the distinctive defining feature of mental strength. As a matter of fact, certain brain exercises are formulated as games so you can enjoy yourself as you learn.

Be determined

Determination is the capacity to remain in course despite the unfavorable conditions. If you are not determined, you can never win. One way to remain determined is to know the significance of what you want to accomplish. Once the importance of your objective is evident, you can look at it. You will pass through every barrier that appears if you do not allow diversion between you and your aim. You will do all you need to do to overcome the difficulties. It has many other elements of mental toughness. This resolve is highly strong. For instance, you are constantly hopeful that what you want to do is feasible when you are determined. You won't complain about the condition either. You are aware that you are going to remove the barrier, pass through it, or in any other manner. What's important is that you won't stop anything.

Flexibility

Change is constant. Although the declaration is an oxymoron on the ground, it nevertheless paints an image of change. So how do you deal with this, particularly given that changing your plans often amounts to nothing? The response is flexibility or adaptability. You understand that you have to modify your plans anytime if you are flexible. You have perhaps produced the best plans, but the situation changes and your plan is not valid anymore. This is going to occur in your life many times. You have better chances of success if you can make changes and make them rapidly. This is very crucial in circumstances where you have made a decision without all information. As new information comes and events unfold, you will soon realize that your current plan cannot be continued. So, what do you do? What are you doing? You will rapidly modify your plans and determine which previous activities need to be altered and which actions can be abandoned. You will have less struggle with the needed modifications in your lives if you have this characteristic. This implies that you save time by taking fresh choices rapidly and implementing them appropriately.

Remain focused

If all job is to be well done and finished rapidly, it requires undivided attention. You have to focus on the work on which you work in order to achieve this. Multi-tasking is often praised as an excellent ability to demonstrate your skill, but it isn't. Multi-tasking is a wonderful distraction, particularly when you work on something that demands concentration. As long as your focus is divided into two or more tasks, your mind can't do its best. Multiple tasks can be fun. It can even appear to get a job done more quickly. But this is true only for pcs, not for people. You are likely to be wrong in the job you do if you are not concentrated. Errors are often expensive to reverse and some are so large that companies can lose heavily. These are the kind of errors that cause products to be recalled and major PR campaigns planned to calm down angry clients. However, you prevent unnecessary distraction and save time by attaining objectives more quickly when you keep the present job and your objectives in focus.

Few things in life are comparable to having mental toughness and emotional resilience. Though you may have to put in much effort, it is a worthy investment in the long run that opens u your path for success and a healthier lifestyle.

CHAPTER 9: ASSESSING YOUR MENTAL STRENGTH

Are you mentally tough? Do you have what it takes to be mentally tough? Do you wish to be mentally tough? If so, why? There are numerous misconceptions about what mental toughness means and why everyone should purpose to master its art. As explained in this book, mental toughness is about having the ability to manage your emotion at the face of adversities and the ability to uphold productive behavior always despite the circumstance surrounding your environment. Just like developing physical strength, building mental strength requires a lot of hard work, time and energy input. Additionally, just like you track your physical workout progress, it is also advisable to track your mental toughness progress and determine the areas where you have improved and where you need to put in more effort. However, assessing mental toughness may not be as simple and straightforward as assessing physical workout results. This is because you can determine a person's physical strength and workout progress just by looking at them which is not the case when it comes to mental toughness assessment. In some cases, a qualified psychologist may be required to conduct a thorough mental toughness assessment on an individual especially among elite athletes who rely on their mental toughness to win. However, for people who are trying to develop mental toughness for their own benefit, it is possible to assess progress at home by answering a few crucial questions as noted herein. The effects of mental toughness are felt by an individual and are more internal than external. Therefore, an honest self-reflection exercise is paramount to developing and maintaining mental toughness. It helps in understanding your strengths and determining the areas that require more input in order to enhance your mental strength. Start by answering the following questions.

Are you good at regulating your thoughts?

The personal conversations you have when alone are core ate boosting your overall well-being. Though is common to be harsh to yourself at times, talking to yourself about some of the issues that affect you or the challenges you may be facing like you would to a best friend is actually very healthy and core at developing mental toughness. However, it is important to reason realistically because having negative thoughts always can be damaging and prevent you from being productive or achieving your goals. On the other hand, too much positive thoughts can also be harmful because they do not prepare for negative eventualities. Your brain is only prepared for success and not a failure. So, when failure occurs, it will be hard for you to accept and move on. Answer the following questions to assess your mindset.

What is the inaccurate conclusion you have about yourself?
• Are there things you beat yourself up for?

• What excuses do you allow yourself to make?

• How do you define success?

• What do you tell yourself when experience failure?

• What do you base your self-worth upon?

• What do you feel and think when you face rejection?

• Do you experience any type of self-doubt?

• When do you feel confident with yourself?

How well do you manage your emotions?

Unlike what most people think, mentally tough people do not suppress their emotions whether they are good or bad. On the contrary, they are always aware of their emotions and above all, they understand how their emotions determine their thoughts and actions. As such, they are open to facing uncomfortable emotions like anxiety and fear when they are required to in order to achieve bigger goals. They do not escape or avoid uncomfortable and painful emotions. Instead, they apply healthy coping skills to address any distressing situations they encounter. To determine how you manage your emotions, answer the following questions.

- How do you react to emotional pain?

- What type of emotion is most likely to get to you?

- What type of fears bars you from achieving your greatest potential?

- What are the emotions you avoid most?

- When do you feel happiest?

- What emotions make you behave out of character?

- What strategies can you use to boost your spirit when feeling down?

- Can you recognize when your emotions are starting to get out of control?

- What do you do when you start experiencing self-pity?

How do you keep your behavior productive?

Developing mental toughness is all about understanding when you should change your behavior and when you should change your environment as well. There are times when you can work on improving self-discipline so that you are able to deal with temptation better and there are times when the only thing you can do is change your environment so that you can bring out the best in you. Other times, productive behavior entails doing the things that you would not wish to do. It may also be about performing behavioral experiments that help you in proving your negative predictions false. Mastering mental toughness helps a person to respond to different hardships effectively as well as overcome obstacles with ease. This way, you are able to make better choices about yourself and when the decisions you make are not very popular. Answer the following questions to determine whether your behavior is productive.

- When do you give up fast?

- When do you hold on longer than you should?

- Do you recognize when your behavior does not sync with your values?

- Do you take good care of your body so that the mind can be as tough as possible?

- What mistakes do you make over and over again?

- Do you make short term solutions that cause long term problems?

- Do you dedicate enough time and energy to doing things that you deem important?

- Do you sabotage yourself?

Why assessing your mental toughness is important

Mental toughness differs from other personality concepts in that it defines "how we believe and reason." Most character models and organizational development measures describe "What we do when faced with occurrences." Of course, it's helpful but maybe not very helpful as "why we do things the way we do." Mental toughness offers the chance for this insight. If we need to modify behavior and know why something causes a problem for us, but not for others, then it is fundamental. Professor Clough Peter, who created the 4-Cs framework now the most commonly accepted in the globe, usually defines it as "the way of mind to cope with life as it occurs, taking steps backward, and realizing that the ups and downs of life will come, but we can see opportunities even in the dark." Mental hardening is a spectrum as well. Mental toughness at one end and mental sensitivity, at the other end. Both extremes have their strengths and weaknesses and we all fall somewhere in their spectrum. A mentally delicate person can be efficient and successful given he or she knows his or her psychological hardness and develops methods for using what he or she learns. The same applies to the hard of mind. Without the same self-confidence, they can fight.

Behavior can be easily observed but it is hard to know what a person is thinking in their head. This can be easily misdiagnosed and it occurs more often than we think. This enables consumers to create a level of self-conception that is hard, perhaps impossible, to accomplish by other means. It enables them to work with customers. In addition, this measure is a normative measure that allows for an evaluation of where a change happened before and after a program. Similarly, the evaluation of mental toughness and aggregated outcomes with organizations and entire populations is feasible to gather views on a main aspect of culture. That is essential as well. There is a clear link between cultural and behavioral impact. While the study demonstrates that our mental toughness has a genetic factor, our mental toughness is also a reflection of our experiences. We have learned to be mentally hard or emotionally delicate based on the events that have unfolded in our lives. Consider the present "snowflake generation" discussion. It's a warning. There is no implicit necessity for our mental hardness to evolve. Instead, self-awareness and reflection are essential to our life-long journey. Some mentally delicate people will gladly stay as they are and profit from studying and adopting methods that the mentally difficult ones will embrace. In this sense, they often learn to deal with situations and embrace their strengths. Others will identify some aspect of mental toughness that will benefit from change and will strive to change it in some way. You learn to cope with your state. Whether it is exposure to or through training, reflecting on experiences, previous and present, and drawing learning from them, experiential learning is very efficient here. Many are also well-known for the type of actions that allow mental growth and positive thinking, anxiety control, attention control, visualization, etc. Interestingly, it is also possible to assess the mental strength of an individual more accurately by using MTQ. It allows us to focus on more specific interventions.

In the face of overwhelming barriers, people who are mentally tough and resilient have pursued their visions. They did not allow problems to diminish their drive and commitment to stand in their manner. They may not have achieved anything tangible for years, but the greatest lesson they have learned is the importance of their mental habits for the achievement of their goals.

The first thing that is useful for mental resilience is to get up every morning and get out of bed ready for action. You go to bed and wake up soon so that you can carry out the duties required to achieve your goals. They do not silence the alarm 10 times because they've been out at night partying late. They are not concealed under the cover of ruminating about previous mistakes or things that have gone wrong in their life. The power is gathered to block any negative effects and get out of bed soon. Throughout this day, mentally tough individuals already have a game plan ready. They already understand their duties and start working on them immediately. This does not mean that they always like what they are required to do but, they always get down to work because they are responsible for their daily duties.

Mentally tough and resilient people start the day without fear of the unknown or failure because they understand that failure is part of the success process. For them, it's a learning experience. You take notes and learn what you can't do in the future. Even if they fail, in future plans they generally will have learnt certain fresh abilities. These people are going to brush off, get up and begin again. They are, of course, not sultry with fun because things have not turned out as they wished, but they are not mentally ruined.

When things do not go in the way they plan, the mentally resilient individuals do not take it personally. They acknowledge that they do not have the right to automated achievement and that difficult work, planning, implementation, and luck are needed where luck isn't on their side sometimes. It won't prevent them from working on their goals, because if they keep trying and refuse to give up, they are certain that things will eventually turn out to their favor. Mentally resilient individuals spend a lot of time considering how their objectives will be achieved. They then prepare a match plan for a period of time with benchmarks. They adhere to the plan and are insane in fulfilling the deadlines. All the hateful and the adverse individuals who want them to fail are ignored.

They don't let it go to their heads when the company or their careers really go well. They do not boast about your riches, your fame, your fortune and everything you have bought lately. Still, if things don't work outright, they don't let themselves be despondent. They remain collected, calm and cool. You know there are higher and lower ones and you are attempting to ride with grace and professionalism. They have their own views and they don't care whether the majority disagree with them. Such people don't follow their dreams and passions, rather they pursue them. They are immune to pressure from peers. It's not simple, but it's difficult for them. If individuals see them as being insane, they brush them off because they do not really care about other people's opinions of them.

People with mental resilience understand how to postpone gratification. They save cash to boost their company or career. They can prefer to live with their parents after college or have lots of roommates in affordable parts of the city in order to save up the cash. These people will not buy expensive vehicles and buy the McMansions showy only to gain praise from their neighbors. They want ready cash to finance their efforts and dreams. Mentally robust individuals might be scared, but nevertheless, they are making progress. They're not going to let fear derail them from fulfilling their wishes. It's not simple, but that's what they do things. Our smartphones and everything else around us can easily distract you. Tough-minded people block foreign noise and hyper-focus on what needs to be done.

One of their mantras, "Don't sweat over tiny things." Like most of us, they're not worried about small nonsense. A filthy look from a trained stranger, a driver who cuts you off, a cashier that takes too long to catch up is all not a bother to a mentally strong individual. You can't let these irritants waste your energy. They spare their energy for significant struggles that have significant outcomes. For mentally tough persons, continuous learning is essential. You want to understand all about your sector. They also want to know stuff that will enhance them and make them better informed in life.

It's hard to turn off opportunities, however, but they know when to say "no." They will have the courage to turn things down humbly because they acknowledge that something doesn't fit in with their game plan or long-term objectives. We are all under pressure, but it doesn't break the mentally resilient individuals. They work hard to be able to cope with the difficult times physically and mentally. All these features are interesting because they look so simple and feasible and can be achieved. Everything comes down to the commitment to achieve it. Most of these individuals are not incredibly brilliant or charismatic. They often begin from the modest beginnings and against our perceived concepts of riches. They hold dear the mental strength they require to evolve and operate like hell is what they abound in, notwithstanding all reverses and failures. The incredible thing is that we can do this all as well.

Hence, it is evident that we not only need to develop mental toughness and resilience but we must be willing to assess our mental strength progress in order to know where we stand as well as what needs to be changed in order to tap into our optimum mental hardiness. There are numerous mental toughness exercises that an individual can complete; they are designed to test different aspects of mental toughness and resilience.

CHAPTER 10: MENTAL TOUGHNESS TRAINING

Experts define mental toughness as a crucial factor required in order to succeed under highly stressful work and life environments. When fighting challenges, mental toughness is what helps you to remain in control of things, cope with adversities effectively and sustain a significant level of performance geared towards a predetermined goal. But what happens if you do not have a mentally tough psychological state? Do you accept and agree to fail when working under stressful conditions? Or do you find ways to develop mental hardiness? The good news is that mental toughness can be trained, mastered and developed in order to help you deal with what life throws at you with much ease and effectiveness.

Working under stressful conditions is never an easy task. This is because, people overlook the fact that your environment is stressful and expect you to work efficiently, effectively and fast to outdo your competition. Due to such expectations under poor working conditions, it is possible for the best performer to switch from excellence to feeling exhausted, overworked and at the blink of burning out. In light of this, there are people who cannot perform under mounting pressures and they recognize that fact. However, they also know that though they cannot do much to change the stressful working environment, they can develop skills in order to change their response to the harsh working environment. This is referred to as the dual nature of stress where a situation is triggered by external pressures and a person reacts accordingly through their internal response. As such, people who have mastered the art of mental toughness emphasize on developing their internal response adaptability and what they can do to improve it. Mental toughness is defined by traits like; confidence, positive attitude, the desire to succeed, focus, determination, perseverance, and emotional regulation. It is what differentiates those who thrive and those who crack under pressure.

Be a self-starter

Motivation is at the root of mental strength. Those considered to be mentally tough usually show what sports psychologists refer to as the' inherent' motive. This is defined by a research carried out in Psychology of motor behavior. People who are inherently motivated are self-starters who are prepared to push hard for the love of what they do and want to accomplish. They need little encouragement to do their best and often set their own objectives. This does not happen to all of us, of course. Some people can only get their heads into a match if the rivalry is under pressure. They thrive at the opportunity to compare themselves with others.

The people have "motive for accomplishment": all things equal between two rivals, and those who are more motivated by accomplishment, are better at what they do. "The calling of an individual driven to prevent a pantywaist from failing if he does not get 10 representatives on his next series of Squats makes him feel that his virility is being demeaned." Achievement motivation features two opposing mentalities that are capable of driving a person to develop mental resilience. Both are present in every individual but a person leans to one or the other. Individuals who are driven by the desire to succeed tend to gather their energies better when they know that a great opportunity is about to present itself. Even when the probability that the opportunity will turn out right is low, they believe that they can utilize it if they work harder.

The opposite of that is known as the reason for preventing failure. These people can only respond to their ego-threatening difficulties. Calling an individual who is motivated to prevent a pantywaist from failure if he does not get 10 of his next set, causes him to feel that his manhood is under attack. It makes sense for people to know that success is simple to attain when focusing on circumstances. If the job looks straightforward, their trust is high. But if an obstacle is seen as an extreme challenge, it can also be coped out, because you don't think it can be overcome.

Understanding which of these two characteristics dominates for you is the key to enhancing your mental toughness training and to endure more challenges along the way. Most coaches report that successful players don't need to be taught or persuading when chips are running out in a game; they view it as a chance for turning stuff around and being heroes. Players whose focus is to prevent failure, however, need that direction. You need guidance to know what to do so you feel that if you are back in a corner you can respond properly. If not guided, they feel like they lack an opportunity to thrive. Take your average soccer game, for instance.

In the final seconds of the match, one team is up by two points. The opponent team got the ball and just got over the center of the field. An excellent trainer or quarterback must inform the players who most probably concentrate on failure precisely what to do to cover their land in an area defense or simply to work on their footwork while covering their passes. This type of instruction removes a player's self-induced stress so that he can concentrate on the job in hand.

This logic is not confined to athletic cases only. You might also discover the power inside and lift an intimidating weight by concentrating on simple techniques and strategies that would make the lifting seem easier especially if you are fearful of failure and you are going on for another max. You can remember to let your body fall back as the hips move forward and to take a monstrous load to activate glute and hamstring. If you feel overwhelmed with imminent office deadlines, generate an overview list to help you save time. Do everything possible to eliminate possible stressors and facilitate productivity.

Determine your zone

Consider this: "World-class endurance sportsmen react to the pressure of a race by reducing brain-wave activities that resemble meditation," says the strong and conditioning coach and triathlete Rachel Cosgrove." The average individual reacts to race pressure by increasing brain wave activities which are limited to panic." This is a prime instance of how getting into "zone" athletes can create a whole difference in your performance. The cool-headed state, which enables an individual to perform in an optimal manner even in high pressures. Realizing that state and sticking to it for self-preservation, despite distractions, suffering and your own instincts boosts mental toughness.

Remain positive

Your mind is on a dialog every day whether you realize it or not. The thinking generally combines outside stimuli with your own views about yourself. Some of them are going to be negative, but in order to succeed, you must concentrate on those that make you feel better. It sounds like heartfelt advice, but you would find it difficult to find a successful individual who does not practice this. For instance, if you believe you cannot finish a marathon, then you certainly will not even attempt to try. One simple way to be in a positive mood is by creating a mission statement that pumps you.

In this case, take the time to consider why you should run a marathon; compete in a specific competition, add 10 pounds of muscle, or gain recognition. Make why your mission statement and keep repeating it during your training sessions. Each time you feel like slacking and demotivated, repeat the mission statement in your head.

Have self-talk

You ought to be your own mental toughness trainer. In the second person, encourage yourself with statements, like,' You'll give all that you've got,'" It can simulate additional motivation as compared to what your mental toughness coach would offer. It can also regulate encouragement offered by your trainer; as mentioned above, you can better react to one type of advice than to another. It is important to learn to speak favorably with yourself when things get hard. Remind yourself that but you're better at doing things and everything will turn out just right. You should be in a position to speak to yourself and encourage yourself just before an important event that requires much dedication and is bound to drive towards winning.

Visualize

Before you even set out to begin working towards your goal, your goal should be achieved mentally. This is by visualizing all the steps that you should take to get to the right position and achieve your goals. Visualize the physical input you require and rehearse in the mind to ensure that you are mentally prepared for any eventuality. It is important to visualize yourself as a winner and an achiever. This gives you a unique level of motivation to attempt even the hardest tasks that you would otherwise not even think of trying. Feed the mind what the body should do and expect then get down to action.

Meditate

Diverse types of meditation, including stress reduction, enhanced mental clarity, and easy relaxation were used for almost thousands of years for almost every purpose. But to make it work, you don't have to go all the way and have a meditation room like setup. Skip the candles and Enya's songs and concentrate on clearing your mind of foreign ideas and preparing for the next competition or confrontation mentally. When they begin to meditate one of the greatest problems is to know if you are doing it properly. In some

cases, you may feel you cannot focus sufficiently well to enter a meditative state. The trick is to ensure that you are completely calm and relaxed before starting the meditation. Meditation heals the mind and helps you to into the deep mental parts that are responsible for enhancing
mental toughness.

Get uncomfortable
You cannot be comfortable with a routine that constantly gets your down and expects to go far. If you are attempting to be more mentally tough, you need to exercise the brain little longer or more quickly than you are accustomed to a couple of times a month. The mental toughness training sessions should be random just like wearing your running shoes one day and deciding to challenge your running or jogging limits. The same applies to the weight space and to life as a whole. Take action classes, go skydiving, or learn the tango. As progression is a significant component of your practice, using any challenge stimulus in your life provides you with a better capacity to cope with all types of stress and develop mental toughness. You learn new skills and the importance of critical thinking prior to reacting to adversities.

Always be prepared

Endurance athletes say: "Nothing is fresh during race day." That means, if you are all ready for it, you will be ready. You ought to understand what to eat, wear, and even think about that day well ahead of a challenge. Of course, you cannot be ready for every event, but it is crucial to attempt it anyway. Think about any issues that might occur and come up with a solution. For instance, during the triathlon, challenges would be something like; flat bicycle pneumatics, your glasses can be shot while you're swimming or getting blistered. It will be mentally helpful if you know that you have done all you can to reach your objective by being prepared to deal with challenges that arise along the way.

Maintain a trusted inner circle

A trusted inner circle is not just a group of people you believe cannot betray you by putting your dirty laundry out in the public. If you want to be successful and above all develop mental toughness, it is crucial that you have a group of the trusted inner circle that challenges you to be a better version of yourself. This includes having mentors and strong career network team that can easily help you get to the next phase of success. Such people also understand the importance of maintaining a positive and clean public image. Therefore, they would readily be there to assist you with cleaning your dirty laundry before it escalates to real problem or gets to the wrong hands.

Importance of Mental Toughness Training

So how do you handle the mental toughness training and application in real life? When things go your way, it's simple to feel strong and powerful. Your brain is already designed to give you a strong and relaxed mentality in the event of exterior conditions in your favor. But how do you get the right brain cocktail mix for yourself, regardless of what happens, so that your mental state doesn't depend on outside conditions? The key is to train and keep a positive, vigorous attitude so it doesn't matter. The scientists discovered that expanded, open postures promote greater testosterone concentrations and reduced cortisol concentrations, whereas closed, shrinking and restricted positions are contrary. They even discovered it helpful to take overly open positions before stressful circumstances. But while such a fake it till you make it last-minute trick can do a bit of a difference, it will not take you very much to imitate open positions. This is because the main issue is not to hit your knees and sit directly. The posture and body language of the average person is profoundly constrained by chronic neuromuscular tension, which forms an inner barrier and permanently and profoundly transforms your mental toughness state.

The inner opponent is a neuromuscular full-body armor that grows in early adolescence over a lifetime and is manifest not only as chronic muscular or neurological tension but as fear, ego, anxiety, stress, and concern. It gives your mind continual signals that it is in physical and real risk, and it allows your mind to run in circles to try to fix an issue of survival that does not exist. That is the root of all mental issues at the base of the depth, the oldest part of the brain. And this cortisol-soaked, reptile, fight-or-flight-anxiety influences your brain far more than any beneficial thinking, statements or motivational quotes you can give. Therefore, in order to develop mental toughness, it is important to dissolve the neuromuscular tensions so as to reclaim your nervous system and trigger the body to mutate to the original primal and relaxed posture. If you achieve this, the brain slowly adopts the core mental toughness traits; low stress and high dominance.

That's what Neuromuscular Release Work (NRW) is doing, and why it has been applied for years as the main technology for mental education and coaching. It is a kind of exercise that dissolves these profound, chronic layers of neuromuscular tensions to create effortless, natural and primal mental resilience by breaking the physical, neurological mind code. You can feel that your psychic toughness is changing your attitudes, actions, and performance during this phase. And it's also felt by other individuals around you. Push it far enough and you can easily reach the flow state, or area; the zero resistance and peak performance state which occurs randomly and rarely. When you achieve this, you have attained a unique level of mental toughness and you are bound to experience the world differently.

Perhaps the most important task for mental toughness training is to find out what it is. It looks like a simple question, but ask everyone what mental strength is, and see how many "uhs" and "um" are needed before there comes a halfway coherent answer. Indeed, go ahead and see whether you can come up with a concept yourself before reading. Is every element of the mental game taken into consideration? Is it consistent and unified? Is it accurate and concrete? If we are to approach instruction in mental toughness as a science, we must understand precisely what we are doing. We need a precise, scientific and operational definition, not just a loose definition. For instance, take trust. When we see it, we all understand it or believe we do. But can you bring a person into a workshop and measure their level of confidence, resilience or motivation? No, it is not possible. These are all excellent characteristics and worth striving for, but they are unclear, slippery and immeasurable. It is difficult to know whether you really have them, if you only have them sometimes, or if you have more or less of them today than you did yesterday. That's why so many mental qualities are called "intangibles." This is the stalemate where some people throw their hands up and say it is not possible to train for mental toughness.

But what if basic mental toughness parameters were measured? Qualities which are essentially physical and are at the root of all these intangibles. What if you could train qualities as accurately as you train strength, speed, or mobility? Well, this is actually possible. The main mental toughness parameters are; high dominance and low stress. These qualities may at first appear to be as intangible as any other. However, the testosterone (the hormone in dominance) and cortisol (the stress hormone) do have a real, physical and measurable presence. Recent scientific research confirms the qualities that are mainly based on the levels of these two hormones, which are associated with "alpha" individuality and feelings of power, risk tolerance, leadership ability (in our language, mental toughness) adhere to the levels of the two hormones. When there are high levels of testosterone and low levels of cortisol, people perform under pressure well. They show all the qualities we connect with mental toughness. The reverse of the recipe is poor performance, fear, and frayed nerves. Hardcore, physical realities define these hormones. From your thoughts, they are not open to negotiation because they act before your thoughts can take effect and before you gain conscious awareness. They determine how you deal with different circumstances, how you perform, how you react to issues as well as how you think.

At any given moment, they dictate who you are. They are the essential and fundamental elements of thinking, and in some abstract mental world, they are not present. They are present in your blood and in your brain. All those intangibles—confidence, focus, motivation, capacity to act under pressure—come naturally and without effort, when you have them dialed in. They don't if you don't. That's because the intangibles, rather than their cause, are consequences of mental toughness. Therefore you cannot think, hope, and imagine your way into true mental hardness. The good news is that you are not obliged to. If you have a genuine, systemic approach to training mental hardness in the brain, you do not need a motivational speech or coach to get you to act. It will be easy and natural to pick the right mental toughness traits and develop them for your own good.

CHAPTER 11: HOW TO PRACTICE STOICISM?

The philosophy of stoicism is designed such that it encourages and helps people to lead the best version of their life. It is a philosophy that actively tries to optimize the positive emotions you experience while minimizing any negative ones and thereby helping you to hone your character.

Stoicism provides the skeletal framework essential to lead a good life regardless of where you are at life. Stoicism was created deliberately to understand life and come up with actionable goals that are practical and attainable.

These days, it feels like stoicism is having a renaissance in the modern world. From politicians to entrepreneurs and everyone else in between seems fascinated with the concept of stoicism.

Stoicism is an ancient philosophy that can be traced back to ancient Greece and Rome during the early parts of the 3rd Century BC. It is quintessential that you keep in mind that the thought process was quite different back then. The primary concern for many was to avoid leading an unfortunate life. Therefore, they were more interested in doing things, thinking such thoughts and behaving in such a manner that will increase their satisfaction in life. You must remember that in the ancient world, no one automatically assumed that by earning money and acquiring materialistic things, they will gain happiness. At that time, all those people simply desired to find a way in which they can have an excellent soul.

Stoicism is a popular school of thought that managed to answer compelling questions related to anxiety, fear, stress, the meaning of life, and the purpose of life. The answer to all this was that you must lead a virtuous life to attain happiness and tranquility in life.

For instance, a person can hone their virtues by giving more importance to their deeds instead of their words. Stoicism is based on the belief that positive behavior helps create a positive life experience and vice versa. This school of thinking prescribes a particular way of thinking and living. The primary focus of stoicism is on leading a virtuous life, on finding happiness and reducing any negative emotions.

When we think of followers of a certain philosophy or thinking or order, we always visualize how they look. So since we are talking about Stoicism and Stoics, do you have any idea what a Stoic looks like? Do they wear white robes? Do they carry a Stoic bible? Do they meditate all the time?

Some people who have only heard the tip of the iceberg of Stoicism or Stoics for that matter, often have negative perceptions mainly due to the indifference and the emotionless principles that they have on certain scenarios.

Think of all the stiff upper lip, resting bitch face kind of personalities you often see on TV or in movies, celebrities like Kanye West or Anna Kendrick and Kristen Stewart are people who look like they repress all their emotions. Think Christina Yang of Grey's Anatomy or Scarlett O'Hara in Gone with the Wind. They may look like they don't care or do not have emotions but deep down, they are people that care a lot for the people closest to them which is what the Stoic principle endorses.

The Ultimate Stoic Characteristic

To the Stoics, true beauty lies the in the character of the person. The ideal Stoic doesn't walk around with a halo around their heads or a bible in their hands. The Adonis of Stoicism is a perfectly wise and good person.

Donald Robertson, a Modern Stoic who describes the ideal Stoic as:

- supremely virtuous

- The epitome of a perfect human being

- The moral approximation to Zeus

- A good person with total serenity

- Attainment of perfect Happiness and fulfillment, or eudaimonia

- Lives in total harmony with themselves and the people around them

- Lives according to Nature's virtues

- Follows reason and graciously accepts fate

- Rises above irrational desires and emotions

- Achieves total peace of mind

- Enjoys the joys of life

- Completely unafraid of their own death

- Possesses supreme practical wisdom, benevolence, justice, and courage

- Has self-discipline

- Praiseworthy, beautiful and honorable

These characteristics summarize the Stoic principles. These characteristics are used by the Stoic as a fictitious ideal in order to compare and contemplate against their own characteristics. The Stoics build this ideal role model that they can compare themselves against and make progress to reach the virtues that they want.

Socrates was the role model for Epictetus as Socrates was the real-life epitome of the Stoic Sage. During his lifetime, Socrates advised his students to live like his ideals. Socrates filled his life by making sure his thoughts were focused on reasoning everything that came his way.

He preached to his followers, that although they have not yet attained Socrates's level, they should still live as someone who wants to become a Socrates.

In other words, we should all try to attain life like Socrates.

In your life, a great help is to ask oneself 'What would a Stoic Sage do in a situation like this?'. This question can be tweaked to fit the various daily issues we face. For example, you could ask yourself 'What would the perfect parent do? Or 'What would the perfect friend do?' or 'What would the perfect boss do?''.

It may seem far-fetched to say perfect but the Stoics keep an exemplary all the time so that they would always remember to live as an example and come each day, closer to reaching a virtuous life.

Seneca said, "Without a ruler to do it against you won't make the crooked straight."

A Stoic can be anyone that embodies virtues- it could be a stay-at-home dad or a businesswoman or a school teacher or a mechanic. Anyone can become a Stoic, trying to reach virtues on many different levels of Stoicism.

CHAPTER 12: EUDAIMONIA AND EMOTIONAL RESILIENCE

Eudaimonism is termed as a type of moral philosophy that denotes the right action on needs to take to attain wellbeing in an individual. It is part of the virtue ethics system of Greek Philosophers, where you practice virtues all your life in every day activity and resolve any dilemmas or conflicts by practical wisdom, allowing individuals to flourish well and lead a happy and good life, which is eudaimonia.

In Greek, Eudaimonia means happiness, but it is better denoted as good life, flourishing of humanity or wellbeing. In general, the term denotes any theory that emphasizes on happiness and the fulfilling life of a person with ethics as the central core. Thus, it can be related to egoism and ethical individualism.

Stoics have a bad reputation when it comes to emotions. If you call someone stoic in normal conversation, you usually mean that they repress their emotions or that they are emotionless. Sometimes it is a compliment, but often it isn't a very good thing. If you are stoic as a partner or a friend, for instance, people might think they lack emotional intimacy with you.

Further, if we are to return to the schema that we've discussed throughout the book—the difference between things that are up to you and not up to you—emotions seem to mess things up. We normally think emotions have a vital influence on our happiness and most people think of our emotions as somehow not up to us. Sadness or anger happen to us, they aren't within our control.

For the Stoics, however, emotions are within our control. Emotions are products of judgments and therefore they are subject to control. This is the sense in which the colloquial meaning of stoic has some accuracy. Stoic philosophy does think that you should have control over your emotions, but it does not think that you should not have them. Because emotions are a product of judgment, there are some situations where it is appropriate to have an emotion. If a beloved relative died tragically, it is appropriate to have the emotion of sadness.

But emotions often don't feel much like judgments. It is easy to think of times in our lives when we have felt overcome by emotion, in much the same way a physical force can push us down.

If you imagine a seafaring philosopher in a great storm, he might feel terror. He observes a wave taller than his head and that physical set of affairs makes an impression on him. Unconsciously, we add a value judgment to our impressions that says, "There is a wave taller than my head and that is terrible." If we assent to this value-laden impression, we will have an emotional response. The philosopher, however, can refuse to assent to the value judgment. He might be briefly overcome by terror, but once he consciously recognizes that he has added the value judgment to the true impression of the thing, he can reject it and return control to his emotions.

This "first movement" of terror before he is able to regain control of his emotions is an important part of the story. For the Stoics, this first reaction is not a genuine emotion. It is not a judgment. It is a physical response that people have before they have a chance to make a judgment and thus, form a proper emotion. If there is a sudden noise, a lot of people would jump. This is not the emotion of fear. If the noise happens in your house in the middle of the night with no explicable cause, then you will first jump out of reflex before making the judgment that fear is appropriate and feeling the emotion of fear.

It is important to keep this distinction in mind because it allows us to both respond to the lived experience of thoughtless reflex and create the space necessary for us to have control over our emotions. Because emotions are a product of us assenting to a judgment about the world, they are within our control and things that we should control. Many emotions are products of faulty reasoning and therefore are a type of disease of the soul. Often, emotions are the result of poor reasoning on our parts. The actions we take out of emotion can also have grave consequences.

This relationship between judgment and emotion has a great deal of resonance with the modern psychological theory of "cognitive behavioral therapy." This theory relies on the space between things happening in the world and our judgment about those things in order to help people have more adaptive responses to problems. Maladaptive behavior often results from the feeling that we are forced to act in certain ways by the actions of others and events in the world. If we feel someone cutting us off in traffic causes anger, we might feel justified in tailgating the other driver or otherwise driving dangerously. These actions might lead to negative consequences.

The best way to gain control over our lives is to refuse to let ourselves off the hook. Emotions, especially emotions that feel like they compel us to action, are choices. We can choose to affirm these emotions or to reject them, even if the first physical reaction is beyond our control.

CHAPTER 13 : SOME PRACTICES OF STOICISM

Cultivating a state of mindfulness is one of the fundamentals of applying Stoicism to everyday life. It is defined as a state in which you are actively paying attention to the present moment. If you've ever tried to practice mindfulness for any period of time, then you know how difficult it can be. It is very hard to tame our minds and focus our attention. But the benefits of practicing mindfulness are vast. It allows us not to give in to our emotions, since we can observe them from a distance. Mindfulness also lets us fully enjoy our lives by living in the present. As Marcus Aurelius said, those who do not observe how their minds move must be unhappy.

There are six mental exercises that Stoics have used to develop the self-discipline needed to practice mindfulness:

Reflect in the Morning

Practicing mindfulness in the morning is a great way to be prepared for the rest of the day. Very often, when we start the day we feel stressed because we are getting ready to go to work and we feel rushed, we feel pressured because we are afraid we are going to be late, we are thinking about the traffic and other problems we're going to encounter. If you're a mother, you have to get the children ready to go to school, they have to get dressed and you have to make them breakfast. With all of this facing us, it's no wonder we feel a little crazy.

Marcus Aurelius also suffered from the problem of having to get up in the morning and having to face the day. He was emperor and had an empire to run! So what does he suggest? Tell yourself: I have to go to work. Of course, he also prepared himself for the difficulties that he would face by reminding himself: today I will be meeting ingratitude, insolence, selfishness, interference and ill-will – all due to the offender's ignorance of good and evil. By doing this, his intention was not to start his day on a sour note, but rather to prepare himself to face things as they were, and not as he wanted them to be.

How can we begin our day on a more positive note? By making time for mindfulness practice. You can do so by setting your alarm clock to wake up thirty minutes earlier, for instance.

What activities can you do to practice mindfulness? The simplest one is to take a short walk around where you live. You don't even need to get out of the house if it's not practical or safe for you to walk outside; you can even just walk around your home. What is important is that while you are walking, you are completely in the moment, actively aware of what you are seeing, feeling and hearing.

You can also keep a mindfulness journal. Don't let the word "journal" intimidate you, since you can choose the form in which it will take. For instance, you can use it to supplement your mindfulness walk by writing down, in as much detail as you can, what you observed while you were walking. Or you can write about a memory from your past, putting down everything that you can remember about it.

Alternately you can just write down 500 words on a topic. It doesn't even have to make sense; what is important is that you just let the words out on the page. The purpose of this exercise is to help you remove blocks to your creativity by writing without prejudging what you're writing. Just write and be in the moment.

Here is a simple writing prompt to help you get started. Start by writing down the words "I feel". Complete the sentence and then continue from there. Let's say you write, "I feel bad". Then you can write about why you feel bad, how you feel about feeling bad, and so on.

You can also integrate mindfulness into your morning routine by doing a chore while being in the present. For instance, let's say you're making coffee. Instead of just doing this task automatically or thoughtlessly, you can do it mindfully. Pick up the jar of coffee and note how it feels in your hand. Note how cool the bottle feels and how the curve of it fits into your hand. Then when you turn the lid to open it, note how much pressure you have to exert and what your hand feels like. Then pick up a spoon and note how that feels in your hand. When you dip the spoon in the jar, note what noise it makes and the slight pressure as the spoon penetrates the coffee granules.

No matter what method of journaling you choose, what is important is that you make it a regular habit. One way that you can do this is to set aside a particular time to do your journaling during which you know you won't be disturbed.

Focus on Your Goals

One of the problems with living in the modern world is that there are so many distractions that it can be hard for us to keep our attention focused on the moment at hand, much less on achieving our goals. For instance, our smartphones are constantly beeping, telling us that there is an SMS that has just come in, or there is a new tweet from someone we are following or a new email has come into our inbox.

In addition, there is the pressure for us to be 'multi-tasking' since otherwise we feel we are not doing enough. These days, young people no longer pay full attention when they are watching TV or a movie since they are constantly looking down at their phones, answering messages or playing games. And of course, there is the natural human instinct to procrastinate. When we have a task that we have to complete, and the deadline is not yet close, there is a tendency for us to put it off until the time that we actually have to finish it.

How can you use mindfulness practice to help you focus and achieve your goals? One obvious way is to cut up your goal into smaller, doable tasks, and then do them one at a time. Instead of allowing yourself to be overwhelmed by how much you have to do, focus on a more achievable task that you have to do.

Another method that you can use to help you achieve goals is to turn them into 'non-goals'. What this basically means is that, instead of making long-term plans to achieve your goal, you instead focus on the present and how to integrate into your daily life small methods of meeting your goal.

To illustrate, let's say you want to eliminate your credit card debt. The traditional ways to do so would include making a budget to control your spending and creating a repayment plan. But these methods are all future-focused and require you to be in a state of unhappiness since you are constantly thinking about how much longer you have to go before you are finally debt-free.

Instead, focus on things that you can do in the present. For instance, you can set up an automated debit at the bank to pay for your outstanding balances. You can cut up your cards and only pay for things with cash. And when you are buying things, be conscious about why you are buying them. For instance, you can ask: do I need this, or do I just want it?

Using this method of achieving your goals helps keep you focused in the present moment instead of constantly thinking about your problem and how it's affecting you.

Accept the Natural Way

One of the painful realities of life is that we will eventually lose everything that we love, including our own lives. Everything passes, and we have to accept it. It is the way of nature, wherein things die and move on.

Obviously, accepting loss is very difficult for most people. In fact, even thinking about losing something they love is sure to make them distraught. This is why Stoics prepare themselves to accept loss.

Epictetus advised Stoics to try this mental exercise: imagine a cup that you like. Now imagine that it breaks. You think to yourself, it's just a cup and I can bear the loss. Apply this exercise to everything else that is meaningful to you – your house, car, loved ones, even your pet.

Epictetus pointed out that most people treat others' losses as part of the natural order and say, it happens. But when it happens to them, then it becomes more difficult to deal with the loss. Loss is the way of nature. By yielding to it, you won't blame nature for what happens, but instead focus on what lies within your power to affect.

One way you can deal with loss is to take the long view. Consider the story of the Daoist philosopher Zhuangzi. After his wife died, a friend visited him and found him singing and going happily about his normal routine. His friend was shocked at the way he was acting, and asked him how he could do such a thing.

Zhuangzi explained that, at first, he was distraught. Then he considered that at the start of the universe, his wife did not exist. But then she was born and she existed for a while. Then things changed and she died. If he were to cry, then it would show that I have not accepted the laws of nature.

Marcus Aurelius also advised Stoics to remember that in the long term, not only will you have forgotten everything, but the world will also move on when you're gone and everyone will forget you. Consider how many people were famous in their time, but have been virtually forgotten today.

CHAPTER 14: HOW TO DEAL WITH YOURSELF WHEN LIFE GETS TOUGH?

You must learn that once you decide to do something, the only time you stop is to take a break, or when you have failed. In these cases you are pausing (not stopping) to review and learn from what you have just failed at, or achieved. In the first two scenarios, you take your break, or you pick yourself up, analyze your failure, and you get back to it. In the third scenario, you analyze your success.

For the first two, a break gives you the respite you need to stay fresh and gain perspective. If you fail, you must look at the steps that got you there and tweak your next attempt and get back to it.

There are two things you must do. Firstly, take the failure as a lesson and not a strike against yourself. Never feel regret or feel depressed.

Secondly, you must reflect on the actions preceding the failure and figure out the cause of the failure. The more you learn, the more you know how not to do something. When asked about his failure when inventing the bulb, Edison said that he just found ten thousand ways how to not make a bulb. Imagine that. Imagine if he had given up at eight thousand. Most people may have given up at eight.

When you misunderstand the nature of failure, you will always find excuses, and you will always find exits. When you misunderstand the importance of your existence, you will turn into a consumer, not a contributor; a spectator, not a gladiator.

To properly understand the nature of failure you need to first stop thinking of failure in negative terms. Failure is not an inadequacy in itself; it is merely the consequence of your own inadequacy in knowing the full extent of what you are doing. And that's not a bad thing. When a child is born, do you expect it to read? Does that mean they're inadequate? Certainly not. Just because the child is not able to instantly remember and recite the alphabet after you spent the day teaching them, does not mean the they should stop learning to read. Do you see the absurdity of the suggestion?

That's how absurd it is to see failure as a reason to stop continuing or finding the way to your goal. You do not stop trying just because things are not going your way. You make yourself keep going, pick yourself up, dust yourself off and try again — success is yours. That's all there is to it!

The one-thousandth fall is just a stand-in to describe many failures. It describes the point of fracture. For some people it could be ten while for others it could be three, but for a few, that number is non-existent because they have made a hard and fast rule that they will not give up in anything once they start.

CHAPTER 15 : 3 EXERCISES

1) **How to Deal With Grief**

Another misconception we tend to hold about happiness is that it's an all-or-nothing state. We tend to think that in order to be happy, we should not only feel positive emotions but also experience a lack of negative feelings such as sadness, uncertainty, and grief. This leads to the typical Western scenario in which we look around at our secure homes, access to clean water, 24/7 entertainment and wonder why we can't "just be happy."

We forget that we are human, and there is room for us to feel negative emotions along with gratitude and happiness. Our moods are often subject to variables beyond our control, and sometimes we must accept that there is no immediately obvious reason why we feel the way we do. Have you ever woken up one morning feeling unusually cheerful but then found yourself more downcast a few days later? This is completely normal, but we tend to forget that not everything needs an explanation. If you make self-discipline a priority, these day-to-day fluctuations won't bother you. You'll be too busy making sure that you are meeting your goals and obligations.

By now, the limitations of our Western ideas of suffering and happiness should be clear. We cannot hope to become happy by avoiding all suffering, as we often try to do, because some of it is unavoidable. In reality, happiness can only be attained when we manage to avoid the unnecessary suffering. How can we manage this? Self-discipline! Self-discipline allows you to be as happy as a person can reasonably hope to be, given that you will inevitably come up against obstacles in every area of your life. Even better, good self-discipline actually helps you find a kind of enjoyment and pride in overcoming setbacks. It takes a great deal of bravery to face up to the reality of suffering, but since it is inevitable anyway you may as well resolve to take a rational, balanced view of life in which happiness is an experience to be enjoyed but never taken for granted.

2) **Be calm and courageous**

Courage is another fundamental virtue of Stoicism. Courage is essential, as you should have the ferocity to survive any situation that comes to your life. You should manifest this virtue in both mental and physical aspects of your life.

Mental courage denotes a strong will that can help you to fight life adversaries. Being mentally strong is always essential, because you need to face the hurdles of life. Take note that nothing is permanent and everything will undergo change at their own time. What you have today may not be there tomorrow, and that involves both people and material possessions. Hence, developing attachment to them will not bring you joy. You need to remain strong and not be too much concerned when you lost them. You should develop a formidable will power and never allow other people to push you around.

Another form of courage that you should develop is physical courage. This will help you find the courage to conquer this world and cope up with the physical challenges you may face. This includes agony, physical pain, sickness, and disability. No one is perfect. Everyone has its imperfection that could bring a person down. You should combat through it and have the right courage to combat it. Too much worrying will only make things worse, but with the right mindset, you can mitigate it. Hence, it is crucial to lessen the physical issues and improve your physical capacity.

3) Do Good, Be Good and Grateful

Another stoic virtue is to measure your life based on virtues and morals and not based on your awards and rewards. These things are fleeting and will not bring you long-lasting joy. You should learn how to keep track of the morals and virtues that you have learned to develop through the years and how these virtues could help you get through unfavorable situations in life. You should always be guided by your virtues and morals, regardless of the situation. It is ideal to learn how to harness your power as much as possible to always prevail in doing the right thing and minimizing the chances to do wrong things. This will ultimately bring you long-lasting happiness.

Honesty is a Great Virtue

Even though you have the freedom to choose the virtues you want to follow in leading your life, it is ideal to consider honesty as the best virtue for your life. Honesty has the ability to bring out the best in a person. If you are constantly dishonest, you will always feel worried and anxious about life and the possible outcome if your dishonesty will be exposed. It is also ideal to surround yourself with people who are also honest and trustworthy, and build a healthy relationship with them. You can go to these people during those times that you are caught in choosing what is right or wrong. Be sure to value their opinion and be sure to work hard to keep your loyalty to those who add value to your life and the principles you believe in.

We Create Our Own Emotions

This is among the most crucial philosophies of Stoicism. The stoics believe that emotions are nestled deep within our minds, and are merely created by our own feelings and thoughts.

Many people believe that their emotions are created by what they hear and see from the external world. But how could these external factors create emotions deep within? It could only feed you with thoughts that could trigger emotions. But once you control your thoughts, then you can easily gain control of your emotions. Hence, it is essential to examine your inner self if you want to understand yourself including your thoughts, and stop blaming the world for your ordeals.

Results are Also Within

Your desired results could be initiated by mere thought. You can achieve the results that you want by starting to form an image about it deep inside your mind and working hard towards achieving it. It is given that life is full of roadblocks, but it is highly doable for you to go over these obstacles. You just need to develop enough determination as well as will power to achieve the results that your mind has set upon. If you just wait for the results of an action to come through without clearly thinking what you want it to be, then you will just experience a lot of negative emotions such as worry and disappointment. But if you know precisely what you can expect then you can take charge in improving your life.

CONCLUSION

As broadly explained in this book, mental toughness entails having the psychological edge that pushes you to perform optimally and efficiently to meet the demands that are placed on you by your own goals, bosses at work or life in general. Note that, the characteristics and benefits of mental toughness are highly evident when you have great demands to fulfill. Some of the characteristics that define a mentally tough person include; self-control, poise, self-confidence, self-motivation, calmness, leadership, determination, composure, concentration, persistence, positive energy, and determination. As well explained, having mental toughness does not mean that you are always destined to win. As a matter of fact, you mainly use the mental toughness attributes when you are faced by adversities that threatened to pull you down or demotivate you to quit working towards your life goals.

To effectively develop mental toughness, you must be willing to practice all the attributes that lead to mental toughness. I wish there was a universally recognized formula for developing mental toughness but there is none. However, that does not mean that it is impossible to achieve mental hardiness. It requires patience, time and the will to learn and adopt new traits. In addition, it is important to surround yourself with the right company and leadership that will make your road to mental toughness and resilience much easier. Notably, most people develop mental toughness after experience failure or facing challenges that made them reevaluate their plans and how they intend to achieve their goals. When a person chooses to accept the outcomes and learn from it instead of blaming people or different life circumstances, they are on the right track towards achieving mental toughness.

Critical elements towards developing mental toughness and maintaining a strong and focused mental state are defining a strong why for everything you do. If you plan on achieving a huge task that you do not have a well-defined why for, you are set to fail. This is because, you will find yourself discouraged, distracted and disengaged from the task as soon as the first challenge set in. Think about the resolutions or goals you have set out to work on previously and things did not turn out right and you had the thought of giving up because you felt like you did not have what it takes to achieve the goals. The truth is, most good and achievable personal goals fail because people do not have a strong why.

According to psychologists, one of the greatest mental drains is having to work towards a goal that you lack definitive why for. In such a case, you will find yourself seeking external motivation and questioning your willpower to achieve the goal. In most cases, people set goals because they like the idea of having resolutions and life goals and not the reality of working towards achieving their goals. Unfortunately, if you cannot connect to your why, you cannot motivate yourself intrinsically to achieve highly challenging goals that hold the key to your success in life. Intrinsic motivation is the desire that burns inside you to pursue something and in most cases, it occurs when you are working on a goal that satisfies you above everyone else or the society at large.

For instance, you could be trying to quit smoking because you are well aware that it is bad for your health. But, you really like smoking and the quitting goal may be close to impossible regardless of the level of mental toughness and willpower you have. On the other hand, if you purpose to quit smoking because you are expectant or just had a baby and you do not want the baby to grow knowing that their parent is a smoker, you will have a strong why that acts as your intrinsic motivation to quit smoking, in such a case, it will be very easy to achieve your goal. Evidently, intrinsic motivation is more powerful than having stubborn willpower to do something. Moreover, it is far much easier to maintain intrinsic motivation in the long run.

Therefore, if your purpose to develop mental toughness and resilience, it is important to connect a definitive why to everything you purpose to achieve. This ensures that you reduce the energy and effort you need to achieve your se goals. Once you establish a strong why for your life goals, you will automatically have more energy and motivation to take on difficult challenges that arise. You will not allow anything to hinder you from achieving your goals.

Printed in Great Britain
by Amazon